THE POLITICS OF
WORLD COMMUNICATION

COMMUNICATION AND HUMAN VALUES

Series editors

Robert A. White, Editor, Centre for the Study of Communication and Culture, London, UK
Michael Traber, Associate Editor, World Association for Christian Communication, London, UK

International editorial advisory board

Binod C. Agrawal, Development and Educational Communication, Space Applications Centre, Ahmadabad, India
Luis Ramiro Beltran, International Development Research Centre, Bogotá, Colombia
James W. Carey, University of Illinois, USA
Marlene Cuthbert, University of Windsor, Canada
William F. Fore, Communication Commission, National Council of Churches of Christ, New York, USA
George Gerbner, University of Pennsylvania, USA
James D. Halloran, University of Leicester, UK
Cees Hamelink, University of Amsterdam, The Netherlands
Neville D. Jayaweera, World Association for Christian Communication, London, UK
Emile G. McAnany, University of Texas, USA
Walter J. Ong, St Louis University, USA
Breda Pavlic, Culture and Communication Sector, Unesco, Paris
Miguel de Moragas Spa, Autonomous University of Barcelona, Spain

Also in this series

THE POLITICS OF WORLD COMMUNICATION

A Human Rights Perspective

Cees J. Hamelink

SAGE Publications
London • Thousand Oaks • New Delhi

First published 1994

 SAGE Publications Ltd
6 Bonhill Street
London EC2A 4PU

SAGE Publications Inc
2455 Teller Road
Thousand Oaks, California 91320

SAGE Publications India Pvt Ltd
32, M-Block Market
Greater Kailash – I
New Delhi 110 048

British Library Cataloguing in Publication data

A catalogue record for this book is
available from the British Library.

ISBN 0 8039 7822 7

ISBN 0 8039 7823 5 (pbk)

Library of Congress catalog card number 94-068163

Typeset by Photoprint, Torquay, Devon
Printed in Great Britain by Biddles Ltd, Guildford, Surrey

Contents

Preface

In early 1990 I began work on the present book. All the environmental signs augured very well for a smooth completion. I had the honour to be appointed the Walter Schmidt Visiting Professor at Santa Clara University, Santa Clara, USA. This meant visiting a beautiful campus, meeting marvellous colleagues and having time to think and write. Particular thanks for that period are due to Thom Shanks, Paul Soukop, John McManus and Chris Bracken. My optimism was somewhat premature. From August 1990 I took over the IAMCR Presidency and working on the manuscript was restricted to a few odd hours in airports and aloft.

Another honourable appointment made all the difference. In early 1993 the Ohio State University, Columbus, USA through its Distinguished Visiting Professorship offered the opportunity to complete the manuscript. Thanks are due to Brenda Dervin, Rohan Samarayiva, the PhD students in the class I taught, the exchanges with Joe Foley, Thom McCain, Joe Pilotta, the long walks with Steve Acker, and the meetings with Tetsunori Koizumi, Sven Lundstedt and Chad Alger. All this communication helped to clarify matters and stimulate the completion of the manuscript.

I am also grateful to the reviewers for their criticism and suggestions, and to publisher Stephen Barr and editor Bob White for their interest and encouragement.

The book is in many respects a logical sequence to earlier writings. Most of my work has been concerned with issues of human rights and world communication. A basic motive throughout the years has been the observation that in the political arena ordinary people do not count. This also guided my inquiry into the politics of world communication.

The book will be published shortly after the end of my tenure as the President of the International Association for Mass Communication Research. Part of my mission as President was the promotion of a more active presence of the communication research community in public policy. This was largely motivated by my conviction that communication researchers have an obligation to generate knowledge that benefits society at large. This obligation finds its rationale in the standard of international law that all people are under a responsibility to strive towards the respect for human rights.

Some people prefer not to be mentioned in prefaces and even less to figure as the person to whom a book is dedicated. I obviously respect this and will only say that I am deeply grateful.

Cees J. Hamelink
Amsterdam

List of Abbreviations

BIAC	Business and Industry Advisory Committee
BSS	broadcast satellite services
CCIR	International Consultative Committee on Radio
CCITT	International Consultative Committee on Telegraph and Telephony
CIB	Council for International Business
COPUOS	Committee on the Peaceful Uses of Outer Space
CSCE	Conference on Security and Cooperation in Europe
ECHR	European Court of Human Rights
ECHRF	European Convention for the Protection of Human Rights and Fundamental Freedoms
EDI	electronic data interchange
EMS	electromagnetic spectrum
FCC	Federal Communications Commission
FSS	fixed satellite services
GATS	General Agreement on Trade in Services
GSO	geosynchronous orbit
HDTV	high-definition television
HF	high frequency
ICC	International Chamber of Commerce
ICCPR	International Covenant on Civil and Political Rights
ICERD	International Convention on the Elimination of All Forms of Racial Discrimination
ICESCR	International Covenant on Economic, Social and Cultural Rights
ICJ	International Court of Justice
IDTBS	international direct television broadcasting by satellite
IFBR	International Frequency Registration Board
IFPI	International Federation of Producers of Phonograms and Videograms
IIPA	International Intellectual Property Alliance
IPR	intellectual property rights
MSS	mobile satellite services
RPOAs	recognized private operating agencies
SBSS	sound broadcast satellite services

TAs	telecommunication administrations
TRIPs	trade-related intellectual property rights
UCC	Universal Copyright Convention
UDHR	Universal Declaration of Human Rights
UNGA	United Nations General Assembly
WARC	World Administrative Radio Conference
WATCC	World Administrative Telegraph and Telephone Conference
WIPO	World Intellectual Property Organization

Major Players

The title 'major players' suggests that this is not a comprehensive listing. I have selected those actors that figure prominently in the present study.

United Nations General Assembly
COPUOS	Committee on the Peaceful Uses of Outer Space
CPI	Committee on Public Information
UNCITRAL	United Nations Commission on International Trade Law
ECOSOC	Economic and Social Council
CHR	Commission on Human Rights
CHR	Committee on Human Rights
CTNC	Commission on Transnational Corporations

United Nations specialized agencies directly involved
Unesco	United Nations Organization for Education, Science and Culture
ITU	International Telecommunication Union
UPU	Universal Postal Union
WIPO	World Intellectual Property Organization

United Nations specialized agencies indirectly involved
UNCTAD	United Nations Conference on Trade and Development
ILO	International Labour Office
IMO	International Maritime Organization
UNDP	United Nations Development Programme
FAO	Food and Agricultural Organization
WHO	World Health Organization

Intergovernmental organizations not related to the United Nations
GATT	General Agreement on Tariffs and Trade
OECD	Organization for Economic Cooperation and Development
CSCE	Conference on Security and Cooperation in Europe

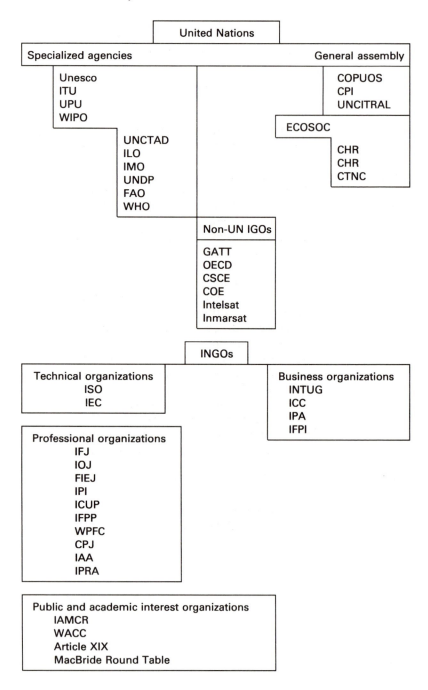

COE   Council of Europe
Intelsat   International Satellite Consortium
Inmarsat   International Maritime Satellite Organization

International non-governmental organizations

Technical organizations
ISO   International Organization for Standardization
IEC   International Electrotechnical Commission

Business interest organizations
INTUG   International Telecommunication Users Group
ICC   International Chamber of Commerce
IPA   International Publishers Association
IFPI   International Federation of Producers of
               Phonograms and Videograms

Professional interest organizations
IFJ   International Federation of Journalists
IOJ   International Organization of Journalists
FIEJ   International Federation of Publishers
IPI   International Press Institute
ICUP   International Catholic Union of the Press
IFPP   International Federation of Publishers of
               Periodicals
WPFC   World Press Freedom Committee
CPJ   Committee to Protect Journalists
IAA   International Advertisers Association
IPRA   International Public Relations Association

Public and academic interest organizations
IAMCR   International Association for Mass
               Communication Research
WACC   World Association for Christian Communication

Introduction

This book finds its origin in a collection of regulatory instruments produced by international governmental and non-governmental organizations. The texts in this collection deal with mass communication, telecommunication, data communication, intellectual property protection and technology transfer.

The collection was put together as a contribution to the chapter on trends in regulation for the Unesco World Communication Report (Unesco, 1989). The complete texts have been published as a compendium of texts on the regulation of world communication (Hamelink, 1994). Since it was not possible to publish complete texts of regulatory instruments in the present book, I shall refer to the compendium for the original materials. Together these texts comprise the majority of basic ordering principles and rules of conduct that the world community has adopted for the transborder movement of data, information and knowledge. Over 1500 pages of regulatory instruments represent the reflection of some 150 years of policy making in an increasingly crucial domain of world politics.

A substantial body of conventions, resolutions, codes and recommendations forms the core of the political practices through which the conduct of actors in world communication is actually governed, or at least may be expected to be governed.[1] These practices are the objects of analysis and assessment in the present study.

The exercise has been motivated by a remarkable feature of world politics which is not exclusively restricted to the communications field. The arena of world politics has little to offer to its largest constituency: all the individuals and their communities that constitute the world's population.[2] They comprise the millions whose daily lives are affected by the developments in world communication. They watch foreign television programmes, use the international telephone lines and mail systems, buy recorded music and read the international news. CNN newscasts, Madonna, Rupert Murdoch's empire, satellite telephony or transborder data flows all touch upon people's daily lives around the world. The political decisions taken in the arena of world communication are important to governments and to business corporations. They also concern ordinary people. The politics of world communication determines the variety of contents in the media, the representation of diverse social interests, the access to public libraries, the charges for use of telephone and postal services, and the quality of information networks. Political decisions shape the cultural environment in which people live. They bring knowledge or deepen ignorance, create benefits for a few or for all, promote accurate news or sanction disinformation.

Yet, the largest client community is no party to the processes of world politics. More often than not, its concerns are not adequately expressed, let alone accommodated.[3] Critical negotiations, such as the GATT Uruguay Round on international trade, largely evolved behind closed doors away from the scrutiny of the world's citizens. Ironically enough, though, the international regulatory texts often justify their proposed measures with a reference to the interests of individuals and their communities. It is routinely stated or implied that the community of people is the ultimate beneficiary. Many preambles to regulatory texts claim to address 'all members of the human family', 'all human beings', 'all peoples' or just 'everyone'. Over 150 years of multilateral policy making is full of people-centred discourse. It is necessary, therefore, to ask: how far do the prevailing political practices address the interests of the world's people? Whose interests are served by the multilateral agreements or by the absence of such arrangements? Are the interests of ordinary people served by the collective practices of world communication politics?

The leading question of the book thus became: do people matter in the actions and processes of world communication politics? To address this question I have chosen to assess the politics of world communication from a human rights perspective. I propose a method of analysis that judges whether the political arrangements of the world community measure up to the standards set by international human rights law. Following the analysis and assessment the book concludes with a proposal for a political practice inspired by the recognition of people's fundamental right to communicate. This would be the basis for a politics of world communication 'as if people mattered'.

The basic reasons for writing this book are the belief that 'all people matter' and the observation that the world's political institutions do not usually reflect this belief. If all people mattered these institutions would provide effective means of enforcement through which people could seek redress in case their basic rights are violated. The book is also motivated by my conviction that scientific work should contribute to the protection and promotion of human rights standards.

The book is organized in the following way. Chapter 1 looks at the origins of multilateral policy making and describes the emergence and evolution of world politics in the field of world communication. It deals with the most essential factors and features of world communication politics in the period from the mid nineteenth century to the late 1980s. It also explains how world communication got on the agenda of world politics.

Chapter 2 introduces the basic framework for the study of the politics of world communication. It identifies as relevant units of analysis the prevailing practices in the major issue areas of world communication. It proposes a human rights perspective for the normative analysis of these collective practices.

Chapters 3 to 9 analyse issues, positions and prevailing practices in the issue areas of telecommunication, protection of intellectual property, mass media, culture, development, transborder data flows and standardization of communication technology. The order in which these areas are treated largely reflects the chronology of their advent on the world political agenda.

Chapter 10 gives an overview of the prevailing practices in the key issue areas of world communication. Borrowing from a variety of theoretical insights it aims to illuminate the development of specific practices in different areas. Chapter 11 measures the prevailing practices in world communication politics against a human rights perspective. It also provides the outline of a politics of world communication that is based upon a human rights perspective.

Notes

1 I prefer the term 'world communication' to other concepts such as 'global communication' or 'international communication'. The adjective 'international' is too restrictive. What I address goes beyond the (communicative) relations between or among states. It involves the interactions of a multitude of states and non-state actors. The arena of these interactions is more adequately described as 'world politics' than as 'international relations'. Cross-border politics can no longer be understood as relations between nation-states as exclusive actors. The world political arena contains multiple actors. They include intergovernmental organizations, transnational corporations, social movements and individuals. For this reason I shall also use the notion of 'world community' rather than the more common 'international community'. The latter is too closely tied to a state-centric conception of the world and ignores the fact that more players than nation-states are affected by the issues this book deals with.

But why not refer to global communication? In my view there are certainly processes of globalization, for example in the cultural arena, but (as yet) there is no global culture. Globalization suggests the movement towards a one-world community. We are only on the way, whereas the use of the term 'global' suggests we have achieved this condition. A global civil society is an aspiration, not a reality. Global communication represents a goal rather than a reality.

The term 'world communication' in this book refers to all cross-border traffic of data, information and knowledge. In this way the analysis is not unduly restricted to such components as news flows. World communication encompasses a large variety of contents and at the same time it is a phenomenon distinct from other transborder interactions.

2 The world's population in this study is referred to as 'people'. The concept 'people' is preferred above other possible notions such as 'citizens'. Although it would be possible to refer to 'world citizens', this concept remains too strongly tied to a limited national understanding which tends to exclude certain categories such as stateless people. The present study focuses on the interests of all human beings. The concept 'people' refers to human beings both as individuals and as members of their communities.

3 In some domains of world politics there has been in recent times an increasingly significant contribution by organizations representing people's interests. The field of world environmental politics is a relevant illustration.

1
World Communication Politics: Origins and Evolution

Multilateralism

Throughout human history people traded and fought. Commerce and war made many people travel great distances. Most people, however, stayed home. For much of world history the capacity of remote cultures to interact was very limited. Ideas and people may have moved between ancient Rome and the China of the Han dynasty. Yet, contacts were so superficial that such interaction could remain unregulated. Even when in the seventeenth century an international system began to develop, the state of the world remained anarchic. Since the Peace of Westphalia (1648) which (together with the Treaty of Utrecht in 1713) laid the basis for a Eurocentric international economy, contacts between European governments increased. But apart from the more than 60 wars fought between 1648 and 1800, most contacts were of a rather shallow and formal diplomatic nature. The bulk of contacts was in fact conducted through international traders and merchants. No institutional arrangement evolved to address issues stemming from the states' international relations and indeed little need was felt to regulate these relations. The Westphalian system of sovereign units had no common conventions or norms and rules. Equally the world outside Europe did not establish forms of multilateral politics for its international relations.[1]

The creation of international organizations that function as forums for multilateral policy making by states is typically a nineteenth century phenomenon. Throughout the seventeenth and eighteenth centuries the conduct of states remained largely defined by the narrow interests of nationalism and individualism. Although these interests continue to be forceful in the late twentieth century, socio-economic developments of the nineteenth century made states more aware of the need to regulate their relations. The 'interaction capacity' (Buzan, 1993: 331) between states increased and the prevailing anarchy began to cause too much inconvenience. With more contact and more conflict between states a desire for minimal rules in such areas as the control of force emerged. A first clear point in time was the Vienna Congress of 1814–15. This congress established the rules for international diplomacy and agreed to meet at regular intervals in peacetime in order to prevent war. The industrial revolution was an important factor in the increase of interaction capacity. The development of mass production, improved communication and transport, and population growth meant that markets expanded within Europe and between Europe and other parts of the world. At the same time another revolution hit Europe. The French revolution fostered nationalism in Europe and reinforced the sovereignty of the nation-states. These two developments created a peculiar tension between the rapidly increasing cross-border movements of goods, capital and people and the firm national control over these movements. The first multilateral institutions accommodated this tension by providing international interaction under norms and rules controlled by independent nation-states. These institutions were the Congress of Vienna of 1815, the Hague conferences of 1899 and 1907, and the administrative bodies that dealt with issue areas such as post, telegraph and intellectual property. The nineteenth century also saw the rise of a considerable number of public and private multilateral associations.

All this international activity could not prevent the First World War. At the end of this war the victorious states gathered at the Versailles Peace Conference of 1919 in order to create an international system that would employ peaceful means in the resolution of inter-state conflicts. An important task of the 1919 Peace Conference was the establishment of multilateral institutional arrangements that could promote international cooperation and contribute to the achievement of peace and security. The basic desire was to shape the kind of post-war international relations that could prevent a collapse of the international system into another devastating war. The most important multilateral institution was the League of Nations.[2]

Telecommunication

The postal system
From the sixteenth century a postal system had developed in Europe that served several countries. The system was governed through bilateral arrangements that accommodated the specific needs of the countries involved. The technical developments in railway transportation and steam engines for shipping began to necessitate changes in the complex set of bilateral rules for the

calculation of rates in different currencies and according to different scales. In the nineteenth century the awareness arose that with the modernization of transport, the administrative formalities would also have to be standardized. The first international meeting to address this was convened in 1862 by the US Postmaster-General, Montgomery Blair. The conference, held in Paris on 11 May 1863, brought delegates together from Austria, Belgium, Costa Rica, Denmark, France, the Hanseatic towns, Italy, the Netherlands, Portugal, Prussia, the Sandwich Islands, Spain, Switzerland, the United Kingdom and the United States of America. Several general principles were adopted by the conference as the first step towards a common postal agreement. These principles were to regulate the conventions that postal administrations would conclude between each other. However, the application of commonly accepted principles within bilateral agreements failed to meet the demands imposed by changing international relations. In 1868 Heinrich von Stephan, a senior official in the postal administration of the North German Confederation, prepared a proposal for an international postal union. Through his government this plan was submitted to a plenipotentiary conference that was held at the invitation of the Swiss government at Berne on 15 September 1874. The 22 countries present at the conference founded, through the Treaty of Berne, the General Postal Union.[3] The convention entered into force on 1 July 1875. In 1878 the name of the organization was changed to the Universal Postal Union. The 1874 Berne conference introduced basic norms and rules that still hold today. Among these were the guaranteed freedom of transit within the territory of the Union, and the standardization of charges to be collected by each country for letter-post items addressed to any part of the Union's territory.

Telegraphy
The development of telegraphy in the early nineteenth century brought about the need for standardization and cooperation across national borders. The first telegraph lines stopped at the border and messages had to be transcribed and then carried across the frontier by hand. A similar problem was faced by early railway traffic when countries deployed different sizes of rails.

By 1849 the first electrical interconnections between telegraph networks were installed and by the early 1850s most European countries had established domestic telegraphy networks regulated by their post offices. The need for standardization first occasioned the conclusion of a series of bilateral treaties, such as between Prussia and Austria in 1849. As well as for standardization, inter-state cooperation was necessary to guarantee the free passage of messages and to organize international tariffing.

A first extension of the bilateral agreements was probably the Austro-German Telegraph Union established in 1850 by Prussia, Austria, Bavaria and Saxony. In 1855 France, Belgium, Switzerland and Sardinia created at Paris the West European Telegraphic Union. In 1858 the WETU – in the meantime expanded with the Netherlands – signed a Telegraph Convention at Berne on 1 September, which was largely the basis for the 1865 International Telegraph Convention.

By 1865 the need was felt to substitute a multiplicity of bilateral, trilateral and quadrilateral arrangements by a multilateral agreement. In that year France invited the European states to an international conference that became the founding meeting of the International Telegraph Union (17 May 1865). With the establishment of this predecessor of today's ITU, the first treaty to deal with world communication was also adopted: the International Telegraph Convention. The original text of the convention stated that the signatories desired to secure for their telegraphy traffic the advantages of simple and reduced tariffs, to improve the conditions of international telegraphy and to establish a permanent co-operation among themselves while retaining their freedom of operation.[4]

The convention adopted as the first international telegraph standard the Morse code. Among the basic norms that were adopted were the protection of the secrecy of correspondence, the right of everybody to use international telegraphy, and the rejection of all liability for international telegraphy services. The contracting parties also reserved the right to stop any transmission that they considered dangerous for state security, or in violation of national laws, public order or morals.

In 1868 the Vienna International Telegraph Conference established the Bureau International des Administrations Télégraphiques which began operating on 1 January 1869. The Vienna conference also recognized private telegraph operators and as a result the United Kingdom (initially excluded as its telegraph network was privately owned) acceded to the Union.

In 1875 the St Petersburg Telegraph Conference (attended by 24 member states and sixteen recognized private operators) revised the convention and resolved that the Telegraph Regulations could be revised in the future by administrative conferences and would not need plenipotentiary diplomatic conferences. In fact between 1875 and 1932 (when the International Telegraph Union was merged with the International Radio-Telegraph Union into the International Telecommunication Union) there were only administrative conferences. Although the USA remained outside the Union, basically because of a lack of interest in this Eurocentric affair, US observers were present at all these conferences. At the 1885 Berlin Telegraph Conference telephony was put on the Union's agenda, and at the London Telegraph Conference in 1903 telephony was to be fully incorporated in the Union's work.

In the same year (1903) the first conference on the regulation of wireless radio-telegraphy took place, the Preliminary Radio Conference of Berlin. This field had been outside the scope of the ITU mainly since it was controlled by private operators in maritime communications. Radio communications was practically monopolized by the Anglo-Italian Marconi Wireless Company. Motivated by this monopoly control and by some incidents that resulted from this (ships with Marconi equipment were prohibited from communicating with stations using other equipment) the German government convened the 1903 conference. The participants were Austro-Hungary, France, Germany, Italy, Spain, Russia and the USA.

A special incentive for the conference seems to have been the annoyance that Prince Henry of Prussia experienced when he wanted to send a radiogram from the vessel *Deutschland*. He travelled on this ship back to Europe after a visit to the USA where he had been hosted by President Theodore Roosevelt whom he wished to thank. The British coast station to which the message was sent refused to transmit it owing to the incompatibility of the telegraphs on board and at shore. The Prince relayed his story to the convenor of the conference, the Emperor. The conference resolved that coast stations should be bound to transmit and receive telegrams for ships at sea 'without distinction as to the system of radio used by the latter'. The conference also agreed that tariffs for radio-telegrams should be internationally determined, and the final protocol made reference to the provision to ensure that there would be no interference with the service of other stations.

After the participants had reported to their respective governments, the Berlin Radio Conference was convened in 1906 which was to draft and sign the Berlin Radio Convention. Twenty-nine countries met in this first international attempt at management of the radio frequency spectrum. The conference allocated frequency bands to specific services and required signatories of the convention to report frequencies they used to the ITU administration in Berne to which the Radio Union entrusted the work of its own international bureau. The 1906 conference decided to hold a revision conference in 1912 at London. The London conference was mainly concerned with safety at sea as it convened two months after the *Titanic* disaster.

As a result of significant technical inventions made during the First World War, radio advanced rapidly in the years immediately after the war. Radio became an attractive commercial commodity and a vital tool for propaganda. All this contributed to the post-war need for domestic and international regulation. In particular the emergence of short-wave broadcasting made it necessary to formulate standards for international radio communications.

The first Radio Conference after the First World War was held at Washington in 1927. Eighty countries attended to draft a new Radio Convention and Radio Regulations. A key element of contention at the conference was the different perceptions of the role of the state in telecommunication. Whereas 'the companies in the United States did not want a document that would further broaden the appearance or reality of government control over them', most of the participating governments 'viewed state control as necessary in order to maximize equitable use of the medium' (Luther, 1988: 28). The conference established the International Technical Consulting Committee on Radio Communications, just as two years earlier the Paris Telegraph Conference had established the International Consultative Committee on Long-Distance Telephones and the International Consultative Committee on Telegraphs. These committees were in fact the predecessors of the international consultative committees which would become so crucial after the Second World War in the development of the International Telecommunication Union.

The Paris conference had also begun to discuss the fusion of the Radio Union with the Telegraph Union, and in Washington it was resolved to call on the participating governments to consider the merger of the two conventions and to set the next meeting of the Radio Union for Madrid in 1932 when the International Telegraph Union would also meet. In 1932 the Thirteenth International Telegraph Conference and the Fourth International Radio-Telegraph Conference were held at the same time at Madrid. The joint meetings did lead to the adoption of a single convention and to the establishment of the International Telecommunication Union.

The protection of intellectual property

The historical development of author's rights
Although intellectual production is known throughout most of human history (in such forms as music, drama, poetry), there is no

early historical record of a legal protection of rights to intellectual property. It would seem likely that the first legal recognition of proprietary rights to intangibles was the protection that was granted to printers by the late fifteenth century republic of Venice (Cavalli, 1986: 14).

A real need to provide protection through privileges or rights arose with the advent and spread of the printing press. The speed and volume of multiplication increased, the number of people able to read grew and the trade of printing and publishing developed. Throughout the sixteenth and seventeenth centuries the granting of monopoly rights to printers and booksellers became common practice in England, mainly for censorship reasons and more for the benefit of crown and publishers than for individual authors. This was a convenient arrangement between publishers who wanted to protect their investments and authorities who could censor publications through the granting of privileges to a restricted group of beneficiaries.

Although in the eighteenth and early nineteenth centuries many countries enacted forms of intellectual property protection (the German states, Belgium, Spain, France, England, Italy, Switzerland and the USA), the piracy of literary works was rampant. Classical cases were the German states and the USA. In the USA, the Copyright Act of 1790 did not protect foreign authors. As a result almost half of the best-sellers were pirated mainly from English novels.

Already in 1738 the idea of international author's rights protection had been expressed by Johann Rudolf Thurneysen in his book *De recusione librorum furtiva* (Cavalli, 1986: 69). The idea was first implemented through the adoption of bilateral treaties (between 1840 and 1866 over 88 such treaties were signed) before in 1886 the First International Convention on Copyright could be concluded in Berne, Switzerland.

The emergence of the need for multilateral arrangements on author's copyright in the nineteenth century is linked with the expansion of international trading and the related need to protect works created in one country and sold in another. The expansion of international contacts increasingly confronted authors with the fact that intellectual property rights had very limited value if there was no international recognition and if the crucial question of the treatment of foreign authors was not resolved.

In the early bilateral treaties there was recognition of the principle of 'national treatment' or 'assimilation'. Foreigners were granted the same protection as nationals. Gradually, however, this shifted to the adoption of the 'reciprocity' principle. This meant that foreigners could only be awarded the right they might enjoy in their home countries. Generosity gave way to the mundane preference to treat foreigners no better than they would be treated at home. The French-Russian treaty of 1861 left little doubt about the significance of the reciprocity norm. The text said: 'it is understood that the reciprocal rights accorded only extend to those authors whose countries extend the same rights' (Cavalli, 1986: 77).

The bilateral treaties did assist the proliferation of the notion of legal protection of author's rights, but at the same time the proliferation of treaties created a very complex situation that was not always to the benefit of authors who could not as a rule grasp all the legal implications of so many arrangements.

More important, however, was the problem that several treaties were primarily based upon trading relations between states and the force of the copyright arrangement would largely depend upon the quality of commercial relations. In addition to this, the possibility of war between states seriously eroded any legal security for authors. International protection could easily be undermined as a result of national politics. The protection of foreign authors was limited because the reciprocity principle applied and because many states had a priority interest in the commercial protection of their domestic authors rather than in promoting the international accessibility of literature.

The inadequacy of the bilateral arrangements pushed the creation of the Berne Union. Its establishment was also facilitated by a series of literary and artistic congresses that had addressed the urgency of multilateral arrangements. A significant preparation for Berne was the First International Conference on Copyright at Brussels in 1858 which resolved among other things that the principle of the international recognition of the property of literary and artistic works should be applied on the basis of national treatment.

In June 1878 the International Literary Congress organized by the Société des Gens de Lettres en France took place in Paris. The society, set up in 1838, had among its members famous authors like Honoré de Balzac and Victor Hugo. Using the occasion of the 1878 Universal Exposition at Paris, the society convened a congress that primarily focused on an international right for the protection of literary property. One of the tangible results of the congress was the establishment of the International Literary and Artistic Association (ALAI). The association – which still exists today – had as its first objective the defence of the principle of literature as intellectual property. The participants of the congress stressed the national treatment principle in one of the resolutions and they proposed the initiative for a multilateral convention on literary property.

The next step towards Berne was the International Congress on Artistic Property of September 1878 in Paris. Again the principle of national treatment was supported, but more importantly the congress proposed the constitution of a multilateral union for the adoption of uniform legislation on literary property (Cavalli, 1986: 138).

The first series of annual conferences of ALAI (London in 1879, Vienna in 1881 and Rome in 1882) provided yet another form of support for the international recognition of author's rights. The Rome conference proposed to establish a union for literary property that would resemble the International Postal Union, and recommended that a conference be held in Berne to discuss the implementation of the union project.

In 1883 the conferences of Berne began with the congress promoted by the ALAI. This was followed by three diplomatic conferences in 1884, 1885 and 1886. The ALAI Berne meeting adopted the draft for a multilateral treaty with the title of Convention Establishing a General Union for the Protection of the Rights of Authors in their Literary and Artistic Works. This draft was sent to 'all civilized countries' through the Federal Council of the Swiss Confederation, with a plan for a diplomatic conference in 1884 to adopt a formal treaty. The third diplomatic conference (6–9 September 1886) adopted the earlier drafts for a convention, an additional article and a final protocol. These three texts were signed by Belgium, France, Germany, Haiti, Italy, Liberia, Spain, Switzerland, Tunisia and the UK. These founder members created a Union which was open to all countries. The Berne treaty provided international recognition for the national treatment principle. As Article 2(1) stated: 'Authors who are subjects or citizens of any of the countries of the Union, or their lawful representatives, shall enjoy in the other countries for their works, whether published in one of those countries or unpublished, the rights which the respective laws do now or may hereafter grant to natives.' In the field of copyright the Berne convention remained the only multilateral treaty until 1952. Since 1886 it has been revised at diplomatic conferences in 1896 (Paris), in 1908 (Berlin), in 1928 (Rome), in 1948 (Brussels), in 1967 (Stockholm) and in 1971 (Paris).

In the development of author's rights the basic principles have been to ensure remuneration for an author by protecting his work against reproduction (for 50 years after the author's lifetime), to demand respect for the individual integrity of the creator, to encourage the development of the arts, literature and science, and to promote a wider dissemination of literary, artistic and scientific works.

*The historical development of industrial property
protection*

Although distinctive marks are found on Greek and Roman
paintings, vases, pottery and medals, and although there was
extensive craftsmanship and international trading, there are no
indications of an early legal basis that would recognize what would
later be called 'trade marks'. The Middle Ages knew some form of
trade marks that were specifically imposed with the emergence of
the guild system as protective measures for the public against fraud.
From the fifteenth century it became customary for authorities to
extend monopolistic privileges to the manufacturing and sales of a
great variety of articles (Ladas, 1930: 8–9).

The first recorded legislation was enacted at Venice in 1474. This
was at the height of Venice's role in international trading. The
Venetian document recognized that inventors needed to be protected lest they would deploy their talents somewhere else. The
rules implied that an inventor would inform the city council about
his invention. Forthwith it was prohibited for others during a period
of ten years to imitate the invention. In case of violation a fine had
to be paid and the imitation would be destroyed. This was clearly
meant to protect Venice's economic interest.

The Statute of Monopolies of 1623 in England was probably the
first real legislative act of protection of the rights to industrial
property. The statute provided the foundation of modern patent
law. It recognized proprietary rights to industrial inventions,
extended these rights to 'the true and first inventors' (these could be
non-nationals) and also limited the protection to a period of
fourteen years.

In the USA the first act to protect industrial inventions was
passed on 10 April 1790. This was the Act to Promote the Progress
of Useful Arts. President Washington was a strong promoter of the
act. He stated in his first annual address to Congress, on 8 January
1790, 'I cannot forbear intimating to you the expediency of giving
effectual encouragement, as well to the introduction of new and
useful inventions from abroad as to the exertion of skill and genius
at home.' Out of dissatisfaction with the act and its implementation,
new legislation was prepared and eventually in 1836 (on 4 July) a
law was enacted 'which has served as a model for the patent systems
subsequently adopted by nearly all the leading nations of the world'
(Weber, 1924: 9). In his history of the US Patent Office, Weber
observes that the act 'provided for the first time in any country, the
means of protecting the rights of inventors in an intelligent,
scientific, and adequate way, by giving the patent grant a prima

facie standing of validity and by inaugurating a proper examination system, authorizing a personnel sufficiently trained to examine claims intelligently, and otherwise providing the machinery and directing the procedure for the protection of such rights' (1924: 11). In the eighteenth and nineteenth centuries the dominant economic thinking gave great importance to the granting of industrial protection. This was generally seen, by Adam Smith and Jeremy Bentham, as imperative for the competitive position of a nation. Following this thinking, many countries began to enact patent laws: Austria in 1810, Prussia in 1815, Spain in 1820, Bavaria in 1825, Sweden in 1834 and Portugal in 1837.

Evidently, the protection of inventions and industrial designs only acquired significance with the emergence of industrial production in the late eighteenth and the nineteenth centuries. In the first period of the industrial revolution (1790–1870) crucial inventions such as the steam engine, textile machinery, large-scale iron production and electricity introduced new forms of transport (railway and steamship), production (factory), and communication (telegraphy and telephony).

With the growth of international trade obviously the question of treatment of foreigners came up. This was addressed very differently in national legislations. Some countries recognized the principle of assimilation; some provided protection dependent upon reciprocity; other countries would exclude foreigners from any protection. In search of international protection, provisions were included in commercial agreements between countries. However, this did not provide adequate legal security since trading relations were subject to change and instability. Moreover, in countries where domestic legislation would not extend sufficient protection to foreigners, the power of trading treaties was not enough to supersede municipal arrangements.

In the nineteenth century patent holders were increasingly confronted with a wide variety of national industrial property protection standards and with countries where no protection existed. In order to acquire protection across borders, inventors had to apply for the granting of patents in separate countries following the legal rules prevailing in those countries. This was a complex and costly process that required an international solution.

Steps leading away from the unsatisfactory situation of divergent municipal regimes and a series of bilateral treaties, and towards the conclusion of a multilateral treaty, began at Vienna in 1873 with the International Industrial Exposition. This occasion was used to organize a congress of experts to discuss the much needed patent law reform. The Congress of Vienna for Patent Reform convened 4–9 August 1873 with the objective to achieve uniform patent legislation in all countries. One resolution of the congress stated that: 'the necessity of reform is evident, and it is of pressing moment that Governments should endeavour to bring about an international understanding upon patent protection as soon as possible'.

Then at the occasion of the International Exposition at Paris in 1878 the French Minister of Commerce convened the International Congress on Industrial Property which drafted an instrument for an industrial property protection union. The French government sent the draft to other governments and convened a conference at Paris in 1883 for final revision and adoption.

On 20 March 1883 Belgium, Brazil, France, Guatemala, Italy, the Netherlands, Portugal, Salvador, Serbia, Spain and Switzerland signed the Convention for the Creation of the Union for the Protection of Industrial Property. The Paris convention dealt with three categories: industrial inventions and designs; trade marks and service marks; and unfair competition.

The convention recognized the principle of assimilation. Article 2 of the treaty stated: 'The subjects or citizens of each of the contracting States shall, as regards patents, industrial designs, trade marks and trade names, enjoy the advantages that their respective laws now grant, or may hereafter grant, to nationals. Consequently, they shall have the same protection as the latter and the same legal remedy against any infringement of their rights, provided they observe the formalities and conditions imposed upon nationals by the domestic legislation of each State.' Article 3 added to this that: 'Subjects or citizens of States not forming part of the Union, who are domiciled or who have industrial or commercial establishments in the territory of one of the States of the Union, are treated in the same manner as subjects or citizens of the contracting States.' The convention of Paris was revised at conferences, in 1891 (Madrid), in 1900 (Brussels), in 1911 (Washington), in 1925 (The Hague), in 1934 (London), in 1958 (Lisbon) and in 1967 (Stockholm).

In the development of industrial property protection the basic principles have been the recognition of the proprietary right of the inventor and the need to encourage industrial invention through a system of securing return on investment. The basic rationale for this form of protection has been that the community should benefit as industrial innovation is encouraged through the granting of legally enforceable monopoly rights. The monopoly is not absolute since, at the end of the period of privilege, the object is brought into public possession.

Growth of the mass media: social concerns

With the proliferation of printed and especially broadcast media in the late nineteenth and early twentieth centuries, serious concerns about the social impact of the mass media emerged. There was considerable excitement about the positive and constructive contribution of the media to peaceful international relations. Such positive expectations were expressed in the 1933 Convention for Facilitating the International Circulation of Films of an Educational Character. This convention was signed at Geneva on 11 October 1933. The contracting parties to the convention, which was registered with the secretariat of the League of Nations, considered highly desirable the international circulation of educational films which contribute 'towards the mutual understanding of peoples, in conformity with the aims of the League of Nations, and consequently encourage moral disarmament'. In order to facilitate the circulation of such films the signatories agreed to exempt their importation, transit and exportation from all customs duties and accessory charges of any kind.

There was however also a serious concern about the negative social impact of the mass media. A moral, educational concern was expressed regarding the spread across borders of obscene publications. This concern resulted in the adoption of the 1910 and 1924 treaties on traffic in obscene publications. The 1924 International Convention for the Suppression of the Circulation of and Traffic in Obscene Publications declared it a punishable offence 'to make or produce or have in possession (for trade or public exhibition) obscene writings, drawings, prints, paintings, printed matter, pictures, posters, emblems, photographs, cinematograph films or any other obscene objects'. It was also punishable to import or export said obscene matters for trade or public exhibition and persons committing the offence 'shall be amenable to the Courts of the Contracting Party in whose territories the offence . . . was committed'.

Concern about the negative impact of the mass media also arose from the increasing use of the mass media (in the course of the nineteenth century) as instruments of foreign diplomacy. Although this was particularly the case with the newspapers, the development of wireless radio did increase the potential for this new form of diplomacy. Increasingly diplomats shifted from traditional forms of silent diplomacy to a public diplomacy in which the constituencies of other states were directly addressed. In most cases this in fact amounted to the propagandistic abuse of the medium. During the First World War, extensive use was made of the means of propaganda. This psychological warfare continued after the war had ended and international short-wave radio began to proliferate.

By 1923 American radio amateurs had discovered the long-range features of high-frequency (HF) transmission and conducted two-way transatlantic communications. Soon several states began to use HF for international broadcasting. By 1926 in Europe there were already 26 stations that sent international transmissions. The Dutch began with broadcasts to the East Indies colonies in 1929; the French started their overseas service in 1931; the BBC followed suit with an empire service in 1932; and the Belgians commenced in 1934. In 1930 the USSR began using short-wave broadcasting to reach foreign audiences.

In the immediate post-war period the League of Nations initiated discussions about the contribution of the international press to peace. The underlying concern with the role of the press in international relations found expression in a resolution that was adopted on 25 September 1925 by the Assembly of the League of Nations. This resolution called for a committee of experts representing the press of the different continents 'with a view to determining methods of contributing towards the organization of peace, especially: (a) by ensuring the more rapid and less costly transmission of press news with a view to reducing risks of international misunderstanding; and (b) by discussing all technical problems the settlement of which would be conducive to the tranquillisation of public opinion' (Kubka and Nordenstreng, 1986a: 71). The resolution referred to the press as 'the most effective means of guiding public opinion towards that moral disarmament which is a concomitant condition of material disarmament'.

In August 1927 the League convened a first conference of press experts in Geneva to deal with such problems as the provision of information that would 'calm down public opinion in different countries' (Kubka and Nordenstreng, 1986a: 54). The conference made an appeal to the press 'to contribute by every means at its disposal to the consolidation of peace, to combat hatred between nationalities and between classes which are the greatest dangers to peace, and to prepare the way for moral disarmament'. In September 1931 the Assembly of the League of Nations adopted a resolution that requested the Council of the League to consider the possibility of studying, with the help of the press, 'the difficult problem of the spread of information which may threaten to disturb the peace or the good understanding between nations'. The increasing concern of the League for moral disarmament evidently reflected the actual historical developments of the period, such as the emergence of Nazism in Germany. When the World Disarmament Conference opened in February 1932 the press was given great importance in moving public opinion towards moral disarmament. A second conference with press experts was convened in Copenhagen in 1932, and one of its resolutions addressed among other issues the problem of inaccurate news. Following the Copenhagen conference, a conference of governmental press bureaux and representatives of the press was held at Madrid in November 1933. This conference adopted a resolution on the right to correct false information.

In 1931 the League of Nations decided to ask the Institute for Intellectual Cooperation (the predecessor of Unesco) to conduct a study on all questions raised by the use of radio for good international relations. In 1933 the study was published (*Broadcasting and Peace*) and it recommended the drafting of a binding multilateral treaty. Under the war threat emanating from Germany after 1933 the treaty was indeed drafted and concluded on 23 September 1936 with signatures from 28 states. The fascist states did not participate. The International Convention Concerning the Use of Broadcasting in the Cause of Peace entered into force on 2 April 1938 after ratification or accession by nine countries: Brazil, the United Kingdom, Denmark, France, India, Luxembourg, New Zealand, the Union of South Africa and Australia. Basic to the provisions of the convention was the recognition of the need to prevent, through rules established by common agreement, broadcasting from being used in a manner prejudicial to good international understanding. These agreed rules included the prohibition of transmissions which could incite the population of any territory 'to acts incompatible with the internal order or security of contracting parties' or which were likely to harm good international understanding by incorrect statements. The contracting parties also agreed to ensure 'that any transmission likely to harm good international understanding by incorrect statements shall be rectified at the earliest possible moment'. In 1994 the convention was still in force and had been ratified by 26 member states of the United Nations.

Early world communication politics and the INGOs

The development of industrialization and urbanization in late nineteenth century Europe brought about important social changes. A modern society was constructed with 'a new sense of self, of subjectivity and individuality' (Eyerman, 1992: 38). This modern society gave rise to the emergence of a multitude of voluntary, non-state associations, such as the trade unions.

The following sections emphasize the important role played by these non-state actors in the negotiations leading towards the first multilateral agreements on world communication already described.

Telecommunication
The 1865 ITU convention recognized the possibility for private companies to become a contracting party to the Union. In 1868 the Vienna International Telegraph Conference recognized private telegraph operators and as a result Great Britain acceded to the Union. The St Petersburg Telegraph Conference in 1875 was attended by 24 member states and sixteen recognized private operators.

In 1903 the first conference on the regulation of wireless radio-telegraphy took place, basically to address the problems implied in the monopoly control by private operators in maritime communications. The first Radio Conference after the First World War was held at Washington in 1927. Eighty countries attended to draft a new Radio Convention and Radio Regulations. Private companies were prominently represented and they practically wrote the Radio Convention (Luther, 1988: 28). The private players forcefully lobbied against legal rules that would permit public control over their operations and pleaded the 'first come, first served' approach to radio frequency spectrum management. The convention followed their preferences.

In the early telecommunication conferences, firms such as AT&T did not have an independent vote in the policy negotiations but were represented by their home governments. AT&T played a role in US delegations to ITU conferences from the 1930s on. AT&T was especially important since it not only was heavily involved in international telephone traffic, but also played a key role in technological innovation in the telecommunication field.

Intellectual and industrial property protection
In the preparations for the Berne convention on copyright the non-governmental organization ALAI played an essential role. The first series of annual conferences of ALAI (London in 1879, Vienna in 1881 and Rome in 1882) provided support for the international recognition of author's rights. The Rome conference proposed to establish a union for literary property, and recommended that a

conference be held in Berne to discuss the implementation of the union project. In 1883 the diplomatic conferences of Berne began with the congress promoted by the ALAI. In the development of industrial property protection, non-governmental organizations were also present and influential. The first non-governmental organization to be admitted to a Paris revision conference of the Treaty on Industrial Property in 1925 (The Hague) was the International Chamber of Commerce.

Mass media

Towards the end of the nineteenth century the increasingly international character of journalism stimulated the organization of journalists across national borders. In a number of European capitals associations of foreign correspondents were founded and in 1893 the first international press congress took place at Chicago. Among the topics addressed by the congress participants was the international role of the press. The following year an international congress at Antwerp (7–12 July 1894) established the first international organization, the International Union of Press Associations (IUPA). The congress was attended by journalists, press owners and publishers from seventeen countries (Belgium, France, Argentina, Spain, Denmark, Norway, Sweden, Germany, Austria, Italy, Russia, the UK, Portugal, the Netherlands, Switzerland, New Zealand and the USA). The IUPA was to address many different issues, such as property rights, work on Sundays, women's emancipation, wages, working conditions, professional training, professional ethics and the problems of international dissemination of false news and war propaganda. In the early 1920s many new international organizations were set up; the IUPA became marginalized and held its last assembly in 1936.

Meanwhile the International Federation of Newspaper Publishers Associations (FIADEJ) had been established in 1933; after the Second World War it was replaced by the International Federation of Editors of Journals and Publications (FIEJ). Other organizations appeared in this period: the International Association of Journalists was accredited to the League of Nations in 1921, the International Sporting Press Association (ISPA) in 1924, the International Federation of the Periodic Press (IFPP) in 1925, and the International Catholic Union of the Press (UCIP) in 1927.

In 1926 the French Journalists' Syndicate took the initiative for the establishment of an international organization of journalists. At a conference in Paris (June 1926) it was decided that this organization would be formally constituted as the International Federation of Journalists (IFJ) by a congress in Geneva at the ILO headquarters.[5] This congress took place in September 1926 and was attended by journalist organizations from several European countries and representatives of the ILO, the League of Nations and the International Institute of Intellectual Cooperation.

In 1926 the League of Nations commissioned the ILO to study the working conditions of journalists. When this study was published in 1928 (*Conditions of Work and Life of Journalists*) it pointed among others to 'an evil from which journalism has suffered since its beginnings, but which was becoming more and more threatening as the profession developed – incoherence, arbitrariness, the absence of a code which would define rights and duties, and which would introduce a little order, and at the same time a little justice, in the conditions in which this great modern profession is unfolding. The absence of a code, which is beginning to be remedied in certain countries, is a veritable anachronism' (Kubka and Nordenstreng, 1986a: 95).

The second congress of the IFJ in November 1928 at Dijon discussed the establishment of an international tribunal of honour for journalists and decided to mandate the permanent commission to elaborate a professional code and to set up a tribunal of honour (Kubka and Nordenstreng, 1986a: 60). The next year the IFJ executive committee discussed at length the principles to guide the tribunal (October 1929 at Antwerp), and at the third IFJ congress the establishment of the tribunal was a key item on the agenda. The Berlin congress of 1930 adopted a fundamental declaration with the principles for the judgements by the tribunal. The preamble referred to the wish to create an institution which sought to establish and maintain a good understanding among peoples, to uplift professional dignity of prescribing special duties for journalists and to secure the legitimate rights of the members of the professional organizations. Alongside the declaration was adopted a procedural code formulating the rules of dispute settlement by the tribunal.

The International Journalists' Tribunal of Honour was solemnly inaugurated at The Hague (in the Palace of Peace) on 12 October 1931. In his inaugural address the president of the tribunal, the Dutch jurist B.C.J. Loder, mentioned that the 'great danger for the people, even in our modern times, the source of many of their conflicts, is that they do not know each other, do not understand each other, that they see only that which divides them instead of being aware of that which could unite them' (Kubka and Nordenstreng, 1986a: 68). The tribunal consisted of a president, a vice-president, two permanent judges, four alternative judges, a public prosecutor, and two alternative prosecutors. The tribunal was to deal with disputes relating to honour which might arise between journalists of different nationalities, or between a journalist and a non-journalist of different nationalities.

In 1937 the issue of a deontological code was on the agenda, and the seventh and last FIJ congress in 1939 at Bordeaux adopted a Professional Code of Honour for Journalists. In addition, the organization of publishers was concerned about the issue of professional responsibility and especially about the spreading of false information. It drafted a convention in 1933 that included the immediate correction of false news. By 1938 the convention was adhered to by member associations from eight countries.

Developments since 1945

It is always somewhat hazardous to identify the key components of historical processes and there is probably always an element of subjective preference and (by implication) of distortion in the exercise. Surveying the past decades of world politics in substantive issue areas of world communication it would appear that among the most important factors affecting its development and orientation are the real-world environment in which world politics takes place; the multilateral institutions that to a great extent are the negotiating forums for state and non-state actors; the growing importance of the non-state actors; and the economic and technological changes in the world. These factors will be briefly discussed before turning to a closer analysis of the distinct issue areas of world communication in the following chapters.

The real-world environment

Two features stand out in the environment of world communication politics since 1945: the expansion of the world system and the great tensions in the system across the East–West and North–South axes.

Since the end of the Second World War the number of active participants in the world political arena has dramatically grown. With the advent of new multilateral institutions there was also the development of larger and more heterogeneous constituencies that began to bring an increasingly diversified set of claims to the diplomatic negotiations. Multilateral diplomacy had been used to a relatively homogeneous European cultural climate. The dialogue between states took place within a state system that shared a large measure of similarity. This fundamentally changed with the advent of the socialist bloc countries and the post-colonial societies. A large group of new states entered the arena and brought new claims as well as challenges to the existing arrangements. In addition an increasing number of non-state actors became heavily involved in political negotiations on issues of information and culture. A primary tension that affected all these actors was the development of a bipolar world locked into a 'Cold War'. The East–West confrontation had a significant influence on the multilateral negotiations. Its overall effect was that most of the issues on the political agenda were located in the context of the superpower conflict which made their resolution complex and often unattainable. For example, Cold War suspicion and distrust made it difficult to reconcile different positions on the management of the radio frequency spectrum and largely obstructed planning for the high-frequency bands. It also brought special regulatory issues to the agenda such as those related to the phenomenon of 'jamming'. When in 1947 the Voice of America established Russian and Eastern European language services, the Soviet Union decided to begin operating full-time jamming against these services. With the heating up of the Cold War, jamming increased, and as it continued throughout the 1950s and 1960s multilateral efforts to negotiate a settlement remained unsuccessful.

The fundamental debate on freedom of information was strongly affected by the East–West adverse positions, as were the debates on Third World demands for a restructuring of the international provision of information. During those decades there was in many instances an allegiance between the position of the Soviet bloc and the Third World community. On the one hand this meant that the hegemonic positions of the Western bloc (particularly the United States) could be challenged with at least the (largely theoretical) capacity to outvote the minority of affluent market economies. On the other hand, the alliance did not necessarily benefit the developing countries, as their legitimate demands were incorporated into the unproductive bipolarity of mutually exclusive world views.

In addition to the East–West tension, the demise of the colonial powers could not fail to have an impact on the politics of world communication. In the post-war period a large number of new, post-colonial states emerged in Asia and Africa. In their struggle to become sovereign entities they confronted, in addition to political and economic dependencies, the cultural legacy of former colonial relations.

The first generation of post-colonial nationalist leaders was intent on creating national integration in state structures that were internally threatened by the existence of multiple nationalities (often artificially thrown together) and externally beleaguered by a forceful cultural diplomacy enacted through Western foreign policy and business interests. In the early 1950s the first collective action by the post-colonial states began. In those years the political cooperation between African and Asian countries, in particular, was at stake, as the 1955 Bandung conference demonstrated. In the 1960s this coalition was extended to include the Latin American countries, which in particular brought economic problems to the agenda. In fact, since the mid 1960s the non-aligned movement has given increasing attention to strategies for the development of economic links among the countries of the South. Alongside the non-aligned movement, the so-called Group of 77 came into existence at the first UNCTAD conference in 1964. These two overlapping groups were both affected by the conflicting efforts of the South to strengthen horizontal linkages and to cope with the remaining links with the former colonial powers.

It became clear in the early 1970s that these latter links had an important cultural component. In particular, the non-aligned summit in Algiers (1973) began to extend South–South cooperation to the area of cultural development.

Throughout the 1970s the debate on the information issue (which took place primarily in Unesco) developed in the context of an economic dialogue between the North and the South which was largely inspired by the threat of a North–South confrontation over oil prices. Because of this threat the United Nations General Assembly adopted (in 1974) the Declaration and Programme of Action on the Establishment of a New International Economic Order. In the same year the Charter of Economic Rights and Duties of States was adopted. In 1976 the UNCTAD IV at Nairobi adopted the Integrated Programme for Commodities and a new financial institution was created to support the effort to stabilize the world's commodity markets, the Common Fund.

In the reality of world politics all this meant very little. In fact, by the end of the 1970s the North had withdrawn from this dialogue as the oil threat had subsided. The UNCTAD V in 1979 at Manila marked the point at which the North–South round of negotiations on a fundamental restructuring of the world economy effectively ended. A few efforts to renew the dialogue in the early 1980s (such as the Cancun summit of 1981, or the UNCTAD VI in 1983) met with no success.

In the earliest meetings of the Economic and Social Council the inadequacy of information facilities in the less developed countries was highlighted. Diplomats representing these countries stressed that with the existing disparities there could be no reciprocity and equality in world communication. The General Assembly in 1958 requested ECOSOC to formulate 'a programme of concrete action and measures on the international plane which could be undertaken for the development of information enterprises in under-developed countries'. The specialized agencies were invited to contribute to this initiative. Unesco was assigned to survey the problems involved in the development of communication.

Among the other specialized agencies to become active in North–South issues was the International Telecommunication Union. In 1959 the ITU convention made reference to the need for cooperation and coordination related to development assistance. In addition the Universal Postal Union became involved with development assistance. This was seen to fall within its mandate to contribute to the organization and development of postal services and the fostering of international postal cooperation. Through the United Nations Development Programme (UNPD) the UPU contributed to various training programmes and institutions for postal administrations and to technical cooperation among developing countries. Other UN agencies that became engaged in development assistance in the communications field were the FAO (particularly assistance to development support for communication projects), the WHO (projects on media and health/nutrition), UNFPA (communication in family planning), Unicef (communication for social development projects) and in particular UNDP.

Development cooperation was also initiated in the field of copyright protection. As the payment of copyright fees turned out to be a real problem for poor countries, Unesco created a system by which governments in rich countries may reimburse their own authors for the publication of their copyrighted materials in poor countries. Additionally the Committee for International Copyright Funds was created by Unesco to assist the payment of copyright fees through loans. The Joint Unesco/WIPO Consultative Committee on the Access by Developing Countries to Works Protected by Copyright was established in November 1979 by an agreement between WIPO and Unesco. One of the tasks of the committee was to improve awareness about the importance of copyright for poorer countries. The main purpose of the work was to facilitate the negotiation and conclusion of publishing and translation contracts between publishers in developing countries and copyright owners who are nationals of industrialized countries.[6]

The developing countries did not merely provide the incentive for cooperation programmes; they also challenged the existing international industrial property system and the conventional copyright conventions. Similar challenges were launched against dominant telecommunications arrangements. For example, they took issue with such conventionally adopted policy principles as 'first come, first served' in resource allocations. In the field of space resources the developing countries were instrumental in introducing the concept of 'common heritage' in the 1979 Moon Treaty. Herewith a claim was laid to equitable access to space resources following the formulation in the 1967 Outer Space Treaty of such basic principles as: 'The exploration and use of outer space, including the Moon and other celestial bodies, shall be carried out for the benefit and in the interests of all countries, irrespective of their degree of economic or scientific development, and shall be the province of all mankind.'

The new multilateral institutions

United Nations With the creation of the United Nations and its specialized agencies a crucial group of institutions for multilateral policy evolution and policy coordination entered the international system. The General Assembly of the UN (particularly through the International Law Commission and several sub-commissions) and the International Court of Justice became the primary movers in the progressive development of the norms and rules that make up the current system of international law.

The UN General Assembly has contributed to world communication politics through a vast number of resolutions that address such divergent issues as the jamming of broadcasts, the protection of journalists on dangerous missions, direct satellite broadcasting, and the human rights aspects of science and technology. Among the key standard-setting instruments adopted by the General Assembly that are pertinent to world communication are the basic human rights covenants, declarations and conventions against discrimination and treaties on outer space law.

Among the various organs of the UN General Assembly, special attention to communication matters is located in the Third Committee of the General Assembly (responsible for social, humanitarian and cultural matters) and the Economic and Social Council. The Economic and Social Council was established as the principal organ to coordinate the economic and social work of the United Nations and the specialized agencies. In the subsidiary bodies of the Council communication issues are addressed, especially in the case of the Commission on Human Rights or the Commission on Transnational Corporations.

Of particular importance was the establishment by the General Assembly in 1959 of the Committee on the Peaceful Uses of Outer Space. This body became the focal point for UN standard setting in outer space law with important references to world communication politics through regulatory instruments addressing satellite broadcasting.

In 1966 the General Assembly established the Commission on International Trade Law (UNCITRAL) with the mandate to facilitate the harmonization of the law of international trade. With the increasing importance of computer technology in international transactions, the Commission has been required to address such problems as legal validity of computer records and liability in electronic funds transfers.

In 1978 the UN General Assembly established the United Nations Committee on Information which received its mandate through a resolution adopted on 18 December 1979 (34/182). The committee has contributed to a series of resolutions on the new international information order and the public information activities of the United Nations.

The specialized agencies Multilateral policy is also made by the specialized agencies of the United Nations, and several of these became important regulators for the field of communication. This is particularly true for such organizations as the ITU, the UPU, Unesco and WIPO. To a far lesser extent the ILO became involved through employment questions relating to communication professionals, and the WHO and FAO through work in the field of standards for advertising and marketing of health and food products.

Standards affecting world communications are also set in the International Civil Aviation Organization (ICAO) which has adopted rules for aircraft telecommunications systems, and the International Maritime Organization (IMO) which has addressed issues of maritime communications. In addition to the already existing multilateral forums that became UN specialized agencies, new regulatory bodies were established such as the Intergovernmental Bureau for Informatics (IBI) (since defunct) and the United Nations Conference on Trade and Development (UNCTAD), which has adopted standards in such fields as intellectual property and transfer of technology.

An important multilateral organization which does not belong to the United Nations family is the General Agreement on Tariffs and Trade. Among the other important multilateral bodies with participation of national governments are the organizations that have been established for the operational application of space telecommunications technology. These are primarily the intergovernmental satellite systems, established by treaty, of Intelsat and Inmarsat.

Three other intergovernmental multilateral institutions should be mentioned, although they are not as broadly representative and are more regionally oriented. However, they have made very significant contributions to world communication politics. These are the OECD, the Conference on Security and Cooperation in Europe and the Council of Europe. In such fields as the freedom of information and the protection of transborder flows, the standard-setting work of these organizations has had an important impact at a world level.

The non-governmental organizations
In the post-1945 phase of the evolution of world communication politics an important contribution was offered by a rapidly growing group of international non-governmental organizations (INGOs). These INGOs are in part truly international in terms of membership and activities, and in part national but with activities that have an international impact. Obviously, they do not have the legal power to issue binding decisions, but they can influence the policy making processes of the intergovernmental organizations as expert groups or as lobbying agents. They can also define standards for their own conduct which may have a political significance beyond the members of the group they represent. Illustrations are the efforts of the international professional bodies in journalism to arrive at a self-regulatory code of conduct, and the self-regulatory codes that are adopted by the International Public Relations Association and the International Advertising Association.

The United Nations and its specialized agencies have from their inception involved non-governmental organizations in their policy making processes. In the development of international human rights law, for example, the INGOs have played a very important role. INGOs, such as Amnesty International have contributed to a crucial instrument for the implementation of human rights standards: 'the mobilization of shame'. Another example is provided by those INGOs that keep the World Health Organization informed of acts by multinational companies that violate the WHO code on the marketing of breastmilk substitutes. In the field of development cooperation new policy insights have been forced upon public institutions through INGO pressure in such fields as women, population, health and environment. Various resolutions by the UN General Assembly have accorded special significance to the contributions of organizations representing scientists, employers and workers' unions in the negotiations on a code of conduct for transnational corporations.

In the UN, agencies such as the ITU, WIPO and Unesco INGOs have made very significant contributions to the formulation of world communication politics.

The world economy
Trading across borders grew exponentially after 1945 and added to the volume of movements of goods, services, capital, people and information world-wide. World exports increased from US $63 billion in 1948 to over US $400 billion by 1977. The need to regulate world trade did lead to the establishment of such important trade and monetary negotiating forums as the GATT, the IMF and the OECD. Vital actors in the world economy became the transnational corporations. Since the early 1950s there has been a rapid rise of transnational industrial and financial companies. These spread their affiliates across the globe and began marketing, advertising and trading in many of the developing countries. As part of the growing world business system, the branch of communication conglomerates developed into one of the leading sectors.

Increasingly, the world flows of news and entertainment began to be controlled by ever fewer companies, often closely interlocked among themselves and with other industrial and financial interests. The increase in scope of industrial activities led to a rapidly growing need for extensive information networks. Telecommunications became critical to the coordination of the dispersed activities of transnational corporations. To support marketing, advertising and public relations, large companies began to develop their own media production capacities. As a result of these developments the transnational business system emerged as a formidable lobby in multilateral negotiations.

The world economy also created a new environment for world communication politics. The increase of private consumption of goods and services implied a growth of information-intensive activities such as airline reservations, hotel bookings, entertainment, consumer electronics and the use of credit cards.

The increasing significance of these services and their trading across borders raised new regulatory issues.

The technological innovations
Rapid developments in the field of communication technology created the need to fill a regulatory vacuum in several areas. Technology also became economically more significant and this brought about a greater need to protect national economic interests and a greater pressure to enact industrial property protection legislation. The international patent system became increasingly important to the transnational corporations.

The years after the Second World War also saw the emergence of an international telephone system that developed from a situation of largely uncoordinated and fragmented national systems. Next to the internationalization of telephony (and later of data communications) the most important technological development was the growth of television.

Technology played a double role. It gave rise to new regulatory controversies, such as the allotment of the geosynchronous orbit (GSO); but it also resolved problems, for example through enlarging the radio frequency spectrum (RFS) capacity.

Particularly influential for the development of world communication politics were the innovations in space technology, reproduction technology and computer technology.

Space technology The development of space technology raised new and complex questions about access to and control over space resources, such as orbital slots and radio frequencies. The feasibility of direct broadcasting from space and the possibility of remote resource sensing by satellites created the need for a new set of standards. A new legal speciality was developed, space law; this had important implications for world communication.

Satellite communications also raised new questions with regard to the free flow principle. Controversial regulatory debates in the ITU, COPUOS and Unesco addressed the question of whether direct broadcasting by satellite should involve free transmissions from space to any receiving point on earth or whether receiving states should have the right of 'prior consent'.

Reproduction technology A crucial piece of equipment that confronted intellectual property protection with new challenges was the photocopying machine. It exacerbated the implied tension in copyright law between the interests of authors, publishers and the general public (particularly in the field of education). The improved techniques for reprography (the shift from carbo-copying and stencil machine to the xerographic machines of the early 1960s) and for reproduction of audiovisual materials (audio compact cassettes and video recording equipment) provided an unprecedented dissemination of copyrighted works and theoretically a proportional increase in remuneration for their authors. At the same time, however, these techniques began to erode the system of protection.

Computer technology This most advanced communication technology raised very complex regulatory issues in such fields as privacy, crime, trade and financial transactions. Particularly through the merger with telecommunication technology, the new phenomenon of transborder data flows emerged from the 1950s and brought new policy concerns to the world political agenda.

Significance of world communication

Since the mid nineteenth century, world communication has acquired status on the agenda of world politics. As world communication moved into the arena of world politics, the politics of world communication emerged as a political playing-field with distinct players, claims and negotiations. This development was largely caused by the increasing dominance of information traffic in relation to other forms of transborder movement.

A common typology of transborder traffic distinguishes between the movements of goods, money, people and information. Among these four main types of cross-border movement, the movement of information has become increasingly dominant as other transactions became dependent upon it or evolved themselves into information transactions. In fact, a large volume of cross-border transactions today is supported by communication capacity and by information-based services such as advertising. The transport of goods and people across borders has in fact become impossible without such services. The cross-border movement of goods has become reliant upon electronic data interchange. Computer-to-computer exchanges process trade contracts, transport bills of lading, transmit invoices and arrange for payments. The significance of information traffic is also demonstrated by the fact that according to a *Communications Week* survey (21 May 1990) the annual expenditures of the top 100 telecommunication users (among them the top world traders in goods) range between US $1 billion and US $20 million annually. In the movement of finance the delivery of communication capacity and information services is actually the main product line. Money traffic is to a large extent a flow of data and information. Financial transactions in the world have become dependent upon telecommunication facilities, electronic data processing systems and electronic information services. Some US 9×10^{12} in electronic funds transfers take place annually through telecommunication facilities. The credit card business centres around the trading of information.

The cross-border movement of people is information intense, as the airlines passenger traffic demonstrates. On board a Boeing 747 from Amsterdam to New York there are on average some 30,000 messages connected to the transported passengers. As a result the privacy sensitivity of such transborder data flows has become a regulatory concern of the IATA. It is unthinkable for today's airlines to operate without access to computerized reservation systems. The linking of these systems with hotel and car rental reservation systems provides their owners with the tools to control a key resource in the world economy: information. Tourism is increasingly dependent upon the usage of information and communication technologies. These are essential to the industry. 'Tourism has become a complex global process in the high-speed movement and management of data and capital as well as of literally millions of individuals' (Mowlana and Smith, 1990: 316).

The increasing significance of world communication can also be explained by reference to its economic role. In 1980 the total world market for communication hardware and software could be estimated at some US $350 billion or some 18 per cent of total world trade. In 1986 the total world market for equipment (consumer electronics, telecommunication equipment, computers and semiconductors), services (telecommunication services, data processing services and advertising) and mass media (broadcasting, publishing, film and recorded music) created a business of over US $1600 billion. Within three decades the information industry became big business for big companies and big markets. In 1992 *The Economist* predicted that by 2000 the international media industry would reach the US $3 trillion mark.

The significant contribution of the communication industry to the world economy inevitably places its regulation on the agenda of world politics. Over the past decades, information has become a key resource in the world economy, and by implication the cross-border movement of information has become a key trade issue. The importance of information on the agenda is also reflected in the changes in its institutional environment. The big telecommunication users, and the vendors as well as the service suppliers, have demanded representation in the multilateral forums. As the movement of information became critical to the world economy, the trade policy makers moved into an arena formerly the privileged domain of telecommunication regulators and intellectual property rights negotiators.

Over the past decades, with dramatic exceptions like the Gulf War, the world political arena has moved from muscle to nerve. The nervous system has begun to replace the muscular system in high politics. World politics consists of a great variety of interactions in which actors communicate with the intention to influence other actors. The effectiveness of this interaction depends largely upon the quality, credibility and efficiency of the transborder movement of information. This type of cross-border interaction has become a crucial component of the conduct of world politics.

International publicity more than ever before has become an essential instrument in the conduct of the business of world politics. World communication is the predominant source of the perceptions that decision makers and their constituencies hold about events in the world. Coverage (with its biases and omissions) of international events, such as the Gulf War, has an important influence in shaping the world views that promote and legitimate concrete action. Mass media, films, literature, radio and TV have an impact on the ways in which citizens and governments shape images about other countries.

> Most people depend on second-hand experiences or information for what they know or want to know about foreign countries. And for most of them this information is not important to shaping their lives, i.e. there is no need to try to obtain primary, first-hand information. Since most people's scope of experience is naturally limited and their knowledge of complex social processes in foreign countries comes mainly from the mass media there is always the danger of manipulation. Mass media reporting can create a 'reality', an image, of its own, and there can be very big differences between media reality and 'reality'. The media select just a few of the countless occurrences in the world, disseminate information about them and so construct an impression of social reality. The influence of the mass media is especially great when no other source of information is available; especially great, too, if there is no possibility of checking on media 'reality'. In this respect television appears to make a particularly powerful impact, at least on average recipients, because of its pictorial documentary character. (Kunczik, 1990: 27)

It can also be observed that the adoption of world communication on the agenda coincides with the increasing significance of issues of 'low politics', such as welfare, common heritage and human rights. It reflects the extension of world politics beyond the conventional 'high politics' of armament and security issues.

Summary

Since the mid nineteenth century, world communication has developed into an important concern on the agenda of the world community. The substantive issue areas of world communication politics have expanded. Today they encompass the fields of mass communication, telecommunication, data communication, intellectual property and communication technology. World communication politics is initiated, amended, debated and implemented by a variety of multilateral forums including both governmental and non-governmental organizations. For specific issue areas, distinct multilateral institutions have become responsible.

World communication in the 1990s continues to confront the world political arena with complex and controversial policy concerns that demand resolution through multilateral bargaining.

The next chapter introduces a framework for the analysis and assessment of the politics of world communication.

Notes

1 As Archer notes, the one possible exception may have been the Greek amphictyonic councils (1983: 5). Nicolson describes these councils as 'something between a Church Congress, an Eisteddfod and a meeting of the League of Nations . . . Although the main purpose of these conferences, as of the permanent secretariat which they maintained, was the safeguarding of shrines and treasures and the regulation of the pilgrim traffic, they also dealt with political matters of common Hellenic interest and, as such, had an important diplomatic function' (1969: 18–19). The ancient Greek councils were an early attempt to establish a multilateral cooperative arrangement that was to prevent warfare among its participating actors.

2 Signatories of the covenant of the League (part of the 1919 Versailles Treaty of Peace) were the USA, Belgium, Bolivia, Brazil, the British Empire (UK, Canada, Australia, South Africa, New Zealand, India), China, Cuba, Ecuador, France, Greece, Guatemala, Haiti, Hejaz, Honduras, Italy, Japan, Liberia, Nicaragua, Panama, Peru, Poland, Portugal, Romania, the Serb-Croat-Slovene State, Siam, Czechoslovakia and Uruguay.

3 The countries present at the conference were Austria and Hungary, Belgium, Denmark, Egypt, France, Germany, the United Kingdom, Greece, Italy, Luxembourg, the Netherlands, Norway, Portugal, Romania, Russia, Serbia, Spain, Sweden, Switzerland, Turkey and the United States of America.

4 The following states did attend: Austria, Baden, Bavaria, Belgium, Denmark, France, Hamburg, Hanover, Italy, the Netherlands, Portugal, Prussia, Russia, Saxony, Spain, Sweden-Norway, Turkey and Württemberg. The United Kingdom was excluded as its telegraph network was privately owned. Consequently it was also decided in 1858 by the Unions that French and German were to be the official languages for international telegrams.

5 In French: Fédération Internationale des Journalistes (FIJ).

6 Essential in the development cooperation of WIPO has been the development of human resources. A special effort has been made in individual on-the-job training. Several member states and copyright organizations have contributed towards meeting the costs of instructors, teaching materials, travel and accommodation, and meeting facilities. Since 1976 a special body has been established (by a decision of the conference of WIPO) called the WIPO Permanent Committee for Development Cooperation Related to Copyright and Neighboring Rights. Its main task is to monitor the permanent programme that sets out 'to promote, in favor of developing countries, by all means within the competence of the World Intellectual Property Organization (WIPO) (i) the encouragement in developing countries of intellectual creation in the literary, scientific and artistic domain, (ii) the dissemination, within the competence of WIPO as defined in the WIPO Convention, in developing countries, under fair and reasonable conditions, of intellectual creations in the literary, scientific and artistic domain protected by the rights of authors (copyright) and by the rights of performing artists, producers of phonograms and broadcasting organizations (neighboring rights), (iii) the development of legislation and institutions in the fields of copyright and neighboring rights in developing countries'.

2
World Politics: Practices, Processes and People

Since world communication has achieved agenda status in world politics, the question arises of how the world community has decided to deal with the major issues in this arena. In response to this question I intend to study the main issue areas of world communication politics and identify the positions that the key players have taken.

The context

The politics of world communication is part of the broader arena of world politics. Two features are essential to this arena. The first is that the key players are no longer states only. Although state actors may still be the principal rule makers, more and more non-state actors have come to play an increasingly significant role in world policy making. The nation-state now shares the arena with the IGOs, the BINGOs, the PINGOs and even with individuals. The second feature is the connection between the world arena and the local space in which most people live.

The multiple-actor arena

The new players in the world political arena challenge the conventional 'realist' view of international relations. This view departs from the premise that world society is anarchical and that world politics is about the establishment and maintenance of order between states. 'This traditional view of international relations also holds that the object of study is the behaviour of states towards other states, and the outcome of such behaviour for states: whether they are better or worse off, less or more powerful or secure.' In the reality of world politics the 'who-gets-what questions must also now be asked – about social groups, generations, genders, and not least, about firms and the sectors in which they operate' (Strange, 1992: 11).

State actors: the nation-states

Although in very real terms a multiple-actor system has evolved in the past decades, it would be unrealistic to put the old Westphalian system to rest. The Peace of Westphalia (1648) marked the beginning of a world system of independent, sovereign nation-states.[1] That system is still a formidable component of world politics. As Hocking and Smith argue: 'The state is still a major participant in the arena, generating influential actions and attracting attention. The state system, in consequence, still remains the most powerful set of organizing forces and activities, but it is not the only significant cluster of networks' (1990: 79).

In today's world system the notion of national sovereignty is certainly under siege, but it has not yet surrendered. The form of national sovereignty in which states treat their nationals as they see fit is still powerful in spite of the formal recognition of universal human rights. In fact, the Westphalian arrangement continues to be a major obstacle to the universal respect for human rights.

The most serious attack on nation-state sovereignty would appear to originate with the most powerful protagonists of global integration, the transnational corporations (TNCs). The reality is however more complex and ambivalent. Specifically, these corporations tend to benefit from the maintenance of strong nation-states. There are certainly contentions between states and TNCs but, as Mel Gurtov observes, 'these conflicts should not obscure their overall symbiotic relationship' (1988: 31). National sovereignty helps the TNCs to avoid the creation of genuine supranational regulatory institutions that might control their restrictive business practices. TNCs need national governments to guarantee safe investment environments, to create market opportunities through foreign aid or to promote the trade of their 'national' companies through their diplomatic missions. They may also benefit from supportive national regulation on technical standards, patent and trade mark protection, or acquisitions and mergers. Governments also provide important markets through purchases in defence and information technology sectors. Much corporate research and development depends upon the provision of public finances. Tran Van Dinh and Rosemary Porter strongly argue that the independent nation-state and international capital should be seen as interdependent. For example, 'international capital is at its most cost efficient if it separates itself from responsibility for the expense of reproducing the system (i.e. education, child care, health, and subsistence economies) and relies upon the nation-states and the people themselves to provide these services' (1986: 125). By and large then it would seem that current globalization processes leave the exercise of national sovereignty unhampered. It is even arguable that the currently dominant form of global integration operates largely through the continued existence of strong independent nation-states that conveniently serve the maintenance of an asymmetrical world society.

Despite the fact that states continue to command considerable force and loyalty, it cannot be denied that there is a shift from a single-actor state-centric world system to a multiple-actor polycentric world system. This has signalled the inevitable erosion of the position of the state as the sole gatekeeper between domestic societies and the international system. A great many actors are today involved in the expression and the protection of people's needs and demands. This civic activity is largely inspired by an increasing world-wide awareness of the incapacity of state representatives to articulate and meet the concerns of their people. This is related to the growing complexity of most domestic political systems, but also to the emergence of a vast array of commercial and non-commercial social forces that are actively mobilizing people's opinions and actions.

Non-state actors

The major shortcoming of the state-centric model is that it ignores the role of non-state actors, such as intergovernmental organizations (IGOs), international non-governmental organizations (BINGOs and PINGOs) and individuals. Examples of IGOs include such organizations as NATO, OPEC, OAS, OAU, and the Arab League. PINGOs (public interest organizations) include the international labour unions and such organizations as the International Olympic Committee, the Palestine Liberation Organization, the African National Congress and the Organization of the Islamic Conference. BINGOs (business interest organizations) are transnational corporations such as AT&T and Shell (Table 2.1).

Intergovernmental organizations (IGOs)
Today's world politics is inconceivable without the multilateral institutions. They emerged in the nineteenth century as a response to the growing need of states to collaborate. In the twentieth century they developed into prime forums of world politics as they (particularly the League of Nations and later the United Nations) began to address the perplexing problems created by the First and Second World Wars. Since 1945 there has been a proliferation of

Table 2.1   *Examples of non-state actors*

IGOs	BINGOs	PINGOs
United Nations	AT&T	Greenpeace Int.
NATO	Shell	World Fed. Trade Unions
OPEC	Exxon	Int. Olympic Committee
OAS	General Electric	Amnesty International
OAU	Nippon T&T	World Council of Churches
Arab League	Mitsubishi	Org. of Islamic Conf.
European Union	Sumitomo	PLO

IGOs intergovernmental organizations; BINGOs business interest INGOs; PINGOs professional and public interest INGOs

these institutions in many new terrains of world politics. Between 1956 and 1989 the number increased from 132 to 300 (Saur, 1989).

The IGOs play a significant role in world political agenda setting. They represent the largest forum for multilateral rule making. Most of the standards for the conduct of international actors find their origin with these institutions.

Pentland (1976: 631–56) considers that IGOs perform three functions: they are instruments of nation-states' foreign policy; they serve to modify states' behaviour; and they act as players in their own right. As players with a measure of autonomy IGOs have an impact on the ways in which governments and their officials perceive issue areas. The IGOs also use their own resources to lobby for preferred policies, for example by building coalitions with governments. An important fourth function of IGOs is to provide a level of legitimacy to the operations of other players. The international business corporations (BINGOs) tend to increasingly use the IGOs as instruments to further their interests. As it is often necessary for the transnational corporations to get national governments to agree to their policies, the route through the IGOs helps to legitimize such policies. The non-commercial, public interest international non-governmental organizations (PINGOs) will also often try to influence the multilateral IGOs to initiate policies or alter existing ones.

The power of IGOs to enforce the decisions they take, and their capacity to implement the programmes they propose, differ greatly. Their political impact ranges from the symbolic to the concrete. The mechanisms for compliance with their promises range from simple consultation to sanctions. Most methods used by IGOs are non-binding, such as reporting on the implementation of decisions or examining situations of non-compliance. Only exceptionally can strong punitive measures be applied, such as economic or military sanctions.

INGOs

The INGOs play a variety of roles in the IGOs. They act as lobbyists, experts or programme executors. With most of the UN agencies the major INGOs have consultative status. The non-state actors can be instrumental to the states' desire to achieve a common agreement. They can also influence the type of agreement underlying a collective practice in an issue area. Many political practices are in fact based upon mixed agreements involving both public and private actors, for example in telecommunications.

BINGOs

'Governments must now bargain not only with other governments, but also with firms or enterprises, while firms now bargain both with governments and with one another' (Strange, 1992: 1). Strange calls this a 'fundamental change in the nature of diplomacy'. Contemporary world politics can only be realistically understood if the significant role of such non-state actors as the major transnational industrial and service corporations is taken into account.

BINGOs represent significant economic power. This power is used for political purposes when it is convenient to create tax havens, to encourage beneficial investment climates, or to control labour forces. There are at present over 20,000 business corporations that have commercial activities across borders. Together they control most of the world's technical innovations, handle some three-quarters of world trade, employ over 50 million people worldwide and invest in foreign affiliates over US $50 billion annually. In particular, since the early 1980s large transnational business conglomerates have become increasingly active and effective in the forums where inter-state negotiations take place. They have successfully lobbied in the United Nations Food and Agriculture Organization, the World Health Organization and the GATT.

Between the early 1960s and 1978 a programme functioned within the FAO that was clearly under the control of transnational agribusiness companies. Only as action groups began to expose this did the Industry Cooperative Programme (ICP) have to be dismantled. The ICP was an initiative of the Groupement International des Associations Nationales de Pesticides (GIFAP), a lobbying group for the agrochemical industry. In the early 1970s the FAO and the ICP organized joint workshops in the Third World on the distribution of pesticides. The most prominent participants in the ICP were major chemical industries. Their lobbyists had a good deal of influence upon the formulation of United Nations policy on agriculture. After the closure of the programme the FAO continued to have close liaisons with the pesticide business. As a probable result the standards enacted in the Codex Alimentarius (joint code of the FAO and the WHO) on pesticides are not very stringent. The links between the GIFAP and the FAO remained strong in pursuing largely similar policies. Industry experts were on panels, committees and workshops. In training workshops in Asia and Africa, GIFAP manuals and resource persons were used. Both the FAO and the GIFAP resisted the reduction of pesticides and strove towards registration and control measures that promote sales and application of pesticides. Both the FAO and the industry encouraged global free trading in agricultural products.

The transnational pharmaceutical companies (and particularly the International Federation of Pharmaceutical Manufacturers' Associations) has for a long time been very active in lobbying its case with WHO policy making. A very concrete case of successful lobbying was the deletion of a crucial recommendation on babymilk supplies in a report to the 39th World Health Assembly in May 1986. At the request of the 1985 Assembly a group of experts had looked into the violations by milk companies of the WHO/Unicef International Code on the Marketing of Breastmilk Substitutes. In its report the experts phrased as one of their recommendations that 'maternity wards and hospitals should not be recipients of free or subsidized supplies of breastmilk substitutes'. This recommendation followed from the finding that the transnational babymilk corporations were providing hospitals with large volumes of their products to stir up more demand. As one source in a report by the *International Herald Tribune* (10–11 May 1986) said: 'WHO was under political pressure from the US and from companies that manufacture these products not to be anything but vague.'[3]

There are strong indications that the GATT is evolving into an international forum controlled by the interests of the world's largest trading companies. At any rate, there can be little doubt that the transnational business community has played a very active role in the recent GATT negotiations on world trade and has had an important effect on the agenda setting and the outcome of negotiations. Throughout the Uruguay Trade Round the US administration, for example, cooperated closely with US corporations.

In May 1990 a powerful lobby (the Multilateral Trade Negotiations Coalition) was established by companies such as American Express, General Motors, IBM, Citicorp, Procter & Gamble and business associations such as the National Association of Manufacturers and the US Council for International Business. The business lobby was largely responsible for placing the issues of services and intellectual property rights on the multilateral agenda and for pushing negotiators to resolving those issues within a liberal 'free trade' and 'market access' regulatory framework.

In world communication politics the BINGOs represent a very powerful group of players. They often operate through such business associations as the International Chamber of Commerce, the International Publishers Association and the International Telecommunications Users Group. Within a multilateral public forum, such as the International Telecommunication Union, the industrial organizations have recently even shifted their legal status from mere observers to fully fledged participants.

PINGOs

The public and professional interest non-governmental organizations have proliferated since the early 1950s. Between 1956 and 1989 the number increased from 973 to 4621 (Saur, 1989). They include such moral lobbyists as Greenpeace International and Amnesty International, and professional interest groups such as the International Federation of Journalists.

The PINGO community fulfils a variety of functions in world politics: as publicists, calling public attention to certain concerns; as legitimators, providing credibility to certain claims; as lobbyists, exerting various pressures for the accommodation of preferential claims; as epistemic communities, that is sources of knowledge, expertise, ideas and intellectual support; and as alternative forums, offering opportunities for international discussion and opinion building where the intergovernmental community refuses to put or keep concerns on the agenda. The actions of these non-governmental actors are important as they may over time force a change from existing practice to stronger provisions.

Individuals

For the early writers about international law in the seventeenth century the status of individuals in world politics posed little problem. It was generally assumed that individuals had an international legal personality. 'But in the nineteenth century when positivism was the dominant philosophy, states were usually regarded as the only subjects of international law' (Akehurst, 1991: 72). In the twentieth century this approach began to shift with the judgements of the war tribunals of Nuremberg and Tokyo after the Second World War. The judges of these tribunals established that individuals have criminal liability under international law. The Nuremberg tribunal stated on 1 October 1946: 'Crimes against international law are committed by men, not by abstract entities, and only by punishing individuals who commit such crimes can the provision of international law be enforced.' A remarkable case was the death sentence against Julius Streicher, the publisher of the anti-semitic *Der Stürmer*. The tribunal found Streicher guilty of racist propaganda and incitement to genocide and gave the verdict of death by hanging. Thereby it was juridically established that individuals hold responsibilities under international law towards humanity.

This provision was reinforced by Article 29(1) of the Universal Declaration of Human Rights, which states that 'Everyone has duties to the community in which alone the free and full development of his personality is possible.' The preambles to the two leading international human rights instruments of 1966 added to this 'that the individual, having duties to other individuals and to the community to which he belongs, is under a responsibility to strive for the promotion and observance of the rights recognized in the present Covenant'. This created a legal personality for the individual person. The legal standing of the individual remained however restricted by the prevailing state system. As Akehurst has commented, the international legal personality of individuals 'is still comparatively rare and limited. Moreover, it is derivative, in the sense that it can be conferred only by states' (1991: 75).

In several human rights treaties that were concluded after 1945, rights have been created for individuals. One has to observe however that these rights are not always directly accessible for individuals. Often these rights do not exist directly under international law, but the treaty implies the obligation for states to incorporate such rights in their municipal law. This means that international rights are dependent upon recognition by national states. The limitation of legal personality is made particularly clear by the fact that the individual has no procedural capacity to appear before the International Court of Justice. Article 34 of the statute of the Court states explicitly that 'only states may be parties to contentious cases before the Court'.

There is a possibility for individuals (under an optional protocol to the International Covenant on Civil and Political Rights, 1966) to communicate complaints about violations of human rights to the UN Human Rights Committee. In the optional protocol to the covenant, the states parties agree that: 'A State Party to the Covenant that becomes a party to the present Protocol recognizes the competence of the Committee to receive and consider communications from individuals subject to its jurisdiction who claim to be victims of a violation by that State Party of any right set forth in the Covenant.' The committee however is not a tribunal and the individual plaintiff who initiates the complaint plays no active part in the proceedings. Another obstacle to this procedure is that only 66 of the 114 states that ratified the Covenant on Civil and Political Rights have recognized the right to petition the UN Committee on Human Rights.

The limited legal international personality of non-state actors is also demonstrated by the fact that they cannot – with few exceptions – directly participate in the international standard-setting processes. Even so, it can be argued that an important consequence of the development of international law after 1945 has been the insight that individuals have an international status, albeit it a limited one. Although states remained the core subjects of international law, for the first time on the international level rights and duties for 'everyone' were drawn up, although without adequate procedures for their protection and implementation.

The intersection of world arena and local space

The multiple-actor arena of world politics is connected with the local space in which most people live. This intersection means that decision making on the world level affects local situations, often in dramatic ways. For example, World Bank plans that originate in Washington have a far-reaching effect on local rain forest communities and their chances of survival. The Tropical Forestry Action Plan initiated by the World Bank, the United Nations Development Programme and the US Agency for International Development in 1985 represents a US $8 billion plan to save tropical forests. According to the critical analysis made by the World Rainforest Movement the plan, if implemented, will increase the harm inflicted upon the forest dwellers.

Yet another illustration is the policies of the Food and Agriculture Organization of the United Nations and their impact on the local level. The March–April 1991 issue of *The Ecologist* published an open letter to the FAO Director General informing him about an international campaign to push for a radical reappraisal of FAO policies and a complete restructuring of its organization. As the letter stated, the initiators of the campaign have taken this course of action 'because we are convinced that the policies pushed by FAO . . . are a major cause of world famine, ecological destruction and social alienation'.

Illustrations of the locally damaging global policies on agricultural development can be found in the FAO promotion of the use of pesticides and fertilizers in the Third World, of export crops, of the commercial development of rain forests, or of high-tech fishery techniques. In all these cases the rural poor were badly affected and their plight deteriorated even further. FAO policies encourage the spread of monocultures, resource-intensive and capital-intensive farming systems, trading patterns that favour the rich countries and Third World elites, and the concentration of land in the hands of few owners. By now it has been well documented how the Green Revolution policy on balance led to the concentration of wealth, exacerbated the problem of landlessness, degraded the environment, created dependency upon producers of pesticides and fertilizers, and displaced agricultural labour, adding to the already dramatic levels of unemployment in Third World rural areas. In spite of all the available evidence FAO policies continued to promote the main components of the Green Revolution which in effect benefits the manufacturers of farm equipment, the agrochemical businesses, at the expense of the poor.

Another evident case of the world/local interconnection is the direct impact on people's lives of the structural adjustment policies demanded by the International Monetary Fund. Whenever such policies impose the cutting of expenditures in essential public services, such as for example in Peru in August 1990, the immediate result is a staggering increase of absolute poverty among people in local communities. Many more examples could be given, such as the employment policies enacted on a world level by transnational corporations and their local effect on the workforce.

An important implication of the world/local intersection is that local struggle is not sufficient. If, for example, local communities want to retain an autonomous cultural space, their battleground has to go beyond the local boundaries, since the space for local cultural expression is co-determined by such world politics as GATT decisions on trade in services or on intellectual property rights. The intersection also implies that world politics may find its origin in local issues. Local conflicts, such as the Iran–Iraq war or the Iraq–Kuwait conflict, have decisive repercussions on the world level. It should also be observed that the foreign policy conduct of many governments is dictated by its domestic roots. The domestic politics of powerful lobbies will strongly influence a country's position in world political forums. A case in point is the effective lobbies of industrialists and farmers in Northern countries and their impact in the GATT multilateral trade negotiations.

The multiple-actor arena and its intersection with local interests set the context within which world communication politics operates. We now need to investigate which concrete forms this politics takes.

The framework of analysis

I propose to conduct the analysis of world communication politics on three levels. First, the basic units of analysis are identified and described. Secondly, it is necessary to understand how these emerged. Thirdly, their purpose must be assessed.

As units of analysis I use prevailing practices. Consequently I want to understand how and why specific practices emerge. On the third level I want to judge the purpose of the prevailing practices in terms of the interests they serve. This is particularly motivated by an important normative standard in international law: the provision that scientific, technological and cultural development should be to the benefit of all. In most of the issue areas of world communication we find intellectual and material resources that are considered in international law the province of humankind. The natural resources that are essential to radio and TV broadcasting, the space resources that are needed for telecommunication, the world's cultural resources are all 'common heritage'. To use the phrasing of Article 1 of the Outer Space Treaty (1967), these resources should be used 'for the benefit and in the interest of all countries, irrespective of their degree of economic or scientific development'. On the basis of this commonly adopted legal principle the analysis will have to question how equally the benefits in the issue areas of world communication are distributed.

Prevailing political practices

The players in the world arena use a variety of instruments to respond to the issues they confront. Among these are military, diplomatic, economic and political instruments. In this study I shall focus on the instruments that shape the political practice in different issue areas.

Players may decide to cooperate in the resolution of issues and establish mechanisms to facilitate such cooperation. In some issue areas they will agree on robust and effective forms of agreement. In others they will only agree to establish weak and ineffective forms of cooperation and coordination. They may also agree to disagree. As Susan Strange has argued, the latter is actually the case with many of the world's most pressing issues: 'The reality is that there are more areas and issues of nonagreement and controversy than there are areas of agreement. On most of the basic social issues that have to do with the rights and responsibilities of individuals to each other and the state . . . there is no kind of international regime' (1983: 349).

The cooperative arrangements in some issue areas have been termed by an important theoretical approach 'regimes'.[2] Although it is tempting to use this concept, it has several flaws which lead me to avoid it in the present analysis. I tend to agree with Strange that the regime concept has strong state-centric implications (1983: 349). Much of regime analysis concentrates on collective arrangements established between state actors and bypasses the role and importance of non-state actors. Even when non-state actors are introduced, for example as epistemic communities, the state remains the central concept. As Haufler observes: 'Overall, regime theorists have left out of their analysis the possibility that states might play only a minor role in a regime' (1993: 95). Also private actors can seek and achieve or fail to reach forms of cooperation.

Another serious problem with the concept of regime is its suggestion of order, discipline and consistency. This obscures the reality of the world political arena in which developments and decision making do not usually follow the discipline of a rational agenda. A heterogeneous community of actors with often unclearly divided roles constitutes a muddled playing-field. Cooperative arrangements that govern issue areas of world politics are usually characterized by the absence of elements that are inherent in the notion of a regime: order, stability, coherence. Collective arrangements in the real world are often disorderly, tentative, inconsistent and messy.

The analysis of regimes also tends to focus on areas where cooperative arrangements have been achieved, thus 'ignoring the vast area of nonregimes that lies beyond the ken of international bureaucracies and diplomatic bargaining' (Strange, 1983: 338). A further complication with the regime concept can be illustrated by taking Krasner's analysis of an issue like remote sensing (1991: 349–50). He concludes that no regime has been established on remote sensing and he provides a convincing explanation. There has been (and continues to be) basic discord in the world political community on fundamental principles, and the most powerful players can by and large operate without multilateral agreement on their operations in space. This does not however reflect the real situation adequately. In reality the prevailing practice is characterized by a great deal of multilateral cooperation and strong prospects for its expansion. If we take the concept of 'prevailing political practice' as the unit of analysis we may establish that in Krasner's terms a regime has not been achieved on remote sensing, but we would also observe that in political reality the basic discord does not necessarily hinder multilateral cooperation.

For the purposes of the present study I shall use this notion of prevailing political practices to describe the key units of analysis. This concept has sufficient flexibility to deal with both agreement and disagreement; it can encompass disorder and discord and can easily be applied to both state and non-state actors.

The concept also suggests that political responses to certain issues do not emerge in a vacuum. They are 'nested' (Aggarwal, 1985) in a broader framework of norms, rules and institutions that shape the 'menu of available options' (Young, 1986: 120). There are always existing practices that will co-determine the outcome of political processes through which new practices are shaped. In the effort to create a new political practice the protagonists have to take into account the menu of available practices.

The concept also implies a reference to the actual conduct of actors. This is important since often in the reality of world politics the decisive factor is not the agreement to cooperate – however formal this may be – but the compliance of the more powerful actors with the norms and rules of the accord.

The prevailing political practice of a certain issue area represents the political response through which players deal with issues on their agenda. In this response they express commitments, obligations and expectations, or they fail to do so.

The prevailing political practices in issue areas of world politics can be divided broadly into situations where the players engage in forms of multilateral cooperation and situations where no multilateral cooperation is established. Forms of multilateral cooperation can be extensive or limited. In extensive multilateral cooperation all important players participate; they engage in regular and joint consultation and decision making through mutually recognized and effective institutional forums. Extensive multilateral cooperation implies that most players perceive cooperation as necessary and advantageous and there is a strong tendency to comply with agreed norms and rules.

Multilateral cooperation is likely to emerge where and when the resolution of issues needs cooperation and coordination and cannot be brought about through unilateral coercion. It is essential to the establishment of multilateral cooperation that international players (governmental and non-governmental) perceive certain issues as in need of a collective response. When some players, and certainly the most powerful players, perceive issues as resolvable through unilateral or bilateral action, it is unlikely that a collective arrangement will develop, and the absence of multilateral cooperation will be the prevailing political practice.

Political practices can also be distinguished along the axis of accord versus discord. Multilateral cooperation can be established and reinforced through different modes of agreement among the players. Multilateral cooperation will often be based on an accord that is concluded among the players involved in certain issue areas. Such multilateral accords can be formal or informal. A formal accord is a binding contractual agreement. An informal accord is a non-binding voluntary agreement. The classical manifestation of the formal agreement is the international treaty that legally binds those states that ratify its provisions. In a formal accord there is a contractual arrangement in which the compliance can be assured through punitive measures. Informal agreements are not legally binding. A characteristic informal agreement is the non-binding declaration. 'Informal accords among states and transnational actors are not exceptional. The scale and diversity of such accords indicate that they are an important feature of world politics, not rare and peripheral' (Lipson, 1991: 498). There are several advantages to the conclusion of informal agreements: they are flexible; they can easily be changed or abandoned; and they can be reached quicker than binding agreements. If one follows Lipson's suggestion that international agreements are basically 'promises about future behavior' (1991: 498), one appreciates why actors often prefer to avoid the publicly visible commitment to a promise.

A peculiar example of an informal common agreement is the CSCE Final Act of Helsinki (1975). The act states clear commitments but not in the form of a binding treaty. It is likely that the Soviet government accepted the strong provisions on human rights (in the so-called 'third basket') since these did not construe treaty obligations. In actual fact, the Helsinki accord turned out to be a very effective informal agreement. This may have greatly surprised the Brezhnev government. One should also note that an instrument such as the Helsinki act may not itself be legally binding, but may contain provisions that are already incorporated in binding international law. Thus instruments, such as recommendations, that in themselves have no legal status may be significant in so far as they refer to legal material that has formal status. (Brownlie, 1990: 578)

Multilateral accords are also concluded among non-state actors. This was done at the UNCED in Rio de Janeiro in 1992 when the NGOs presented at the Global Forum a number of alternative treaties. This resulted from the growing confidence in the NGO community that it has a legitimate and pertinent claim in the world political arena. The NGOs presented alternative treaties on environmental education, alternative economic models relating to consumption and lifestyle, and an alternative non-governmental agreement on climate change. The Treaty for Non-Governmental Organization Cooperation and Sharing of Resources provided that the signing NGOs were committed to certain actions but without a compliance mechanism or a secretariat to administer the treaty. Although such accords are usually informal, it is possible for non-state actors to conclude contractual agreements among themselves with binding provisions on compulsory arbitration. Contractual agreements are also made between IGOs and INGOs when the latter execute projects commissioned by the former.

The fact that a common agreement is formal does not by itself mean that it is a robust effective arrangement. The binding nature of an agreement does not mean very much by itself. A binding commitment may risk the costs of non-compliance but does not change the reality of non-compliance. There are binding treaties that lack effective enforcement. Although there is some fetishism about binding rules in debates on international law, the binding character of normative provisions is not necessarily decisive. There are binding agreements with generous space for escape and reservation. In many cases it is easier– given the variety of interests and/or the rapidity of technological developments – to achieve a non-binding arrangement which, if perceived by parties as the most beneficial instrument, can *de facto* have binding effect. It may also be that arrangements that are initially non-binding evolve in time into binding law. There are also important illustrations of non-binding instruments that have had a strong impact on domestic law making. A case in point would be the 1981 OECD Guidelines on Privacy and their influence upon Australian legislation (Kirby, 1987: 81).

The force of multilateral accords can be judged on a number of variables. The most important are the normative provisions, the enforcement procedures, the institutional mechanisms for implementation of the agreement, and the compliance of players.

The normative provisions of a multilateral accord articulate the standards of conduct for the players in the arena. They encompass principles, norms and rules that require, prohibit or authorize conduct. These provisions can be divided very broadly into binding and non-binding provisions. Binding provisions may be peremptory (*ius cogens*) for all international actors or may be binding only on those actors who entered contractual obligations under a multilateral treaty, and they may allow for derogations by the contracting parties. Non-binding provisions vary from resolutions adopted by multilateral governmental institutions (that may evolve into binding law), to self-regulatory rules (in a variety of forms ranging from codes of practice within individual companies to rules adopted through a multiple-party agreement), and to mere guidelines. In addition to the legal provisions created by the multilateral state institutions, there is also a growing body of regulatory instruments that are designed and adopted by the community of non-state actors. The norms and rules in these instruments may not have legally binding force, yet they can have an important moral impact on the constituencies of non-governmental institutions (for example, norms and rules established by such voluntary associations as the Roman Catholic Church).

The procedural provisions of multilateral accords deal with the enforcement of the adopted standards. They encompass the variety of measures that facilitate the compliance of players with the normative provisions. The procedural provisions of multilateral accords have varying levels of force. They may range from very strong provisions for legal enforcement (with mechanisms for sanctions and dispute resolution), to non-legal forms of intra-organizational enforcement (with rules for binding arbitration), to weak instruments of enforcement (in the form of mechanisms for monitoring, information exchange, coordination), to a complete absence of enforcement procedures.

The role of multilateral agreements as collective responses to international issues will depend not only on the strength of their normative and procedural provisions, but also on the institutional context within which the collective practice is implemented. An essential factor among the institutional conditions is also the strength of the organs that are responsible for carrying out the provisions. The nature and effectiveness of these organizational arrangements will have an important impact upon the actual performance of the political arena.

The effectiveness of multilateral accords will also be determined by the level of actual cooperation among players. A formal multilateral accord with strong normative provisions and procedures for enforcement does not automatically guarantee extensive multilateral cooperation. A formal accord with robust provisions can still be undermined if major actors do not comply. Equally actors can strengthen an informal accord with weak provisions if they decide to comply with the accord in their actual conduct. Therefore, it is not sufficient to establish that actors agree to cooperate; it should also be tested whether they indeed cooperate. In spite of fairly robust agreements on free trade, for example, the actual conduct of very powerful actors in the world economy is highly protectionist. Actors may also in actual conduct comply with even a soft and informal agreement, if they consider the costs of non-compliance too high. Acceptance by actors is important as this largely determines the legitimacy of a multilateral accord. It makes a considerable difference which parties support an international arrangement. For instance, strong provisions on technology transfer that are not supported by the key producers of technology do not create adequate conditions for implementation of those provisions.

In the analysis of multilateral accords all four variables (standards, enforcement procedures, institutional mechanisms and compliance) need to be taken into account. Their significance will largely depend upon the mutual strengthening of the four dimensions. Strong rules with binding force have little meaning if there are no effective instruments of enforcement or if the major players decide not to comply. Equally it might be the case that non-binding norms in combination with effective dispute resolution procedures establish a robust accord. Voluntary standards can have an important significance – even without legal enforcement – if there are strong self-imposed organizational sanctions and if most actors concerned decide to comply. The crucial variable is common acceptance by actors. In principle, this means that an accord can be robust even if it is of a voluntary nature and the norms and rules are not based upon a contractual arrangement.

In summary then it can be said that players in world politics engage in extensive, limited or no multilateral cooperation, and they conclude different types of accord or agree to disagree.

Formal (binding) or informal (voluntary) accords are robust if the parties to the agreement share the common acceptance that the adopted norms and rules have a binding impact upon their actual conduct. Accords are weak if the parties to the agreement do not share this common acceptance or if the major players do not support the accord. It is therefore possible to distinguish between four types of multilateral accord. There are robust binding accords, weak binding accords, robust voluntary accords and weak voluntary accords.

In certain issue areas players may only agree to disagree. In these cases their discord can be either basic or marginal. Discord either revolves around fundamental differences on matters of principle or results from minor – sometimes politically convenient – divergencies. In the case of a basic discord it is not likely that a common accord can be reached between actors, although forms of multilateral cooperation are not excluded. For example, as long as the disagreement about the NIIO was about basic principles, no agreement was reached. When the debate shifted to more pragmatic concerns an agreement could be achieved. Marginal discords are often about procedures and logistical issues, such as whether the IPDC should be a multilateral fund or a clearing house. In the UNCTAD negotiations on the Code of Conduct on Transfer of Technology, the basic discord is about basic principles; the marginal discord is about the modality of the agreement. This is not unimportant, but the question about a binding treaty versus a voluntary code can be resolved in bargaining.

In the negotiations on the Code of Conduct on TNCs, radical differences about such principles as the rule of international law and non-discriminatory treatment of the TNCs created obstacles to reaching a common agreement. This is not to underestimate the importance of procedural differences. These can for example significantly undermine the mutual confidence of negotiators. However, usually they can be resolved in the bargaining process. This may take time and cause delay in the negotiations. This happened for example in the preparations towards the Uruguay Round of multilateral trade negotiations when the controversy about traded services postponed the beginning of the negotiations. 'The dispute on services did not concentrate on the substance and possible merits of multilateral action in this field, but became a procedural and institutional battle which was finally resolved by a procedural compromise that allowed the negotiations to start but did not entirely remove the possibility of future conflicts' (Feij, 1989: 107). Even so, the differences were resolved and eventually a common agreement was concluded on trade in services (December 1993). Often marginal discord takes a considerable time to resolve because of the practice in many IGOs to seek consensus.

It should also be noted that procedural disagreement may not always be so easy to resolve. At the core of the remaining issues in the UNCTAD negotiations on the Code of Conduct on Transfer of Technology is the issue of whether the instrument should be a binding treaty (the developing countries) or a set of voluntary guidelines (the Western countries). The parties involved are fundamentally divided on this issue, so it is a robust disagreement. However, there may still be a common agreement if the most powerful actors manage, as they often do, to coerce or persuade, or both, the less powerful actors to make a concession on the legal form of the code. In 1979 the developing countries accepted the code as a non-binding instrument if concessions on such substantial issues as restrictive business practices were made by the Western countries. So far these concessions have not been made.

	FRA	FWA	IRA	IWA	BD	MD
EMC						
LMC						
NMC						

EMC   extensive multilateral cooperation
LMC   limited multilateral cooperation
NMC   no multilateral cooperation

FRA   formal and robust accord
FWA   formal and weak accord
IRA   informal and robust accord
IWA   informal and weak accord
BD   basic discord
MD   marginal discord

Figure 2.1   *Political practices*

Prevailing practices in world communication politics can be described along the axis of multilateral cooperation versus no cooperation and the axis of multilateral accord versus discord (Figure 2.1). This means that there can be multilateral cooperation among the different players based upon robust or weak formal accords and upon robust or weak informal accords. There can be situations where no multilateral cooperation is established because players have basic or marginal disagreements about cooperation or about the terms of cooperation. It is also possible that there is no multilateral cooperation although players have concluded formal or informal accords. It is also conceivable in world politics that players decide to cooperate in spite of basic or marginal disagreement.

Decision making processes

The next question for the analysis is through which processes the prevailing practices emerge.

Political decision making never emerges in a vacuum. There is always a specific historical context within which actors articulate their positions in connection with issues they (and other players) perceive as in need of resolution. The process usually begins with the dissatisfaction that exists regarding existing solutions or the lack of solutions. This dissatisfaction leads actors to claim the amendment of existing arrangements or the establishment of new arrangements that would accommodate their interests more adequately. As transborder problems do not emerge in a disinterested ambience and have their specific historical-political location, the actors involved may have very different perceptions on similar problems or indeed very different ideas as to what constitutes a relevant problem. Often the key players in world politics have vested interests in the resolution of their preferred problems and in their preferred modalities of resolving these problems.

If all actors had only interests that never moved beyond their national boundaries, or if all interests of all actors were in perfect harmony and would spontaneously find orderly arrangements by which all would optimally benefit, or if one hegemon could simply tell all other actors what to do, there would be no need for world politics. If the pursuing by all actors of the optimization of their claims made all better off, there would be no need for collective governing arrangements. In the real world, players only rarely share similar claims to the desirability and the terms of multilateral cooperation. The more common situation is that players have divergent claims to the need of multilateral cooperation and/or to the terms of this cooperation. Players often have rival interests that need arbitration or mutual interests that need cooperation. In the real world, even the hegemon often finds the opportunity costs of exercising coercion less attractive than a form of negotiated agreement. Arrangements to accommodate divergent interests will therefore usually require bargaining among players through various institutional forums. These bargaining situations are complicated as players may have disagreements on fundamental principles or on decision making procedures or on both. Moreover, there may be great differences in bargaining strength. All these factors will contribute to the outcome of the decision making process and thus to the shape that world politics takes in certain issue areas.

World politics can then be conceived as a decision making process between (often unequal) players that tend to have contending positions on certain issues. The positions taken imply claims to an optimal accommodation of what players perceive as their interests. Optimality in the context of world politics may imply that players expect their preferred outcome to be implemented. It may also mean that all players agree to a less preferable outcome if they would all be worse off if there was no agreement. Optimality may also stand for those outcomes that are sub-optimal, but that at least do not benefit another player.

Decision making in world politics confronts consensual and rival claims. Players may have similar claims based upon consensual interests, yet the perception of the root causes of the issues they address may be starkly different. As a consequence their preferred solutions may also strongly diverge. There may be a consensual interest to share and conserve the common human heritage. There may alike be claims to resolve transborder problems involving the commons (for example the near-universal claim to stop the ozone layer destruction), but the preferred solutions may be very different. If the claims of all players involved converge, it may not be too difficult to formulate basic principles and rules that all can agree upon. In such cases, it may well be that the agreement exists only on the level of rhetoric and the effort to implement the universally adopted policy measures may run into serious trouble. Illustrative is the case of the three multilateral conventions on the reduction of aerial piracy and the illegal diversion of aircraft.[3] The basis for the conventions was a consensual interest in the international community to protect the freedom of the air. A reciprocity of interests between states was at stake and all states participated in the drafting of the treaties. Since opinions were divided as to the political causes of aircraft hijacking, several states failed to actually sign or ratify the conventions.

In the reality of the decision making processes some claims will be better accommodated than others. Some demands are not accommodated at all; others are met at a lower level of legal formulation and/or political implementation than their protagonists had aimed at. The concerns of the different client communities in the world political arena are only rarely settled in equitable ways.

We find that the practices that emerge from the decision making processes reflect the preferences of some actors better than those of others. The type of practice that prevails in issue areas is the outcome of decision making processes in which a variety of variables can be identified. This requires a theoretical approach, as Chapter 10 will explore. An analytical effort has to be made to explain the different modalities of the prevailing practices and the differential distribution of their benefits.

World politics and the world's people

This raises the third question about the purpose and function of the prevailing practices. Whose interests do they serve?

As we will see later, the prevailing practice in space technology is a form of multilateral cooperation in combination with a weak voluntary accord. There is consensus in the world community that this practice has not benefited all countries equally. As a result the developing countries have claimed the need for a new arrangement that ensures equal benefits for all countries.

A specific question I would want to pursue on this level of the analysis is: how do the prevailing practices of world communication politics serve the interests of ordinary people? World politics affects people's daily lives in often dramatic ways. It is obvious that in areas such as peace and security, trade and finance, environment and humanitarian relief, common agreements – or the lack thereof – shape the conditions of people's present lives and their prospects for the future. This is less immediately visible in the arena of world communication politics. Here the decisions by the world community seem very remote. Yet, some cases from the issue areas that will be discussed later can illustrate how the politics of world communication affects people's daily lives.

In the issue area of communication development, action by the world community on the availability of mass media affects a large number of the world's people. It determines their access to information, education and entertainment.

In the area of telecommunication, people's access to telephony and its possible life-saving use depends upon negotiations in multilateral organizations that are very distant from people's daily lives. Yet the outcome of such political processes directly impinges on the quality of their lives.

In the politics of transborder data flows, the rules and standards adopted by the world community determine the protection of people's privacies. Without adequate multilateral regulation, person-related information is unprotected against its abuse by states and business operators. The politics of standardization of consumer electronics affects the quality and price of consumer products. The model of intellectual property protection that is proposed for the whole world by the most powerful players implies the dispossession of knowledge held by people in local communities in developing countries and militates against the independent development of their local knowledge. The standard of market access achieved in the trade in services negotiations has profound implications for people's local cultural space and the diversity of cultural products they will have at their disposal.

I conclude therefore that the political practices in world communication matter to ordinary people. It is thus a legitimate question to ask how the interests of ordinary men and women are served by the politics of world communication. In other words, do people matter in the actions and decision making processes of world communication politics?

A complex problem with an assessment against the standard of the 'people's interests' is that this is not an unequivocal category that is expressed in a singular way at a clearly identifiable forum.

Therefore, one has to infer people's interests from an identifiable set of standards upon which all people can agree. This would seem almost impossible given that in a multicultural world with multi-layered societies people will have divided interests and will make different preferential normative choices. However, despite the temptations of a normative relativism and the justified suspicion about unitary value judgements, it is possible to infer people's interests from universally accepted standards. These are the standards of international human rights. Human rights provide currently the only universally available set of standards for the dignity and integrity of all human beings. It is in the interests of all people that they be respected.

The provisions of international human rights law represent the interests of ordinary men, women and children, as individuals, as groups and as collectivities. In applying a human rights perspective to the politics of world communication the premise is that the interests of ordinary people are better represented the stronger is the 'human rights content' of the prevailing practices.

A human rights perspective

On 10 December 1948 the General Assembly of the United Nations adopted through its Resolution 217(III) the Universal Declaration of Human Rights (UDHR). This first comprehensive international standard on human rights was prepared by the United Nations Commission on Human Rights. It expressed the concern for protection of human rights which emerged after the Second World War in response to the atrocities of Nazism. The first indications of this concern were signalled by the charters of the war tribunals at Nuremberg and Tokyo and in the United Nations charter of 1945.[4] Article 55 of the UN charter states: 'the United Nations shall promote universal respect for, and observance of, human rights and fundamental freedoms for all without distinction as to race, sex, language or religion'. The origins of the declaration are found in European history; its philosophical undercurrent is the tradition of the eighteenth century Enlightenment. Its prime mover was a European-initiated war and its first proponents were Western governments with strong European roots. In spite of this biased beginning and despite the continuing debate about the need to redress the European bias in human rights thinking, the declaration is recognized by all member states of the United Nations as the 'common standard of achievement for all peoples and all nations'. The declaration does not constitute binding international law but its universal recognition as a standard of conduct renders its provisions moral obligations for all peoples and all nations. The adoption of the Universal Declaration signals the beginning of a dynamic development of human-rights-based standards in world politics.

It is common to refer to the classical civil and political rights as the first generation of human rights. These represent the freedom of citizens from state interference or their rights to perform certain activities while the state observes the duty of non-intervention. The historical roots of the first generation are the Magna Charta (1215), the American Bill of Rights (1791), and the French Déclaration des Droits de l'Homme et du Citoyen (1789). The economic, social and cultural rights are referred to as the second generation which represents the right to claim an active involvement of the state.

The first and second generations of human rights are formulated as binding international law in two conventions that were drafted in the 1950s, adopted in 1966 and came into force in 1976. These are the International Covenant on Civil and Political Rights (ICCPR) and the International Covenant on Economic, Social and Cultural Rights (ICESCR). Together with the Universal Declaration of Human Rights, these instruments constitute the International Bill of Rights. In addition to the Bill of Rights, the UN General Assembly has adopted the International Convention on the Elimination of All Forms of Racial Discrimination (1965), the Convention on the Elimination of Discrimination against Women (1979), the Convention against Torture and other Cruel, Inhuman or Degrading Treatment or Punishment (1984), and the Convention on the Rights of the Child (1989).

In the development of international human rights a third generation has also emerged. This addressed the question of the need for a separate category of human rights in which the dominant individualistic orientation of human rights instruments would be complemented by the recognition of collective rights. This would imply that peoples can be holders of human rights. It has been argued that this logically flows from the acknowledgement of an intrinsic link between the notion of human rights and the principle of collective self-determination. This principle is embodied in the UN charter, Articles 1 and 55, and in Article 1 of the two human rights covenants. As collective rights have been proposed the right to peace and security, the right to development, the right of minorities to their own culture and language, and the right to communicate. The African Charter on Human and Peoples' Rights (1981) refers both to the rights and freedoms of the individual and to those of peoples.

Among the difficulties that the proposed collective rights raise is the identification of the holders of these rights. Related to this is the question of how far collective holders of rights can be seen as having the power to implement their entitlements and how far they can be held responsible if these rights are not enforced. In the development of human rights it is important that the United Nations World Conference on Human Rights of 1993 has reaffirmed the right to development as a universal and inalienable right and has also decided to strengthen its implementation. The Vienna Programme of Action 'welcomes the appointment by the Commission on Human Rights of a thematic working group on the right to development and urges that the Working Group . . . promptly formulate . . . comprehensive and effective measures to eliminate obstacles to the implementation and realization of the Declaration on the Right to Development and recommend ways and means towards the realization of the right to development by all States'.

Collective claims to human rights are contested and are not normally incorporated in international arrangements. The emphasis in international law is on individual claims. Article 27 in the ICCPR, for example, provides protection to minorities, but through individuals belonging to minorities.

The collective rights recognized by the United Nations are the basic right to self-determination (UN charter, Articles 1 and 55, and the ICCPR) and the right to physical survival of 'national, ethnical, racial or religious groups' (Convention on the Prevention and Punishment of Genocide). The collective right to development was first proposed in 1972 by the Senegalese lawyer Kéba MBaye. It is founded on Articles 25 and 28 of the UDHR and Article 11 of the ICESCR.

In 1977 the UN Commission on Human Rights recommended the Economic and Social Council to invite the UN Secretary General together with Unesco and other competent agencies 'to undertake a study on the subject "The international dimensions of the right to development as a human right in relation with other human rights based on international co-operation, including the right to peace, taking into account the requirements of the New International Economic Order" '. This study was presented to the Commission in 1979 and led to the establishment of a working group to study the scope and contents of the right to development and the most effective means to ensure its realization. The working group had nine meetings in the period 1981–4 and presented in 1984 a report which was the basis for the Declaration on the Right to Development, adopted by UNGA Resolution 41/128 of 4 December 1986: 146 states voted in favour, eight states abstained and one state (the USA) voted against.

The declaration proclaimed that: 'The right to development is an inalienable human right by virtue of which every human person and all peoples are entitled to participate in, contribute to and enjoy economic, social, cultural and political development, in which all human rights and fundamental freedoms can be fully realized.' The declaration also states that: 'All human beings have a responsibility for development, individually and collectively . . . and they should therefore promote and protect an appropriate political, social and economic order for development.' The 1993 World Conference on Human Rights in Vienna confirmed the right to development by declaring in its final statement (Article 10): 'The World Conference on Human Rights reaffirms the right to development as established in the Declaration on the Right to Development, as a universal and inalienable right and an integral part of fundamental human rights.'

An inclusive perspective
The core of international human rights law is the simple though powerful notion that 'all people matter'. This idea represents the fundamental novelty in world politics that was introduced with the adoption of the UN charter in 1945. The charter provided the basis for the recognition of the entitlement of all human beings to the protection of dignity, integrity, liberty and equality. Herewith it proposed an 'inclusive' interpretation of human rights.

Earlier human rights entitlements had always been defined in an 'exclusive' manner. During most of world history most people did not matter. They were slaves, serfs, workers, women, children, aboriginals, blacks. They did not matter. In the political arena they were 'non-persons'. When fundamental rights were awarded, there always was this category of non-persons that was not included. The Bill of Rights of the State of Virginia provided in 1776 fundamental freedoms to the 'good people of Virginia'. The good people did not include the black slaves and the indigenous Americans.

A supranational perspective
The United Nations charter made human rights not only an inclusive, but also a 'world' affair. No longer was the protection of human rights a matter for domestic governments only. The world community was given the duty to intervene in internal affairs when people's human rights were violated. Before 1945 global human rights policies were absent. The covenant of the League of Nations, for example, made no reference to human rights. This was not accidental, but 'the direct result of a system of world order based on the sovereignty of territorial states' (Donnelly, 1993: 28). Since the constitution of the modern society of states in the seventeenth

century, a key principle of international relations was 'the sovereign prerogative of each state to treat its citizens as it saw fit' (1993: 29). Unfortunately, the realities of world politics after 1945 never permitted this new approach to develop into a robust and enforceable multilateral practice. International human rights law remained a weak and largely non-enforceable arrangement. It should not be ignored that this was a conscious political choice. Most nation-states have shown little interest in interference with their human rights record. As a result today's world system remained largely a case of criminals policing themselves. The state-centric arrangement of world politics in which states are unwilling to yield power over their citizens is still dominant and stands squarely in the way of universal respect for human rights. In current world politics, states still retain a considerable measure of sovereignty in the treatment of their citizens. Yet, the United Nations World Conference on Human Rights of 1993 has reaffirmed that 'the promotion and protection of all human rights is a legitimate concern of the international community'.

It remains a much contested issue in world politics whether intervention by states in the affairs of other states can be justified by the humanitarian purpose of such intervention. The defence of human rights could lead countries to wage wars or contemplate invasions for the good cause. In proceedings before the International Court of Justice (*Nicaragua vs the United States*, 1986) the USA justified its military activities against Nicaragua with the right to use armed force to protect human rights in a foreign country. Intervention for humanitarian purposes will often imply the use of physical force. This has been strongly condemned by the International Court. In its conclusion to the *Nicaragua vs the United States* case, the Court stated: 'The protection of human rights, a strictly humanitarian objective, cannot be compatible with the mining of ports, the destruction of oil installations, or again with the training, arming and equipping of the Contras. The Court concludes that the argument derived from the preservation of human rights in Nicaragua cannot afford a legal justification for the conduct of the United States.'

Obviously, there are other means of humanitarian intervention of a non violent nature, such as economic sanctions or cultural boycotts. World communication in its various forms can represent a non-violent intervention justified by humanitarian purpose. International broadcasting which denounces human rights violations, for example, constitutes intervention and will often be seen by the receiving state as unacceptable interference with internal affairs.

The different arguments in this debate emphasize either the global nature of human rights or the respect for self-determination. The former position argues that states have voluntarily reduced their national sovereignty by adopting human rights standards; the counter-argument stresses that human rights are internal affairs to be ruled by domestic legislation and judiciary. The prohibition of intervention in the internal affairs of other states is a basic principle of international law. As the Declaration of Principles of International Law Concerning Friendly Relations and Cooperation among States proposes, 'armed intervention and all other forms of interference . . . are in violation of international law'.

In actual political practice the prohibition of interference is not absolute. Certain violations of human rights are seen by the world community as such serious threats to peace that they become a legitimate international concern. It has been accepted by the Security Council and the International Court of Justice that forms of intervention are justified in cases of gross violations of human rights. In such cases, for example the past politics of apartheid in South Africa, a violation of obligations with *erga omnes* effects is at stake. These are breaches of obligations with serious effects on all members of the world community. This raises the problem of how to distinguish between gross violations and those with no *erga omnes* effect. The case of apartheid may have been clear, but there are many other appalling violations which threaten international peace, life and security where the world community would find less consensus.

A universal perspective

An intriguing question in the human rights debate is how we should interpret the universality of human rights. Does universality mean the confinement to the universal validity of one human rights concept? Or could universality mean the recognition of the concurrent existence of different concepts? Does it mean that one interpretation of such standards as dignity, equality or liberty is superior to other interpretations? The latter position may obscure a 'human rights colonialism' that abuses human rights principles in the justification of a preferred political position. The claim to universalism can easily be used as a convenient instrument of an expansive foreign policy. However, the opposite, more relativist position is also fraught with risks. This position stresses the variety of cultural settings and the equality of different interpretations of human rights. This has the intellectual attraction of avoiding the fallacies of ethnocentrism. Yet, apart from the consideration that relativism is the typical European intellectual response to the Eurocentrism of colonial politics and science, the relativist position obstructs any form of solidarity with the dissidents in other cultural milieus.

The importance of accepting a minimal standard of universal validity is precisely the possibility to intervene in situations where the victims cannot speak for themselves. It should be borne in mind that the belief that there are no universally shared basic moral concepts is usually proposed by elites that are not representative of ordinary people. The relativist argument is in most countries around the world easily defeated if one only inquires among the victims of human rights violations. As Donnelly observes: 'ordinary citizens in country after country in the Third World have found internationally recognized civil and political rights essential to protecting themselves against repressive economic and political elites' (1993: 35). This is what Ramcharan has called the democratic test of universality: 'Just ask any human being: would you like to live or die? Would you like to be tortured or enslaved? If there is any critic of universality who would argue that an individual would choose death to life, and serfdom to freedom, let us hear from that critic' (1989: 26). I would add to this that an even more convincing test of universalism is the 'victim test'. If anyone is in doubt about the desirability of the universal application of basic human rights, he or she should ask the victims of human rights violations.

It is important that the United Nations World Conference on Human Rights (1993) has reaffirmed the universality of human rights. The final declaration states 'The universal nature of human rights is beyond question.' In the preparatory process of the conference the universality concept had been challenged by several actors. In the Cairo Declaration on Human Rights in Islam (9 June 1993) the member states of the Organization of the Islamic Conference made human rights subordinate to Islamic religious standards. The declaration provided that the rights and freedoms it stipulated are subject to the Islamic Shari'ah.[5] The Bangkok declaration of the Asian preparatory conference stated that, in the protection of human rights, differences in national, cultural and religious backgrounds had to be taken into account. The declaration recognized that while human rights are universal in nature, they must be considered in the context of a dynamic and evolving process of international norm setting, bearing in mind the significance of national and regional particularities and various historical, cultural and religious backgrounds. The Vienna declaration recognized that universality does not equal uniformity, and reminded that 'the significance of national and regional particularities and various historical, cultural and religious backgrounds must be borne in mind'.

Why a human rights perspective?

The selection of an inclusive, supranational and universal perspective on human rights for the assessment of world communication politics can be justified on pragmatic and normative grounds.

A pragmatic justification

There is an international political consensus about human rights. The world political community has recognized the existence of human rights, their universality and indivisibility, and has accepted a machinery for their enforcement. Despite all the turmoil, the Vienna World Conference on Human Rights (1993) managed to reinforce that the standard of human rights is universal. This tells us that international human rights law represents – however ineffectual – a set of moral claims that is accepted universally. Therefore, it provides us with a legitimate international standard against which to assess the performance of world communication politics. Only if politics measures up to this standard can it be considered legitimate.

This pragmatic justification can be reinforced by the observation that it is common practice to associate communication with human rights values. As Pekka Tarjanne, the Secretary General of the International Telecommunication Union, has stated: 'From its very beginning the telecommunications industry has been closely associated with certain values – most notably freedom of expression, reciprocity between individuals and universality of access' (1992: 45). In line with Tarjanne's remark, one can establish that many regulatory instruments on world communication contain explicit references to human rights standards.

A normative justification

A general premise for this justification follows the earlier analysis that world politics is no longer the 'who-gets-what arena' for state players only. Contemporary world politics is also about the concerns and interests of a wide variety of non-state actors, individuals and their communities. Not only states bring their claims to benefits, protection and liberties, but also the non-state actors. International human rights represent claims made by individuals and their communities against states as well as against other individuals and other communities. Therefore, it is relevant to analyse whether and to what extent such claims are accommodated in the practices of world politics.

The more specific basic premise of the normative justification is that the interests of ordinary people should be accommodated. This premise proposes that communication structures and processes are not just ends in themselves. The most efficient, effective and universally available means of communication can be used for very destructive purposes. As Justice Kirby has phrased it: 'Dictators can build magnificent highways and sometimes provide sufficient telephones: all efficiently susceptible to official interception' (Kirby, 1993a: 262). Therefore, if we accept that 'all people matter', it is imperative to assess communication policies in the light of their contribution to the protection and promotion of the dignity of all people.

Notes

1 The Peace of Westphalia refers to the treaties concluded in Osnabrück and Münster between the German Emperor and Sweden and France on 24 October 1648. These treaties concluded the Thirty Years War, which was largely a religious war. The Peace of Westphalia is seen by most historians as the beginning of the European system of sovereign nation-states and as an essential factor in the development of the European political structure.

2 A common definition of regimes that has been widely used in the literature on international organization is suggested by Krasner: 'Regimes can be defined as sets of implicit or explicit principles, norms, rules, and decision making procedures around which actors' expectations converge in a given area of international relations' (1983: 2). In this definition principles stand for beliefs, norms for standards of behaviour, rules for prescriptions, and decision making procedures for practices in connection with making and implementing collective choices. Principles and norms are considered the basic defining characteristics of a regime. Changes in principles and norms are changes of the regime itself, whereas changes in rules and procedures are changes within a regime. In a simpler definition proposed by Donnelly (1986: 602) regimes are 'norms and decision making procedures accepted by international actors to regulate an issue area'.

3 Tokyo convention of 1963, The Hague convention of 1970, and Montreal convention of 1971.

4 The tribunals concluded that under international law individual responsibility could be recognized, and that individuals could be charged with offences against international peace. The judgement by the international military tribunal at Nuremberg of 1 October 1946 reads: 'That international law imposes duties and liabilities upon individuals as well as upon States has long been recognized . . .'

5 Shari'ah is the holy law of Islam.

3

Telecommunication

Telecommunication emerged among the first issue areas on the agenda of world communication politics. For more than a century the world community has addressed concerns about the guaranteed provision of international telecommunication services (see Chapter 1). Since the early twentieth century there has been a related concern in telecommunication politics about the allocation of natural resources. Much later in the 1970s the issue of remote sensing appeared, and in the 1980s the trading of telecommunication services achieved a significant status in the political arena.

Availability

The availability of telecommunication services to the general public has been a basic standard in international regulation since the ITU convention of 1865. Already in this first multilateral accord the right of everyone to use international telegraphy was formulated. Also in the national legislation of many countries it has been recognized that minimal telecommunication services should be provided on a universal basis. The US Communications Act of 1934, for example, proposed 'to make available, so far as possible, to all people of the United States, a rapid, efficient, nationwide and worldwide wire and radio communications service with adequate facilities at reasonable charges'.

The world community has expressed its political choice on the availability of telecommunication services in a landmark resolution on space communications in 1961 (UNGA Resolution 1721D(XVI)). The resolution provides that: 'Communication by means of satellite should be available to the nations of the world as soon as practicable on a global and non-discriminatory basis.' The agreement for the operation of the satellite consortium Intelsat (signed by parties at Washington on 20 August 1971 and entered into force on 12 February 1973) made reference to this resolution in its preamble: 'Considering the principle set forth in Resolution 1721D(XVI) that communication by means of satellite should be available to the nations of the world as soon as practicable on a global and non-discriminatory basis.'

The standard of availability obviously demands international coordination. It requires that telecommunication networks are technically compatible and that common rules are adopted about access to and use of these networks. From the mid nineteenth century to the 1970s this coordination was governed by a stable and robust multilateral accord. The world community had adopted common standards on the technical compatibility of networks and the price setting for access to and use of these networks. This public service type of agreement was based upon the principles of natural monopoly and cross-subsidization. Monopolies of equipment and services were seen to provide efficient and equitable public service. Cross-subsidization meant that tariffs for small users were not based upon real costs, but were kept affordable by subsidies from such revenue generating operations as international telephony.

This arrangement was fundamentally challenged by technological innovations which inspired the profound regulatory reforms of the 1980s. The merging of telecommunication with computer technology, the optical fibre cable, the fax machine, and the erosion of the distinction between voice and data contributed to a rapid growth of telecommunication and to increasing pressure from the largest users to reduce tariffs. These users discovered that cost reductions were possible if they used alternatives to the networks controlled by the national monopolists. In some countries technological and commercial pressures began to have an effect on national policy. This was clearly the case in the USA where the Reagan administration formulated its 'open skies' policy in 1984. This deregulatory policy initiated a change from a national monopoly arrangement based on cross-subsidization to a practice based on market principles and cost-related pricing.

Deregulation became the key policy orientation in telecommunication. A wave of telecommunications deregulation found concrete expression in privatization and liberalization. As telecommunication users began to realize their growing dependence on telecommunications, they organized strong lobbies to achieve regulatory change in line with their interests. By and large the regulators affirmed business users' demands. In the 1980s telecommunications systems in the USA, the UK and Japan shifted to deregulatory policies.

This began with Judge Harold Greene's landmark decision on the break-up of the long-distance services, local services and equipment manufacturing of the giant telecommunication operator AT&T. On 1 January 1984 AT&T was broken up into its 22 local companies. In exchange AT&T was now at liberty to enter into new types of business. In 1985 the sale of 51 per cent of Britain's nationally owned British Telecom shares to private sector interests was authorized by the UK government. Also in 1985 Japan developed a new policy towards the liberalization of its telecommunications operations. The largest operator, Nippon Telephone & Telegraph, lost its monopoly in exchange for permission to begin new competitive lines of communication business. Part of the government's ownership of NT&T was sold to the private sector and new local voice carriers were allowed in the marketplace.

This ushered in a new era of competition in the provision of equipment and services (both basic and enhanced), new rules for the conduct of the former monopolies, new contenders in a competitive marketplace for carriers, and a shift to cost-based pricing strategies. The leading reformers, the USA, the UK and Japan, 'have also promoted the expansion of international capacity through the licensing of new satellite competitors and transoceanic fiber-optic cables' (Aronson, 1990: 20).

Following these deregulatory policies, concern began to be expressed about the availability of telecommunication services in a climate of privatization and liberalization. 'Under liberalization cost-based pricing involves a reduction in long-distance tariffs, an increase in local call charges and an increase in the charges levied on individual subscribers (these subscribers being once again made responsible for meeting the cost of the local loop)' (Hills, 1989: 134). Although there is not sufficiently strong evidence of large numbers of subscribers being forced off the network, there is some evidence that privatization and liberalization have not increased the penetration of telephone networks. This is largely due to the fact that deregulation tends to increase the costs of connection, rental and usage. 'In the USA consumer groups argue that the divestiture of AT&T has disenfranchised groups of consumers from use of the telephone by the rebalancing of charges and the liberalization of the local network monopoly – these groups are the elderly, the poor and those living in high-cost rural areas' (1989: 139). A number of initiatives have developed to address this, such as subsidization schemes; however, consumer groups argue that these emergency measures are not adequate. They provide access to the 'emergency box', but this does not constitute a universal service. 'The argument adopted by consumer groups in the USA is that access is not universal service – that the telephone should be priced at a level which makes it possible for disadvantaged groups to use it for social reasons rather than simply as an emergency service' (1989: 141). The data on penetration in the USA suggest that since the AT&T divestiture national telephone penetration has not decreased (Fuhr, 1990: 187), but this may be different for actual usage. 'Consumer groups claim that usage of the telephone has decreased among lower-income groups, such as the elderly. The American Association of Retired Persons argues that one in five people over the age of 55 years have had to reduce their telephone usage' (Hills, 1989: 142).

Deregulation of telecommunication may also have an impact on international tariff structures. The concern has been raised that the new competitive climate for Intelsat could lead to so-called 'cream-skimming' on the dense routes and consequently problems for the financing of the thin routes (in particular for Third World traffic). 'Through an economic policy of global price averaging, Intelsat has ensured affordable communications on a worldwide basis. To accomplish this, Intelsat takes revenues derived from high-traffic routes (e.g. the North Atlantic region, USA to Europe) and subsidizes the less profitable traffic routes that interconnect geographically isolated and/or developing nations' (Gershon, 1990: 249). Deregulation means that Intelsat will have to compete with other satellite operators, but also increasingly with fibre optic cable operators that will apply pricing systems based on high-density routes. This may raise critical problems for the integrated global pricing system of Intelsat. Since its very beginning Intelsat has enjoyed a near-monopoly status in the delivery of satellite communications. According to Article II of its statutes, Intelsat provides all regions on a non-discriminatory basis. This implies the need to cross-subsidize thin traffic routes through revenue from the dense traffic routes. Competition to the monopoly began with the emergence of regional satellite systems (Eutelsat and Arabsat) and national satellite systems (like the Indonesia Palapa system which provides regional services). The more serious threat came with the open skies policy of the Reagan administration (in 1984) which claimed that new private entrants on the transatlantic satellite market would be in the national interest. Intelsat defended its monopoly status in satellite telecommunications by arguing that more participants would increase costs and decrease efficiency. Intelsat also referred to the damage to its cross-subsidization if others were allowed to skim the cream. By the mid 1980s a number of applications for the provision of satellite services had been received by the US Federal Communications Commission. The major applicants were Orion Satellite Corporation (March 1983), International Satellite Inc. (August 1983), RCA (February 1984), Cygnus Corporation (March 1984) and Pan American Satellite Inc. (May 1984). Only the PanAmSat application asked authorization for international carrier services between the USA and Latin America. The others were only interested in the provision of private

satellite services (information traffic within a network owned or
leased by the customer) in the North Atlantic region. Even so,
Intelsat began to feel uneasy about the prospect of cream-skimming
competitors.

The positions
The concern about availability in terms of both technical functional-
ity and provision of services is universally shared. The major agents
of this concern have been the telecommunication administrations
(TAs), the recognized private operating agencies (RPOAs), the
ITU, and the business community of large telecommunication
users. Recently, some consumer groups have also expressed their
interest in the availability of telecommunication services.

The issue of availability is largely motivated by public service
interests and by economic interests. The standard of 'universal
service' is not only advocated from a public interest angle, but also
promoted by private interests. The latter, however, tend to argue
that 'if individual subscribers are too poor to meet the increased
costs of access then they must forfeit the telephone service and drop
off the network. If governments wish the network to be "universal"
then they must pay a subsidy to have these people kept on' (Hills,
1989: 134).

Since the early 1980s rival claims have been brought to the
regulatory agenda. By and large the provision of telecommunication
services in many countries had been organized on the basis of
different patterns of monopoly (public or private) and on cross-
subsidization as the pricing strategy. Governments had a great
interest in telecommunication revenues and in the creation of
reliable markets for their national telecommunication equipment
manufacturers. The overriding claim was that connectivity was most
efficiently and effectively secured through monopoly institutions,
such as the state-run or para-statal public monopolies of the PTTs,
or such private monopolies as AT&T in the USA. It was generally
argued that the provision of telecommunication services demanded
such a large economy of scale that it was most efficient if one
operator provided the service to all. This was corroborated by the
fact that telecommunications offered an undifferentiated service,
the plain old telephone service (POTS). Technological developments, especially digitization, changed this and led to the provision
of a range of differentiated services to which different arrangements
could be applied. The effective claim to a monopoly arrangement
based upon cross-subsidization began to be challenged in the 1980s
by a *laissez-faire* position based upon competitive and cost-based
tariffing arrangements. In response to this position the tendency in

many countries has been to retain forms of monopoly control over basic services and open up the market for so-called enhanced services.

Thus, in current debates on international telecommunication regulation, the rival claims that confront each other are the restrictive, regulatory position and the permissive, *laissez-faire* position. The restrictive position argues that in the competitive battle between private entrepreneurs, given the levels of expenditure, there might not be sufficient commercial incentive to meet the public obligation of universal service. Without regulatory measures, it is expected that the competitive reduction of international charges might stop the cross-subsidization of local calls. Competition on crowded traffic routes, such as the transatlantic route, might lead to capacity glut on dense routes, and cream-skimming might make the operation of thin routes less feasible. The expectation is that the adoption of new pricing policies leads public service ideals into grave jeopardy.

The claim to regulation is also defended by pointing to the loss of national control and the need to protect national sovereignty. In particular, developing countries have presented the case that new developments in international telecommunication lead to the concession of control over national networks to foreign operators. They fear that international private service providers could bypass the national network through the use of sophisticated lease-line arrangements which would be beyond their control. They also fear that network by-pass could result in economic losses and that countries might be obliged to adopt the policies of other countries.

The restrictive position proposes that private networks should be subject to international regulation and to the same technical and operational requirements as the public networks. This position is shared by many telecommunication administrations. Contrary to this, the private operators oppose any inclusion of private networks in such regulation. The defence of their *laissez-faire* position is that 'the mandatory application of extensive performance and operational standards to either private or public networks runs contrary to market approaches taken by some countries, especially the USA' (Rutkowski, 1986: 71).

The claimants for the permissive position base their claim on the need to change an unacceptable cost structure for large international users, to advance the slow rate of technological innovation in monopoly markets, and to achieve global market access. These agents (mainly representatives of the leading reform countries, and large user groups such as INTUG) argue that a competitive, largely private telecommunication market is well suited to provide an optimal range and quality of telecommunication services. They counter the argument about their alleged low interest in the provision of universal service by stating that the public monopolies have often not provided universal service either.

They argue that telecommunication tariffs should be on a cost-based system in order to avoid excess charges on large business users for the conventional cross-subsidization of residential users. The liberalization claim also states that technological innovation has created a differentiation of products and services which can no longer adequately be supported by monopoly providers.

Prevailing political practice
World telecommunication was governed from the mid nineteenth century to the 1970s by a stable, robust and effective collaborative arrangement. This political practice is today in transition. In many countries the conventional national monopolies are still in control, but their operations are under siege. The collective practice is shifting from a robust multilateral accord based on the principle of national monopoly and controlled pricing to an accord based upon competition and market-oriented pricing. The emerging political practice will have a strong free trade orientation. It is likely to be a robust accord that will be effectively implemented through the enforcement mechanisms of ITU and GATT and supported by the major private players in the field.

In recent multilateral decision making on telecommunication the basic standard of general availability has been confirmed. The World Administrative Telegraph and Telephone Conference of 1988 stated in the final acts (Article 1.3): 'These Regulations are established with a view to facilitating global interconnection and interoperability of telecommunication facilities and to promoting the harmonious development and efficient operation of technical facilities, as well as the efficiency, usefulness and availability to the public of international telecommunication services.' The conference also adopted a resolution on the continued availability of traditional services which considers: '(d) that keeping in mind the universality of communications, it would be desirable to ensure to the greatest extent possible, in the absence of the establishment of new services in many Member countries, that the public in those countries should have continuing effective use of traditional services to communicate on a world-wide basis; (e) that certain rural areas and developing countries, in particular, may need to rely on existing widely available services for international communications for a relatively long period of time; resolves that all Members should co-operate to ensure that . . . provisions should be made to allow, through available communication infrastructures, continued availability of traditional services so as to enable effective communications on a world-wide basis.'

The final acts of the Plenipotentiary Conference of the ITU in 1989 (Nice) provided in the constitution of the ITU in Article 22: 'Members recognize the right of the public to correspond by means of the international service of public correspondence.' Article 27 added to this that 'Members shall take such steps as may be necessary to ensure the establishment, under the best technical conditions, of the channels and installations necessary to carry on the rapid and uninterrupted exchange of telecommunications.'

The telecommunication annex to the General Agreement on Trade in Services (December 1993) has binding provisions on access and use of public telecommunication networks and services: 'Each Member shall ensure that no condition is imposed on access to and use of public telecommunications transport networks and services other than is necessary: to safeguard the public service responsibilities of suppliers of public telecommunication transport networks and services, in particular their ability to make their networks or services available to the public generally; to protect the technical integrity of public telecommunications networks or services.'

For the issue of availability the current shift from the conventional restrictive regulatory position to a more liberal trade position poses the question of how the emerging practice will accommodate the commonly adopted standard of availability. One of the open questions in this connection is which telecommunication services should be included in a universal service obligation. After initial disagreements on the issue, the ministers who approved the final act of the Uruguay Round (December 1993) also adopted a decision on negotiations on basic telecommunications. A negotiating group on basic telecommunications was established and its mandate is to study basic telecommunications in the light of the 'progressive liberalization of trade in telecommunication transport networks and services'. The aim of these negotiations is to bring basic telecommunications under the standards of the Uruguay accord. This would mean that access to basic telecommunication markets in member countries would be liberalized.

Frequency allocation

The allocation of natural resources is a basic issue in telecommunication politics. It has always been a major concern in telecommunication that different services should not interfere. The basic principle of non-interference required international coordination in the allocation of such natural resources as radio frequency bands in the electromagnetic spectrum and slots for satellites in the geosynchronous orbit. Since these are limited resources, the world community faced a classical distributional problem of 'who gets what, why and how'.

Spectrum allocation is an evident agenda item for multilateral negotiation. The radio spectrum is a limited resource. This remains so in spite of digital compression techniques that facilitate a more efficient use of bandwidth but cannot possibly keep pace with the exponential demand for spectrum use. It is also a shared resource. Its adequate utilization demands that interference is avoided and that it can be effectively used by such mobile users as aeroplanes and ships. The essential institution for negotiation about spectrum allocation is the International Telecommunication Union (and its World Administrative Radio Conferences).

The earliest collective practice for frequency allocation was agreed upon by the Berlin Radio Conference of 1906. It implied that an administration would notify which maritime stations it operated and these notifications would then be published by the International Bureau of the International Telegraph Union (ITU). The administrations would have to consult the ITU notifications before operating new stations. Since 1906 most governments have agreed to notify the Berne bureau of the ITU. The Berlin conference allocated frequencies for public correspondence in the maritime service, for long-distance communication by coast stations, and for mobile services for the military. In line with these arrangements, the Radio-Telegraph Conference of 1920 in Washington DC provided in its decisions that frequencies would be chosen such 'as to prevent, so far as practicable, interference with international services carried on by existing stations the frequencies of which had already been notified to the International Bureau'. The Washington conference adopted a table of frequency allocations. The following Radio-Telegraph Conference at Madrid in 1932 gave official status to the international frequency list and provided that administrations were obliged to notify all frequencies assigned to stations that could cause international interference.

In this first phase of international allocation politics, the allocation of frequency bands was largely based upon a 'first come, first served' (or *a posteriori*) practice. A telecommunication administration that planned to use a frequency notified this to the bureau of the ITU. If the frequency request could be granted, this was recorded and the requesting administration had the right to use the frequency. Others could not interfere with this use.

After the Second World War there were so many radio stations operating on frequencies that had not been registered that telecommunication regulators had to find a solution to this problem. First, a new international frequency list had to be drawn up; and secondly, a body had to be created to take care of future additions to the list. The ITU Atlantic City conference of 1947 established this body in the form of an eleven-member International Frequency Registration Board (IFRB). The conference installed the board and gave it the assignment to draw up the new international frequency list.

The first world conference after the Second World War (at Mexico City) about frequency allocation focused on the high-frequency (HF) portion of the radio spectrum. This was especially important for international broadcasting and other forms of long-distance communications. The HF band was also a restricted international resource and there had been an ongoing concern about its unfair use. With the number of parties interested in this resource growing it became increasingly difficult for administrations to get access to the overpopulated HF band. A crucial problem facing the Mexico City High-Frequency Broadcasting Conference in 1948–9 was that required frequencies greatly exceeded available space in the radio spectrum. The creation of an allotment plan turned out to be very difficult, almost impossible. The Mexico conference achieved only a partial solution (for only one region) and this was seriously emaciated by the refusal of the USA to sign the agreement. Among the reasons given were the fact that the USSR carried out jamming activities and that the plan allotted more frequency hours to the USSR than to the USA. The Second International High-Frequency Broadcasting Conference was equally unsuccessful in reaching an agreement. This conference took place at Florence/Rapallo in 1950 and, apart from the Soviet walk-out from the conference, there was still the problem of too many requests and too little space.

In the following decade, the IFRB worked extensively on the issue and attempted to design an allotment plan that would be acceptable to all administrations. Draft plans were submitted to the 1959 WARC which was called upon to revise the table of frequency allocations that had been drawn up at the 1947 Radio Conference at Atlantic City. The plans were rejected. However, the conference adopted a procedure that became the prevailing practice and decided to create a master international frequency register to contain older assignments together with new plans. A full new frequency list was seen as not feasible, since as a result of technological and economic developments the demands for frequencies increased and continued to greatly exceed available capacity.

From the late 1950s the concern about frequency allocation began to be extended to the issue of radio frequencies for space communications. The development of space technology raised new and complex questions about access to and control over space resources, such as orbital slots and radio frequencies, and motivated the concern that space services might cause interference. Space regulation became an international issue with the launching of the first satellite, the Soviet Sputnik 1, in 1957. As Sputnik caused various forms of signal interference it created the need for space frequency allocations. A year later the United Nations General Assembly adopted its first resolution (UNGA Resolution 1348(XII), 1958) on outer space which declared that 'recent developments in respect of outer space have added a new dimension to man's existence and opened new possibilities for the increase of his knowledge and the improvement of his life'. The General Assembly also recognized that outer space is the common interest of mankind and should be used only for peaceful purposes and for the benefit of all mankind. An *ad hoc* committee was set up that became in 1959 the Committee on the Peaceful Uses of Outer Space (COPUOS). Herewith a new regulatory forum was created. Mainly as the result of the work done by COPUOS a body of space law was developed that encompasses five multilateral treaties.[1]

The first ITU conference to become involved with frequency allocation for space services took place in 1959. It allocated thirteen frequency bands to the new space and earth-to-space services. Also at this WARC in 1959 Third World countries began to question the *a posteriori* practice. The conference took no decision on the matter.

The next conference to deal with this was the 1963 Extraordinary Administrative Radio Conference for Space Radiocommunications (EARC). This was the first major effort to allocate frequencies to space services and to devise procedures for their use. At this conference two frequency bands were allocated solely to space services. This was accepted by a majority of delegations, with the exception of some twenty countries that indicated the need to retain these frequency bands for other services. Also frequency bands for shared use between terrestrial and space services were assigned. The EARC decided that for satellite communications a notification and recording procedure should be used as had been developed for terrestrial services. Frequencies to be used should be notified to the IFRB, which would examine notifications in the light of the ITU convention and the Radio Regulations, and in view of possible harmful interference. If acceptable, registrations would be entered in the master international frequency register. The EARC also passed a resolution on equitable use of the spectrum, stating that: 'All members and associate members of the Union have an interest in and right to an equitable and rational use of frequency bands allocated for space communications . . . the utilization and exploitation of the frequency spectrum for space communications [should] be subject to international agreements based on principles of justice and equity permitting the use and sharing of allocated frequency bands in the mutual interest of all nations.'

In spite of these shared principles there were clearly opposing positions on the actual allocation of frequencies. The *a posteriori* position was supported by the USA, Western Europe, Latin America and Japan. The developing countries favoured an *a priori* planning practice, but there was no concerted Third World voting on the controversy. The major clash on the issue occurred at the Space WARC in 1971. The USA maintained its *a posteriori* position, but France and the UK began to claim an *a priori* planning practice for certain bands. Also Latin America shifted to the *a priori* position. Overall, Space WARC 1971 maintained the *a posteriori* position. However, the Third World got a resolution (Spa-WARC Resolution 2-1) which secured equal rights to the use of the EMS. The norm adopted by the resolution was that 'All countries have equal rights in the use of both the radio frequencies allocated to various space radiocommunication services and the GSO for these services.' The 1973 ITU Plenipotentiary Conference in Malaga gave support to the *a priori* principle by incorporating in the ITU convention the notion that radio frequencies are 'limited natural resources' that 'must be used efficiently and economically so that countries or groups of countries may have equitable access to both in conformity with the provisions of the Radio Regulations according to their needs and the technical facilities at their disposal' (Article 33.2).

The basic principles established by the 1971 conference were to be implemented by the 1977 ITU WARC (the so-called Geneva 1977 plan), at least for regions 1 (Europe, USSR, Africa) and 3 (Australasia, Oceania). Planning for region 2 (the Americas) was achieved in 1983. The 1977 plan was also based upon a specific political assumption: the need to ward off TV's threat to national sovereignty. This matched perfectly with the technical assumption that given the needed high-power transmitters on board satellites, the signals would beam to limited geographical areas only. Broadcast satellite services (BSS) would be nationally confined. The 1977 plan was firmly based on the concept of limited national coverage and the principle of equity, and led the ITU to assign the same number of frequencies to all countries: five per country, irrespective of likely service requirements. 'Almost from the beginning it was apparent that the overwhelming majority of the 111 delegations in attendance were planning to create a formal, long-term *a priori* plan which would allot to each of the members of the ITU a portion of the 12 GHz frequency band allocated to satellite broadcasting and the appropriate geostationary orbital positions' (Codding, 1990a: 103).

The USA argued for a more flexible method of planning. When the argument failed, the delegation persuaded other members in region 2 to postpone allotment for this region until a later date. With the support of Canada and Brazil this worked. For regions 1 and 3 allotment plans were designed which implied that in future the right to use space resources would depend upon a system's compatibility with the *a priori* plan and not its date of notification. The region 2 conference took place in 1983 in Geneva. It drafted an *a priori* plan for frequency and GSO allotment in region 2.

Meanwhile, the WARC of 1979 had addressed the allotment for fixed satellite services (FSS). The USA stated – as before – that a fixed plan would hamper the development of new services and new technologies. This time also other developed countries supported this position. The developing countries proposed to deal with this issue at an administrative radio conference in two parts. These became the 1985 and 1988 WARC-ORBs.

The 1979 WARC also again raised the issue of frequency allocation for HF broadcasting, approved an increase in the spectrum bandwidth for HF broadcasting services, and proposed another WARC to establish planning principles for HF allocation. These WARCs would be held in 1984 and 1986 as conferences for the planning of HF bands allocated to broadcasting services. At the 1979 conference several proposals were submitted for an equitable allotment plan by Yugoslavia, India, China, Nigeria, Algeria and Syria. The developing countries argued in favour of an *a priori* planning approach since they felt that the existing procedure did provide special advantages to the developed countries. Their lack of resources hampered an effective participation in the procedure. Therefore, they proposed that a special conference should allot frequencies according to the needs of countries. The developed countries generally argued that the optimal solution was an improvement of the current procedure. In particular, the USA claimed that an allotment plan would hinder the introduction of new technologies that might ultimately resolve the problem.

In the end, the 1979 WARC did not really resolve the issue of the rival claims to *a priori* versus *a posteriori* allotment. The conference decided to request yet another conference that would 'guarantee in practice for all countries equitable access to the geostationary satellite orbit and the frequency bands allocated to space services'. The resolution also stated that the geostationary satellite orbit and the frequency bands allocated to space services are 'limited natural resources'.

The 1979 WARC was very much influenced by the spirit of the 1970s debates on a new international economic and information order. To some extent the conference proved a success for the Third World countries which found their claim to *a priori* planning on an equitable basis accepted. The 1979 conference also gave the Third World preferential access to the frequency bands for HF broadcasting. Provisions of preferential access were incorporated into the ITU Radio Regulations (RR 1218 procedure). These were clearly considerable political achievements for Third World negotiators.

In the 1980s, however, the gains largely withered away and turned out to be mainly symbolic as a result of political factors (especially the lack of Third World coordination and cohesion, plus a rapid proliferation of privatization and liberalization policies), deteriorating economies (and as a result the inability to actively participate in ITU technical debates), and technological developments. The debt problem acquired staggering proportions and Third World differentiation only increased. Also in the Third World the trend towards deregulation became the wisdom of the day. A comprehensive Third World solidarity was replaced by region-based or sub-region based bargaining related to shared needs and interests.

In 1982 the ITU Plenipotentiary Conference reinforced the equitable access provision by changing Article 33 of the convention, which would now read: 'In using frequency bands for space radio services, Members shall bear in mind that radio frequencies and the geostationary satellite orbit are limited natural resources and that they must be used efficiently and economically, in conformity with the provisions of the Radio Regulations, so that countries or groups of countries may have equitable access to both, taking into account the special needs of the developing countries and the geographical situation of particular countries.'[2]

The WARC-ORB of 1985 managed to find a compromise between *a priori* and *a posteriori* positions. There would be planning for FSS, but no planning for other services. The first session of the WARC-ORB concluded with a compromise allotment plan, 'a plan with *a priori* characteristics, but only in completely non-controversial segments of the spectrum' (Savage, 1989: 117). Even so, the developing countries emerged 'optimistic as they received certain guarantees . . . and ensured access to space services' (1989: 118). The 1988 WARC-ORB reached agreement on an allotment plan for the FSS in specific bands (prepared by the IFRB), and an improved procedure for bringing satellite communication systems into service in certain frequency bands. The conference also decided to allow greater participation of the common user's organizations (such as Intelsat and Inmarsat) in multilateral planning meetings.

A future conference was to decide on world-wide frequency allocations for bands to be assigned to satellite high-definition TV and to sound broadcast satellite services (SBSS). This was the 1992 WARC which took place in Torremolinos, Spain from 3 February to 3 March. In fact, allocation concerns were the essence of this conference, which was attended by some 1500 delegations from 127 countries and observers from over 30 international organizations. On its agenda the conference had the extension of the spectrum bands that were allocated to HF broadcasting and EMS allocations to sound broadcasting by satellite, HDTV, mobile satellite services, and FSS.

Crucial factors leading to the need for these allocations were technological developments (such as digitization, spectrum compression techniques, spectrum reuse techniques, fibre optics and miniaturization), the rapidly increasing demand for the utilization of radio waves, and the proliferation of new services. Such services include emergency services, personal communications, world-wide paging, security monitoring and the exchange of electronic data (EDI). For several new services new consumer electronics need to be manufactured, for example for digital TV or for digital SBSS. In order to successfully market such equipment it is critical to obtain world-wide frequency allocations. Also service providers have a vested interest in obtaining world-wide standardization of frequencies to service a global market.

This conference was the first WARC since 1979 to revise a part of the EMS and the first attempt to accommodate new regulatory demands raised by technological innovation at one major meeting. The conference managed to allocate frequencies to a large volume of recently emerged wireless technologies. In recent years a set of mobile satellite services has emerged (for maritime, aeronautical and land mobile use) that operate on a global basis and require additional use of the electromagnetic spectrum. These requirements in fact dominated the Torremolinos conference agenda. Its outcome implies far-reaching changes in telecommunications as it will become increasingly independent of cable. Mobility and portability will greatly increase. That mobile services became the focus of conference action is explained by the rapid growth and proliferation of mobile technologies and their related services on a world market. More than 12,000 mobile satellite terminals are in use on ships, oil rigs, aircraft and trucks, and with disaster relief organizations and news gathering organizations. For the 1990s a phenomenal growth of this community of users is expected. Inmarsat expects to have well over a million users by 2005 (Poskett and McDougal, 1990: 356). Mobile systems have among other factors been strongly pushed ahead by the overwhelming success of cellular radio systems. Maritime telephone traffic has grown in the past years at an annual 50 per cent. There has also recently been a rapidly growing interest in public telephone traffic from aircraft aloft.

Since the spectrum is a limited resource, the new mobile services contested the frequency bands allocated to conventional services. Those promoting the new services proposed to redesign frequency allocation to accommodate their interests. Conventional services are point-to-point fixed radio communication services. Since mobile services demand transmissions through the radio spectrum they are more in need of frequency allocations than fixed services which can also utilize cables. The protagonists of mobile services argue that with such advanced technologies as optical fibre, the fixed services should have no difficulty in using cable as a transmission medium or should find frequencies in different bands. WARC 1992 decisions clearly pointed to the prioritizing of new services over existing interests. In the battle between fixed radio services and mobile services for frequency bands, the latter came out as winners. Among the reasons for this is probably the overall development of the telecommunication infrastructure in many of the developed countries. These countries are developing optical networks to accommodate the digital services their societies require and to transmit broadband television. In many developed countries (for example the USA, Belgium and the Netherlands) television is today mainly transmitted through cable networks and no longer by the airwaves.[3] Moreover most of these systems still use coaxial cable and not yet optical fibre. The transformation (the so-called Negroponte switch) means that what today mainly goes by air (images) should go by cable, and what goes by cable (voice and data) should go by air. The argument is strengthened by the broadband requirements of HDTV and the increased use of new cellular services.

WARC-92 was unequivocally one of the most contentious conferences in the history of the International Telecommunication Union . . . The conference was characterized by a struggle between the world's different regions to establish and defend their own interests and to get what they considered best for themselves. WARC-92 also saw an unprecedented industry influence. Wealthy international corporations that were vying for a piece of the spectrum sent fleets of lobbyists to the conference to try to tilt its decisions in their favour while their home governments engaged in formal diplomatic negotiations on their behalf. (Sung, 1992: 624)

On various allocation issues the positions of delegations differed sharply. For example, for SSBS, only on the last day of the conference could an agreement be reached. Allocations for SBSS are important in view of the possibility of broadcasting with digital audio quality, and this is expected to push the demand for a new generation of radio sets. Digital audio broadcasting (DAB) means that in both terrestrial and satellite radio services the analogue signal is replaced by the improved quality of the digital signal.

On frequency allocations for HDTV, different positions also emerged, but no common solutions were achieved. For ITU region 2 a band has been assigned which is different from that in the rest of the world. This was mainly due to the fact that the currently assigned bands would be only available by 2007 and thus imply postponement of HDTV for regions 1 and 3.

As the 1992 event approached it was clear that there would be little Third World policy coordination or coalition formation and that the agenda was largely dominated by Western interests, for example clashes between the USA and Europe about allocations for mobile services. The political context of the last allocation exercise in 1979 was very different from the 1992 environment. Little if anything was left of the earlier political controversy in connection with Third World demands for a more equitable world communication order. The Torremolinos conference provided a new type of environment in which commerce and pragmatism prevailed.

The positions
The concern about frequency allocation is shared by all members of the world community. A basic motive for this universal concern is the common interest in the interference-free utilization of a limited natural resource. More recently, commercial actors have been motivated to actively lobby for frequency allocations to support a range of new services. Many of these services are privately operated and companies which have invested large amounts in their development are obviously very concerned about getting those world-wide frequencies allocated to their services that allow access to global markets.

Two rival positions have confronted each other in the resolution of the frequency allocation issue. There is the *a posteriori* approach which claims the 'first come, first served' practice as the most efficient solution for utilization of the EMS. This claim is mainly defended with reference to the norm of economic efficiency, and in particular the big telecommunication users (the main agents for this claim) contend that an *a priori* planning approach is inefficient and hinders their future use of the spectrum. They have argued that a fixed plan would hamper the development of new services and the kind of new technologies that might ultimately resolve the problem of spectrum scarcity.

The rival position proposes an *a priori* allotment plan. This approach involves the design of an allotment plan that is *a priori* negotiated between telecommunication administrations and that allocates frequencies in line with their needs. The *a priori* allotment position is based upon the principle of equitable sharing. This is further defended with the argument that the EMS is a non-terrestrial resource, and as such is a common heritage that is not to be appropriated by any state.[4] The main claimants for the *a priori* approach (the developing countries) have argued that the existing *a posteriori* practice gave special advantages to the developed countries. Their own lack of resources hampered an effective participation in this practice.

Although international bargaining in the 1970s and 1980s seemed to have accommodated the allocation concern in line with the preference of those who claimed the *a priori* approach, the business community has recently begun to claim that technical developments lead to renewed reflection on the issue of *a priori* planning. There are increasing pressures to reconsider the ways in which in the 1970s and 1980s the claims for equitable sharing of the EMS resource have been accommodated. These pressures originate with an increasing demand for receiving equipment for private use, for instance in hotels, and with the world-wide trends towards liberalization of the trade in film and TV programmes. The big users and operators claim that the *a priori* planning that was adopted earlier as collective practice does constrain the development of world communication. In effect, this means that rival positions on EMS utilization are still on the world political agenda.

Prevailing political practice

During the 1906–71 period the *a posteriori* approach was the accepted collective practice for the accommodation of the frequency allocation concern. This was a robust and binding multilateral accord since all actors wanted to avoid interference and understood that, without collective agreement, interference-free operation of radio stations would be in jeopardy. Moreover, the adopted rules had the legal force of treaty provisions, were enforced by an effective international institution (ITU), and were supported by a powerful constituency.

The first multilateral agreement was the Berlin Radio Conference of 1906. The principle of registration was 'first come, first served'. In the 1960s Third World delegates began to challenge the principle and proposed *a priori* planning instead. They argued that the *a posteriori* norm would lead to supremacy of the technology leaders (which was in fact the situation in the early 1980s as 90 per cent of the EMS is used for 10 per cent of the world population). At the 1971 Space WARC the collective practice began to shift to an arrangement based upon the *a priori* position. Frequencies came to be seen as limited resources, the norm of equitable access was adopted, and the position of latecomers was taken into account.

In the 1980s a compromise was reached. There would be *a priori* planning for the fixed satellite services, and *a posteriori* practice would hold for the BSS (i.e. for most of the frequencies). The change towards an *a priori* allotment practice was partial only and, moreover, is recently again under siege. Recent discussions about the privatization of the EMS and about auctioning off segments of the spectrum to private operators make a return to the *a posteriori* arrangement most probable.

Overall, it should be concluded that the essential objective of interference-free operation in the EMS has been effectively achieved. There is currently serious compliance by all international actors with the table of frequency allocations and the other provisions of the Radio Regulations. There are procedures for obtaining coordination or agreements of other administrations. There is notification, publication and recording of frequency assignments in the master register.

In sum, the world community has established for the allocation of frequencies in the EMS a practice of effective multilateral cooperation based upon a robust and binding common accord. The accord has not resolved the controversy of the contending claims to *a priori* versus *a posteriori* practices. Although *de iure* the world community has adopted a practice based upon *a priori* planning, the most powerful players continue to operate *de facto* the *a posteriori* practice. Current economic and technological trends strengthen this practice.

Geosynchronous orbit allocation

Directly related to the frequency allocation issue is the problem of allocating orbital slots for satellite services. For the provision of space communication services, access both to the appropriate bands of radio frequencies and to the appropriate orbital positions is essential. The geosynchronous orbit (GSO) is the optimal location for broadcasting satellites. This is at some 36,000 km above the equator where satellites rotate at the same speed as the earth and where – as a result – they remain fixed over the same spot on earth. They cover in this position some one-third of the earth's surface and their transmitting and receiving equipment can remain directed at the same point. Geostationary satellites can easily be observed from the earth and do not need complicated tracking equipment. This is important when a satellite no longer holds its position and poses the risk of collision. Although the GSO satellite was theoretically designed by Arthur C. Clarke as early as 1945, the first real GSO satellite was Syncom in 1963, contracted to Hughes by the NASA. In 1964 the famous Syncom III satellite relayed the Olympic games from Tokyo to the USA.

The demand for slots in the GSO has rapidly increased since the 1960s. The GSO offered excellent opportunities for military communications and reconnaissance (some 40 per cent of the orbit has on average been used for such purposes) as well as for commercial services such as sound broadcasting by satellite or mobile satellite services.[5] Allocation in the geostationary orbit has increasingly become a concern to Third World countries, although the expense of satellite manufacturing, launching and maintenance has kept them out of access to space resources. By the late 1970s the Third World countries became afraid that occupations of orbital slots could prejudice their access in time and they began to resist the 'first come, first served' policy that was customary practice. This was reinforced by the recognition of the limited nature of the resource. The 'Clarke belt' is finite and, unless slots and frequencies in the GSO are shared, signals can interfere. The WARC 1971 for Space Telecommunications found itself confronted with the controversy about the rival claims to GSO positions. Although the conference adopted a resolution that provided an 'equal right' to the use of the orbit resource and resolved that its use by latecomers should be ensured, the conventional *a posteriori* norm was adopted for GSO positions. The ITU Plenipotentiary Conference of 1973 established the principle of 'equitable access' to the GSO.

In 1976 a group of eight equatorial states (Brazil, Colombia, Congo, Ecuador, Indonesia, Kenya, Uganda and Zaire) claimed sovereignty over 'their' geostationary orbital positions. The Bogotá declaration they signed on 3 December 1976 stated: 'Equatorial countries declare that the geostationary synchronous orbit is a physical fact linked to the reality of our planet because its existence depends exclusively on its relation to gravitational phenomena generated by the earth, and that is why it must not be considered part of outer space. Therefore, the segments of geostationary synchronous orbit are part of the territory over which Equatorial States exercise their national sovereignty.' The signatories of the Bogotá declaration resolved 'to proclaim and defend on behalf of their peoples the existence of their sovereignty over this natural resource'. This declaration contradicted norms adopted by the ITU and the provisions of the 1967 Outer Space Treaty, particularly the rule on 'appropriation'. The 1967 treaty stated in Article II that 'Outer Space . . . is not subject to national appropriation by claim of sovereignty.' The eight countries proposed a formal appropriation claim against the *de facto* 'appropriation' of the GSO by those countries that controlled space technology. The Bogotá declaration was contested on grounds of the Space Treaty standards, but also on the basis of the 'common heritage' principle that was so vigorously defended by Third World countries.

When in 1979 at the WARC the debate about the *a priori* allotment versus a 'first come, first served' approach flared up again, the conference passed a resolution reconfirming equitable access to space resources. Resolution 3 adopted by the conference called for a conference to 'guarantee in practice for all countries equitable access to the GSO'. The 1982 ITU Plenipotentiary Conference authorized the conference which would take place in 1985.

Meanwhile the geosynchronous orbit and its equitable use had become an even more urgent issue since more countries launched geostationary satellites in the 1980s. By the late 1980s some 133 satellites were in the GSO transmitting voice, data and video. More domestic satellite systems became operational with launchings by India (1983), China (1984), Mexico (1985) and Colombia (1986); the Arabsat regional system became operational (1985), and the legal arrangements for the European regional system Eutelsat entered into force (1985). In the allocation of the GSO the common user organizations, such as Intelsat, Inmarsat and Intersputnik, began to be actively involved.

In 1985 the first session of the WARC-ORB focused on the use of the geostationary satellite orbit and the planning of space services using it. The conference came to a compromise between *a priori* and *a posteriori* positions. There would be a guarantee of access to the GSO when states required it. 'The developing countries emerged optimistic as they received certain guarantees of orbit allotment equitability, including a minimum of one allotment per country and ensured access to space services' (Savage, 1989: 118). Following the provisions of the 1988 WARC-ORB final acts, both early and late arrivals in space would find adequate protection for the use of space resources.

The positions
It has been generally recognized by all relevant players that the allocation of slots in the GSO needs multilateral cooperation. There is a common interest in the interference-free use of this finite natural resource.

Just as with the EMS allocation, the shared concern about the GSO did not exclude a strong controversy about its optimal mode of accommodation. The contending positions represented claims to a practice based upon *a priori* planning versus a practice based upon *a posteriori* allocation. The *a posteriori* claim has been mainly defended (by the space technology countries) on the basis of the economic and effective use of space resources and the desire not to allow planning procedures to slow down technological development. The *a priori* claim has been strongly argued by Third World countries on the basis of the equitable use of space resources. This defence followed the formulation of basic principles in the 1967 Outer Space Treaty (see note 1 to this chapter). It was also based on the concept of common heritage as recognized in the 1979 Moon Treaty. In line with the common heritage principle, it was argued that an allotment approach was more appropriate than the 'first come, first served' policy, since it demanded that resources such as orbital slots were equitably distributed through some form of planning.

Prevailing political practice
Initially the collective practice was based on *a posteriori* allocation. This changed with the adoption of compromise positions in the 1985 and 1988 WARCs which guaranteed equitability in orbit allotment and protection for latecomers. This shift to the accommodation of an *a priori* preference had been prepared by a series of United Nations resolutions (UNGA Resolutions 1721 in 1961 and 1802 in 1962) that contained the essential norm for GSO allocation: the non-discriminatory access to space for all nations. In line with this provision the special space conference (Space WARC) in 1971 had adopted a resolution that emphasized an 'equal right' to the use of the orbit resource. The conference also resolved that the use of the resource for latecomers should be ensured. The 1973 ITU Plenipotentiary Conference recognized the issue of 'equitable access'. Article 33(2) of the ITU convention stated clearly that this meant

the fair and just sharing of the orbit resource among all countries. The article also stated that the GSO should be treated as a limited natural resource to be used efficiently and economically so that countries or groups of countries may have equitable access. In connection with the allocation of the GSO resource, the body of space law also defined essential standards. The concept of 'common heritage' in the 1979 Moon Treaty, for instance, reinforced that benefits should be distributed equitably. The concept implied that 'there is a basic obligation that falls upon States carrying out space activities to be responsive to the interests of developing countries and to provide for some method of distributing the benefits derived from such activities' (Matte, 1982: 78). In 1982 the UNISPACE (the Second United Nations Conference on the Peaceful Uses of Outer Space) resolved that the GSO was a 'limited resource and therefore its optimum utilization required planning and/or arrangements'.

The prevailing practice on GSO allocation is guided by multilateral accord. In line with the basic principles of non-interference and non-discriminatory access to space services there is a need for all players to coordinate. The rules of the accord have shifted from an *a posteriori* approach to an *a priori* approach. This shift was largely motivated by the interests of the developing countries in acquiring equitable access to space broadcasting. Since all actors share the need for interference-free communication the agreement on space resource allocation is perceived as binding and there is general compliance. This does not exclude that the actual conduct of the most powerful players by and large follows their *a posteriori* preference.

Remote sensing

The technical possibility to gather information from outer space has generated a series of complex issues for the international community. At the core of these issues is the question of control over the data collected by this technique. The world community has been divided over the question of whether the 'sensed' states should give their 'prior consent' to being sensed. The possibility of collecting data from space has also raised a concern about the availability of such data, the lack of access to data about the resources of sensed countries, and the possibility of use of such data by third parties. This concern has become even more urgent with the commercialization of remote sensing activities and the unrestricted sales of data to whoever can afford to pay. The developing countries became particularly concerned about the effect of the 'commercial availability of data on their economic resources and on activities related to their national security' (Jasani, 1991: 23).

Remote sensing has been carried out since the late 1950s for both military and civilian purposes. The sensing of atmospheric conditions was conducted in 1957 by Sputnik 1, and the first US earth observation satellite for cloud cover and weather was launched in 1960 (Tiros 1).

The military application of remote sensing technology was from the beginning an important component of the superpower conflict. The capacity for observation from outer space facilitated, for both the USA and the USSR, forms of mutual control over their nuclear arms systems. It can be argued that this capacity to monitor and verify had a stabilizing function. Military remote sensing was largely controlled by the USA and the USSR until the 1970s when the People's Republic of China launched an observation satellite. In the 1980s France (in collaboration with Italy and Spain) also decided to develop a remote sensing capacity for military use, and other countries (among them the UK and Israel) began to entertain similar plans.

In the civilian field remote sensing developed a wide range of applications, including very successful multilateral cooperation since the 1960s in the World Meteorological Organization. The first earth resource technology satellite, the ERTS-A (later in 1974 named Land Satellite, LANDSAT 1), was launched on 23 July 1972. The LANDSAT programme was conducted by the NASA and the NOAA (National Oceanic and Atmospheric Administration) and has been privatized through the Land Remote Sensing Commercialization Act of 17 July 1984. With the privatization the programme was transferred from the NOAA to the private company EOSAT (Earth Observation Satellite Company).[6] Among the applications of the LANDSAT programme were the exploration of iron formation, the measurement of sugar cane and rice crops and the mapping of river sediments and forests, as well as oceanographic and demographic mapping. The general policy of the programme has been that its data were (against cost) available to everyone from the Earth Resources Observation Systems (EROS) in South Dakota, USA. In 1986 a French programme for civilian remote sensing was started (with the participation of Sweden and Belgium), the Système Probatoire d'Observation de la Terre (SPOT). The data generated by SPOT satellites are sold through a company called SPOT-Image. Other countries that became involved in civilian remote sensing included the Soviet Union, which in 1987 began to market its space data through the trading company Soyuzkarta. With a few exceptions (such as China, India and Brazil) remote sensing technology has been the exclusive domain of the more powerful industrial countries. The Third World countries have shown great interest in the technology for the exploitation of their natural resources.

In the late 1960s the remote sensing issue was put on the agenda of the United Nations. Discussions about the issue took place at the First UN Conference on the Peaceful Uses of Outer Space in 1968 at Vienna, and in 1969 the Scientific and Technical subcommittee of COPUOS called attention to the use of remote sensing techniques for the planning of global resources. The first formal proposal for rule making on remote sensing was made in June 1970 by Argentina. In September 1971 the first meeting took place of the COPUOS working committee on remote sensing. At the second session of the committee in 1973 the Argentinian draft international agreement and a preliminary draft of legal principles submitted by the USSR (co-sponsored by France) were considered. In the 1973 progress report by the committee the positions ranged from complete freedom to gather data by sensing states to a right to prior consent by the sensed state. With regard to the receipt and processing of primary data the positions covered complete freedom of the sensing state to exclusive rights for the sensed state. Also concerning the dissemination and interpretation of data there were important differences. Some states favoured universal dissemination of analysed information; others proposed that the sensed states should enjoy exclusive rights on the end product. By 1975 the Legal Subcommittee of COPUOS had begun to identify a number of common elements in the documents submitted by various countries, and in 1978 a set of seventeen principles was proposed that since then has formed the basis for negotiations (United Nations, 1978).

In the following years basically four positions emerged. One group of states defended the legality of remote resource sensing activities. A second group took the position that remote sensing should be treated as a violation of their national sovereignty. Yet other states reasoned that they accepted the legality of remote sensing but wanted to be able to give prior consent or wanted minimally to be informed in advance. The fourth group of states accepted remote sensing but did not want data collected about their resources to go to third parties. This was qualified by some that claimed that they wanted prior access to the data before third parties could use them.

Several countries proposed amendments to the principles, and eventually in December 1986 the United Nations General Assembly adopted UNGA Resolution 41/65 entitled Principles of Remote Sensing. The principles recognize that remote sensing is permissible without the prior consent of the sensed countries. The prior consent approach that was preferred by the developing countries was not accepted. The advanced states were best able to secure their interests. By and large their political preference for an open skies policy was adopted and private interests were allowed to participate in the remote sensing activity. Important also is the fact that the principles do not extend the principle of permanent sovereignty over natural resources to information about natural resources. The developing countries were not able to influence the established liberal practice by their references to national sovereignty over natural resources or data about these resources. The principles were endorsed by the UN General Assembly, but not considered binding by such major sensing states as the USA, the Soviet Union and Japan.

In the early 1990s the concern about remote sensing was still on the agenda of the world community. 'The developing countries continue to express the hope that their needs will be met through dissemination at a reasonable cost and in a timely manner of information and data obtained through the remote-sensing process. They have also urged that there should be free access to data from meteorological satellites' (Christol, 1990: 154). The open skies policy principle has been adopted by consensus in spite of the fact that several developing countries in the 1988 and 1989 sessions of COPUOS have repeated their concerns about a form of commercialization of the sensing process that involved no prior consultation and no form of financial compensation for the sensed countries.

The positions

Remote resource sensing raised questions about the control over data collected from outer space, the control over national resources (and information about these resources), the protection of political and economic security, and the desire to reap benefits from sensing operations.

In the negotiations on remote sensing, contending positions have been taken on a restrictive versus a permissive accommodation of the questions involved. The restrictive position claimed the need for prior consent. This was based upon the defence that if remote sensing (and the utilization of its gathered data) was not controlled by the sensed countries, it could pose threats to the national sovereignty of these countries. Most Third World countries claimed the priority of national sovereignty over the freedom to collect data through remote sensing satellites. Some countries that had originally supported the claim to a prior consent practice changed their position as they themselves developed space programmes. Good illustrations of this shift were the USSR, France, India and Brazil.

The claim to some form of control over remote sensing and the collected data was also defended by reference to the principle of sovereign control over natural resources. This principle had been established by various United Nations instruments.[7] Third World countries extended this principle also to information about their natural resources and were initially supported in this by the USSR and France. These two countries stated in a submission of 1974 that there was an inalienable right 'to dispose of . . . national resources and information concerning those resources'. Against this position most Western countries argued that territorial sovereignty could not be extended to information about national resources. In general, Western countries laid claim to a liberal practice for remote sensing. They defended this by reference to the freedom to conduct space activities as established by the 1967 Outer Space Treaty. Third World countries emphasized the earth impact of remote sensing and claimed accordingly that sensed states have a right to exercise their sovereignty in the protection of their resources. Against this position Western countries claimed that remote sensing was basically a space event and restrictions that might emerge from the principle of territorial sovereignty did not apply. Since outer space is not controlled by the principle of territorial sovereignty, they saw remote sensing as a lawful act.

Prevailing political practice
The principles that were adopted in 1986 represent a weak voluntary accord. There are no binding provisions and no effective enforcement mechanisms. Most important, however, is that the major players announced their intention not to comply. Despite many years of legal and political debate no effective multilateral accord has emerged. This is to a large extent due to the wide disparity in the technological capacity of sensing and sensed nations. Discord continues over such questions as the right to collect data versus the right to control the access to national resources. Despite basic discord about fundamental principles the world community is increasingly cooperating in space programmes through such multilateral bodies as the World Meteorological Organization. Several cooperative ventures have become operational in such areas as early warning for natural disasters. In fact the prevailing practice combines basic discord on fundamental principles with active and

expanding multilateral cooperation. Despite the cooperation, the chances of a multilateral accord would still seem minimal since the activity of remote sensing can be largely conducted without international coordination and the sensed countries in practice have no possibility of interfering with the activity. There are some bargaining cards for sensed countries though, since the usefulness of data collection increases when the sensing state has access to the sensed territory. Territorial access is necessary if the sensed resources are to be exploited and used. To obtain this access some sensing countries have provided information about their sensing operations to countries they had targeted for remote sensing.

Underlying the remote sensing debate was the broader issue of equal access to space technologies for all countries. The developing countries have been very concerned that the benefits of space technology should be distributed in fair ways. They have recently reopened the debate on this in COPUOS and its Legal Subcommittee. Their preference is the establishment of a formal accord on principles for space technology transfer. The industrialized countries prefer the continuation of the existing practice of international cooperative space projects.

Motivated by the discontent of Third World countries over the existing practice in space cooperation, the Legal Subcommittee of COPUOS has since 1988 on its agenda a discussion on the possible codification of rules for cooperation in space activities. The basic legal rationale for this discussion is provided by Article 1 of the Outer Space Treaty (1967) (see note 1 to this chapter). Although there has been an increase in multilateral and bilateral cooperative projects in space, the consensus is that not all countries have benefited equally. In the 1992 and 1993 meetings of the Legal Subcommittee there was a basic disagreement on the desirability of a formal legal instrument to enforce space cooperation. The Third World countries claimed the need for a multilateral formal accord that could ensure access to the benefits of space technology for all countries. In a first working paper (submitted in 1991 by Argentina, Brazil, China, Mexico, Nigeria, Pakistan, the Philippines, Uruguay and Venezuela) the principle of preferential treatment of developing countries was proposed. The paper suggested a set of principles as the core of a new legal instrument. According to the developed countries there was no need for such an instrument, and the best way to increase benefits for all countries would be to expand present cooperation programmes on a voluntary basis. At the 1993 session of the Legal Subcommittee a revision of the 1991 paper was submitted which sought to achieve a consensus. The Third World demands were toned down and the demand for preferential treatment disappeared. In spite of the concessions the divergencies remained and more negotiation is obviously needed.

Some observers expect that in time the present disagreement will shift towards an agreement on a set of principles for cooperation in space. 'There has been a distinct willingness of both sides in this debate to compromise: the developed countries have clearly become more amenable to the idea of formulating a new set of principles to serve as guidelines for international cooperation in space activities and for ensuring equal access to space technology, and the developing countries, in particular the drafters of the working paper, have demonstrated a willingness to back away from their most contentious demands which were contained in the first draft of the principles' (Jasentuliyana, 1994: 15). With the prospect of an agreement there is also the realistic observation that it seems 'unlikely that there will be any reference to the need for special treatment for developing countries' and that any set of principles will not force the major space players 'to share information universally' (1994: 15).

Telecommunication services trade

Over the past decade different concerns have arisen in connection with the world trade in services and with the dual role of telecommunication in this trade. Telecommunication is both a service sector in itself and at the same time the key vehicle for the international movement of other services.

Concerns have emerged about non-tariff barriers to the trading of telecommunication services and about the possibility that governments may use their regulatory authority in the telecommunication field to hinder services trade at large. This has become manifest in the concern that telecommunication users have about access to networks and about the connectivity between private corporate networks and the public networks.

Public telecommunication authorities, on the other hand, have become concerned about the option for users to bypass the public network. Governments, particularly of Third World countries, have expressed concern for the growth of their infant service industries and for the political and socio-cultural implications of losing control over their telecommunication infrastructures. Regulation of service activities is often closely related to specific national aspirations. This is evident in such cases as the regulation of banking and insurance and the operation of telecommunication and airlines.

In recent years international negotiations on telecommunication have been incorporated in the GATT multilateral trade talks and this has begun to impact the future direction of world telecommunication politics. Third World countries in particular have expressed concern that the treatment of telecommunication services under trade rules would not be in their interest. This concern was stimulated by the observation that so far the international trading system had not benefited the developing countries and had been largely inequitable and not mutually beneficial. As a consequence Third World concerns addressed the continuation of exploitative economic relations, the absence of genuine technology transfer, the monopoly role of transnational corporations, Western protectionism and GATT's incapacity to deal with this. Third World representatives have also expressed the concern that it would not seem likely that all Third World countries stand to benefit equally if a GATT trade regime were imposed on telecommunication services. It would be likely that only some of the newly industrializing countries (NICs) might have some advantages in the sense of the improvement of their local infrastructures and the strengthening of their export positions.

Services
Services have become increasingly important in national and global economies. Trade in services in the early 1990s amounted to some US $600 billion a year, which exceeds the combined trade in food and fuel in the world. The largest service exporter is the USA with some 70 per cent of its GDP from these exports. These represent almost 20 per cent of total US exports and almost 12 per cent of total world services exports. The industrialized countries and their TNCs have a distinct advantage in the field of services. This is largely caused by their technological leadership. In developing countries the service sector ranges between one-third and two-thirds of the GDP contribution and has approximately the same share in employment. The largest category of services is wholesale and retail services, followed by public administration and defence services. As a whole these countries show a trade deficit in services and are highly dependent upon the imports of services, often to the extent that some 45 per cent of foreign exchange goes to service imports.

The importation of services tends to exacerbate the burden of their foreign debts. In many countries the sector is too weak for international competitiveness, and there are too few human and capital resources and a lack of specialized knowledge. Both infrastructural services (like transport and telecommunication) and producer services (banking, insurance) are inadequate.

In the early 1980s the USA began to lead a campaign for a freer world trade in services. Developing countries felt that this could imply a threat to their national sovereign control over foreign investment and over their domestic monetary policies.

The GATT and services
Until 1980 there had been no concerted effort to include the trade in services in multilateral negotiations. The OECD member states had already in the convention of 1960 provided to 'pursue their efforts to reduce or abolish obstacles to the exchange of goods and services and current payments and maintain and extend the liberalization of capital movement and services'. In the OECD Code of Liberalization of Invisible Operations (1961) and the OECD Code of Liberalization of Capital Movements and the Declaration of National Treatment (1976), the organization had reinforced its commitment to the promotion of free trade in both goods and services. The codes were only adhered to by the limited membership of the OECD and had no mechanisms for enforcement. Under the 1974 Trade Act, the USA negotiators in the GATT Tokyo Round had the mandate to put trade in services on the multilateral agenda.

There was a lot of pressure from US companies, such as American Express, Citibank, American International Group and IBM, on the US administration to have services included in the Tokyo multilateral trade talks. Most trading partners were not open to the proposition and the USA gave in. However, when the Reagan administration took office in the early 1980s, it launched a set of new efforts to open international negotiations on services trade. The USA began active lobbying among its trading partners and, in spite of limited support from the Western industrial countries and the considerable opposition of the Third World, the November 1982 GATT ministerial meeting decided to invite the GATT contracting parties to conduct national examinations on the role of services and to consider at the 1984 session whether services could be the object of multilateral arrangements.

This preparation of GATT negotiations on services was strongly opposed by Third World countries, especially India and Brazil. They questioned the legal competence of GATT in this field and the applicability of GATT rules to services. They also raised concerns about the economic effects of the opening of Third World markets to foreign service providers and pointed to the serious threats this could pose in terms of destabilizing their socio-cultural development. There was also their worry that services negotiations might focus on the technology-intensive areas in which the industrial countries had a distinct advantage rather than on the labour-intensive service areas where cheap labour constituted a comparative advantage for the Third World. Third World countries were somewhat sceptical about the willingness of the Western countries to offer equitable trade-offs between exports of technology and exports of labour. Support for the US position was forthcoming from Canada, the UK, Sweden and Japan. Only by 1985 did the EC countries also provide strong support for the inclusion of services in trade negotiations. The November 1984 meeting did not reach a consensus on multilateral action.

After more lobbying and a stepped-up effort to divide the Third World opposition, a compromise was reached in 1986 at the GATT ministerial conference in Puenta del Este, Uruguay. In fact, by the time of the Uruguay conference the active group of Third World opponents had decreased to ten countries: India, Brazil, Argentina, Cuba, Egypt, Nicaragua, Nigeria, Peru, Tanzania and Yugoslavia. The compromise formula was that the provision to incorporate trade in services in the global round of negotiations was stated in a separate document, and not by the contracting parties but by the trade ministers. The document also stated the negotiations would seek to expand services trade 'under conditions of transparency and progressive liberalization and as a means of promoting economic growth of all trading partners and the development of developing countries'. The Puenta del Este statement also proposed that the envisioned multilateral framework of principles and rules for trade in services 'shall respect the policy objectives of national laws and regulations applying to services'. The US claim to have services trade put on the agenda was accommodated, but in the context of the recognition of development objectives and the role of national legislation. The claim of the group of ten countries that services negotiations should not take place within the legal framework of GATT was also accommodated. As a consequence, they went along and participated in the services negotiations.

The Puenta del Este declaration stated the need 'to establish a multilateral framework for services, including elaboration or possible discipline for sectors'. Among the sectors identified following the declaration were telecommunication services. Concern about the trade-related dimensions of telecommunication had already been voiced in the period 1982–5 before the Uruguay Round. It became increasingly clear that telecommunication was central to world trade and that telecommunication services were tradable. Telecommunication was seen as essential to an agreement on services because of its double function as a distinct economic sector and as the major means of transport for most other economic transactions. With the growth of internationally transacted services, the importance of telecommunication as the essential mode of delivery of the bulk of these traded services became manifest; and it also became manifest that telecommunication had not only made more services tradable, but also created new kinds of transactions that were independent of time and location. With the growth and internationalization of trade in manufactured goods, the trans-nationalization of industrial production, the globalization of markets, the need for banking and other financial services, market-ing and advertising, the role of telecommunication as facilitator became ever more important.

At the Uruguay Round mid-term ministerial review in Montreal (December 1988), the ministers advised the Group of Negotiations on Services (GNS) that: 'Before the concepts, principles and rules which comprise a multilateral framework for trade in services are finally agreed, these concepts, principles and rules will have to be examined with regard to their applicability and implications of their application to individual sectors and the types of transaction to be covered by the multilateral framework.'

At the April 1989 meeting of the GNS, it was decided that the exploration of sectors would start with telecommunication and construction, followed by transportation, tourism, and financial and professional services. In its meeting of June 1989 the GNS selected the telecommunication sector as a test case for the framework proposed by the Montreal mid-term meeting. This framework encompassed among others such principles and rules as trans-parency of laws, regulations and administrative guidelines; pro-gressive liberalization with due respect for national policy objectives; 'no less favourable' treatment for foreign exporters than is accorded to domestic services or services providers in the same market (national treatment); most favoured nation treatment for all providers; and market access. The framework also stressed the increasing participation of developing countries 'through the strengthening of their domestic services capacity and its efficiency and competitiveness'. The results of the June 1989 GNS meeting were inconclusive. 'There was considerable confusion and some difference of opinion among countries about which telecommunica-tions services should be treated and how, and the way in which specific concepts, principles and rules might be applied to the sector' (Woodrow, 1990: 23).

In late 1989 and early 1990 several delegations to the negotiations began to submit drafts for a multilateral arrangement on services. Proposals were forwarded to the GNS by the USA, the EC, Switzerland, Japan and Brazil, by a group of eleven Latin American countries and by a group of seven African and Asian countries.[8] At the May 1990 meeting of the GNS it was decided to continue negotiations on two levels: one addressing the overall framework agreement and one addressing specificities of eight sectors, including telecommunication. Following this approach the ministerial meeting held at Brussels in December 1990 (which was to conclude the Uruguay Round, but failed owing to the conflict on agriculture between the USA and the EC) had in front of it a draft General Agreement on Trade in Services (submitted by the GNS chairman) and a series of draft annexes on sectors, including telecommunication services. In December 1991 the GNS chairman presented the four years' work of the group to the GATT Director General, Arthur Dunkel. On 18 December the Director General and the GNS secretariat submitted a proposed text for the Uruguay Round final act. To this draft general agreement annexes on telecommunications (produced by the GNS working group on telecommunication services, which was established in March 1990 following a suggestion made by the US delegation) were attached which were not discussed in Brussels. At the conclusion of the Uruguay Round in December 1993 a final version of the annex on telecommunication was agreed upon by the contracting parties.

The positions
Concerns in the world community about the trading of telecommunication services are divided. There is a concern that conventional telecommunication arrangements (both domestic and international) pose non-tariff trade barriers in an increasingly important sector of the world economy. This concern is largely motivated by the observation that telecommunication is a significant economic sector as well as the major means of transport for most other international economic transactions. Key agents of this concern are Western service exporters (in particular the USA, Japan and the EC countries) and the transnational service industries. There is equally a concern that the application of a trade agreement to telecommunication services threatens infant service industries in developing countries and causes the loss of control over national telecommunication infrastructures. This concern is motivated by the desire to maintain sovereign control over essential sectors of the national economy, to lessen dependence upon foreign service providers, and to protect local socio-cultural development. The main agents of this concern are Third World countries such as India and Brazil.

Before the GATS negotiations began there were rival positions with regard to the incorporation of the services sector in a GATT trade arrangement. The USA and the service industry community lobbied hard for the inclusion of services in the GATT agenda. These actors claimed that the world community would benefit from a binding accord on services in the GATT. Such an agreement would prescribe practices for services trading and for the settlement of disputes. It would have to include such principles as national treatment, fair market access, right of local presence for foreign suppliers, dispute settlement and the need for transparent procedures. This claim was opposed by a group of Third World countries (with trade deficits in services and dependence upon foreign providers) that contested the competence of the GATT to address service issues and that were very critical about the alleged benefits for their economies.

From the beginning there was a tension in the services negotiations between the claim to a permissive, free-trade-based multilateral accord and the claim to a more restrictive, development-based arrangement that would allow the right to pursue national policy goals. The free trade position defended the absence of public intervention in world trade and promoted trends towards liberalization and privatization. The Council for International Business, for example, claimed in 1988 that telecommunication 'should receive priority treatment in any services trade negotiations' and 'The removal of policies or practices that create barriers to the movement or the innovative management of information or to the ability of service providers to utilize telecommunications effectively should be addressed during negotiations aimed at establishing a general agreement for trade in services.' In the same year the Business and Industry Advisory Committee of the OECD (BIAC, 1988) claimed that foreign providers of telecommunications services should have the right to 'provide their services from within the host country and from foreign countries, sell their services even when no local firm offers the same or similar services, establish a commercial presence (i.e. opening offices, appointing agents or installing equipment for the purpose of distributing, delivering, facilitating or marketing their services within the host country), and lease, construct or operate equipment within the host country that is necessary for the provision of their services'. The International Chamber of Commerce stated in 1988: 'It will also be essential to recognize that the use of telecommunications services has a central and strategic role in the provision of services in general, and that there must be rules to ensure reasonable and liberal access to and use of public telecommunications services.'

The development position recognized the special position of the Third World countries and proposed to adopt a form of progressive liberalization, with exemptions and conditions on foreign companies, and measures to strengthen their domestic service industries. The Third World countries claimed that without well developed infrastructures and capabilities to master, apply and innovate knowledge, there would be little or no benefit accruing to them from the international telecommunication services. They therefore claimed that the establishment of a multilateral agreement would go together with the equitable distribution of benefits. The development claim also included flexibility for developing countries to promote their service exports, access to technology, preferential treatment without reciprocity, the recognition of agreements among the developing countries themselves, safeguards for infant service industries and control of restrictive business practices.

Prevailing political practice
The key conflict is that of trade agreement versus telecommunication agreement. Prior to the inclusion of traded services in the multilateral trade talks, telecommunication was generally not perceived as a trade issue. Accordingly, the field was regulated for many years by a telecommunication agreement and not a trade agreement. The developments described above indicate that this is changing and that a new collective practice based upon GATT normative provisions and institutional conditions is emerging. Technology, politics and economics converged to create the need to address telecommunication in a trade context. This has raised the inter-organizational jurisdictional competence of ITU versus GATT and exposed the different approaches in trade regulation versus telecommunication regulation.

Telecommunication regulation is characteristically restrictive since it addresses standardization, revenue sharing, harmonization of accounting practices, avoidance of interference, and the allocation of scarce resources. Telecommunication regulation tends to restrict ownership of and control over telecommunication operations. It conceives of telecommunication as a public utility with the obligation to provide universal service. Essential to telecommunication regulators are such concepts as cooperation and interconnectivity.

Trade regulation is characteristically permissive and tends towards liberalization. Its crucial concepts are competition, right of establishment, fair and mutually beneficial trade, and reduction of barriers. Trade regulation provides for ongoing negotiation and dispute settlement.

For conventional telecommunication regulators, domestic laws and practices are usually outside their scope, since they concentrate on international rules for the movement of information across borders. Trade regulators, however, address domestic arrangements whenever they may distort trade. Whereas telecommunication regulators focus on public interest, trade regulators recognize primarily commercial interest. Possible conflicts between the two types of regulators occur when an activity such as standard setting, which is essential to the interconnectivity that telecommunication regulators pursue, causes concern for trade regulators, as the requirements of standard setting can erect trade barriers.

The general feeling seems to be that GATT and ITU rules have to be reconciled. This does raise some inter-organizational competition, as Feketekuty states: 'The road to cooperation will undoubtedly cross a difficult terrain and will not be traversed without passionate arguments over objectives and bureaucratic infighting over turf. Inevitably, we can expect a certain amount of competition between national telecommunication officials and the ITU secretariat on the one side and national trade officials and the GATT secretariat on the other' (1989: 285).

A question to address is whether the trade-based practice is imposed on the conventional telecommunication agreement, or whether the latter is itself 'tilting' towards a trade agreement (Woodrow, 1991a). Part of the answer can be found in the role played by the key multilateral body for telecommunication arrangements, the ITU. As Brian Woodrow has argued, developments within the ITU have demonstrated that the union 'is itself playing a significant role in reforming international telecommunications and in the shaping of a trade regime for telecommunications service' (1991b: 150). It may be that the union was initially somewhat hesitant, or even hostile, or at least concerned about the intrusion of trade negotiators into terrain that was formerly a privileged domain for telecommunication regulators. It is certainly true that the ITU administrators and their constituencies did not look at telecommunications as a trade issue. From June 1987 onwards the ITU began to closely watch the GATT process and got involved on the level of working relations between the secretariats. The ITU attitude towards the negotiations on services during 1988 and 1989 was characterized by both support for the Uruguay Round objectives and annoyance about the role of the new players. Woodrow described the ITU stance as 'schizophrenic' (1991b: 152).

This began to change with the adoption by the 1989 ITU Plenipotentiary Conference of the new telecommunication regulation (proposed by the 1988 WATCC) and by the positions the new ITU Secretary General, Pekka Tarjanne (elected by the 1989 conference), took towards the GATT trade talks. Interestingly, however, the Nice meeting never engaged in debate on the issue of trade in services. After 1989 the relations between ITU and GATT were upgraded and Tarjanne stressed regularly the 'complementarity' between the two organizations. The report of the High-Level Committee in 1991 reinforced this very clearly, as it stated: 'The philosophy and spirit of ITU's evolution are, therefore, not fundamentally different from those emerging in GATS. It is understood that the latest draft Annex on Trade in Telecommunications Services recognizes the role of ITU and the needs of developing countries. There is no reason, therefore, why ITU and the GATT should not continue to proceed along compatible paths' (HLC, 1991). Woodrow concludes: 'Rather than viewing the services trade negotiations as an attempt to impose a trade regime on international telecommunications . . . the international telecommunications regime has in recent years been tilting towards a trade regime' (1991b: 156).

The essential provisions of the emerging collective practice are to be found in the annex on telecommunications of the General Agreement on Trade in Services as adopted in the final acts of the Uruguay Round of multilateral trade negotiations (15 December 1993). The general objective of the annex is to elaborate the provisions of the GATS with respect to the access to and use of public telecommunications transport networks and services. This is done because of the recognition that telecommunication services have the dual role of 'a distinct sector of economic activity' and 'the underlying transport means for other economic activities'.

The essential normative provisions of the annex deal with transparency; access to and use of public telecommunications transport networks and services; technical cooperation; and international cooperation. Transparency implies that 'relevant information on conditions affecting access to and use of public telecommunications transport networks and services is publicly available'.

Access to and use of public telecommunications transport networks and services is to be provided on 'reasonable and non-discriminatory terms and conditions'. Non-discrimination refers to most favoured nation and national treatment. The ensurance of access and use implies that foreign suppliers are permitted 'to purchase or lease and attach terminal or other equipment which interfaces with the network and which is necessary to supply a supplier's service; to interconnect private leased or owned circuits with public telecommunications transport networks and services or with circuits leased by another service supplier; and to use operating protocols of the service supplier's choice in the supply of any service, other than is necessary to ensure the availability of telecommunications transport networks and services to the public generally'. Certain restrictions on access and use are permissible, for instance to ensure the security and confidentiality of messages, but restrictive conditions should not represent 'a disguised restriction on trade in services'. In general no condition may be imposed other than is necessary for instance 'to safeguard the public service responsibilities of suppliers of public telecommunications transport networks and services; or to protect the technical integrity of public telecommunications transport networks and services'.

Under the norm of technical cooperation 'a developing Party may, consistent with its level of development, place reasonable conditions on access to and use of public telecommunications transport networks and services necessary to strengthen its domestic telecommunications infrastructure and service capacity and to increase its participation in international trade in services'. As the annex recognizes the importance of an efficient telecommunications infrastructure to the expansion of trade in services, parties are encouraged to participate 'in the development programmes of international and regional organizations'. Parties shall also 'encourage and support telecommunications cooperation among developing countries . . . and make available, where practicable, to developing countries information with respect to telecommunications services and developments in telecommunications and information technology to assist in strengthening their domestic telecommunications services sector'. Special consideration shall be given to the least developed countries and foreign suppliers are encouraged to 'assist in the transfer of technology'. In the field of international cooperation especially the role of the ITU is recognized, as is the need to promote international standards for network compatibility through cooperation with such bodies as the ITU and the International Organization for Standardization (ISO).

The practice one may expect to emerge after the conclusion of the Uruguay Round negotiations will be largely shaped by the application of the guiding principle of GATS to telecommunication services. These principles are the most favoured nation norm and the national treatment standard. The MFN principle prohibits discrimination of foreign suppliers and national treatment implies that foreign and national suppliers are treated equally. The accord only applies to those services a country specifically identifies. For example the EU countries have brought E-mail, voice mail, on-line information services, EDI and protocol conversion under the provisions of GATS. So-called basic services, such as telegraph, telex and voice telephony, are not included. It remains to be seen what further negotiations will produce in relation to the basic services and how they may eventually be included in the GATS accord.[9]

The current accord opens the way towards a further liberalization of the world trade in telecommunication services. The accord is binding and robust in so far as countries accept certain services to be treated under GATT standards. All countries, even the smaller ones, have a certain space to slow down the liberalization process. The GATT accord was signed in April 1994 at Marrakesh, after which ratifications should follow by participating states. The accord is likely to enter into force by July 1995.

Notes

1 The emerging space law (*ius spatiale*) and its relevant treaties provide an important part of the context within which telecommunication operates. The Outer Space Treaty was signed in January 1967 in the capitals of the three depositary governments, the US, the USSR and the UK. Particularly important are Articles I and II. Article I provides that: 'The exploration and use of outer space, including the Moon and other celestial bodies, shall be carried out for the benefit and in the interests of all countries, irrespective of their degree of economic or scientific development, and shall be the province of all mankind.' Article II states that: 'Outer space, including the Moon and other celestial bodies, is not subject to national appropriation by claim of sovereignty, by means of use of occupation, or by any other means.' This treaty founds international law in the field of space resources.

Other space treaties are: Agreement on the Rescue of Astronauts, the Return of Astronauts and the Return of Objects Launched into Outer Space, 1968; Convention on International Liability for Damage Caused by Space Objects, 1972; The Moon Treaty, 1979 (this treaty provides *inter alia* that: 'The Moon and its natural resources are the common heritage of mankind'); Convention on Registration of Objects Launched into Outer Space, 1975. These treaties state the rights and duties of states with regard to space resources.

In 1961 the General Assembly recommended the following principles to states for their guidance in the exploration and use of outer space (Resolution 1721(XVI), 1961): '(a) International law, including the Charter of the United Nations, applies to outer space and celestial bodies. (b) Outer space and celestial bodies are free for exploration and use by all States in conformity with international law and are not subject to national appropriation.' The same resolution (Section D) also called for the development of the law of space communications. This was further reinforced in Resolution 1802 of 1962 when the General Assembly noted with appreciation the prompt response of the ITU to the request contained in Section D of Resolution 1721 and stressed 'the importance of international cooperation to achieve effective satellite communications'.

2 The last phrase replaced an earlier phrase about present facilities that should take into account future requirements for latecomers that today do not yet have a possibility of using the resource.

3 Illustration of cable penetration rates in European countries: the Netherlands, 82 per cent; Belgium, 89 per cent; Switzerland, 77 per cent; but also Spain, 14 per cent and Austria, 25 per cent. Data in Sung (1992: 617) from the 1992 *Cable and Satellite Yearbook*.

4 An early reference to common heritage is found in UNGA Resolution 1348(XIII) of 13 December 1958 by which the *ad hoc* COPUOS was established. The preamble 'recognized the common interest of mankind in outer space . . . desired to promote energetically the fullest exploration and exploitation of outer space for the benefit of mankind'. Also the resolutions establishing the COPUOS (UNGA Resolutions 1472A and B(XIV) of 12 December 1959) recognize 'the common interest of mankind' in connection with outer space. All the important legal instruments on the use of outer space contain the reference to the interests of all mankind, for instance the Outer Space Treaty (see note 1 to this chapter).

5 It is common to distinguish twelve space services: fixed satellite services (point to point); broadcast satellite services (point to multipoint); mobile satellite services; radio determination satellite services (determination of geographical positions); space operation services; space research services; earth exploration satellite services; meteorological satellite services; inter-satellite services; amateur radio services; radio astronomy services; standard frequency and time-signal satellite services.

6 EOSAT was established as a joint venture by Hughes Aircraft Corporation and RCA.

7 For example by UNGA Resolution 1803(XVII) of 14 December 1962: 'The General Assembly . . . declares that the right of peoples and nations to permanent sovereignty over their natural wealth and resources must be exercised in the interest of their national development.'

8 The Latin American countries were: Brazil, Chile, Colombia, Cuba, Honduras, Jamaica, Nicaragua, Mexico, Peru, Trinidad and Tobago and Uruguay. The African and Asian countries were: Cameroon, China, Egypt, India, Kenya, Nigeria and Tanzania.

9 One problem here is the absence of a generally adopted definition of basic services.

4

Protection of Intellectual Property Rights

Like telecommunication, the protection of intellectual property came on to the world political agenda in the mid nineteenth century (see Chapter 1). Two main types of protection were provided by the multilateral accords concluded in Paris (1883) and in Berne (1886). The Paris convention dealt with the protection of industrial property and the Berne treaty addressed author's rights. The Paris type of protection of intellectual property was extended through a series of multilateral accords administered by the World Intellectual Property Organization (WIPO). Author's rights were protected by Berne and its revisions (administered by WIPO) and the Universal Copyright Convention (UCC of 1952) administered by Unesco.

When the category of author's rights could not adequately protect derivative works such as phonograms, films or broadcast programmes a new set of so-called 'neighbouring rights' was introduced and secured through multilateral accords (Rome, 1961 and Geneva, 1971). This new type of protection extended copyright protection to those who were not the original authors of works. The adequacy of the prevailing practice of protection became an issue in connection with technological advances in computer hardware and software. The desirability of a new type of protection which would be *sui generis* also came up in the context of debates on the preservation of folklore and works in the public domain.

Several issues have confronted the prevailing practice of intellectual property protection. Particularly relevant for the politics of world communication were issues that arose in connection with developments in technology (transmission, reproduction and computer technology), the extension of property rights to new holders of rights and new domains, and the international trade in intellectual property rights.

Transmission technology

The development of new transmission techniques, such as cable and particularly satellite, caused concern about the adequate protection of copyrighted signals transmitted through these vehicles. In the existing copyright conventions (the Berne convention, the Universal Copyright Convention and the Rome convention) there were no references to the distribution of signals through cable networks or by broadcast satellites since these techniques developed and were deployed after the enactment of the treaties.[1]

The challenge posed by these new techniques of transmission was whether they could be considered broadcasting. If these transmissions could be brought under the general concept of broadcasting, then protection of copyrighted works could be provided. Apart from this legal-definitional debate, the new techniques did considerably increase the difficulty of control by copyright owners over the distribution/reproduction of their works.

Both Unesco and WIPO began to discuss the problem of satellite piracy from 1968. The Unesco General Conference in 1968 adopted a resolution which requested the Director General 'to consider, in collaboration with the International Bureau for the Protection of Intellectual Property and in consultation with the appropriate intergovernmental bodies, whether the protection of television signals transmitted by communication satellites requires the modification of existing conventions or the preparation of a new international instrument'. A year later the Unesco Intergovernmental Meeting on International Arrangements in the Space Communication Field (2–9 December 1969 in Paris) decided that the protection of satellite signals against unauthorized use was a priority. Three avenues were explored: the protection under the Rome convention (International Convention for the Protection of Performers, Producers of Phonograms and Broadcasters), the revision of the ITU convention, and the creation of a new convention.

Unesco and WIPO decided to call a meeting of experts to look into the legal problems in the field of copyright, rights of performers and broadcasters as a result of transmissions by satellites. This meeting, held at Lausanne in April 1971, concluded a new convention was needed and drafted the text for it. The third meeting of the experts group in 1973 at Nairobi recommended to hold a diplomatic conference in 1974 in order to conclude a multilateral convention. This conference was convened by Unesco and WIPO at Brussels on 6 May 1974 and it adopted the Convention Relating to the Distribution of Programme-Carrying Signals Transmitted by Satellite. The convention obliges member states to 'take adequate measures to prevent the distribution on or from its territory of any programme-carrying signal by any distributor for whom the signal emitted to or passing through the satellite is not intended'. The convention does not establish rights for the holders of copyright, as it affords protection to the signals but not to the messages they carry. The convention entered into force on 25 August 1979. Several years later, an important WIPO/Unesco meeting of experts (March 1985) confirmed that direct broadcasting of works by means of a satellite should be defined as broadcasting in the sense of the international copyright conventions and should be thus protected. This did not resolve all problems, since the question remained of which 'leg' should be considered broadcasting. Does broadcasting include both the upleg and the downleg stages, or the upleg stage only? This issue was raised again in the context of the negotiations on a protocol to the Berne convention. In the WIPO preparatory document for the third session of the committee of experts (June 1993) it was observed that there is growing support for the inclusion of both legs and for the conception of broadcasting as not only emission but also communication to the public. This statement reflects the so-called Bogsch theory (named after the Director General of WIPO) which claims that satellite broadcasting should be governed by copyright provision of both the emitting country and the receiving (footprint) country. In satellite broadcasting this is relevant since often programmes are emitted from one country and transmitted to the public in another country. 'The answer to the question where the act of broadcasting takes place also determines the identity of the person who has the right to authorize such broadcasting, if that person is not the same in the country or place of emission as in the country or countries where the signals are normally receivable' (WIPO, 1993a: 29). According to the WIPO document and following the Bogsch theory, 'the requirements of two or more laws must be complied with, namely the law of the country of emission and the law or laws of the country or countries where the signals are normally receivable' (WIPO, 1993a: 29). In the discussions on this during the second session of the expert committee (February 1992) there was general agreement that broadcasting by satellite was broadcasting under the Berne convention. The preference of most participants was that only one law should be applied and that this should be the law of the emitting country.

With regard to cable transmissions a WIPO/Unesco group of experts had presented conclusions that became guidance for the international discussion in 1980. They defined distribution by cable 'public communication', and as such the exclusive and specially recognized rights of authors should be upheld whenever copyrighted material was transmitted. It was recommended that national laws provide for 'institutionalized collective administration' of royalties both for copyright and for neighbouring rights. Broadcasting organizations, as holders of neighbouring rights, should be conferred the exclusive right to authorize the distribution of their programmes by cable.

Reproduction technology

The developments in reproduction technology caused concerns about commercial piracy and home taping of copyrighted works.

A crucial piece of equipment that confronted intellectual property protection with new challenges was the photocopying machine. It exacerbated the implied tension in copyright law between the interests of the author and publishers and those of the general public (particularly in the field of education).

The improved techniques for reprography (the shift from carbo-copying and stencil machine to the xerographic machines of the early 1960s) and for reproduction of audiovisual materials (audio compact cassettes and video recording equipment) provided an unprecedented dissemination of copyrighted works and theoretically a proportional increase in remuneration for their authors. At the same time, however, these techniques began to erode the system of protection.

In many countries educational establishments came to rely on un-authorized reproduction of textbooks in order to provide students access to valuable educational materials.

Commercial piracy

In the 1980s copying of copyrighted works developed into largescale piracy, often including 'bootlegging' which is the unauthorized recording of performances and the marketing for profit of such recordings. According to the International Federation of Producers of Phonograms and Videograms the world market for pirated audio recordings reached by the mid 1980s some US $1200 million. Also the pirating of video productions became big business. In the EC countries the average market share for pirated video products was almost 40 per cent in 1986. Growing concern was caused by the pirating of computer programs. The US-based International Intellectual Property Alliance (IIPA) estimated for 1988 losses to the computer software industry of US $547 million.

The WIPO/Unesco committee of governmental experts on audio-visual works and phonograms, meeting in Paris in June 1986, adopted a resolution related to piracy. This stated among other things that piracy is an illegal activity – a form of theft – and, as such, thoroughly antisocial and contrary to the public interest and not merely a matter affecting the private rights of individuals. The manufacture and distribution, including the import and export, of pirated copies of audiovisual works and phonograms, should be expressly forbidden by law, and, where such acts are perpetrated, penalties of sufficient severity should be imposed to act as a deterrent. The committee of experts also proposed a resolution for endorsement by the governing bodies of the Berne convention and the Universal Copyright Convention. The resolution recognized that the enormous growth of the world-wide commercial piracy of audiovisual works and phonograms poses a danger to national creativity, to cultural development, to local industry and to intellectual property rights. It urged therefore that states should in their national laws introduce the rights guaranteed under the international conventions in this field, and invited the states which are not parties to these conventions to adhere to them and bring their legislation up to date so as to take fully into account the new technological uses of intellectual property. The resolution expressed the strong conviction that the adequate and effective protection of all right holders under the conventions requires the provision of criminal sanctions in national law of sufficient severity to punish and deter piracy and the effective enforcement of such criminal sanctions. It also acknowledged that such sanctions should include fines and/or imprisonment terms appropriate to other serious thefts of property in the country concerned, provisions for the seizure and destruction of infringing copies and the equipment used in their production, measures to prevent importation into convention states, and procedures to facilitate the detection and proof of piracy.

In 1989 WIPO established an international register for audio-cassettes and videograms in order to curtail piracy. This was done at a diplomatic conference at Geneva that adopted the Treaty on the International Registration of Audiovisual Works. Preparations towards such a register had commenced in 1984 as a result of a resolution adopted by the 1981 WIPO Worldwide Forum on the Piracy of Sound and Audiovisual Recordings. This introduced the intention to set up an international register of audiovisual recordings into the work programme of WIPO. A meeting of consultants strongly endorsed the urgency of such a register, which would 'greatly increase the security of international transactions, be helpful in identifying right owners, and efficiently further the repression of piracy' (WIPO, 1988). The register was foreseen as a voluntary enterprise. When statements about financing did not come forward from the non-governmental organizations most closely involved, the Fédération internationale des associations de producteurs de films (FIAPF) and the Motion Picture Association of America (MPAA), the Director General of WIPO recommended to discontinue the effort. However, the September 1987 meeting of the governing bodies of WIPO and the Paris and Berne unions decided to continue efforts to establish an international register. A committee of experts meeting at Geneva in 1988 (7–11 March) prepared a draft for a treaty and regulations on application and registration.

Home taping

Although reproduction without consent had been in use since the invention of the printing press, its expansion in the 1960s and 1970s made it into a serious concern for right owners. A particular difficulty arose with the fact that most infringements take place in private homes or other non-public places, such as universities. This made control difficult, if not impossible.

The Berne and the Rome conventions had provided a 'private use' exception that permitted copying of copyrighted works (Berne, Article 9(2); Rome, Article 15(1)(a)). The Universal Copyright Convention (UCC) did concur with its formulation in Article IV bis/2, which accepted exceptions provided these did not conflict with the spirit and provisions of the convention. Where member states provide for exceptions, they 'must accord a reasonable degree of effective protection' to the reproduction right. It would seem, however, that at the time of the formulation in 1971 this referred to the manual and single reproduction of parts of a work. With the spread of the new reproduction techniques, copying was done by machines in multiple form and whole works were copied. On reprography the Stockholm conference of 1967 stated in its report: 'If a small number of copies is made, photocopying may be permitted without payment, particularly for individual or scientific use' (paragraph 85). In 1975 two committees of the Berne union and the UCC concluded a joint study with the observation that 'a uniform solution on the international level cannot, for the time being, be found' and recommended that states should establish their own appropriate protective measures.

Copying of copyrighted material – both sound recordings and audiovisual materials – developed on a large scale in the private home. It has been stated at various meetings that the home copying of music from broadcasts and recordings is a cause of a decline in recording sales, which in turn results in a decline of new releases, especially in the field of classical music. It has been difficult to establish whether this is indeed the case. The sales of recording equipment and of blank tapes have certainly increased, but that does not in itself constitute proof that copyrighted works are being recorded or that this recording hampers the normal exploitation of such works. What seems clear from various national surveys is that most home audio recording consists of the recording of music from records or disks.

With regard to video, most national surveys suggest that the overwhelming majority of recordings are from television material. Films and entertainment programmes are recorded for time-shift purposes. The recording of pre-recorded material for reproduction hardly occurs.

Home taping is seen by some as an infringement of the rights of authors and other right owners. Therefore, persons making copies of musical performances should pay a royalty. These royalties should be collected by the organizations representing the owners of rights: the collecting societies. Obviously, the collection of royalties from private taping poses practical problems and raises the question of whether this could be done without seriously violating individual privacy. As a solution to this, the proposal has been forwarded to provide for royalties on recording equipment and/or blank tapes. In particular, the recording industry, supported by organizations that represent the copyright holders, has argued strongly for measures to compensate for home taping. Legislation to levy taxes on equipment or tapes has been introduced in Austria, Congo, Finland, France, Germany, Hungary, Iceland and Portugal. Similar legislation has been proposed in Belgium, Czechoslovakia, Italy, the Netherlands, Spain and the United Kingdom.

Another opinion, represented by the blank tape industries and supported by some consumer organizations, holds that home taping for private purposes is legal, questions the claim about damage done to right holders, and rejects the demand for compensation. A problem with the levy schemes is the question of to whom the revenues will flow. These could be the already most successful and well-off authors and composers, or public agencies. In the latter case the basic concept of remuneration for individual creation is undermined.

Next to levying schemes, the introduction of technical devices that would prevent unauthorized copying has been pleaded for. This has been particularly the case with the new digital audio tape (DAT) recorder. Digital audiocassette recording makes it possible to copy music from compact disks (CDs) without loss of quality. The producers of phonograms feared that this could lead to infringement of their copyrights and of the rights of performers and to decreasing sales of compact disks. The representatives of the music industry forwarded proposals to the US Congress and to the European Commission for protective measures like the obligation to have all DAT recorders equipped with a technical device so that similarly encoded software could not be copied. Initially, those who opposed the levying schemes also resisted the introduction of such anti-copying devices. They argued that this would hamper technological innovation and market growth, and might have a negative effect on sound quality. More recently, the music industries and the hardware companies have found agreement. In 1989 an agreement was reached (June 1989, Athens) between the International Federation of Producers of Phonograms and Videograms (IFPI) and representatives of the electronics industry to sell DAT recorders with a chip that prevents the copying of more than one copy of any given CD. Crucial to the agreement were hardware firms Sony and Philips, both owners of large music companies, CBS Records and Polygram.

The issue of home taping was discussed during the negotiations about a protocol to the Berne convention (February 1992). Opinions were however so divided that the topic did not come back on the agenda for the 1993 meetings on the protocol. Participants in the meeting of the expert committee in 1992 did not agree on the nature and extent of provisions on a right to remuneration in respect of private reproduction. They also disagreed about the practicality of prohibitions of private copying and the application of copy protection systems or new licensing techniques.

Computer technology

In the field of computer technology the concern has arisen that existing intellectual property protection provisions might not adequately cover computer software, semiconductor products, and such new developments as electronic publishing and electronic data banks.

Computer software

In the 1980s the economic significance of computer programs increased dramatically.[2] By 1985 world-wide sales of software amounted to over US $30 billion, and in 1990 the world market had reached US $43 billion (Wijk and Junne, 1992: 16). Given the costs of program development, the spread of both professional and non-professional uses of the computer, and the proliferation of software theft, the need for adequate legal protection arose. Basically, five legal mechanisms could be tested for their usefulness: copyright, patent law, trade mark, trade secret and a *sui generis* protection.

In 1978 WIPO began to discuss the problems of protection of computer programs during the preparation of the WIPO Model Provisions on the Protection of Computer Software. These provisions proposed a *sui generis* minimal protection, although the commentary to the model provisions stated that this did not mean the need to adopt *sui generis* legislation: protection could also be implemented through copyright legislation. After much debate from the mid 1970s on, and after the drafting of a special software treaty (which was abandoned in 1983), the international consensus preferred the protection through copyright. A meeting, jointly convened by WIPO and Unesco in 1985, concluded that *sui generis* protection was not desirable and that copyright law would be the most appropriate legal arrangement. In spite of the international consensus to treat computer programs as literary and artistic works, some pertinent questions remained to be resolved. The multilateral copyright conventions did not specifically refer to computer programs, although their formulations were sufficiently broad to accommodate them. This, however, made it possible to apply copyright protection to computer programs, but the conventions do not require the member states to do so. This would demand a revision of the instruments with explicit inclusion of computer programs.

Another question addressed the issue of 'artificial intelligence'. If computer programs are generated by computers, who owns the copyright: the computer, the owner of the computer, the original programs that instructed the computer to function as programmed? In law suits, questions have arisen in relation to the original identity of programs. If there are similar programs on the market, can infringement of copyright be proven? Courts faced questions such as: when does software represent an individual identity? When is it more than mere technological development of what already exists? When does it exceed, in choice and systematization of information and instructions, the normal crafts of the average computer programmer?

Another pertinent question was whether the copyrighting of systems software could lead to a monopolization of hardware. This raised the issue of whether in such cases anti-trust law would be applicable or whether those who abuse copyright law for the strengthening of economic positions could invoke such law against infringement of their rights.

An unresolved problem with copyright protection is the possibility of 'reverse engineering'. Copyright legislation provides no protection against the algorithms which are basic to computer programs and does not protect against the use of these 'ideas' in writing compatible software. Under copyright law it is only the expression of ideas that can be protected and not the ideas themselves. Protecting the fundamental ideas of computer programs would create enormous obstacles for the independent design of such programs.

The WIPO preparatory memorandum for the third session of the committee of experts on a possible protocol to the Berne convention proposed that the protocol 'should provide that countries party to the Protocol are obliged to grant copyright protection to computer programs and that the protection must be the same (subject to certain exceptions specified below) as the Berne Convention provides for literary and artistic works' (WIPO, 1993a: 4). At this meeting opinions on the issue of software protection were very divided and no conclusions could be drawn. Positions differed about the nature and extent of provisions on software in the protocol, on the inclusion of provisions on issues such as the decompilation of programs, and the matter of private reproduction of software.

Protection of semiconductor products
Essential to electronic systems are the miniaturized components called integrated circuits or 'chips'. The world market for chips in the 1980s reached the US $1 billion mark. A peculiar aspect of the manufacturing of chips is that their research and development is enormously expensive whereas the cost of their copying represents a fraction of these expenditures. This situation has called for a form of adequate legal protection. Thus the question of the appropriate legal practice arose.

The international consensus has tended towards a preference for a *sui generis* protection. The USA – the leading chip producing country in the world – enacted as first country such a *sui generis* ruling, the Semiconductor Chip Protection Act of 1984. The main motive for enacting a form of protection was the increasing loss of revenue due to chip piracy. The choice of a *sui generis* model was motivated by the inadequacy of both patent and copyright laws. The US law was based on the principle of reciprocity. Without equally strong protection in their own countries, foreign chip manufacturers would not be extended any protection on the US market. Under this threat Japan followed suit with similar legislation on 31 May 1985, as did Sweden in 1986, and France, the Federal Republic of Germany, the United Kingdom and the Netherlands in 1987. In June 1985 the Council of European Communities announced a directive to member states to enact equivalent legislation, and on 16 December 1986 the Council approved the directive on the legal protection of topographies of semiconductor products. One of the reasons why the US chose the *sui generis* approach was that under copyright protection the national treatment clause of the Universal Copyright Convention would have been operative. This would have meant that the USA would have to have provided protection to other members of the convention in the same way as it did to nationals. As a result Japanese chips would have been protected, whereas Japan did not protect US chips.

WIPO began work towards an international treaty in 1985. Between 1985 and 1988 a committee of experts met four times and in 1987 it was decided (by the WIPO General Assembly and the Paris Union Assembly) that a diplomatic conference should be convened. In November 1988 a preparatory meeting for the diplomatic conference took place that prepared the documents, rules of procedure and agenda for the conference. From 8 to 29 May 1989 the diplomatic conference was convened in Washington DC at the invitation of the US government. The conference was able to conclude a treaty entitled Treaty on Intellectual Property in Respect of Integrated Circuits. The treaty met with the approval of developing and socialist countries; Japan and the USA declared opposition; the EC member states supported the treaty but did not sign it. As a result of the conference there is an international agreement to provide a minimal protection for topographies of integrated circuits, but the level of protection does not meet the requirements of the major chip producing countries.

Electronic publishing

The field of electronic publishing raised a key concern about the applicability of present copyright, patent and trade mark legislation to new types of information production and distribution. Traditional legal protection may no longer be adequate for a category of 'work' that is not necessarily fixed or permanent. How can the unauthorized use of information be controlled when a shift takes place from hard copy (printed format) to electronic forms of storage? When a text is published electronically, the text can be stored in a computer and the reader can easily distribute and copy it. In general, copyright laws deal with the work in tangible format and not with the information itself. However, with electronic text valuable information is not expressed in tangible form. The intangible format makes it difficult to prove infringement and makes it unclear when transfer of property takes place.

The reading of an electronic text is actually copying the text. The copy can be shared with others in a network, and it is complicated to establish whether this represents an infringement through unauthorized copying or equates to giving the copy of a book to others to read. Often users of electronic information services may download the materials, i.e. store them in the computer at the receiver's location. The off-line use may be to save telecommunication costs, but it may also be for local reproduction of the material. If downloading leads to reproduction (local machine-readable copies of the material) and the document is copyrighted, then this can only be done with the consent of the author. Since there is the exception for 'private use' in the international conventions and in most national laws, the complicated question is whether indeed private use is the case. Often this will be difficult to establish and current regulation is inadequate in dealing with the grey zones (Bing, 1988: 57–67).

Particularly since national jurisdictions differ on the issue of private use, the international use of electronic publishing does allow a vast scope for copyright infringements. Downloading may also increase the attraction for users to rewrite documents and exploit them for different purposes. This would obviously imply a serious threat to the moral rights of the original authors of such documents. Again, control and enforcement of legislation may prove impractical.

Questions of protection have emerged with the growing economic importance of electronic publishing. It has been estimated that in 1985 the world-wide market for electronic publishing already amounted to US $5 billion.

Electronic data bases
Data bases are compilations of electronically stored information that is made accessible either on-line through telecommunication or off-line through such media as compact disks with enormous storage capacity (CD-ROMs). Globally the number of publicly accessible data bases grew from 400 in 1980 to almost 3000 in 1986. In the USA alone in 1988 there was a total of 3700 on-line data bases. Several countries have begun to study whether their copyright legislation can adequately protect the information that is stored in electronic data bases.

A data base implies the storage of works that may be copyrighted. This is often the case with full-text data bases that contain original texts of textbooks, articles in journals or newspapers, newsletters and encyclopedias. If these originals are copyrighted, then the data base compilers are under the legal obligation to obtain licences for the use of the materials. The situation is equally clear in the case of factual data bases (usually referred to as data banks). These contain mostly non-copyrighted numerical and historical data.

The grey zones are with the data bases using secondary information, such as abstracts from information published somewhere

else. The copyright question here is whether the abstract represents
a mere citation or a substitute of the original work. Problems arise
with newspaper articles where the distinction between the factual
part that is not copyrighted and the editor's additions may be
difficult to make.

The protection of the use of the data is complicated since
copyright guards the particular format of the data base information
and not the data themselves. Thus unauthorized copying of a data
base in its particular format would be illegal. Data bases are
however rarely totally reproduced. Selected pieces of information
are extracted for reproduction.

The items of information in a data base are often in the public
domain. It is difficult to establish the origin of any information item
when data bases are randomly accessed. Enforcing proprietary
rights in an electronic data base would constitute serious problems
of proof. Another issue for debate is whether the principle of fair
use should be applied to electronic data bases. The principle holds
that limited reproduction of copyrighted works, for purposes of
teaching or news reporting, does not constitute an infringement of
rights. There is a need to clarify the right of citation, particularly
since it is easy to cite from electronic data bases and the extent of
the right is unclear. Consideration is also needed as to how far the
copyright principle of exhaustion is sufficiently clear in relation to
data bases.[3]

Normally, it is understood that a legally acquired copy of a
copyrighted work can be freely resold, borrowed or rented. This
supports the free flow of materials and improves their public
accessibility. Can this also be applied to electronic data bases? With
the publishing of data bases on CD-ROMs the possibilities for reuse
in secondary rediffusion schemes are endless and in practice
uncontrollable.

The WIPO negotiations on a possible protocol to the Berne
convention have also addressed the protection of data bases. The
memorandum prepared by the international bureau for the third
session of the committee of experts noted the growing agreement
that data bases deserve protection of the kind provided for under
Article 2(5) of the Berne convention, 'if they constitute intellectual
creations by reason of selection, coordination or arrangement of
their contents' (WIPO, 1993a: 12).[4] An important qualification to
the recommendation to provide Berne protection for collections of
data was that 'the protection of collections of data or other
unprotected material does not make the data or other unprotected
material themselves eligible for copyright protection' (1993a: 13). It
should be mentioned here that this proposal addressed not only

electronic data bases but all data bases, 'whether in print, in computer storage units or any other form'.

Concerns about new rights

New right holders: publishers and film directors
Attempts have emerged to define the role and the status of publishers in international copyright. From the mid 1980s the International Publishers Association (IPA) has expressed as its opinion that the publisher's role should be recognized and sustained. When the IPA introduced its quarterly publication *Rights* in the spring of 1987 the editorial stated: 'The need for full and strong legal protection calls for a reinforcement of the publisher's position . . . A level of protection is needed to provide publishers with a sufficient return in their investment so that they can take the necessary risks and pay the high costs' (*Rights*, 1987: 2–3). The spread of unauthorized copying is seen as especially threatening to publishers and, when their publications are pirated, usually the publishers have to take legal action. Often, and particularly in the case of scientific publications, authors seem less concerned about the publisher's interests than in the wide dissemination of their work.

The publishers were late in asserting their rights as compared with other groups of intellectual property producers and distributors, such as film producers or recorded music producers. These groups have their neighbouring rights protected in the 1961 Rome convention and the 1971 Geneva convention. As the rights of publishers are indeed not author's rights but neighbouring rights, they are as such not protected under the two international conventions. This has raised the question of whether a special treaty for the protection of published editions would be needed. One of the issues raised in this context is whether the notion 'author' does include producers or whether these are separate categories. In the latter case there is no copyright protection for the publishers and a special neighbouring rights arrangements would be due. However, the argument could be made that films and musical records seem to have been increasingly accepted as 'works' which accords them the conventional copyright protection. 'Indeed, the majority of states that protect recordings do so under copyright, and the two greatest producers of recordings – the United States and the United Kingdom – protect recordings as works in the traditional Berne sense of copyright' (Turkewitz, 1989: 7). In this conception the producer is entitled to copyright protection because of a creative and original contribution to the works of the mind.

At a meeting of the committee of experts (WIPO/Unesco, December 1987) it was concluded that the question of a publisher's right should definitely be on the international regulatory agenda. Among the principles the meeting considered was that states should consider granting appropriate protection to publishers in respect of the typographical arrangements of their published editions, irrespective of whether such editions contain works protected by copyright. The issue was again raised at the meeting of the committee of governmental experts on the evaluation and synthesis of principles on various categories of works (Geneva, 27 June to 1 July 1988). The IPA position at the 1991 meeting of the WIPO committee of experts on a possible protocol to the Berne convention contained a strong plea for the protection of publishers and their publications (Baumgarten, 1991: 1–5). It was argued that where the draft protocol introduced a higher degree of protection for phonogram producers, this should also hold for publishers. This would benefit the primary beneficiaries of the Berne convention, the authors. In the IPA view, publishers should be seen as strong allies of authors.

A debate has also emerged as to the rights of yet another group, the film directors. Since under US law the owners of copyright can do as they please with the copyrighted work, the holders of rights can decide to colour original monochrome motion pictures. It is also possible that the coloured version can be copyrighted as a separate work. Colourization is obviously only one of the possibilities; other adaptations include superimposing messages on to films, reduction of cinemascope formats to TV formats, and the insertion of advertisements. In 1987 the European Federation of Audiovisual Film Makers adopted the Barcelona declaration in which the inalienable moral right of directors was claimed to respect for the integrity of their works under all circumstances, in all countries and by all users of their works. The new French copyright law has recognized this problem and provides that directors of audiovisual works are co-authors with inalienable moral rights.

Underlying the discussion is the problem of the definition of the concept of author. Who is ultimately responsible for the existence of an audiovisual work? There is a chain that includes the producer, the writer, the director, the actor, the broadcaster and even the consumer. An intriguing question thus raised is whether consumers could claim a right to see an audiovisual work in its original version.

Lending rights
A number of countries have introduced so-called public lending rights (Denmark as early as 1946). These rights recognize that the

grand-scale lending of works through public library systems may negatively affect the remuneration of the author. This is obviously the case when library loans would decrease the copies of the work bought directly by the public. Under copyright legislation the rights of authors do not extend to resale or rental. The copyright is exhausted with the sale of the copy and its further distribution is not protected except in the case of reproduction. Public lending rights are usually categorized under public support to cultural development. They are part of cultural policy rather than of the copyright system. Yet, they raise copyright-related problems. In most countries that have public lending rights these afford remuneration to citizens or residents of the country only. The principle of 'national treatment' in the two conventions would, however, seem to imply that parties to the treaties would have to grant their public lending rights equally to foreigners whose works are loaned by libraries.

In the WIPO negotiations on the possible protocol to the Berne convention there was disagreement about whether public lending rights should be part of copyright legislation at all. For some participants these rights belonged in the realm of social or cultural rights. Arguments against inclusion of lending rights in international copyright protection are also based upon the fear that the application of the national treatment norm would have very disadvantageous consequences. This norm, which is also referred to as the principle of assimilation, is essential to the Berne convention (Article 5) and implies that parties grant similar levels of protection to nationals and foreigners. Countries that have adopted lending rights will usually try to ignore the national treatment requirement. There is a strong reluctance to adopt an arrangement on public lending that might imply large amounts of compensation to foreigners from countries that do not have lending remuneration schemes.

Right of rental
A right of rental refers to the for-profit provision of copies of a work for a limited period of time. This mainly implies the rental of audiovisual products. At the second session of the expert committee on a possible protocol to the Berne convention there was general support for the inclusion of provisions on such a right in the protocol. However, opinions on the scope of this right (which works should be included) were divided,

Works in the public domain
As soon as they cease to be protected by copyright, literary, scientific and artistic works fall into the public domain and form part

of the heritage of humankind, without anyone exercising any further monopoly on them. From that time, the use of these works is in principle free and unremunerated, as opposed to the situation in force when copyright applies.

At the present time, there is an increasing number of operations in relation to works in the public domain that are considered by many people questionable. These include reproduction of a work or a part of it without attribution of the author's name; adaptation and transformation without notification to the public; and distortion of the essence and spirit of the original work. While the use of a work in the public domain is free and unremunerated, except in relation to remuneration under legislation which has established a *domaine public payant*, this freedom should not permit the distortion of a work or the suppression of the name of its author. Freedom should mean that reproduction, performance, translation or adaptation are permitted without the consent of the author, but on the condition that the essence of the work is not distorted or lost. Freedom does not include the right to destroy the work or impair its nature. A work of art is not an object which may be used in any manner without qualification.

At present, however, apart from legislation which protects moral rights in perpetuity, the status of works in the public domain is characterized by a legal vacuum. A comparison between the right of ownership of the state or of public bodies in respect of goods which are theirs by natural attribution or by legal assignment, and the status of works in the public domain, shows that only the former is organized. The latter does not exist. This is why many governments have expressed the need for a special legal system to protect intellectual work from the pillage and distortion that erode them and to enable them freely to enter the common heritage of the community to which they belong.

Having examined the report and preliminary study on the desirability of adopting an international instrument on the safeguarding of works in the public domain, on the possible extent and scope of such a regulation and on the method which should be adopted for the purpose (report submitted by the Director General to the General Conference of Unesco), the General Conference decided (by resolution adopted at its 24th session, 1987) that the questions of safeguarding of works in the public domain should be regulated at the international level by means of a recommendation to member states. The Director General was requested to convene the special committee consisting of technical and legal experts with instructions to draw up the final draft recommendation on this matter for submission to the General Conference at its 25th session (1989). This General Conference invited the Director General to continue the work on the basis of the past achievements and resubmit the whole question to the 26th General Conference. The conference in 1991 adopted Resolution 3.8, which stated that a final decision would be taken at the 27th session in 1993. This decision would be based on a draft recommendation that proposed some general principles on which the safeguarding of works in the public domain may be based. These principles included that any work in the public domain may be freely used in any form or manner by anybody, either for personal purposes or for public purposes, be it on a non-profit or on a profit making basis, without the need for any authorization whatsoever or payment of any remuneration for such use. This presupposes due respect for the authorship and integrity of the works and for the rights of the proprietor of the material object constituting the work. The principle of free use should preclude any distortion of its underlying essence, character or meaning or adulteration of it to the point where it is stripped of its value, or its cultural identity is destroyed. At its 27th session (25 October to 16 November 1993) the General Conference thanked the Director General for all the work carried out in this field, noted that in view of the few replies and comments most member states did not attach special importance to the draft recommendation, and considered that at the present time 'there is no need to adopt a specific international instrument for the safeguarding of works in the public domain' (Unesco 27/C, Resolution 3.17).

Folklore

The developing countries have addressed the need to recognize folklore as an important cultural phenomenon. This was motivated by the concern that technological development could lead to its improper exploitation, such as by commercialization, without respect for the interests of the communities where folklore originates. To foster folklore as a source of cultural creativity, special legal solutions must be designed for its protection. In certain countries, the attempt to protect folklore under copyright law has not been very effective. Works protected by copyright law must bear the decisive mark of individual creativity and folklore results from continuous, collective efforts. The possibility has also been explored of protecting folklore by so-called neighbouring rights, but this would not prevent the copying of folkloric expressions. It would seem that a *sui generis* regulation is needed. Since 1980, WIPO and

Unesco have worked on the elaboration of model provisions for national laws on the protection of expressions of folklore.

New recording technology
In the WIPO negotiations on a possible protocol to the Berne convention a distinction has been made between the rights of authors and the rights of producers of phonograms, following the conventional distinction between copyright and neighbouring rights. The expert committee that was mandated to address the second group was instructed to study 'the desirability of covering in the protocol the rights of producers of sound recordings in sound recordings produced by them'. The reason to address this group of rights holders was that the existing provisions in the Rome convention (1961) are no longer adequate to deal with developments in recording technology. The introduction of digital recording technology has made conventional definitions of phonograms and producers of phonograms obsolete. Recording today is no longer the fixation of sounds, but is increasingly also the fixation of previously fixed sounds or digital representations thereof. Therefore, the definition of a phonogram as the fixation of sounds is no longer useful if a whole industry is developing for the digital rearranging of earlier sound fixations. As a result not only should legal definitions be adapted but also new forms of protection should be granted.

The WIPO proposals state that 'the widespread practice of digital manipulation of fixations of performances, and the subsequent combination of various fixations . . . seem to justify the grant of a right of adaptation and the right to authorize inclusion of pre-existing phonograms . . . in collections of phonograms, rights recognized in the case of literary and artistic works' (WIPO, 1993b: 16). In the light of new developments WIPO also proposed that the right of first distribution and the right of importation should be explicitly recognized. Although there is a good deal of agreement that phonogram producers should enjoy a higher level of protection, there remain divided opinions as to their inclusion under a protocol to the Berne convention which is a copyright convention. The issue is presently addressed in two WIPO committees of experts. One deals with the possible protocol to the Berne convention; the other studies a possible separate instrument for the protection of the rights of performers and producers of phonograms. During meetings of the committees in 1993, among the topics discussed were public lending rights; rights of rental, distribution and importation; exclusive rights of performers in live performances; and the right of communication to the public. By the end of 1993 no final decisions had been reached.

Table 4.1 *Patents registered in 1992*

Company	Country	Patents (no.)
AT&T	USA	528
GTE	USA	181
NTT	Japan	71
BCE	Canada	94
BT	UK	60
Ericsson	Sweden	53

Trade-related intellectual property rights

In connection with the trade of intellectual property rights, the concern about severe industrial losses to counterfeiting and piracy have been forcefully expressed by intellectual property rights (IPR) exporting countries and representatives of the IPR industry. Against their argument for a stricter protection of intellectual property, others have questioned whether this would benefit the developing countries, the individual right holders and the consumers.

There has always been an interest in the economic dimension of intellectual property, but only in the late 1970s did a real trade concern develop. Various studies on the economic significance of the production and distribution of intellectual property provided a strong economic rationale for strict forms of IPR regulation. In the 1980s the economic significance of the production and distribution of intellectual property became increasingly clear. Skilbeck (1988) in an international survey calculated as an average contribution to GDP some 2.7 per cent. This means that copyright industries were surpassing in economic importance such sectors as automobile manufacturing. In the USA, for instance, the copyright industries are the second largest contributor to GDP and still growing yearly. In 1990 they were estimated to contribute 5.8 per cent to GDP (*Rights*, 1992: 5).

The economic importance of IPRs can also be concluded from the announcement made by Amstrad PLC (a British consumer electronics firm) that it had acquired the Danish company Dancall Radio A/B in September 1993 mainly for the company's intellectual property rights. This is corroborated by the numbers of patents that the leading telecommunication firms have registered in recent years (Table 4.1). The large computer and telecommunication manufacturers are also spending considerable amounts of money on the creation of innovations. The Swedish company Ericsson spent in

1992 some 17 per cent of its overall income on R&D. In most of the large firms the R&D figures increase steadily. This economic value, and in particular the recent losses due to piracy, have provided a strong incentive for strict regulation. On the agenda of both the US government and the EU the protection of intellectual property has evolved into a major issue in world trade relations. The US-based International Intellectual Property Alliance (IIPA) in 1988 estimated the total losses in copyright industries in the USA at over US $1.3 billion.

The world-wide unauthorized illegal reproduction of copyrighted works became a grave trade-political concern. In many countries existing legislation turned out to be inadequate to combat piracy. Several nations began to step up activities against piracy through adjusted regulation, information campaigns, training of law enforcement officers, and increased penalties. Also a series of bilateral agreements were concluded between the US and infringer countries (such as Korea, Malaysia and Thailand) and between the EC and countries such as Indonesia and Korea. Given the unsatisfactory nature of such bilateral accords, the USA began to propose movement towards a multilateral accord for trade disputes on intellectual property. As a forum for such an arrangement the US government preferred GATT over WIPO.

This preference was largely motivated by what was perceived as a serious weakness of international copyright conventions. The existing treaties do not provide for an effective mechanism of implementation and sanction. Under the Berne convention it was made obligatory with the Brussels revision (1948) that disputes between members would have to be brought before the International Court of Justice. However, the Stockholm revision of the convention in 1967 made this optional. Any country that ratifies the convention can consider itself not bound by the dispute settlement clause. GATT on the contrary has a mechanism for the settlement of disputes and for retaliatory measures when GATT rules are broken.[5]

The expressed preference for GATT also reflects the choice to view the protection of intellectual property primarily as a trade issue. With the increasing economic significance of intellectual property, the priority for protection is clearly shifting from the individual creators to the institutional producers. The individual authors, composers and performers are low on the list of trade figures and as a result there is a trend towards IPR arrangements that favour institutional investment interests over individual producers (Cohen Jehoram, 1988). The recent insistence on including intellectual property rights in the GATT trade negotiations demonstrates the commercial thrust of the major actors. Copyright problems have become trade issues and the protection of the author has given ground to the interests of traders and investors. This emphasis on corporate ownership interests implies a threat to the 'common good' use of intellectual property and seriously upsets the balance between the private ownership claims of the producer and the claims to public benefits of the users. The balance between the interests of producers and those of users has always been under threat in the development of collective IPR practices. It would seem, however, that the emerging GATT arrangement provides benefits neither to the individual creator nor to the public. The commercial tendency, for example, to focus resources on types of knowledge that can be protected under the terms of a GATT accord leads in effect to a reduction of available variety for consumers.

The positions
Concerns in the field of intellectual property protection have been expressed on different levels. The existing provisions have been considered inadequate in dealing with new developments, particularly in technology. Important agents of this concern were actors in the business community, such as electronic chip manufacturers, software companies and phonogram producers. The existing provisions have been seen as too limited for the inclusion of the interests of important actors and domains. Here the vocal actors have been such professional groups as publishers and film directors. It has been argued – mainly by companies in the IPR industry – that the existing provisions are too weak to protect trading interests. Developing countries have pleaded that existing provisions are too biased to accommodate their specific interests in access to knowledge or protection of the cultural heritage. These concerns were motivated primarily by economic and moral interests, and to a lesser extent social interests (as in the case of public lending rights).

Although the world community has consensually recognized the principle that creative work warrants a form of protection, contending positions have been taken in the accommodation of this principle. Rival claims emerged as a moral approach versus an economic approach, and a development approach versus a trade approach.

Moral versus economic
In the original versions of the Berne convention and the Paris convention the main motive for the protection of intellectual property is economic. There was a basic recognition of rights to the

economic exploitation of literary and artistic works and industrial inventions. Intellectual property protection secured a benefit for the creator and provided an incentive to invest in innovation and creativity. Only in the 1928 revision of the Berne convention (Rome act) was Article 6 bis introduced, which refers to the author's moral rights. During the debates at the Rome conference, the extension of author's rights from economic rights to moral rights was introduced by the French, Italian and Polish delegates and the International Institute of Intellectual Cooperation. The French position was that the conference should express its wish that all the signatory countries of the Berne convention introduce as soon as possible in their respective legislation formal provisions whose object is to institute the moral rights of authors in their works. To the French delegate it seemed desirable for this right to be declared inalienable and for its conditions to be fixed in an identical manner in every country. According to the Italian position the author should always have the right to claim authorship of the work, the right to decide whether the work may be published, and the right to object to any modification of the work which is prejudicial to his moral interests. Poland proposed amendments to the convention by which the author should have the right, despite any stipulation to the contrary, to object to any attempt to undermine his character of author as well as to any transformation or mutilation whatsoever which might distort the way in which his work was intended to be presented to the public. The Italian delegate in his intervention referred to 'the recognition of this principle that a work of the mind does not only have a market value, but especially a spiritual and moral value'. The delegations from common law countries protested since these proposals were incompatible with the general principles of English law. In the negotiations a compromise text was achieved which became Article 6 bis.[6] By and large the moral approach has been defended by the civil law tradition which focused more on the individual authors, whereas the economic approach has found the strongest support in the common law tradition which has included the interests of producers and investors.

The moral rights approach recognized that the works represent the intellectual personality of their authors. It is recognized that this moral right exists even after transfer, which in essence means that it is non-transferable. The Brussels revision of the Berne convention in 1948 extended the moral rights provision further by establishing the continuation of moral rights after the death of the author. The Stockholm revision conference (1967) strengthened this by granting the moral rights the same protection as the economic rights until the expiry of the latter. Stockholm also designed a compromise formula to address the problems of member countries whose legislations would not in principle protect moral rights within the system of copyright protection. In the common law countries moral rights might not be recognized in copyright legislation, but they could yet be recognized by the courts under other legal titles, such as the principle of equity. Although the convention did now grant international protection to the author's moral rights, the remedy was left to national legislation and no commitment was made to incorporate this into municipal law.

When the USA began (in 1986) to consider accession to the Berne convention, a coalition of publishers started lobbying against adherence to the convention. It was especially feared that the recognition of author's moral rights could have negative commercial effects. This right would enable journalists, writers, photographers and artists to oppose interventions in their work. This would threaten the widespread practice of editors of books and magazines to radically change texts, shorten them and use them in advertisements without consulting the authors. Parties to the coalition were companies like McGraw-Hill, Meredith, and Reader's Digest. Against this lobby a group of US authors, artists and directors began to promote adherence to Berne, since they saw this as a chance to introduce the notion of moral right. On 31 October 1988 President Reagan signed into law the Berne Convention Implementation Act by which US law was placed under the obligation of compliance with the 1971 version of the convention. This did not change US legislation in line with a recognition of the moral rights approach. The prevailing opinion was that US laws on defamation, privacy and unfair competition could adequately deal with the issue of moral rights to intellectual property.

In the past years trade figures have become more prominent in the politics of intellectual property protection. If one compares the relative contribution of copyright holders to the overall economy, the institutional groups such as printers, publishers, computer services, broadcast companies and advertising firms deliver more than the individual authors, composers and performers. The latter group is lower on the list and therefore has a lower protection priority. It remains to be seen what the implications are for moral rights in the prevalent treatment of IPR as tradable commodity.

In current bilateral IPR arrangements corporate producers are favoured over individual authors or composers. There is a trend towards agreements that protect the economic rights of investors, broadcasters, publishers and record producers better than the moral rights of the individual creator.

Development versus trade

The claims made by the developing countries for a revision of both the patent system (see Chapter 7) and the copyright system were defended with arguments related to their national development needs. They made reference to the need of access to patented and copyrighted materials, the necessary protection of their own infant intellectual property industries, and the defence of their cultural traditions. Third World countries in general claimed a lower degree of protection, whereas the industrial countries claimed a higher degree of protection. The latter group and their lobbies of IPR industries promoted the concept of intellectual property protection as a trade issue and claimed that only a trade framework could adequately protect their investment and expand their markets. The GATT Uruguay Round on trade became a crucial arena for the collision between development and trade claims. Third World actors claimed that TRIPs should not be integrated into a GATT framework, that there should be ample space for national remedies and exemptions. They also proposed to balance owner rights with public interest, to strengthen compulsory licensing and to impose obligations on right holders. The industrial countries claimed that intellectual property protection should be under GATT jurisdiction, and that there should be world-wide uniformity of legislation (with a few exceptions), no obligations for right holders, long periods of protection, and mechanisms for retaliation.

Underlying the development versus trade clash were very divided positions on intellectual property. The development position saw intellectual property as a public good and as part of the common heritage of humankind. The trade position viewed it as private property which is owned and exploited primarily for economic benefit.

Prevailing political practice

The protection of intellectual property is provided under the international system of copyright and neighbouring rights, under the patent system, through *sui generis* arrangements, and – most recently – by a trade-based multilateral accord. The latter accord has been particularly motivated by the ineffectiveness of the conventional practice.

The patent system comprises the protection of industrial property through patents, industrial designs, trade marks, service marks, trade names, indications of source or appellations of origin, and the repression of unfair competition (for more discussion on the patent system, see Chapter 7).

The international system of copyright and neighbouring rights provides protection of the rights of authors, performers, producers of phonograms and broadcasting organizations. For more than 100 years a system of protection has been developed that offers the incentives, rewards and recognition for individual producers of knowledge that stimulate the development of knowledge. It represents the economic incentive to invest in innovation and creativity, and provides the inducement to publish the results for a wide audience. The classical principle of the protection of intellectual property is 'to promote the progress of science and the useful arts by securing for limited times to authors and inventors the exclusive right to their respective writings and discoveries' (formulation in the US constitution). The protection of intellectual property implies a delicate balance between a public principle (to promote public welfare by the progress of science and arts) and a private principle (to protect individual ownership).

Multilateral cooperation in this issue area has been guided by a series of binding but weak agreements.[7] There are binding normative provisions in the conventions, but in practice no mechanisms for enforcement or dispute settlement. Although one should not underestimate the significance of the conventions for the promotion of intellectual property rights, the prevailing practice has been unable to stop large-scale infringements around the world and has equally been unable to protect the interests of a large portion of the world community, the developing countries. By and large the existing arrangements have also been insufficient to guarantee the rights of individual creators to the fullest extent.[8]

Recently world politics began to shift towards a new practice. This was especially pushed by the large IPR producing and exporting players. They moved the negotiations to the GATT forum in order to obtain a trade-based robust and binding multilateral accord that would effectively secure their interests. In the final act of the Uruguay trade negotiations (December 1993) provisions on TRIPs were incorporated in the new GATS framework. The new accord is binding upon the contracting parties. It will have effective mechanisms for enforcement, and a powerful constituency of the world's leading IPR industries will support it. The new arrangement was most needed by the powerful players and in spite of their hegemonic position its compliance demands considerable bilateral pressures and compromise bargaining. Non-compliance can be punished with (cross-) retaliatory measures but even so the threat remains that less powerful actors have considerable scope to render the accord less effective and to reduce the effectiveness of the new practice.

Notes

1 The new transmission techniques posed the complex problem of the legal definition of the operation performed by broadcast satellites. The nature of the rights involved and accordingly the determination of applicable national law would be dependent upon this definition. In the two international copyright conventions there is a distinction between 'public communication' and 'broadcasting'.

The UCC in Article IV bis distinguishes between the exclusive right to authorize public performance and the exclusive right to authorize broadcasting. The implication is that the scope of the exceptions to these rights may be different. The Berne convention separates the exclusive right to authorize broadcasting from the right that applies to other forms of public communication. Article 11 confers exclusive rights on the author to authorize the public performance of works. As such these rights can be claimed in any country should national legislation have omitted such protection. Article 11 bis confers the exclusive right to authorize broadcasting but leaves it to national legislation to specify under which conditions protection is granted. According to this article there is in the case of broadcasting no right 'specially recognized' by the convention, but the author has to rely on national law.

Another problem was posed by the fact that the Radio Regulations as annexed to the International Telecommunication Convention (adopted at Malaga-Torremolinos in 1973 and revised at Nairobi in 1982) defined a broadcasting satellite service as a 'radiocommunication service in which signals transmitted or retransmitted by space stations are intended for direct reception by the general public'. The copyright conventions, however, did not contain the notion of the general public. It was unclear whether the general public is those people who have access to special decoders to decode signals, or those who receive signals through complex individual equipment.

When, in addition to the existing fixed satellite services (FSS) that allow for satellite-to-cable transmission, direct broadcasting services through signals from geostationary satellites became available, new copyright questions had to be answered.

2 In a simple definition a computer program can be said to be 'a set of instructions the purpose of which is to cause an information processing device, a computer, to perform its functions' (from the Green Paper on Copyright and the Challenge of Technology, Commission of the European Communities, COM (88), Brussels, 1988, p. 70). WIPO provided in 1977 the following definition in its Model Provisions on the Protection of Computer Software: '(i) "computer program" means a set of instructions capable, when incorporated in a machine-readable medium, of causing a machine having information-processing capabilities to indicate, perform or achieve a particular function, task or result; (ii) "program description" means a complete procedural representation in verbal, schematic or other form, in sufficient detail to determine a set of instructions constituting a corresponding computer program; (iii) "supporting material" means any material, other than a computer program or a program description, created for aiding the understanding or application of a computer program, for example problem descriptions and user instructions; (iv) "computer software" means any or several of the items referred to in (i) to (iii).' The US Computer Software Copyright Act of 1980 defines a computer program as 'a set of statements or instructions to be used directly or indirectly in a computer in order to bring about a certain result'.

3 Exhaustion is a general principle in the legal protection of intellectual property. It is generally accepted that the principle has universal application, unless right

owners have made territorial restrictions (Cohen Jehoram, 1987: 28). A work legally acquired in country A (provided there is no geographical restriction in the publisher's contract) can freely be resold in other countries. The doctrine of exhaustion is theoretically founded by German lawyer Joseph Kohler. It provides the compromise between intellectual protection and the right of property of those who acquire copies; it delimits the rights of right holders to prohibit further use of their works. As the US copyright law states: 'the owner of a particular copy or phonorecord is entitled, without the authority of the copyright owner, to sell or otherwise dispose of the possession of that copy or phonorecord' (Article 109(a)). Limits to the exhaustion principle are that those who acquire possession by rental or otherwise may not use the same privileges of exhaustion. Moreover, the author retains exclusive rights of reproduction and performance and therefore the reuse is restricted. You can rent your legally acquired CD, but not multiply it for commercial sales. In several countries this has given rise to the establishment of remuneration schemes for book loans from public libraries. Similar schemes for phonorecords and videograms are also under consideration.

4 Article 2(5) of the Berne convention provides that: 'Collections of literary or artistic works such as encyclopedias and anthologies which, by reason of the selection and arrangement of their contents, constitute intellectual creations shall be protected as such, without prejudice to the copyright in each of the works forming part of such collections.'

5 Meanwhile, WIPO has proposed to establish a new treaty on the settlement of intellectual property disputes between nations and a mechanism to resolve disputes between private parties. This proposal for the dispute settlement mechanism is believed to be the WIPO response to the challenge from GATT.

6 Article 6 bis (1) of the Berne convention provides: 'Independently of the author's economic rights, and even after the transfer of the said rights, the author shall have the right to claim authorship of the work and to object to any distortion, mutilation or other modification of, or other derogatory action in relation to, the said work, which would be prejudicial to his honour or reputation.'

7 The major copyright conventions (the Berne convention and the Universal Copyright convention), the conventions on neighbouring rights (the Rome and Geneva conventions), the Paris Convention for the Protection of Industrial Property (and a related series of treaties on the protection of patents, trade marks and industrial design), the Treaty on the Protection of Intellectual Property in Respect of Integrated Circuits, and the Agreement on Trade-Related Aspects of Intellectual Property Rights, Including Trade in Counterfeit Goods, of the final act embodying the results of the GATT Uruguay Round of multilateral trade negotiations.

8 The conclusion that in the context of WIPO and Unesco a largely ineffective form of multilateral cooperation existed seems somewhat unfair in view of the undoubtedly important work done by the two bodies. They have contributed in large measure to the promotion of recognition and respect for intellectual property in the world. Their standard setting, work on model laws, anti-piracy programmes and assistance to developing countries should not be minimized. However, the appropriate enforcement measures have remained noticeably weak.

5
Mass Communication

Radio broadcasting: the issue of harmful communication

The technical possibility of directly reaching out to vast audiences made the world community aware of both the opportunities and the risks this entailed. International radio broadcasting raised in particular the issue of the right of sovereign states to prevent the reception of signals they consider harmful to their interests. This issue came up very strongly in the context of hostile political propaganda.

Obviously the use of propaganda as a foreign policy instrument has a long history. It has been systematically practised since the fifteenth century. In particular the eighteenth century provides many illustrations of hostile propaganda. However, only in the twentieth century has it become an issue that demands a collective response. Although propaganda was exercised through newspapers, magazines and movies, radio broadcasting became the essential medium. 'The invention of radio in the late nineteenth century totally altered for all time the practice of propaganda' (Jowett and O'Donnell, 1986: 82). In spite of the availability of more advanced communication technologies, radio broadcast propaganda is still today a vibrant activity engaging vast sums of money around the world. There is an estimated audience of between 100 and 200 million listeners world-wide. Radio programmes are transmitted abroad for a variety of reasons. Among them are the contacts with nationals in foreign countries, the international dissemination of news, the distribution of information about a country's politics, economy and culture, and hostile propaganda.

During the First World War extensive use was made of the means of propaganda. This psychological warfare continued after the war had ended and international short-wave radio began to proliferate. Germany began with international radio broadcasting in 1915 and was followed in 1917 by the Soviet Union. During the 1920s there was a rapidly growing interest in international radio broadcasting and more nations became involved. By 1939 some 25 countries were actively engaged in broadcasting to foreign countries in a multitude of languages. Many broadcast programmes in this period contained propaganda, and most of it was hostile. Programmes defamed other governments or their leaders, made attempts to subvert foreign leadership or incited to war.

From its establishment the League of Nations (predecessor to the United Nations) was concerned about the role of the mass media in international relations and addressed such problems as the contribution of the press to peace. In 1931 the League of Nations had decided to ask the Institute for Intellectual Cooperation (the predecessor of Unesco) to conduct a study on all questions raised by the use of radio for good international relations. In 1933 the study was published (*Broadcasting and Peace*) and it recommended the drafting of a binding multilateral treaty. This treaty was indeed drafted and concluded on 23 September 1936 with the signatures of 28 states. The fascist states did not participate. The International Convention Concerning the Use of Broadcasting in the Cause of Peace entered into force on 2 April 1938 after ratification or accession by nine countries: Brazil, the United Kingdom, Denmark, France, India, Luxembourg, New Zealand, the Union of South Africa and Australia. Basic to the provisions of the convention was the recognition of the need to prevent, through rules established by common agreement, broadcasting from being used in a manner prejudicial to good international understanding. These agreed rules included the prohibition of transmissions which could incite the population of any territory 'to acts incompatible with the internal order or security of contracting parties' or which were likely to harm good international understanding by incorrect statements. The contracting parties also agreed to ensure 'that any transmission likely to harm good international understanding by incorrect statements shall be rectified at the earliest possible moment'.

The Second World War led to an enormous expansion of radio propaganda and this continued in the years after the war. 'As the dynamics of world politics were being played out, international radio broadcasting became a prominent weapon in the arsenal of propaganda' (Jowett and O'Donnell, 1986: 86). In response to harmful broadcasting there were attempts to impede the reception of radio signals from abroad. 'Jamming' has been practised by many countries. Governments have tried to manipulate the effective receiving range of radio sets. Usually most of these attempts have not been very successful.

Immediately after the Second World War the issue of harmful broadcasting was discussed at the United Nations Conference on Freedom of Information in 1948. From this conference evolved the Convention on the International Right of Correction (adopted by UNGA Resolution 630(VII) on 16 December 1952). The convention desired 'to protect mankind from the scourge of war . . . and to combat all propaganda which is either designed or likely to provoke or encourage any threat to the peace, breach of the peace, or act of aggression'. The United Nations General Assembly adopted a series of resolutions addressing the problem of war propaganda and the diffusion of false or distorted reports 'likely to injure friendly relations between States' (UNGA Resolution 127(II) of 1947). The concern about propaganda was codified in Article 20 of the International Covenant on Civil and Political Rights. Also the Unesco General Conference adopted a series of resolutions on the role of Unesco in generating a climate of public opinion conducive to the halting of the arms race and transition to disarmament. For example, Resolution 1878 (twentieth session) recommended '. . . to pay particular attention to the role which information, including the mass media, can play in generating a climate of confidence and understanding between nations and countries as well as increasing public awareness of ideas, objectives and action in the field of disarmament'.

The positions
On the issue of harmful broadcasting contending positions were taken by most of the Western countries against the developing countries and the Soviet Union. These positions followed largely the 'freedom of information' versus 'social responsibility' controversy that will be discussed later in this chapter.

Prevailing political practice
If one adopts the distinction proposed by Whitton (1979: 217–29) we can consider the collective responses to subversive propaganda, defamatory propaganda and war propaganda.

The category of subversive propaganda which incites to revolt has been recognized in various legal instruments as an illegal act. It has been seen as a form of illegal intervention and as a form of aggression. A large number of multilateral treaties urge states to refrain from this type of propaganda.

The category of defamatory propaganda in which foreign leaders are vilified has also been ruled illegal and a danger to international peace. A special problem in this context has been 'the question of the publication of defamatory – especially false – news by the independent press and radio of a country'. Although there is general agreement in the world community that false news should be prohibited, 'there is wide discord over the best method to accomplish this' (Whitton, 1979: 223). There is no unequivocal collectively adopted agreement on this type of propaganda.

The consideration of propaganda for war as illegal is a typical development of the twentieth century. Earlier, 'to declare war was considered one of the sovereign rights of every state' (Whitton, 1979: 225). War propaganda came to be seen as a serious danger to international peace by the League of Nations and later by the United Nations. The preliminary draft of the General Convention to Improve the Means of Preventing War by the League of Nations stated that aggressive propaganda could 'take such offensive forms and assume such a threatening character as to constitute a real danger to peace'. In various instruments the world community expressed its concern about war propaganda, but it never managed to establish a robust multilateral accord on the issue.

A peculiar problem in this area has been the fact that much hostile communication originates with private actors and opinions have been very divided over the extent of state responsibility in such cases. Moreover only a limited number of states have adopted the prohibition of war propaganda in their domestic legislation. It remains a matter of dispute whether a state can be held responsible when independent media under its jurisdiction were guilty of warmongering. There is also a lack of clarity about the precise definition of propaganda for war.

By and large the political practice has been characterized by discord and ambivalence. The ambivalence is clearly articulated in UNGA Resolution 424(V) of 14 December 1950. In paragraph 3 the resolution invites the governments of member states to refrain from interference with the reception of certain signals originating beyond their territories. At the same time it invites all governments to refrain from radio broadcasts which would mean unfair attacks or slander against other peoples anywhere. In several UN instruments jamming has been condemned but this was never codified in binding law. Equally there is no multilateral accord that would limit the contents of international radio broadcasts. In fact, it has been the prevailing practice of most players to broadcast as they wanted, largely unhindered since attempts at barring broadcast signals have usually been ineffective.

Direct satellite TV: the issue of prior consent

The possibility of international direct TV broadcasting by satellite (IDTBS) raised the hot political issue of 'prior consent'. The world community has been divided on the question of whether direct satellite transmissions need the consent of receiving states.

The international negotiations on IDTBS raised some difficult questions on the impact of international telecommunication. Can international telecommunication have 'harmful effects' and, if so, can these be regulated? Can IDTBS imply damage to a state's political, commercial and cultural interests? If so, who is to be held responsible? Are states responsible for TV transmissions originating in their territories with private institutions? Are recipient states responsible for the protection of the integrity of their territories and as such responsible for incoming TV signals?

The possibility of the transmission or retransmission of signals by space stations intended for direct reception by the general public was already recognized in the early 1960s. Direct reception of satellite signals would be possible both in the form of individual reception by simple domestic installations and as community reception by installations which may be complex and intended for a group of the general public at one location or through a distribution system covering a limited area.

The development of direct TV broadcasting by satellite (DTBS) was much slower than initially expected. The first attempts in North America ran into serious problems (the United Satellite Communications Inc.) and the most widespread use of satellite broadcasting turned out to be 'space piracy' – the interception of satellite transmissions. 'By March 1984 USCI only had 1000 paying subscribers, and in July 1984 Western Union, CBS and RCA took the hint and effectively pulled out of DTBS by failing to file applications on time with the FCC' (Forester, 1987: 111). Japan launched DTBS in 1984 for use by NHK. In the UK, despite early enthusiasm, in August 1983 the BBC could no longer pay for two DTBS channels. A special joint BBC-IBA project to develop three channels for satellite TV collapsed in 1985.

DTBS takes place mainly as a national or regional operation, and has not yet developed as an operational project on the world level. The technology for IDTBS is available, however, and has put the question of international legal provisions for its use on the United Nations agenda since the early 1960s. The IDTBS issue first emerged in a United Nations Committee on the Peaceful Uses of Outer Space (hereinafter cited as COPUOS) meeting in November 1963. This meeting was preparing the draft Declaration of Legal Principles Governing the Activities of States in the Exploration and Use of Outer Space. In connection with the draft Outer Space Declaration, the delegate from Brazil stated: 'The Declaration should also incorporate a ban on the utilization of a communication system based on satellites for purposes of encouraging national, racial or class rivalries and a reference to some international scrutiny of global satellite communication' (COPUOS, 1963). Also the Soviet delegate proposed a provision regarding the contents of space communication: 'The use of outer space for propagating war, national or racial hatred or enmity between nations shall be prohibited' (COPUOS, 1963). These interventions articulated a demand to impose restrictions on programme content in IDTBS. The Outer Space Declaration did not incorporate the demand when it was passed by the General Assembly on 13 December 1963 (Resolution 1962(XVIII)). The resolution, however, made a reference to the earlier UNGA Resolution 110(II) of 3 November 1947, which 'condemned propaganda designed or likely to provoke or encourage any threat to the peace, breach of peace, or act of aggression'. The resolution also recognized that the anti-propaganda provision was applicable to outer space. It was, however, not explicitly stated that this standard on programme content was to be imposed on space communication. In fact, the Outer Space Treaty that was to follow from the declaration (and that became the leading legal document on the use of space resources) does not mention space communication. There is a reference (in the eighth preambular paragraph) to UNGA Resolution 110(II), but IDTBS is not mentioned.

The space communication issue had been raised, however, and would soon be put on the agenda of the Legal Subcommittee of COPUOS. UNGA Resolution 2222 of 19 December 1966, to which the Outer Space Treaty was annexed, contained a request to COPUOS 'to begin . . . the study of questions relative to the definition of outer space and the utilization of outer space and celestial bodies, including the various implications of space communications'. In response to this request, COPUOS recommended in 1964 to the General Assembly that it had decided 'to consider questions relating to the use of satellites for transmitting radio and television programmes for direct reception by the general public'. Four years later, on 20 December 1968, the General Assembly unanimously adopted Resolution 2453(XXIII) by which the COPUOS working group on direct broadcast satellites was created. The working group was 'to study and report on the technical feasibility of communications by direct broadcast satellites and the current and foreseeable developments in the field, including comparative user costs and other economic considerations, as well as the implications of such developments in the social, cultural, legal and other areas'. In this resolution the General Assembly made reference to its earlier Resolution 1721D(XVI) of 20 December 1961 (communication by means of satellites should be available to the nations of the world as soon as practicable on a global and non-discriminatory basis) and 'recommended that States parties to negotiations regarding international arrangements in the field of satellite communication should constantly bear this principle in mind so that its ultimate realization may not be impaired'. The working group would meet annually and report to COPUOS and the General Assembly.

In the report of its first session in 1969, the working group recognized both the positive effects ('the promise of unprecedented progress in communications and understanding between peoples and cultures, e.g. improved health and education and a greater flow of news and information') and the adverse effects ('as resulting from the receipt of basically television programs in the territories of states whose governments do not wish to have them received . . . programs aimed at achieving certain political objectives, e.g. propaganda, incitement and interference; programs that are objectionable because they use materials or techniques outlawed in the receiving states, e.g. violence, libel, obscenity; programs that are unwanted mostly because they are foreign and have the potential to undermine national integrity, e.g. news or public information programs'). At this first session all members of the working group, except the USA, were in favour of some form of standard setting for direct satellite broadcasting. The USSR had already submitted a draft of provisions for the utilization and exploitation of satellites for broadcasting. However, no consensus was achieved save the minimal acceptance (at the working group sessions in 1969 and 1970) of the major sources of international law that would be applicable to IDTBS. These were: the UN charter, the Outer Space Treaty, the ITU convention and Radio Regulations, the Universal Declaration of Human Rights and relevant resolutions of the UN General Assembly. This was endorsed by the General Assembly in Resolution 2733. The resolution also pointed to the issue of responsibility for IDTBS as it recommended in Article V 'that the COPUOS should study through its Legal Sub-Committee, giving priority to the Liability Convention, the work carried out by the Working Group on Direct Broadcasting Satellites under the item on the implications of space communications'.

In the first session of the working group it was also proposed that a distinction would be made between the deliberate broadcasting into the territory of another state and unintentional 'spill-over' into the territory of another state. In the second session (1969) the issue of programme content was discussed under the headings of political programmes, cultural and social programmes and commercial programmes. The dominant theme in discussing these three categories was the two-sided assessment of the impact of IDTBS: potential benefits versus adverse effects.

In 1970 the French delegation to the COPUOS presented a Code of Good Conduct relative to space communication. This code, while accepting the right of states to broadcast from space, stated a number of restrictions that would all need the prior consent of the receiving state. Programmes which would be considered illegal were identified in the code. These were programmes with propaganda detrimental to international peace, programmes undermining individual dignity, cultures, religions or traditions, and programmes that would interfere with domestic or foreign policies of other states. The code also proposed restrictions on advertising and recommended that advertisements should demonstrate an artistic or educational interest and contain truth. The French proposal was not accepted. It did bring clearly to the surface, however, the essential issues involved in IDTBS negotiations: a controversy about the principle of prior consent, and a controversy about the question of state responsibility.

In the ensuing debates on IDTBS three major positions emerged. The first emphasized prior consent, sovereignty and non-interference (held by, among others, France, the Soviet Union, and developing countries). The second opposed prior consent and defended the human right to freedom of information as prohibitive of any interference with direct broadcasting (especially the USA). The third advanced the possibility of a compromise agreement, largely based upon bilateral arrangements between sending and receiving countries (Canada and Sweden).

In 1972 the Soviet Union submitted a draft convention on principles governing the use by states of artificial earth satellites for direct television broadcasting. Article 5 of the proposed convention read that satellite broadcasts should be contingent upon 'the express consent' of the receiving states. The Soviet proposal also promoted control over programme content. In the debates that followed, a Soviet resolution calling for a binding treaty on IDTBS was amended to UNGA Resolution 2916 (adopted by the General Assembly in 1972) on preparation of an international convention on principles governing the use by states of artificial earth satellites for direct television broadcasting. The only dissenting vote came from the USA.

In 1972 Canada and Sweden proposed a compromise approach in order to overcome the IDTBS controversy between those who wanted to regulate space communication strictly and those who abhorred this. The proposal adopted the principle of consent, but as a form of licensing for international IDTBS operations (similar to national licensing schemes) and with participation by and close cooperation between broadcasting and receiving states. It was suggested by the initiators of the compromise solution that this position would make a provision on programme content super-fluous. The hope was that the provision on 'consent, participation and cooperation', would satisfy the pro-regulation countries and that the absence of a programme content provision would satisfy the anti-regulation countries. The compromise remained just that. It was still too restrictive and impractical for the free flow protagon-ists, and unsatisfactory for those who felt that the principle of consent would still need to be expanded with standards on pro-gramme content since international cooperation among states would not be a guarantee against 'unlawful' broadcasts.

In 1972 Unesco adopted a declaration that reflected largely the position of the countries that felt there should be express obligations for the operation of international IDTBS. The Declaration of Guiding Principles on the Uses of Satellite Broadcasting for the Free Flow of Information, the Spread of Education, and Greater Cultural Exchange did prescribe a set of standards for IDTBS. Its preamble made references to Article 19 of the Universal Declara-tion of Human Rights as well as to the anti-propaganda resolution of 1947. Article V stated that the objective of satellite broadcasting for the free flow of information is to ensure the widest possible dissemination, among the peoples of the world, of news of all countries, developed and developing alike. While stressing the freedom of information principle, the declaration also recognized the prior consent principle in Article IX: 'In order to further the objectives set out in preceding articles, it is necessary that States, taking into account the principle of freedom of information, reach or promote prior agreements concerning direct satellite broadcast-ing to the population of countries other than the country of origin of the transmission.' The declaration also stated explicitly the inter-national nature of space communication by providing in Article III: that 'The benefits of satellite broadcasting should be available to all countries without discrimination and regardless of their degree of development.' The declaration was adopted with 55 votes in favour, 22 abstentions and seven against: Australia, Canada, Costa Rica, Denmark, the FRG, the UK and the USA. A strong protest against the declaration was expressed on behalf of the cooperating broad-casting unions. 'They in turn elaborated a code of conduct related to IDTBS and which stressed professional collaboration amongst national broadcasting organizations' (Taishoff, 1987: 164).

The prior consent principle was again stressed in a 1974 proposal made by Argentina for a draft international convention on direct broadcasting by satellite. This proposal attempted to accommodate both the prior consent and the free flow principles and stressed the need for regional agreements (UNGA document A/Ac.105/134, 5 July 1974). A different position was taken in the draft convention presented by the USA in the same year. Article 3 of the draft convention stated that all states had the right to emit international broadcasts by means of IDTBS. The proposal promoted the free flow of information principle. In the COPUOS debates the US delegate explained that according to his country's view international law did not contain any obligation of prior consent. In 1976 the General Assembly adopted a resolution (31/8) by which the COPUOS was requested to draft principles for IDTBS as a matter of priority.

In February 1977 the final acts of the WARC 1977 were signed containing rules on prior consultation in the case of spill-overs. This reflected the more technical approach to IDTBS which was taken within the ITU through the World Administrative Radio Conference for the Planning of the Broadcasting Satellite Service (WARC 1977). The conference drew up a detailed plan for space communication and confirmed the consultation procedures that had been established at the 1971 WARC. These procedures implied that the transmission of signals to the territory of other countries should be reduced unless previous agreement had been reached between the countries concerned. The pertinent Radio Regulation 7, Section 428A reads: 'In devising the characteristics of a space station in the television broadcasting satellite service, all technical means available shall be used to reduce, to the maximum extent practicable, the radiation over the territory of other countries, unless agreement has been previously reached with such countries.' At the WARC the USA had no objection to this form of prior consultation. There were different views on whether the ITU type of prior consultation made the provision of prior consent in the draft principles on IDTBS superfluous. Some countries held the view that the technical agreements that had been reached under the ITU plans made further agreements unnecessary. For the US delegation these provisions were seen to provide adequate protection. Another claim (by the USSR delegation) was that coordination agreements under the ITU regulations covered exclusively technical matters and that they in no way concerned regulatory questions on the political and legal level. Given the claim by the majority of states that they did not wish to accept foreign radio and television interference through space communication unless previously agreed upon, the ITU technical standards were not sufficient to satisfy this claim and further work on guiding international legal principles for IDTBS activities remained necessary (Matte, 1982: 191).

An important argument by those who felt the ITU arrangements were sufficient was that the 1977 WARC defined satellite broadcasting largely as a national operation with limited international ramifications. The plans for IDTBS adopted in the WARC 1977 final acts were for national satellite broadcasting (and a few regional arrangements) and provided for permission for a small number of states to engage in state-to-state broadcasting. For most countries in the world IDTBS would in fact be national broadcasting and would need no special protection. As the ITU representative in the meeting of COPUOS stated in 1977, the ITU plans for allocation of frequencies and orbital slots were not primarily for international broadcasting but they were for the domestic services of individual countries (Stewart, 1991: 137). Although the ITU plans reduced IDTBS mainly to national services, several delegations felt that this would still not pre-empt the need to elaborate standards for programming policies (e.g. Chile). Moreover, it was also recognized by some actors in the debate (for instance the European Broadcasting Union (EBU)) that the 1977 plans had provided for permission to some ten countries to engage in cross-border broadcasting by satellite, so that IDTBS was still on the agenda. In its 1977 meeting the working group attempted to reconcile the prior consent versus free flow positions by replacing the 'consent and participation' principle with a 'consultation and agreement between states' principle. With the new formulation the issue of prior consent had not disappeared, however, and it remained a basic impediment to reaching a multilateral consensus on IDTBS.

In 1978 the COPUOS Legal Subcommittee presented twelve draft principles on IDTBS which were subsequently discussed in 1979, 1980 and 1981. In 1979 the Canadians and the Swedes tried once again to mediate with a proposal for draft principles governing the use by states of artificial earth satellites for direct television broadcasting. The proposal accommodated the prior consent positions by referring to the prior consent requirement and by stating that 'each nation should bear international responsibility for television broadcasting carried out by state entities or private broadcasters under their jurisdiction'. The free flow position was accommodated through Article 14 which stated that the principles were agreed upon 'in order to facilitate the freer and wider dissemination of information of all kinds and to encourage cooperation in the field of information and the exchange of information with other countries'. The compromise was not accepted as it remained too restrictive for the free flow position.

Neither at the 1980 nor at the 1981 sessions of the IDTBS working group was progress towards a consensus made. By the end of the

1970s the different approaches continued to create a serious legal impasse. The free flow approach was undoubtedly a minority position but, given with the agreement that COPUOS would operate by consensus, it could not be overruled by the majority.

The fifth and final meeting of the working group completed its mandate. The working group submitted its report to COPUOS and recommended the basic draft for the principles. COPUOS (at its seventeenth session) accepted the report and was unable to reach an agreement on the future of the working group. The General Assembly (UNGA Resolution 3234(XXIX) of 12 November 1974) noted with appreciation the work done by the working group and recommended that COPUOS should consider reconvening it if or when it deemed this useful. The draft principles were then discussed by the Legal Subcommittee, and replaced by the text proposed by a group of twelve delegates. COPUOS was unable to reach a consensus on the text. The text of the draft principles to govern IDTBS activities was finally sent to the General Assembly. The 1982 session of the General Assembly adopted with a majority vote UNGA Resolution 37/92 (10 December 1982) on the Principles Governing the Use of States of Artificial Earth Satellites for International Direct Television Broadcasting: there were 107 votes for, thirteen against, and thirteen abstentions. This was the first time that a resolution on legal principles related to space had not been adopted with consensus. The basic legal instrument for IDTBS had been adopted, but the controversy continued.

Since 1982 no serious progress has been made in the IDTBS negotiations. The 1982 principles in fact formalized the underlying controversy of national sovereignty versus free flow. It is not certain whether an elaboration of the principles into an international convention may take place. At the 1983 meeting of the COPUOS several delegations to COPUOS proposed that the Committee and the Legal Subcommittee should work towards the development of a binding instrument on IDTBS.

Basically, the concern about international TV signals remained unresolved. There were stark differences between the claim that states had the responsibility to protect their national sovereignty against external interference and the claim that state responsibility for IDTBS content would imply a sanctioning of state censorship. The notion that states have a responsibility to watch over the legitimate interests of the territories they govern is a well established principle in international law. In line with this it has also become accepted practice that states put certain restrictions on the imports of technologies that may have adverse effects. The quintessence of the IDTBS negotiations was whether an agreement could be designed that would adopt this practice in the field of TV broadcasting by satellite without obstructing a free international provision of information not hindered by arbitrary governmental censorship.

The positions

The IDTBS issue has been contested in the sense that it has been more strongly expressed by receiving states than by states from whose territories broadcast signals originate. Concerned agents have mainly been Eastern European and Third World countries, and a minority of Western countries (such as France). The concern has been largely motivated by the potential of the adverse political and cultural effects of direct TV broadcasting.

In the IDTBS negotiations strongly contending claims confronted each other. On the one hand there was a restrictive, prior consent claim (mainly defended by Eastern European and Third World countries). On the other hand a permissive, *laissez-faire* claim was made by countries such as the USA and by the large broadcast organizations. The restrictive position claimed that broadcasts from foreign territory by satellite should be subject to the prior consent of receiving states. The permissive position claimed that IDTBS should be free from state interference.

The prior consent position was defended with reference to the recognition that TV programmes can be considered a form of external interference (*inter alia* based upon UNGA Resolution 2916) and that interference constitutes a violation of international law provisions on national sovereignty. This position claimed the right of states to define their own communication and culture policies and the implicit restriction this right imposes on the freedom of information standard. The prior consent position was further argued on the basis of the principle of the illegality of broadcasts and the right to restrict such materials.

The counter-claim argued that the obligation of prior consent was not established in international law and that in effect it would violate the right to freedom of information as enshrined in Article 19 of the Universal Declaration of Human Rights. The *laissez-faire* position was also defended by reference to the principle of national sovereignty, as provisions on contents would violate sovereign rights of states to determine what should or should not be pro-gramme contents. This was in fact a classical conflict between free flow of information claims and national sovereignty claims.

This controversy was recognized in UNGA Resolution 2916(XXVII) of 9 November 1972 in which the General Assembly requested COPUOS to prepare draft principles on IDTBS and considered that 'the introduction of direct television broadcasting by means of satellites could raise significant problems connected with the need to ensure the free flow of communications on the basis of strict respect for the sovereign rights of States'. Implicit in this controversy were obviously divergent positions on the question of the illegality of broadcasts. One view was that programmes transmitted to foreign territories without the prior consent of the receiving state, and with materials that according to international law are not admissible, should be considered to be illegal and to incur the international liability of the broadcasting states. Another view held that the concept of illegality would only give rise to international problems as there would be no consensus on objective standards for its assessment. Moreover, the restrictive approach to IDTBS would endanger fundamental human rights principles.

Prevailing political practice
The basic legal instrument to govern IDTBS is UNGA Resolution 37/92 of 4 February 1983 on: Principles Governing the Use of States of Artificial Earth Satellites for International Direct Television Broadcasting. This is an instrument adopted with divided votes, without a strong constituency or an efficient executive institution, and without procedures for enforcement. It is therefore a weak, voluntary and largely ineffective accord that is characterized by a very limited perspective on IDTBS. The emphasis in the principles is very much on a restrictive approach, on what programmes should be excluded. As Stewart has explained, this was largely due to the fact that work in the Legal Subcommittee and COPUOS was strongly influenced by the draft Soviet convention which focused more on protective provisions for IDTBS than on its positive purposes (1991: 22–7). Another limitation to the approach taken by the Legal Subcommittee and by COPUOS, and eventually by the General Assembly, was that DBS was not really addressed as a world phenomenon. In spite of the global nature of the technology, and in spite of UNGA Resolution 1721D(XVI) of 1961 and the reminder of the global principle in UNGA Resolution 2453B of 1968, the emphasis was rather more on implementation for national (or regional) objectives. As Stewart rightly notes, when Article A(2) of the principles mentions the assistance to educational, social and economic development, 'the focus appears to refer to national development within each country' (1991: 49). The primarily nationalist orientation of most negotiators impeded the development of a common agreement beyond national or regional interests. This was

reinforced by the technical arrangements decided upon by the ITU, especially the 1977 WARC.

Although the Unesco declaration instrument gave some emphasis to the global dimension of IDTBS (by its reference to UNGA Resolution 1721D(XVI)), its Article III, which mentions benefits to all countries and the need for international cooperation, did not go beyond a framework of national interest and forms of bilateral or regional cooperation. The limited nature of the IDTBS accord is also evident in the fact that the principles only contain an indirect reference to the common heritage standard through a reference to the Outer Space Treaty in Article B(4). Although at various points in the negotiations several participants had recognized the global nature of IDTBS and its significance to the common interest of all mankind, this was not explicitly mentioned in the principles.

The prevailing political practice is the absence of effective multilateral cooperation and a fundamental disagreement about essential principles. This makes it unlikely that a multilateral accord on IDTBS will emerge. This is reinforced by the fact that the most powerful players do not perceive an accord as necessary. They have the technological advantage and stand little to gain from cooperation.

Freedom of information

Concern about the freedom of information is reported as early as 350 BC when the Greek statesman and orator Demosthenes said that taking away the freedom of expression is one of the greatest calamities for human beings. For an early record one could also refer to the Roman historian Tacitus (55–116) who complimented the emperor Trajan for the felicitous times when one could freely express whatever one wanted to say.

It could be argued, however, that a real systematic articulation of the concern began only with the invention and proliferation of the printing press which almost immediately led to censorship. In 1485 the Archbishop of Mainz (where lived the inventor of the printing press, Gutenberg) established the first secular censorship office. In 1493 the Inquisition in Venice issued the first list of books banned by the Church. In 1559 the *Index Librorum Prohibitorum* was made binding on all Roman Catholics and was administered by the Inquisition. Secular powers also followed these examples and issued forms of regulation to control expression. The official rationale for this was greatly inspired by Thomas Hobbes' reflections in his *Leviathan* where he extended state sovereignty to the opinions and persuasions of the governed: 'it is annexed to the Soveraignty, to be the Judge of what Opinions and Doctrines are averse, and what conducing to Peace; and consequently, on what occasions, how farre, and what, men are to be trusted withall, in speaking to Multitudes of people; and who shall examine the Doctrines of all bookes before they be published' (1651: 233).

An example of such sovereign control was the English Regulation of Printing Act for the control of printing and printing presses. This 'licensing law' provided for a system of censorship through licences for printing and publishing. Against this type of regulation John Milton published his *Areopagitica* in 1644. In this famous speech to the Parliament of England on the liberty of unlicensed printing, Milton claimed: 'Truth needs no licensing to make her victorious.' In 1695 the Regulation of Printing Act was revoked. Interestingly enough, Milton's plea for freedom of printing did not apply to Roman Catholics as he felt one should not extend principles of tolerance to those who are intolerant. In Sweden in 1766 an order on the freedom of the printing press was enacted as formal law, including the rights of access to public information. The oldest catalogue of fundamental rights (in the sense of human rights and civil rights that possess a higher legal force) is the Declaration of Rights preceding the constitution of the state of Virginia in 1776. Here the freedom of expression was formulated as press freedom: 'That the freedom of the Press is one of the greatest bulwarks of liberty, and never be restrained by despotic governments.' Following the Anglo-Saxon tradition the French declaration on human and citizen's rights (Déclaration des Droits de l'Homme et du Citoyen) was formulated in 1789. This declaration went beyond the Virginia declaration in stating that the unrestrained communication of thoughts or opinions being one of the most precious rights of man, every citizen may speak, write and publish freely, provided he be responsible for the abuse of this liberty, in the cases determined by law. Then, in 1791, the US Bill of Rights stated in Article I the famous provision that 'Congress shall make no law . . . abridging the freedom of speech, or of the press.'

In the nineteenth century legislation on fundamental rights the freedom emerged in many countries and the freedom of the press became a central issue, primarily in the form of the prohibition of censorship. This was reflected in many national constitutions. Until the twentieth century the concern about freedom of information remained almost exclusively a domestic affair. Interestingly enough, when in the early twentieth century the League of Nations focused on the problems of false news and propaganda, it did not address the protection of freedom of expression. The International Federation of Journalists, however, stated the concern about freedom of information in the first article of its statute in 1926. 'Its purpose is, notably, to safeguard in all possible ways the liberty of the Press and of journalists which it will endeavour to have guaranteed by law.' During the Second World War the professional community would continue to express its concern about the freedom of information. At the second congress of the IFJAFC (International Federation of Journalists of Allied or Free Countries) in 1942 a resolution was adopted on the Charter of the Free Press that in part read: 'The Congress recognises, however, that the freedom of the Press is no greater and no less than the freedom of the individual and carries with it the obligations, which the journalist worthy of the name will freely accept and observe, not to publish false or distorted news, not to do anything likely to discredit his profession, his paper, or himself. To this end, Congress urges the universal adoption of a Code of Professional Conduct as has been done by several of its affiliated organisations' (Kubka and Nordenstreng, 1986a: 83).

When during the Second World War drafts for a post-war international bill of rights were prepared, the freedom of expression figured prominently. This is the case in the draft prepared by a commission of US Department of State in 1942: 'All persons shall enjoy freedom of speech and of the press, and the right to be informed.' During the war the US newspaper industry also began campaigning for freedom of news gathering (Schiller, 1976: 31–2). In June 1944 the American Society of Newspaper Editors (ASNE) adopted resolutions that demanded 'unrestricted communications for news throughout the world', and in September of the same year both houses of Congress stated 'its belief in the worldwide right of interchange of news by news-gathering and distributing agencies, whether individual or associate, by any means, without discrimination as to sources, distribution, rates or charges; and this right should be protected by international compact'. In early 1945 a delegation of the ASNE travelled around the world to promote the free flow doctrine. 'In fact, as the war drew to a close, preparations for the promotion of the free flow doctrine shifted from the national to the international level' (Schiller, 1976: 32).

The newly created United Nations agencies became prime targets for this promotional effort. The US delegation to the UN submitted on 16 February 1946 a proposal to the UN Secretary General, Trygve Lie, that asked the UN Commission on Human Rights to consider the question of freedom of information with the aim of drafting a convention. US delegates did this in response to prompting by the Congress which in turn had been lobbied by the newspaper industry. The media lobby (particularly newspapers and news agencies) was at first very supportive in putting the concern on the UN multilateral agenda. Later they changed their minds and considered a multilateral arrangement on the freedom of information a mistake and in fact a threat to freedom.

The Unesco constitution, adopted in 1945, was the first multilateral instrument to reflect the concern for the freedom of information. The constitution was largely based on US drafts (Wells, 1987: 62). These drafts included among other things a proposal stressing the paramount importance of the mass media and 'the need to identify opportunities of Unesco furthering their use for the ends of peace'. To promote the implementation of the concern for the freedom of information, a special division of 'free flow of information' was established in the secretariat in Paris.

In 1946 the delegation of the Philippines presented to the UN General Assembly a proposal for a resolution on an international conference on issues dealing with the press. This became UNGA Resolution 59(I) which was adopted unanimously in late 1946. According to the resolution the purpose of the conference would be to address the rights, obligations and practices which should be included in the concept of freedom of information. The resolution called freedom of information 'the touchstone of all the freedoms to which the United Nations is consecrated'. It described the freedom of information as 'the right to gather, transmit and publish news anywhere and everywhere without fetters'. Already freedom of information began to shift away from the concern about the individual's freedom of speech to the institutional freedom of news gathering by news agencies.

In 1947 the United Nations General Assembly adopted additional resolutions that were to be placed on the agenda of the Conference on Freedom of Information. One dealt with measures against propaganda and incitement against war, the other was concerned with false or distorted reports. Already by 1947 the UN had indicated a concern for both freedom and social responsibility in matters of information. In 1948 at Geneva the United Nations Conference on Freedom of Information took place from 23 March till 21 April. Fifty-four countries were officially represented and on the initiative of the UK practising news people were also included. The USA was interested only in a convention on news gathering. France was mainly interested in a convention on the international right of correction. The UK preferred a convention on freedom of information. Eventually the French text became a convention, but with only a few ratifications.

As Caroll Binder – a member of the American Society of Newspaper Editors – commented: 'our initial attempts to commit the United Nations to [the US concept of freedom of information] were successful beyond expectation' (Wells, 1987: 61). As the USA had taken the initiative, the Soviet Union and its allies were put in a reactive position. They responded to the US proposals for a free flow with demands for regulation. They were a minority in the UN bodies and most of their motions to qualify the free flow standard were defeated. This was also a result of the emerging Cold War antagonism. The conference produced numerous resolutions and three draft treaties on freedom of information (proposed by the British delegation), the gathering and international transmission of news (proposed by the US delegation), and the international right of correction (proposed by the French delegation). The six Eastern European countries voted against all three conventions; the USA abstained only from the freedom of information convention. This was based on the problems the Americans had with the list of limitations on the freedom of expression (Article 2) which they found too restrictive.

The draft convention on the gathering and international transmission of news was modified and subsequently approved by ECOSOC (Resolution 152(VII)), and then discussed at a meeting of the Third Committee of the General Assembly (at New York in April 1949) which decided to join the draft with the draft convention on the international right of correction. Then the joint texts were adopted by the UN General Assembly (Resolution 277(III)C) in 1949 but not opened for signature. The right of correction draft was subsequently separated from the gathering and transmission text and was opened for signature in 1952. After ratification by six countries the convention entered into force on 25 August 1962. By 1993 only eleven UN member states had ratified the convention.[1] The third draft convention on the freedom of information was adopted by the UNGA in 1949 (Resolution 277(III)A) after modification and adoption by ECOSOC and modification by the Third Committee, which abandoned work on the convention after approval of its preamble and five articles. The convention was never opened for signature and got lost in protracted ideological confrontation. In 1959 ECOSOC – urged by the USA – drafted a set of principles as the basis for a declaration on freedom of information. In 1960 the General Assembly received the principles, but took no action.

At the 1948 conference there were confrontations between those who advanced a largely liberal-economic position in defence of newspapers and news agencies, and those who challenged this as sanctioning of commercial monopolies and propagandistic practices. Serious objections were made by the Soviet Union against a concern for the freedom of information that was exclusively based upon commercial claims. The Soviet Union Minister of Foreign Affairs, Andrei Gromyko, claimed that the proposed freedom of information was in fact the freedom of a few monopolies. The doctrine of the free flow of information obscured, in his opinion, the interests of bankers and industrialists for whom Wall Street represented the summit of democracy. The Soviet Union also claimed that the freedom of information could not mean freedom for fascist propaganda. Other delegations equally stressed the need to prevent the establishment of news monopolies under the guise of freedom. Some nations, such as Yugoslavia, drew attention to the wide disparities in available means of mass communication and claimed that freedom should be linked with the standard of equality.

Following the 1948 conference, one of the articles of the Universal Declaration of Human Rights was dedicated to the freedom of expression. This became the well known Article 19, which states: 'Everyone has the right to freedom of opinion and expression; this right includes freedom to hold opinions without interference and to seek, receive and impart information and ideas through any media and regardless of frontiers.' An important observation is that the authors of the article constructed freedom of information from five components. The first is the classical defence of the freedom of expression. The second is the freedom to hold opinions. This provision was formulated upon the American insistence on protection against brainwashing, the forced exposure of a political conviction. The third is the freedom to gather information. This reflected the interests of the US news agencies to secure freedom for foreign correspondents. The fourth is the freedom of reception. This has to be understood as a response to the prohibition of foreign broadcast reception during the war. The fifth is the right to impart information and ideas. This is a recognition of the freedom of distribution in addition to the freedom of expression.

The Article 19 formulation became important guidance when later international documents articulated the freedom of information concern. Important illustrations are the European Convention for the Protection of Human Rights and Fundamental Freedoms (1950), the International Covenant on Civil and Political Rights (1966), the American Convention on Human Rights (1969) and the African Charter on Human and Peoples' Rights (1981).[2]

Following the importance attached to the concern about 'the free flow of ideas' in its constitution, Unesco prepared two multilateral agreements on the circulation and the importation of educational, scientific and cultural materials: the Agreement for Facilitating the International Circulation of Visual and Auditory Materials of an Educational, Scientific and Cultural Character (the Beirut agreement of 1948), and the Agreement on the Importation of Educational, Scientific and Cultural Materials (the Florence agreement of 1950 and the protocol to the Florence agreement of 1977). The Beirut and Florence agreements were intended to promote the implementation of the free flow policy. The Beirut agreement, for example, provided for the exemption of visual and auditory materials of 'an educational, scientific and cultural character' from customs duties, from quantitative import restrictions, and from the need to secure import licences. The agreement was adopted with a small majority, largely owing to conflicting claims to imports of profit making materials. Several countries, notably France, held that the exemptions should only apply to non-profit materials. It was feared by countries such as India that the Beirut agreement provided no protection against the imports of Hollywood-type commercial materials. The Florence agreement both extended the range of materials (to include books and other printed materials) to be exempt and limited the exemption to materials consigned to non-profit making institutions and licensed as such by the importing state.

The free flow of information remained a recurrent concern with Unesco, and in the debates (of the 1970s) on the Third World demand for a new international information order the concern became a leading controversial issue. In particular, under pressure from Third World representatives the free flow concept was broadened to include the notion of balance. In the first years of the freedom of information debates the Third World countries were practically absent or had no common claims to offer. This began to change in the 1970s when Third World nations succeeded in getting Unesco to change the 'free flow of information' formula to the standard of a 'free and balanced flow of information'. This shift first surfaced at a Unesco conference of experts (representing 61 member states) in December 1969 with the recommendation to 'making the flow of visual news in the world more balanced, particularly with regard to providing news coverage to and from, as well as between, developing areas'. The Unesco Mass Media Declaration of 1978 used the concept of a 'free flow and wider and better balanced dissemination of information' and also referred to 'a new equilibrium and greater reciprocity in the flow of information'. These notions represent a reformulation of the earlier 'freedom of information' concept as the basis for a new world information and communication order (NWICO). The Unesco General Conference in Belgrade in 1981 for instance stated in its Resolution 4.19 the following as being among the basic principles of the NWICO: the removal of the internal and external obstacles to a free flow and wider and better balanced dissemination of information and ideas; the plurality of sources and channels of information; the freedom of the press and information; and the freedom of journalists and all professionals in the communication media, a freedom inseparable from responsibility.

In line with the extension of the freedom of information with the notion of balance, a new thinking also emerged that sought to extend the existing provisions into a 'right to communicate'. The discussion on a right to communicate will be treated more extensively in Chapter 11. In the early 1990s freedom of information was highlighted on Unesco's agenda through regional meetings to promote the development of free media. These meetings were held in 1990 in Windhoek, Namibia and in 1992 in Alma Alta. Special attention to the concern about freedom of information has been paid by the CSCE since 1975. In the final act of the CSCE in Helsinki, 1975 a great variety of issues on the CSCE agenda was distributed over three baskets. The first dealt with security matters; the second addressed cooperation in economics, science, technology and environment; and the third covered human rights, information and culture. For the concern on the freedom of information the final act contains the most important provisions in the third basket. The participating states expressed their conviction that 'increased cultural and educational exchanges, broader dissemination of information, contacts between people, and the solution of humanitarian problems will contribute to the strengthening of peace and understanding among peoples and to the spiritual enrichment of the human personality without distinction as to race, sex, language or religion'. In the field of information the participating states acknowledge 'that a wider dissemination of information contributes to the growth of confidence between peoples and therefore emphasizes the essential and influential role of the press, radio, television, cinema and news agencies and of the journalists working in these fields. The participating States aim to facilitate the freer and wider dissemination of information of all kinds, to encourage co-operation in the field of information and the exchange of information with other countries, and to improve the conditions under which journalists from one participating state exercise their profession in another participating state.'

In the Helsinki final act the states decided to continue the multilateral process, and since 1975 a large number of CSCE meetings have taken place. On the freedom of information the following were important: the Ottawa meeting 7 May to 17 June 1985 on human rights and fundamental freedoms (no concluding document); the Cultural Forum 21–5 November 1985 in Budapest (no concluding document); and in particular the Information Forum in London 18 April to 12 May 1989. The latter forum was an exceptional exchange of opinions between diplomats and media professionals. There was no concluding document, but a listing of some 70 proposals for the improvement of the working conditions of media personnel. Freedom of information was also addressed in the Conference on the Human Dimensions of the CSCE, held in three subsequent meetings in Paris (30 May to 23 June 1989), Copenhagen (5–29 June 1990) and Moscow (10 September to 4 October 1991). The final document of the Helsinki follow-up meeting in 1992 stated that the participating states decide that 'under the guidance of the CSO [the Committee of Senior Officials which was established at the Paris summit of November 1990], the Office for Democratic Institutions and Human Rights will organize CSCE Human Dimension seminars which will address specific questions of particular relevance to the Human Dimension and of current political concern.' In order to launch the new CSCE human dimension seminars without delay, the participating states decided that the Office would organize the four following seminars: migration, minority issues, tolerance and free media. All four were to be held before 31 December 1993. The seminar on free media took place in November 1993 in Warsaw, Poland.

The concern for freedom of information has also been on the agenda of the non-governmental organizations. After the Second World War the Cold War caused polarization among the community of professional journalists and the disintegration of their unity. Several Western countries left the IOJ and by 1952 they had decided to set up the new International Federation of Journalists (8 May 1952 at Brussels during the World Congress of Journalists). The constitution adopted by 49 delegates from fourteen countries read in part that IFJ objectives were 'to do all in its power to safeguard the freedom of the press and the freedom of the journalists engaged in their legitimate professional activities, and to preserve the standards of the profession'.

The concern about the freedom of information has been particularly strongly expressed in connection with the protection of journalists on dangerous missions. This issue was raised by a series of killings and kidnappings in countries where conflicts take place and where journalists are unwelcome. In the 1980s countries like El Salvador and Lebanon provided dramatic examples. In 1992 the IFJ reported that 84 journalists were killed in 23 countries.

The need to protect journalists while on perilous missions was put on the agenda of the Unesco International Commission for the Study of Communication Problems (the so-called MacBride Commission). In May 1979 a special seminar was held under the auspices of the Commission for which draft texts were submitted by the Inter-American Association of Broadcasters, the World Press Freedom Committee and the International Press Institute. In its final report (1980) the Commission recommended:

> The professional independence and integrity of all those involved in the collection and dissemination of news, information and views to the public should be safeguarded. However, the Commission does not propose special privileges to protect journalists in the performance of their duties, although journalism is often a dangerous profession. Far from constituting a special category, journalists are citizens of their respective countries, entitled to the same range of human rights as other citizens. One exception is provided in the Additional Protocol to the Geneva Conventions of August 12 1949, which applies only to journalists on perilous missions such as in areas of armed conflict. To propose additional measures would invite the danger entailed in a licensing system since it would require some body to stipulate who should be entitled to claim such protection. Journalists will be fully protected only when everyone's human rights are guaranteed. (Recommendation 50)

The Chairman of the Commission (Sean MacBride) added to the recommendation: 'I consider this paragraph quite inadequate to deal with what is a serious position. Because of the importance of the role of journalists and others who provide or control the flow of news to the media, I urge that they should be granted a special status and protection. I also urge that provisions should be made to enable a journalist to appeal against a refusal of reasonable facilities.' The Commission suggested that further studies should be made for the safeguarding of journalists in the exercise of their profession: 'The possibility might be explored for setting up some mechanism whereby when a journalist is either refused or deprived of his identity card he would have a right of appeal to a professional body, ideally with adequate judicial authority to rectify the position. Such studies should also look into the possibility of the creation of an international body to which a further appeal could be made in the final resort' (International Commission for the Study of Communication Problems, 1980: 274).

In connection with the Commission's recommendation, Unesco convened a consultation with IFJ and IOJ on the protection of journalists on 21–2 January 1980 in Paris. The meeting addressed the definition of a journalist, the protection of journalists on dangerous missions, the protection of journalists on assignments abroad, and the protection of journalists in their home countries. The debate on adequate regulatory measures to protect journalists on dangerous missions remained unresolved, and the fear was expressed that protection implies licensing and control over the profession. The participants of the Voices of Freedom Conference of Independent News Media (organized in 1982 at Talloires, France) stated on the topic of protection for journalists: 'We seek no special protection or any special status and oppose any proposals that would control journalists in the name of protecting them . . . Licensing of journalists by national or international bodies should not be sanctioned.' The professional organizations have recently concentrated their efforts on monitoring and documentation activities. At the initiative of the International Federation of Journalists (1988) an electronic mailbox system has been established that uses the UN's DEIN computer as host and point of exchange. The idea is to use the computer exchange when one organization requests help and information from other organizations in such cases as the detention of a journalist.

The positions
The concern about freedom of information originated in a long-standing philosophical tradition that seeks to protect individual expression against state censorship. Its codification in national legislative instruments began in the eighteenth century; its codification in international instruments took place after the Second World War. In the development of world politics after 1945 the concern was adopted as one of the basic standards to guide the conduct of states. In its development the concern became strongly linked with the defence of the professional rights (of media personnel, in particular journalists) and the commercial interests of corporate information providers. The concern widened in its history from freedom of expression, to freedom of information, to free and balanced flow of information, and to the right to communicate. In essence, there is almost universal support for the need to accommodate the concern.

The concern is largely consensual and its main agents are individual intellectuals, government representatives, institutions of the professional community, and commercial operators. Key motives are based upon the defence of individual human rights, the protection of professional rights, and business interests. The collective consensus on the need to protect freedom of information is challenged by rival claims to the mode of its accommodation. The contending positions can be distinguished as permissive versus restrictive.

The permissive position claims that freedom of information can only be optimally accommodated if there are no restrictions imposed upon its exercise. The classical formulation of this claim is found in the US constitution: 'Congress shall make no law . . .

abridging the freedom of speech.' Also measures to enhance freedom, such as provisions for the protection of journalists on dangerous missions, are considered a potential threat to freedom. The permissive mode argues that all speech is entitled to protection, including commercial speech as in advertising.

The restrictive position claims that no right can be absolute and that freedom should be balanced with a measure of social responsibility. Sovereignty, security and stability need to be protected against an unlimited expression of ideas. Freedom of information has also to be seen in the light of the very real inequalities in access to the world's resources. Without constraints, freedom of information could be the monopoly of commercial and propagandist interests.

The claimants for a more permissive practice included a majority of Western governments, part of the professional community, and the business interest community. The restrictive practice found its constituency among most of the Eastern European and Third World governments, and part of the professional interest NGOs. Both positions were justified by arguments based upon moral and legal norms and preferred conceptions of government. The permissive mode is also defended by arguments based upon professional and economic interests. The restrictive mode uses arguments based upon considerations of national political sovereignty and economic and cultural protectionism.

Prevailing political practice
There is no comprehensive, binding multilateral accord on freedom of information. Efforts in this direction never moved beyond the drafting stage. There are important normative provisions in such instruments as the Universal Declaration of Human Rights and the International Covenant on Civil and Political Rights. There are however no effective procedural provisions on enforcement, although the optional protocol to the ICCPR offers the possibility of individual complaints about violations to the UN Human Rights Committee. On the world level no procedures for redress and remedy have been implemented. There is no International Court of Human Rights comparable to the European Court of Human Rights to which individual citizens have recourse against their own governments. It remains to be seen whether the appointment of a UN Special Rapporteur on Freedom of Expression (1993) will strengthen enforcement of the current norms and standards.

The actual conduct of the major players does not concur with the adopted standards. There is widespread censorship exercised by many states both developing and developed. There is also commer-

cial censorship by private actors. In the international mass media
the economic interests of media 'bosses' often override professional
journalism. There is also widespread professional self-censorship.
There is no effective multilateral cooperation in the area of freedom
of information. There are binding standards but they operate in the
context of weak and largely voluntary agreements.

Media responsibility

The debates on freedom of information have always had an
association with reflections and viewpoints on the social responsibility of the media of mass communication. The key normative
provisions on freedom of information permit freedom of expression
'without fetters', but also bind this to other human rights standards.
The clear recognition of the right to freedom of information as a
basic human right in the Universal Declaration of Human Rights
was positioned in a standard-setting instrument that also asked for
the existence of an international order in which the rights of the
individual can be fully realized (in Article 28). This implies that the
right to freedom of information is linked with the concern for a
responsible use of international media. This linkage laid the basis
for a controversy in which one position emphasized the free
flow principle, whereas another position stressed the social duty
principle.

Already the Unesco constitution, adopted in 1945, contained the
tension between the two approaches. It accepted the principle of a
free exchange of ideas and knowledge, but it also stressed the need
to develop and use the means of communication toward a mutual
understanding among nations and to create an improved factual
knowledge of each other. This could also be seen in the post-war
development of the professional field. The wartime IFJAFC had
(26 March 1946) convened a World Congress of Journalists that was
held at Copenhagen on 3–9 June 1946. This congress was attended
by some 165 delegates from 21 countries. In the invitation letter the
Executive Committee of the IFJAFC indicated among the purposes
of the congress, 'to discuss methods of assuring the freedom of the
press' (Kubka and Nordenstreng, 1986b: 10). The discussions
largely focused on the establishment of a new international professional organization; a provisional constitution was unanimously
adopted and the International Organization of Journalists was
created.

Special attention was given to the debate on the liberty of the
press, and at the end of the congress a statement of principle on the
freedom of the press was adopted: 'The International Congress of

Journalists affirms that freedom of the press is a fundamental principle of democracy and can function only if channels of information and the means of dissemination of news are made available to all' (Kubka and Nordenstreng, 1986b: 115). The statement stressed 'the responsibility of every working journalist to assist by every means in his power the development of international friendship and understanding and instructed the Executive Committee to examine the various codes of professional ethics adopted by national bodies, particularly in respect of any journalist deliberately and knowingly spreading – whether by press or radio or news agencies – false information designed to poison the good relations between countries and peoples'.

The social duty dimension was even more strongly present in the resolution on press and peace, which stated that 'this congress considers the cementing of lasting international peace and security the paramount aim of humanity, and calls upon all the 130,000 members of the IOJ to do their utmost in support of the work of international understanding and co-operation entrusted to the United Nations'. The provisional constitution read, under aims and objectives, Article 2: '(a) Protection by all means of all liberty of the press and of journalism. The defence of the people's right to be informed honestly and accurately. (b) Promotion of international friendship and understanding through free interchange of information.'

As the Cold War was already warming up by 1948 the social duty principle and the free flow principle collided in the early UN debates largely as East–West ideological confrontations. For instance in the General Assembly of 1947 the Yugoslav delegation proposed legislation to 'restrict false and tendentious reports calculated to aggravate relations between nations, provoke conflicts and incite to war'. This was unacceptable to the Western delegations and eventually a compromise text (proposed by France) was adopted that recommended the study of measures 'to combat, within the limits of constitutional procedures, the publication of false or distorted reports likely to injure friendly relations between states' (UNGA Resolution 127(II)).

After 1948 the principles of freedom of information and social responsibility largely followed separate paths and could be found as separate provisions in subsequent standard-setting instruments. Some instruments also linked the two principles, such as the International Covenant on Civil and Political Rights (1966) and the Unesco Mass Media Declaration (1978). Article 19 of the covenant, for example, acknowledges the freedom of information, whereas Article 20 states important restrictions: 'Any war propaganda shall be prohibited by law . . . Any advocacy of national, racial or religious hatred that constitutes incitement to discrimination, hostility or violence shall be prohibited by law.'

The origins of concern with the social responsibility of the mass media are found in the late nineteenth century. They are related to the increasing use of the mass media as instruments of foreign diplomacy and the emergence of journalism as an independent profession in this period. The emergence of the culture of professionalism in Europe stemmed from the rise of the middle class in the eighteenth and nineteenth century. This class resisted the aristocracy and needed emancipatory symbols in this struggle. Such a symbol was the existence of a class of independent professionals. The idea of the independent profession proliferated rapidly in the late nineteenth and early twentieth centuries in such fields as medicine, law and the clergy. Also journalism developed as a profession. For many professions the formulation of an ethical code was the legitimation of autonomy and the recognition of a public status. Out of the development of professionalism grew the ethics of journalism. The first formal ethical code was probably formulated by newspaper publishers in Kansas in 1910. The oldest international code of conduct for journalists was probably the Code of Journalistic Ethics adopted by the first Pan-American Press Conference at Washington in 1926. This code was confirmed in October 1950, in New York, by the Inter-American Press Conference as the guideline for the Inter-American Press Association (IAPA). The IFJ made serious attempts at professional self-regulation through the establishment of the court in 1931 and the adoption of a professional code of honour in 1939. Also other professional organizations adopted principles of conduct, such as the International Union of Press Associations in 1936. In the mid 1920s the International Federation of Journalists asked the League of Nations and the International Labour Office (with the International Association of Journalists accredited to the League) to study the position of journalists throughout the world in respect of their material conditions of work and in terms of professional status and social responsibilities.

After the Second World War the 1948 UN Conference on Freedom of Information at Geneva articulated normative prescriptions for the conduct of the mass media. After the conference the United Nations Sub-Commission on Freedom of Information and of the Press became involved in a very extensive attempt at the formulation and adoption of a professional code of conduct.

In 1950 a group of experts serving on the Sub-Commission drafted an international code of ethics that was sent by the UN

Secretary General to some 500 professional organizations in the mass media field. Based on the replies, which in majority indicated that respondents thought a code would be useful, the Sub-Commission produced a second draft which it submitted (in 1952) to the ECOSOC. In the same year the Council adopted the draft international code of ethics as Resolution 442B(IV). The code proposed that the media should strive towards factual accuracy, desist from wilful slander, plagiarism, calumny, and libel, be responsible and devote themselves to the public interest. The draft international code of ethics was sent to professional associations and mass media enterprises. Commercial organizations such as the Motion Pictures Association of America and the US National Conference of Business Paper Editors had no objections to the code. Also in 1952 the UN General Assembly called upon media professionals to arrange for a conference to elaborate the draft and to discuss its implementation (UNGA Resolutions 635(VII) and 736(VII)). No further action was taken and the proposed code never developed beyond its draft status.

In the 1970s Unesco also entered the debates on journalistic ethics. The organization convened a consultation on ethical principles in 1973 and a consultative meeting with working journalists in 1978.

Discrimination
An important provision in international law that affects the social performance of the mass media concerns discrimination. Article 20 of the International Covenant on Civil and Political Rights contains, in addition to the propaganda provisions, a paragraph that states: 'Any advocacy of national, racial or religious hatred that constitutes incitement to discrimination, hostility or violence shall be prohibited by law.' This was even more strongly formulated in Article 4 of the International Convention on the Elimination of All Forms of Racial Discrimination (adopted as UNGA Resolution 2106A(XX), 21 December 1965). Here 'all dissemination of ideas based upon racial superiority or hatred, incitement to racial discrimination, as well as acts of violence or incitement to such acts against any race or group of persons of another colour or ethnic origin' were declared criminal offences. Essential to these provisions is that states are also required (in Article 4b) to declare illegal any organizations which promote and incite racial discrimination. The Unesco 1978 Declaration on Race and Racial Prejudice in this context specifically mentioned the mass media in Article 5. The declaration provides a strong prescription for media conduct as it urges the 'mass media and those who control or serve them' to 'promote understanding,

tolerance and friendship among individuals and groups and to contribute to the eradication of racism, racial stereotypes, partial, unilateral or tendentious pictures of individuals and of various human groups'. The mass media are also told to be 'freely receptive to ideas of individuals and groups which facilitate communication between racial and ethnic groups'.

The Unesco Mass Media Declaration
The issue of racial discrimination was also addressed in the most extensive regulatory instrument concerning social responsibility in the mass media, the Unesco Mass Media Declaration. This declaration originated from the nineteenth General Conference of Unesco (in 1979 at Nairobi) when there took place a first multilateral discussion about a draft declaration on fundamental principles governing the use of the mass media in strengthening peace and international understanding and in combating war propaganda, racialism and apartheid. The heart of the controversy at that meeting was a proposed Article XII of the draft declaration which stated: 'States are responsible for the activities in the international sphere of all mass media under their jurisdiction.' For many member states this reference to state responsibility suggested the possibility of state control over the mass media. Also the phrasing on 'the use of the mass media' in the title of the draft declaration was deemed unacceptable. In particular for Western member states this meant that standards would be set for the mass media by users, and among those users the state could play a prominent and potentially dangerous role. The draft declaration that was proposed at the nineteenth General Conference had been adopted in 1975 during an experts conference. The Group of Nine EC countries (the Federal Republic of Germany, Denmark, Ireland, Britain, France, Italy, Belgium, Luxembourg and the Netherlands) had walked away in protest from this meeting. For them the text was unacceptable because of its reference to the UNGA Resolution 3379 on Zionism as a form of racism and because of the fact that the state was accorded an important role with regard to the mass media.

During the General Conference of 1976 there were three positions. For the Western countries, Japan and some Latin American countries the draft declaration was totally unacceptable. Several delegations from the East European countries pushed for the adoption of the draft declaration. A group of African and Asian countries supported the draft declaration but did plead for postponement in order to design a new text with better chances for consensus.

The decision taken in Nairobi referred the draft to the Director General and the General Conference invited him 'to hold further broad consultations with experts with a view to preparing a final draft declaration which could meet the largest possible measure of agreement . . . requests the DG to submit such a draft declaration to member states at the end of 1977 or early in 1978 . . . decides to include this item in the agenda of its twentieth session'. It was also decided to establish a commission for 'a comprehensive study on the problems of communication in the modern world'. This became the International Commission for the Study of Communication Problems, usually called after its chairman Sean MacBride, the MacBride Commission.

During the twentieth General Conference of Unesco in 1978 at Paris the amended draft declaration was unanimously adopted as the Declaration on Fundamental Principles Concerning the Contribution of the Mass Media to Strengthening Peace and International Understanding, the Promotion of Human Rights and to Countering Racialism, Apartheid and Incitement to War. The conference also adopted a resolution aiming at practical recommendations concerning the Mass Media Declaration. The resolution proposed the holding of a congress to discuss the application of the declaration and was accepted with 61 votes in favour (the socialist and developing countries), one vote against (Switzerland) and 26 abstainers (all of them Western countries).

During the 1980s there was no follow-up to the declaration. An attempt was made jointly by the leading journalists' bodies, the IFJ and the IOJ, to arrange an international congress to discuss the declaration. Largely owing to the unwillingness to cooperate expressed by FIEJ and IPI, the meeting never took place.

The non-governmental actors
In the non-governmental community the two main professional bodies in journalism did address issues of social responsibility.

The IFJ (founded in 1952) adopted in 1954, at its Second Congress in Bordeaux, an international code of ethics, the Declaration of Principles on the Conduct of Journalists. This Bordeaux declaration stated among its principles: 'The journalist only accepts, professionally, while recognizing the acknowledged right of every country, the jurisdiction of his equals, to the exclusion of any other interference, governmental or other.'

The IOJ adopted, at its various international conferences, resolutions that articulated the organization's concern about journalistic ethics. In 1956 a meeting organized by the IOJ at Helsinki (10–15

June) was attended by 200 journalists from 62 countries who adopted among other resolutions a statement on professional ethics. This read in part:

> The journalist's profession imposes a great moral responsibility on those that exercise it. It demands that he acts in accordance with the aspirations of peoples for peace, mutual understanding and cooperation. Reporting must be truthful and impartial in order to help people understand events taking place in the world and in their countries. A journalist's professional ethics require him to work for a better future for mankind, for peace and for social progress and to oppose war propaganda . . . We believe the ethics of journalism requires every journalist to fight against the distortion of the truth and to oppose all attempts at falsification, misinformation and slander . . . He should support freedom of the press in those countries where it is restricted, should oppose mass communication media monopolies that hamper the discharge of his duty, should protect against the persecution of journalists, their imprisonment, the banning of newspapers and discriminatory press legislation.

The second meeting of journalists organized by the IOJ in Baden-Baden in October 1960 stated: 'We are convinced that professional ethics imply, at the present time, the duty of every journalist not to tolerate the distortion of the truth and to take a stand against all attempts at falsification of information and slander. Each journalist should be aware of the responsibility which rests with him. All journalists should safeguard professional ethics and morality.'

From the Unesco consultative meeting with working journalists in April 1978 in Paris emerged the so-called Consultative Club. This was a network of professional organizations that regularly convened to discuss matters of professional importance, such as ethics. Meetings took place in Mexico City (1980), Baghdad (1982), Prague and Paris (1983), Geneva (1985), Brussels and Sofia (1986), Cairo and Tampere (1987) and Prague (1988). The Club met under Unesco auspices, but without direct involvement of the organization. It also liaised with the ILO and the International Committee of the Red Cross. At the first meeting it was agreed 'to examine possible common grounds for a definition of basic ethical principles of the journalistic profession'. At the second meeting in Mexico this examination produced a draft document that was adopted by the representatives of the attending organizations as the Mexico declaration.[3] The meeting also appointed a working group with the brief to produce a draft international code of ethics. In its preparatory work the working group changed the notion of an international code to a set of ethical principles. It seemed to the group that the concept of a code was more appropriate to national or regional efforts than to an international agreement. The group retained the basic structure of the Mexico declaration and presented a draft at the Prague meeting of 1983. As a result of some reservations expressed by the IFJ it was decided to postpone a final decision on the document till the consultative meeting to be held in late 1983 in Paris. The Paris meeting, after further amendments, decided to adopt the text even in the absence of the IFJ.

The concern with social responsibility has to a large extent addressed the issue of international news provision. This should however not obscure the fact that other media products have also given rise to similar concern. This can be illustrated from the fields of advertising, consumer information and public relations.

When in the late nineteenth century advertising emerged as an industry, it confronted suspicion and opposition. There were accusations of distortion, waste of resources, and the creation of false needs. The establishment of active consumer groups in many countries led to self-regulation of the industry. In many countries national advertising industries developed their own self-regulatory structures and mechanisms. In spite of the fact that advertising is becoming a global business, very little effort has been made to align self-regulatory policies across national borders. Probably the first international attempt was made in 1911 at the Convention of the Associated Advertising Clubs of the World at New York City. This was the Truth in Advertising Resolution. The first comprehensive self-regulatory code was formulated in 1937 by the International Chamber of Commerce (revised in 1973). Among the standards the code sets are: 'All advertising should be legal, decent, honest, and truthful . . . Every advertisement should be prepared with a due sense of social responsibility . . . No advertisement should be such as to impair public confidence in advertising.' The ICC has played a very active role in the past decades to coordinate efforts 'to establish a common ground upon which national systems of marketing self-regulation may be based. It has sought to outline the principles and to encourage business communities in many countries to set up the machinery for their observance' (Neelankavil and Stridsberg, 1980: 7). Efforts at self-regulation have generally been seen by the industry as an attractive way 'to protect both the consuming public against deceptive advertising and themselves against unfair competition on the one hand and overzealous government regulatory bodies on the other' (1980: 2).

At the beginning of the 1980s the effects of the promotion and sales of milk powder as breast feeding substitute, particularly in developing countries, had become an issue for international concern and action. Extensive lobbying on many fronts, through paediatricians, nutritionists, breast feeding action groups, publications (such as *The Baby Killer*) and legal action brought against Nestlé, all assisted the development of a draft International Code on the Marketing of Breastmilk Substitutes proposed in December 1980 by the World Health Organization (WHO). The draft was approved unanimously by the WHO executive board and then adopted by the WHO Assembly at Geneva in May 1981. The vote was 100 to one: the USA opposed the code and claimed that it was 'contrary to the principle of free enterprise'.

The need for guidelines also arose in the field of consumer information. Increasing pressure was mounted by consumer organizations to provide information in a responsible manner. Important steps were the unanimous adoption by the United Nations General Assembly of the Guidelines for Consumer Protection in 1981 and the listing a year later (1982) of products harmful to health and the environment. The increasing concern with consumer information was strongly motivated by accidents due to deficient product information, including instructions for use. It has been estimated that within the EU countries annually there are some 30,000 deaths and 40 million injuries as a result of inadequate information.

As in the advertising field, the world's public relations professionals also felt the need for self-regulation. On 12 May 1965 the General Assembly of the European Public Relations Confederation adopted an international code of ethics at Athens. This so-called code of Athens which has been adopted by all professional PR bodies in the world, provided that all members of the PR profession would observe in the course of their professional duties the moral principles and rules of the Universal Declaration of Human Rights. They would also refrain from 'taking part in any venture or undertaking which is unethical or dishonest or capable of impairing human dignity and integrity'. The preamble of the code refers to the issue of social responsibility by stating that public relations practitioners can substantially help to meet social needs.

The positions
There is no consensus in the world community about the need to set standards for a responsible conduct of information providers. Some actors contest such standards on the grounds that provisions on social responsibility unduly restrict freedom of information and threaten free enterprise. Actors that have promoted the concern have included governments of Eastern European and Third World countries, and to a lesser extent Western countries. Just like the diplomatic community, the professional groups and the business interest groups have been divided on the issue. The major motives for an accommodation of the concerns are based upon the conviction that normative prescriptions for information provisions are

essential to the creation of peaceful and non-aggressive relations between states, peoples, and ethnic and religious groups.

The contending positions on the issue can be separated into the rejection of any kind of regulation, the reference for governmental regulation, and the choice for self-regulation. In general the world community has been very divided on these approaches. The professional community of journalists, for example, has shown different attitudes towards the project of a professional code of conduct.

Prevailing political practice

On the issue of social responsibility no multilateral cooperation was established. Standards have been formulated in such voluntary and weak accords as the Unesco Mass Media Declaration or in the self-regulatory instruments of the professional community.

The Mass Media Declaration A crucial observation about the declaration is that it has little legal significance. Although by themselves declarations have no stronger legal force than recommendations, they are important in international law since they can be forerunners of binding treaties, or can evolve into international customary law. Declarations can also be generally considered as having legal force. There is, however also the possibility that a declaration is too controversial to contribute to international law.[4]

The legal significance of a declaration will largely depend upon whether it is adopted unanimously, is worded in a strong obligatory fashion, is referred to in the debates as important and binding, and is intended to interpret or clarify existing legal principles or rules. On these criteria the record of the Media Declaration is very poor indeed. There was unanimous adoption, but in the explanations of their votes several delegations undermined the legal significance of this unanimous acceptance. Switzerland, Denmark and Austria voiced strong reservations and the Dutch delegation, while congratulating Unesco, stated that 'if it had narrowed its scope to its own interests, it would never have felt the need for an international instrument of this kind'. Also Third World delegates (among others Benin, Indonesia, Jamaica, Nepal, Guinea and Algeria) stated reservations by expressing that they had wanted a more normative instrument. The declaration is not worded in strong obligatory language. It is less prescriptive than other instruments adopted by the international community. The language of the declaration is more liberal than the Unesco constitution, which refers to 'employing the means of mass communication for the ends of peace', or the Universal Declaration of Human Rights, which mentions social duties. The declaration does not seriously interpret or clarify existing legal principles. Consequently, the declaration is not likely to evolve into either a binding treaty or customary law or to be considered legally relevant.

Professional self-regulation   An essential weakness of most self-regulatory professional instruments is that the normative provisions are articulated in terms which are too general and multi-interpretable. An illustration is a formulation such as 'information should be true and correct'. Another problem is that the standards usually address individual behaviour. However, journalism, for example, is practised in large corporate production structures with their own specific demands and rules. The individual is expected to be loyal to the corporate structure of which the moral obligations are not formulated in the code. Other problems are that the definition of professions is often uncertain and the instruments tend to suggest a professional unity that does not exist. There are important differences within the professions in status, power and income. Very critical for the status of self-regulatory codes is that there are usually no disciplinary bodies and procedures through which the enforcement of the normative provisions can be secured.

Concentration of media ownership

The issue of concentration in the provision of information was articulated in 1840 when the author Honoré de Balzac complained that foreign news in France was monopolized by the Agence Havas, the predecessor of the Agence France Press. The first institutional expression of this concern, however, came from the Second Congress of the International Federation of Journalists in 1928. The congress adopted in Dijon (15–18 November) a resolution that stated: 'The congress acknowledges the importance of this phenomenon for the moral and material interests of journalists and requests the national organizations to continue the study of this phenomenon. In this connection it enjoins a special committee of the Federation to follow the development of this phenomenon and to propose immediate measures if necessary.' The phenomenon at stake was the concentration in the printing industry. The IFJ resolution was inspired by the ILO report *Conditions of Work and Life of Journalists* that had been published in the same year. This report pointed to developments in the USA, 'the formation of vast trusts aiming at controlling all or a part of the Press', and it talked about the emergence of 'newspaper kings' just as there are 'steel kings' and 'automobile kings'. With regard to professional journalists employed by these new 'trusts of opinion' the report considered: 'This concentration of the Press, which is already very advanced in the United States and which has begun in Europe, principally in Great Britain, is the subject of anxious comment in the journalists' professional organs. It undoubtedly brings a new element into their life, though one which does not in any way contradict the previous tendencies in the evolution of the Press. Be that as it may, the journalist of our day is dependent on a vast organisation of a more or less industrial type, and this is the power which determines the working and living conditions of journalists.' Concentration in the press was seen in the ILO report as a threat to both the material and the moral conditions of the work of journalists. The freedom that was wrung from the state was now increasingly jeopardized by the industrial organization of the press.

The Second Congress of the International Organization of Journalists (established in 1946 at Copenhagen as the post-war continuation of the earlier International Federation of Journalists) in June 1947 at Prague approved a document entitled *Proposition of IOJ to the Economic and Social Council of the UNO*. In the document the IOJ requested the ECOSOC 'to investigate the tendency towards cartelization and the creation of local monopolies'. Also the draft convention on freedom of information that was formulated at the 1948 UN Conference on Freedom of Information at Geneva contained an article that provided rights to prevent the development of news cartels since this concentration would limit the 'free flow of information'.

In the Unesco debates in the 1970s on a new international information order, concern for concentration was expressed in the report of the MacBride Commission. The report mentioned the threat to the diversity of the press and the labour conditions for journalists. The Unesco General Conference in Belgrade in 1980 stated in its Resolution 4.19 to be among the basic principles of the NWICO the elimination of the negative effects of certain monopolies, public or private, and excessive concentrations.

The large-scale media mergers of the 1980s and early 1990s have given rise to renewed concern about media concentration in many countries. On the international level minimal concern is being expressed, mainly in the European context. In February 1989 the Parliamentary Assembly of the Council of Europe adopted a motion for a resolution on the dangers caused by media concentration for the exercise of freedom of expression and information and for cultural diversity in Council of Europe member states (Document 6021). The resolution referred to 'recent take-overs in the written press and . . . by the rapid development of multi-media ownership at multinational level, inspired by purely economic and financial considerations', and warned that these developments 'are leading to a smaller number of independent publications and to an impoverishment of the cultural diversity in the media'. In September 1992 the European Parliament adopted resolutions which called upon the European Commission to propose regulatory measures to restrict media concentration and to safeguard pluralism. The Commission responded to this in December 1992 with the publication of a green paper entitled *Pluralism and Media Concentration in the Internal Market*. The green paper did not propose specific action; it analysed and considered different options for action, and invited the views of interested parties. The Commission expressed an interest in opinions about three different options it saw as feasible: taking no action; proposing a recommendation to enhance transparency; or proposing the harmonization of national restrictions on media ownership by (a) a Council directive, (b) a Council regulation or (c) a directive or a regulation together with an independent committee.

Media concentration also became an issue on the agenda of the European Commission. The tendency of the Commission has been to balance competition policy against industrial policy. In the perspective of internal European competition, concentration would need regulatory measures against giant mergers. These measures would however be to the advantage of American and Japanese contenders on the world market. A protectionist European industrial policy would therefore need to promote the development of giant European mergers.

The positions
The phenomenon of media concentration is generally acknowledged, but there is no universal concern about its implications. Political, industrial and academic positions on the issue are widely divergent. Scientific research on concentration, for example, tends to focus on the question of effects of media concentration upon media contents. Such research often finds it 'very difficult to demonstrate any link between the two' (McQuail, 1992: 125). This would be relevant if media contents were the core issue. It is however more important to question whether consolidation of media ownership guarantees sufficient independent locations for media workers, enough channels for audience reception and/or access, adequate protection against price controls on oligopolistic markets, and opportunities for newcomers on media markets. Even if the oligopolist could demonstrate quality, fairness, diversity, critical debate, objectivity, investigative reporting, and resistance to

external pressures in his offerings to the marketplace, there would still be reason to provide regulatory correction as the marketplace would effectively be closed for newcomers and thus not constitute a free market.

The players that argue for multilateral regulation of the issue constitute a heterogeneous collective of politicians, academics and professionals. They have a variety of motives for the conclusion of a multilateral accord. There is an interest to protect the labour conditions of employees in the media industries. This motive addresses both employment opportunities and the quality of work in the media. The freedom of the workers in the information market is very dependent upon the strength of the agreements they can negotiate with their employers. Generally, in cases of market concentration the freedom of their professional position is under threat. The need to accommodate the commercial purposes of the company and the political idiosyncrasies of the owners inevitably implies forms of direct and indirect censorship. There is also a constitutional motive. Several US Supreme Court decisions, for example, have claimed that the freedom of the press is undermined because 'the media become so oligopolistic that censorial powers lie in private hands'.

An important motive addresses the extent of independence in information provision and cultural production. Industrial concentration inevitably implies the establishment of power. The large companies are centres of power that are at the same time the subject and the object of media exposure. Moreover, the information industry as a power centre is linked into other circuits of power, such as the financial institutions, the military establishments and the political elite. A specific problem is posed in situations in which mass media that provide news and commentary are part of an industrial conglomerate. The conglomerate may engage in activities that call for critical scrutiny by the media, but which the controlling actors prefer to protect against exposure.[5]

The concern about concentration is also motivated by the threat that oligopolization erodes the diversity of informational and cultural production. In cases where consolidation occurs as vertical integration, meaning that production and distribution are controlled by the same actors, the real danger exists that they will exclusively offer their own products to the market. A common example is the newspaper that as part of a conglomerate places mainly reviews of its own books. The growing influence of institutional investors and commercial interests not genuine to the information sector tends to lead to an emphasis on the profitability of the commodity, rather than on its socio-cultural quality. As a result there is a preference for products that can be rapidly sold on mass markets. An illustration is the tendency among film production companies and recorded music producers to concentrate on 'blockbusters'. This 'Rambo' and 'Madonna' tendency reinforces a homogenization of markets as the less profitable products are avoided.

There are contending positions on the issue of media concentration. The preference for strict regulation clashes with the claim to no regulation at all. The pro-regulation position is defended with the following arguments. Anti-trust legislation in the media field is defensible since concentration diminishes competition and as a consequence there is a negative effect on diversity on the information market. Moreover, anti-cartel measures promote competition, diversity and freedom. Against this position it has often been suggested that mergers lead to stronger companies with more power to protect information freedom. However, mergers are not always successful. They often occur without careful weighing of assets and liabilities. They may be motivated by the personal interests of top management or the short-term interests of small stockholders. On average, out of ten major acquisitions, four or five will be sold again. Often the aims that the merger is expected to achieve are not met. It is quite possible that after the consolidation profits do not increase, market segments do not expand and the innovative potential of the firms may even diminish. As a result of the failed merger, companies may indeed disappear.

Oligopolization in the information industry may also undermine the civil and political fundamental right to freedom of expression. This is the case when concentration actually diminishes the number of channels that citizens can use to express or receive opinions. In oligopolistic markets it becomes easier for the controlling interests to refuse the distribution of certain opinions. It is easier in such situations, for example, to refuse certain forms of advertisement. For oligopolists there is always the tendency to use their market power to raise the costs of purchasing their goods or services after an initial lowering of their prices. This may easily mean that access to information and culture becomes dependent upon the level of disposable income.

It can be attractive for the oligopolist to bring competing products on to the market. This is, for example, quite common in such sectors as cosmetics or detergents. The implication of this intra-firm diversity is that it erects very effective obstacles to the market entry of newcomers. This is important since often a considerable contribution to market diversity originates with new entrants. However, it is true that large firms may support loss making operations by compensating the losses elsewhere in the company accounts. In this way newspapers, for example, that otherwise would have disappeared can be maintained. However, the length of time this compensation will be acceptable to shareholders (and in particular institutional investors) is limited. Moreover, losses accumulate over time and in the medium to longer term the products that are not profitable will have to be removed.

The key arguments against attempts to regulate media concentration are the following. There is no empirical proof that concentration indeed has such negative effects. On the contrary it can be argued that strong consolidated companies can offer much more diversity and can mobilize more independence in their dealings with governments than smaller media. Moreover, strong media can 'rescue' loss making media that otherwise would disappear and thus their contribution to diversity is retained. It is also argued that if there was more competition this would still not guarantee more diversity, as competitors may all try with a similar product to reach the largest share of the market. Even if regulatory measures against industrial consolidation were successful in stimulating more competition, there would be no guarantee of more product diversity. Markets tend inevitably towards identical, though marginally distinct, products since of necessity they address the largest possible number of buyers. A problem is that allowing competition in the marketplace does not necessarily lead to more diversity. There is some evidence that the deregulated, competitive broadcast systems of West European countries reflect less diversity in content than the formerly regulated, public monopolies. This is largely due to the fact that in a competitive market the actors all try to control the largest segment by catering to the rather similar tastes and preferences of that market segment.

Prevailing political practice
After over 60 years the IFJ Commission has still to fulfil its task. Only a few countries have today some form of regulation in connection with media concentration. By and large policies in industrial countries have promoted concentration rather than hindered it.

Governments of such countries as the USA, the UK, Germany and France have in general been benevolent towards large corporations and they have often been willing to exempt the mass media from any measures against cartels they might have enacted. The Motion Pictures Export Association in the USA, for instance, has been organized as a legal cartel and under the so-called Webb-Pomerone Export Trade Act of 1918 it has been exempted from the anti-monopoly provisions of the Sherman Act (1890) and the Clayton Act (1914). The MPEA can thus 'act as the sole export sales agent for its members, set prices and terms of trade for sale of its members' products abroad, and make arrangements for the distribution of these products in overseas markets' (Guback, 1969: 92).

In conclusion it can be said that there is a basic discord in the world community on the issue of concentration of media ownership. There are very divergent positions on the issue and the most powerful players see no need for multilateral regulation to control their operations. The actual conduct of these players clearly demonstrates the trend towards further concentration. Recent events such as the merger between Paramount and ViaCom provide the evidence of this trend.

Trade in media services

The trading of media services has become global business in an expanding and profitable market. *The Economist* has predicted (29 February 1992: 15) that by 2000 the international media market could reach the US $3 trillion mark. This expanding market is to a large extent due to the concurrent processes of deregulation of broadcasting and the commercialization of media institutions. These developments imply a growing demand for entertainment. The related important process is globalization, in terms of markets but also in terms of products and ownership.

There is world-wide an increasing demand for American entertainment. As *Fortune* magazine (31 December 1990) recently observed: 'Around the globe, folks just can't get enough of America.' A remarkable feature of this trend is that Europeans and Japanese are buying into this successful export commodity. Of the global record companies, Warner, CBS, EMI and Polygram, only Warner is an American corporation. A similar trend is showing in the film industry. The Japanese invested in the early 1990s some US $12 billion in the US entertainment companies. In November 1990 Japanese hardware manufacturer Matsushita bought MCA for US $6 billion and acquired with this purchase Universal Studios, Universal Pictures and MCA Records. In early 1991 Paramount Communications negotiated with interested Japanese companies (Pioneer and Sumitomo). Also the Disney company formed a partnership with Japanese investors, among which were Yamaichi Securities and Fuji Bank. By late 1990 an initial US $600 million was provided for film financing.

With these developments the centre of US film production, Hollywood, has begun to globalize. Feature film production had to take serious account of the growing international demand for entertainment products as a result of the proliferation of commercial TV stations. Joint ventures have been initiated between Hollywood firms and co-producers from Japan and the Soviet Union. Foreign investors have acquired traditional US film 'majors', such as Twentieth Century Fox (acquired in 1985 by Rupert Murdoch's News Corporation) and Columbia Pictures (purchased by Japanese Sony in 1989 for US $3.4 billion). Australian and Italian entrepreneurs have been battling over the acquisition of MGM/UA.

The very big media companies have outgrown their saturated home markets and the logical direction for further growth is cross-border expansion. In particular West European and Japanese firms entered the US market loaded with cash from very stable and profitable revenues.[6] An important feature of the trend towards globalization is that the trading by the giant companies is shifting from the international exchange of local products to production for global markets.

Concerns with regard to the world market in media services have been recently expressed in connection with the current Uruguay Round of multilateral trade negotiations. The special focus of these concerns is TV programmes and films and the existing and/or potential constraints to trading them across the world. The concerns focus on forms of national regulation that restrict imports of media services or national policies that protect national media industries. There are however also concerns about trade constraints that address the structure of the international media market, particularly with reference to the large share of market control by only a few transnational operators.

The world's largest exporter of films, the USA, has confronted protectionist measures in its largest export markets since its early beginnings. In Europe, for instance, the massive invasion of American films in the early 1920s caused restrictive measures, first by Germany, later by France and the UK. After the Second World War, with massive imports of US-made films, worries rose in European countries about the protection of national film production and about their balance of payments. These worries motivated measures of import control that largely worked along two lines. The number of imported films was limited (so-called number quotas) and screen time was shared between foreign and domestic films (so-called screen quotas). These protectionist policies changed in the 1960s when US exports declined, the European film industry became stronger, a strong trend towards trade liberalization emerged in Europe, and several co-production and co-investment schemes for film production developed between European markets and the US film industry.

The most active player in the search for solutions to the concern about trade constraints has been the US Motion Picture Export Association. The MPEA has sought unilateral US trade sanctions against countries that raised trade barriers to US produced films, television programmes and home videos. In 1989 the MPEA filed complaints to the US Trade Representative quoting Section 301 of the US Trade Act.[7] It has targeted for retaliatory trade restrictions such countries as Brazil, Colombia, India, Indonesia, the Republic of Korea and Taiwan. Among the retaliatory actions proposed by the MPEA were restrictions on imports of textiles and electronics. The MPEA has identified various non-tariff trade barriers and has considered a lack of adequate intellectual property protection the most serious barrier to free world trade.[8]

In September 1993 the French audiovisual industry took the initiative to protest against the inclusion of audiovisual products in the final text of the GATT Uruguay Round multilateral trade talks. In these negotiations, the USA demanded that the world trade in AV products follow the principles of free trade policy. This would imply that a variety of protectionist measures (such as national import quotas and state subsidies) which are common in European countries would have to be abandoned. Representatives of the French entertainment sector (with the support of the EU ministers of culture) claimed that only removing AV products from GATT rules could save the European film and entertainment industry. An appeal signed by over 4000 professionals in the industry accused the USA of 'cultural dumping'. In the European protest against GATT rules for audiovisual services, important economic interests were at stake. Some 80 per cent of the European AV market is controlled by US producers. The sales of US TV programmes in Europe have increased from US $330 million in 1984 to US $3.6 billion in 1992. In 1991 some 77 per cent of US AV exports went to the European market and this market grows at an annual 6 per cent. It can be expected that the introduction of more advanced AV technology will only lead to more channel capacity and thus more demand. A strong lobby against what was perceived as European protectionism was represented by the Motion Picture Association President Jack Valenti and film producer Steven Spielberg. Part of the disagreement was about the wish of the European Union to use a proportion of box office income to subsidize European films and the rule that at least 51 per cent of TV programmes in Europe should be of

European origin. The European industry expressed as its position that the application of free trade rules would promote the global spread of Hollywood materials and would effectively annihilate European culture.

The positions
Perspectives on the issue of traded media services diverge. Some players claim that this trade should be unhindered and that foreign markets should be freely accessed. Others are concerned that without restrictions on media imports, local cultural industries cannot survive and local cultural heritage gives way to McDonald-ization. The leading media production companies, their associations such as the MPEA, and the governments of exporting countries (especially the USA) have been very concerned about barriers to media trade. The concern about the lack of controls is largely articulated by small producers and by governments of importing countries (Third World countries, West European countries, Canada). Their preference for import restrictions is largely moti-vated by the desire to economically and culturally protect their own media industries. This is reinforced by the fear that transnational control over local distribution and exhibition mechanisms will exert a decisive influence on what cultural product is locally available.

The contending positions are liberal-permissive claims versus protectionist-restrictive claims. The liberal position prefers an arrangement that permits total liberalization of market access for media services. The more protectionist position favours levels of protection from media imports as instruments to support local media industries or protect local culture.

One of the complexities of addressing media services in a trade context is that not all of them have commercial purposes. A part of mass media production is typically oriented towards non-commercial, educational, artistic or socio-cultural goals. Although this is recognized in Article IV of the GATT,[9] the big media exporters define their product in terms of a commercial commodity only. This implies the collision of the claim to the opportunity to increase markets for a profitable commodity with the claim to rightfully regulate media imports and protect national media markets for a variety of reasons.

For developing countries a problem with the liberalization claim is also that since media products are finished products, it is not likely that liberalization will increase labour or technology inputs for them. In contrast to tourism, for instance, media services do not bring employment or training. There is also the problem that market access is likely to be a one-way street. There is, given the economic realities of media production and distribution, little chance of exports from the Third World countries.

Prevailing political practice

At present it looks as if the most likely provisions to emerge for the world trade in media services are GATT rules pertaining to traded services and intellectual property rights. The emerging practice of multilateral trade cooperation will be based upon a binding and robust GATT accord. There is, however, a question as to the appropriateness of such an arrangement, given the distinctions between media services and services at large:

> Firstly, the production of a film or television programme resembles manufacturing. There is an actual physical product, composed of labour – and capital-intensive inputs. So, in comparison with services such as tourism or construction where employment occurs and value is added at the final destination of the service, films and television programmes are finished products which are merely distributed at their final destination. The distancing of production and distribution in these industries virtually eliminates possibilities for technology transfer or highly skilled employment at the point of distribution. In comparison with some services in which developing countries could compete on the basis of a comparative labour-cost advantage, the production of media products is organized in such a way that almost all labour inputs and certainly all skilled labour inputs occur in centralized locations far removed from the distribution point. Secondly, all the costs in making the product are incurred in turning out the first copy of the film or the television programme. Additional copies can be produced very inexpensively. So, profitability in this sector depends on timing and strategic control of the release of the film or programme, a process that has become more complicated as the number of different types of potential distribution outlets has multiplied worldwide. This constraint on potential profit intensifies the need to control distribution very tightly, for example, ownership of distribution networks. (Christopherson and Ball, 1989: 250–1)

A complication is also that film and TV programmes are both goods and services. The contents may be transmitted in tangible formats, but also through intangible media such as airwaves. Moreover, as several studies have noted, it is very difficult to measure in any reliable manner the actual trade volume (Guback, 1969; Widman and Siwek, 1988).

It also remains to be seen whether a GATT arrangement would permit certain trade barriers in the light of cultural policies. This is allowed in the OECD Code of Liberalization of Current Invisible Operations (Annex IV to Annex A) which provides that: 'For cultural reasons, systems of aid to the production of printed films for cinema exhibition may be maintained provided that they do not significantly distort international competition in export markets.'

The GATT accord that was concluded in mid December 1993 did not include the sector of audiovisual services. The most powerful players were divided among themselves and clashed on a free trade perspective promoted by the USA and a cultural policy perspective defended by the EU. The discord is only of marginal significance. There is no basic disagreement among the opponents about the commercial nature of culture and information as marketable commodities. European politics has already for some time established that broadcasting, for example, is a traded service and is subject to the rules on market competition of the EEC treaty. The European claim to exempt culture from international trade rules is not motivated by deep principles. In the bargaining at some point a deal will be made and a trade agreement will emerge. This will also be facilitated since protectionism is not a feasible proposition. The owners of satellite dishes cannot be stopped from receiving US audiovisual fare if they want to do so.

For the time being, the major players have agreed to disagree. However, in February 1994 both key US actors (such as the MPEA) and the European Commission indicated a desire to reconcile their divergent positions on the issue of traded media services.

Notes

1 Ratifications by Cuba, Cyprus, Egypt, El Salvador, Ethiopia, France, Guatemala, Jamaica, Sierra Leone, Uruguay, Yugoslavia.

2 The European Convention for the Protection of Human Rights and Fundamental Freedoms, 1950, Article 10: 'Everyone has the right to freedom of expression. This right shall include freedom to hold opinions and to receive and impart information and ideas without interference by public authority and regardless of frontiers. This article shall not prevent States from requiring the licensing of broadcasting, television or cinema enterprises.'

The International Covenant on Civil and Political Rights, 1966, Article 19: '1. Everyone shall have the right to hold opinions without interference. 2. Everyone shall have the right to freedom of expression; this right shall include freedom to seek, receive and impart information and ideas of all kinds, regardless of frontiers, either orally, in writing or in print, in the form of art, or through any other media of his choice.'

The American Convention on Human Rights, 1969, Article 13: 'Everyone has the right of freedom of thought and expression. This right includes freedom to seek, receive and impart information and ideas of all kinds, regardless of frontiers, either orally, in writing or in print, in the form of art, or through any other media of one's choice.'

The African Charter on Human and Peoples' Rights, 1981, Article 9: '1. Every individual shall have the right to receive information. 2. Every individual shall have the right to express and disseminate his opinions within the law.'

3 Participating professional organizations were the International Organization of Journalists, the Latin American Federation of Journalists, the International Catholic

Union of the Press, the Latin American Federation of Press Workers, the Federation of Arab Journalists, the Union of African Journalists and the Confederation of ASEAN Journalists.

4 Examples of the various categories of declarations are as follows. Declarations that are forerunners of binding treaties: (1) the Declaration of Legal Principles Governing the Activities of States in the Exploration of Outer Space, UN General Assembly, 1963, which led to the Treaty on Principles Governing the Activities of States in the Exploration and Use of Outer Space, including the Moon and other Celestial Bodies, 1967; (2) the Declaration on the Elimination of Discrimination against Women, UN General Assembly, 1967, which led to the Convention on the Elimination of all Forms of Discrimination against Women, 1979.

Declarations that evolve into international customary law: the Universal Declaration of Human Rights, UN General Assembly, 1948.

Declarations generally referred to as binding and legally significant: the Declaration on the Granting of Independence to Colonial Countries, UN General Assembly, 1960.

Declarations which are too controversial to contribute to international law: Declaration on the Establishment of a New International Economic Order, UN General Assembly, 1974.

5 The close interlocks between the US media and the military contractors have been suggested to have contributed to the partisan way in which the Gulf War was reported. The National Broadcasting Corporation (one of the three leading US networks) is owned by General Electric. 'As it turns out, GE designed, manufactured or supplied parts or maintenance for nearly every important weapons system employed by the USA during the Gulf War, including the much-praised Patriot and Tomahawk cruise missiles, the Stealth bomber, the B-52 bomber, the AWACS plane, the Apache and Cobra helicopters and the NAVSTAR spy satellite system. Few TV viewers in the USA were aware of the inherent conflict of interest whenever NBC correspondents and consultants hailed the performance of US weapons. In nearly every instance, they were extolling equipment made by GE, the corporation that pays their salaries' (Lee, 1991: 29). As a former NBC employee observed: 'The whole notion of freedom of the press becomes a contradiction when the people who own the media are the people who need to be reported on' (1991, 29). It could be argued that the core of a democratic society is the presence of a public debate about the distribution and execution of power. It is crucial for democratic arrangements that choices made by the power holders are publicly scrutinized and contested. In the public debate the informational and cultural products play a significant role. If the interests of the information and culture producers and the powers that be are intertwined, a society's capacity for democratic government is seriously undermined.

6 A good illustration is the French publishing giant Hachette, which in 1988 bought the magazine group Diamandis in the US. Hachette now owns 74 magazines in ten countries with a total circulation of some 650 million copies. Also the German group Bertelsmann has expanded into the US market with the purchase of publisher Doubleday and record company RCA Records in 1986.

7 In 1988 amendments were introduced in the provisions of the US Trade and Competitiveness Act. Some of these, commonly referred to as 'Super 301' and 'Special 301', sanction more forceful steps in trade negotiations between the USA and trading partners. Under these provisions the USTR has to identify trade practices that should be eliminated in order to secure US trading interests. If such practices are identified an investigation starts to establish whether they constitute

unreasonable, unjustifiable or discriminatory restrictions to US trade. If the investigation indicates this to be the case and bilateral negotiations do not lead to concessions, the USTR may employ the threat of retaliation which usually amounts to the announcement that imports from the offending country will be restricted. If this fails the retaliation may be effectuated. Through this instrument the USTR can coercively bring countries to concessions. As Raghavan remarks, 'The US is thus negotiating with its trading partners while holding a gun at their heads – the threat of unilateral trade restrictive measures, if they do not yield' (1990: 88). The USA has used threats of retaliation against Japan, Brazil and India. In connection with the TRIPs negotiations in the GATT Uruguay Round, several countries were put on a so-called 'watch list'. Among them were Argentina, Canada, Chile, Colombia, Egypt, Greece, Indonesia, Italy, Malaysia, Pakistan, Philippines, Portugal, Spain, Turkey, Venezuela and Yugoslavia.

8 Other barriers identified by the MPEA are: theft of film prints; pirated videocassettes that reach large shares of markets; theft of broadcast signals, for example the receiving of satellite signals by unlicensed stations; screen quota in theatres; quantitative restrictions on exhibitions of imported materials, e.g. prescribing a number of exhibition days for foreign films; quantitative restrictions on TV programmes; restrictions on the imports of films; local theatrical printing requirement or dubbing requirements in local language; restrictions on home videocassette distribution; discriminatory taxes on foreign films; remittance of earnings restrictions; inability to open distribution offices; censorship measures; or even insufficient supplies of blank cassettes and video recorders.

9 Article IV of the General Agreement deals with special provisions relating to cinematograph films. It rules that quantitative restrictions of films should take the form of screen quotas. For such quotas it determines some specific requirements.

6

Culture

Although the area of culture has been considered 'low politics' for a long time, culture has begun to acquire agenda status in world politics. Over the past decades cultural diplomacy has been adopted as 'the third pillar of foreign policy' (Willy Brandt in Mitchell, 1986: 1). Today most countries have established cultural accords (often bilateral) as a common component of their foreign relations. Culture is often expected to contribute to peace, to improve political relations among countries, to reduce the stereotyped images that people may hold about each other, and to promote trade between countries. In cultural diplomacy states use culture deliberately as an instrument to promote their interests.

The first systematic organization of cultural diplomacy was probably initiated by the French. Beginning with the cultural expansionism of such kings as Louis XIII (1610–43) and Louis XIV (1643–1715), France managed to make its language the dominant diplomatic and scholarly language of eighteenth and nineteenth century Europe. In the early twentieth century France established its educational institutions abroad; this example was followed by many other countries, among them Britain, Germany and Italy. Until 1945 most cultural diplomacy was unilateral or bilateral; multilateral politics in the field of culture emerged only after the Second World War. The first multilateral forum for collective cultural diplomacy was Unesco, established in 1945. Its constitution (1945) commences with the notion that 'wars begin in the minds of men' and therefore 'it is in the minds of men that the defences of peace must be constructed'. Among these mental defences of peace are the 'wide diffusion of culture' and the cultural relations among the peoples of the world. On this basis Unesco is committed to the spread, the protection, the development and the diversity of culture.

The spread of culture

For the implementation of its mandate the Unesco General Conference adopted in 1948 and 1950 multilateral agreements on the circulation and import of cultural materials. In 1948 the so-called

Beirut convention was adopted, the Agreement for Facilitating the International Circulation of Visual and Auditory Materials of an Educational, Scientific and Cultural Character. The key provision of the agreement is that each of the contracting states shall accord 'exemption from all customs duties and quantitative restrictions and from the necessity of applying for an import licence in respect of the importation, either permanent or temporary, of material originating in the territory of any of the other contracting States'.

The 1950 so-called Florence agreement, the Agreement on the Importation of Educational, Scientific and Cultural Materials, stated that the contracting states shall not levy customs duties or other charges on the importation of books, publications, documents and educational, scientific and cultural materials as listed in the annexes to the convention. The contracting states also accepted to grant the necessary licences and/or foreign exchange for the importation of a variety of cultural materials. In 1976 a protocol to the Florence agreement was adopted that extends the materials listed in the annexes especially in the light of the needs and concerns of the developing countries.

In 1976 the Unesco General Conference adopted a recommendation on the international exchange of cultural property. The recommendation urges states to adopt measures to develop the circulation of cultural property among cultural institutions in different countries. The basic rationale for this is the consideration that the extension and promotion of cultural exchanges contribute to the enrichment of the cultures involved. The circulation of cultural property is seen as a powerful means of promoting mutual understanding and appreciation among nations.

The right to culture

The International Bill of Rights (UDHR, IECSR, ICCPR) proposed to articulate entitlements in the area of culture as basic human rights. The Universal Declaration of Human Rights (1948) formulated the right to culture in the sense of participation in cultural life. Article 27 provided: 'Everyone has the right freely to participate in the cultural life of the community.' Article 22 of UDHR stated that everyone is entitled to realization through national effort and international cooperation of the economic, social and cultural rights indispensable for their dignity and the free development of their personalities.

Participation in cultural life has raised difficult questions about the definition of communities, the position of subcultures, the protection of participation rights of minorities, the provision of physical resources of access, and the links between cultural access and socio-economic conditions. Underlying some of these difficulties is the tension between the concept of culture as public good or as private property. These positions can be mutually exclusive when historical works of art disappear into the vaults of private collections.

The inclusive nature of human rights ('everyone') implies a shift away from an elite conception of culture to a view of culture as 'common heritage'. In fact, the Unesco Declaration on Racial Prejudice (1978, General Conference Resolution 3/1.1/2) founded the right to culture on the notion of culture as 'common heritage of mankind', which implies that all people 'should respect the right of all groups to their own cultural identity and the development of their distinctive cultural life within the national and international context' (Article 5). The right to culture thus implies, beyond participation in cultural life, the protection of cultural identity, the need to conserve, develop and diffuse culture, and the need for international cultural cooperation.

In 1968 a Unesco conference of experts considered the question of cultural rights as human rights (Paris, 8–13 July 1968). A statement of the conference was: 'The rights to culture include the possibility for each man to obtain the means of developing his personality, through his direct participation in the creation of human values and of becoming, in this way, responsible for his situation, whether local or on a world scale' (Unesco, 1970: 107). The Intergovernmental Conference on the Institutional, Administrative and Financial Aspects of Cultural Policies (convened by Unesco in 1970) decided that the right to participate in the cultural life of the community implies the duty for governments to provide the effective means for this participation.

A series of regional conferences on cultural policies (in 1972, 1973 and 1975) provided important inputs into the formulation of a Unesco recommendation on participation by the people at large in cultural life and their contribution to it (approved 26 November 1976). The recommendation aims to 'guarantee as human rights those rights bearing on access to and participation in cultural life'. The recommendation questions the concentration of control over the means of producing and distributing culture. Regarding the mass media, the text states that they should not threaten the authenticity of cultures and 'they ought not to act as instruments of cultural domination'. The preamble proposes that measures are taken 'against the harmful effect of "commercial mass culture" ' and recommends that governments 'should make sure that the criterion of profit-making does not exert a decisive influence on cultural activities'. There was strong Western opposition to various elements of the recommendation, such as the mention of commercial mass culture in a negative sense, and the use of the term 'people at large'. In the preparatory meetings and during the Unesco General Conference several Western delegations expressed their concern that the recommendation if implemented would restrict the free flow of information and the independence of the mass media. The strongest opponent was the USA. 'The USA asserted a belief from the outset that access to and participation in cultural life were not fit subjects for international regulation, took minimal part in the drafting process, sent no delegation to the intergovernmental meeting, urged the General Conference to turn down the proposed text and, after its adoption, announced that it had no intention of transmitting the Recommendation to the relevant authorities or institutions in the USA' (Wells, 1987: 165). The Western countries were against, although to a lesser extent; the developing countries and Eastern European countries supported the text. In the drafting process there was little input from the cultural industries. The vote was 62 for, five against and fifteen abstentions.

The preamble refers to the UDHR, the Unesco constitution and the Declaration of Principles of International Cultural Cooperation, and considers cultural development as a true instrument of progress. The recommendation links participation in cultural life with access to culture and claims that 'access by the people at large to cultural values can be assured only if social and economic conditions are created that will enable them not only to enjoy the benefits of culture, but also to take an active part in overall cultural life and in the process of cultural development'. It is recommended that member states 'guarantee as human rights those rights bearing on access to and participation in cultural life . . . provide effective safeguards for free access to national and world cultures by all members of society . . . pay special attention to women's full entitlement to access to culture and to effective participation in cultural life . . . guarantee the recognition of the equality of cultures, including the culture of national minorities and of foreign minorities'. Regarding the mass media the recommendation states that they 'should not threaten the authenticity of cultures or impair their quality; they ought not to act as instruments of cultural domination but serve mutual understanding and peace'. Member states and appropriate authorities should 'promote the active participation of audiences by enabling them to have a voice in the selection and production of programmes, by fostering the creation of a permanent flow of ideas between the public, artists and producers and by encouraging the establishment of production centres for use by audiences at local and community levels', and should 'encourage media to pay special attention to the protection of national cultures from the potentially harmful influence of some types of mass production'.

This line of thought was reinforced by the 1982 World Conference on Cultural Policies held in Mexico City. The Declaration on Cultural Policies adopted by the conference reaffirmed the requirement that states must take appropriate measures to implement the right to cultural participation. In Recommendation 28 on cultural rights the conference participants claimed that governments should take measures 'to strengthen the democratization of culture by means of policies that ensure the right to culture and guarantee the participation of society in its benefits without restriction'. An assessment of the implementation of the recommendation on participation in cultural life in 1985–6 showed that little had been done by many states and that these issues remained relevant.

Several factors explain the emergence of cultural rights in the era after the Second World War. There was the rise of post-colonial states who searched for their identity in the light of both imposed colonial standards and their own traditional values. The issue of cultural identity came up particularly strongly in the process of decolonization. The newly independent states saw the affirmation of their cultural identity as an instrument in the struggle against foreign domination. In their earlier battle with colonialism cultural identity had played a significant role in motivating and legitimizing the liberation movement.

The proliferation of the mass media confronted the risks of cultural uniformity with the possibilities of unprecedented cultural interaction. The spread of a consumer society raised serious questions about the uniformity of a 'world culture'.

Protection of cultural identity

The protection of cultural identity became a particularly hot issue during the 1970s debates on cultural imperialism. In 1973 the non-aligned summit at Algiers stated: 'it is an established fact that the activity of imperialism is not limited to political and economic domains, but encompasses social and cultural areas as well, imposing thereby a foreign ideological domination on the peoples of the developing world.'

Cultural domination and the threat to cultural identity were also treated by the MacBride Commission. The Commission saw cultural identity 'endangered by the overpowering influence on and assimilation of some national cultures though these nations may well be the heirs to more ancient and richer cultures. Since diversity is the most precious quality of culture, the whole work is poorer' (International Commission for the Study of Communication Problems, 1980: 31). In its recommendations the Commission offered very little prospect for a multilateral approach to the issue of cultural domination. Its main recommendation was for the establishment of national policies 'which should foster cultural identity . . . Such policies should also contain guidelines for safeguarding national cultural development while promoting knowledge of other cultures' (1980: 259). No recommendation was proposed on what measures the world community might collectively take. The Commission proposed the strengthening of cultural identity and promoted conditions for the preservation of the cultural identity, but left this to be implemented on the national level.[1]

More recently, the South Commission addressed the issue of cultural identity. According to its report, the concern with cultural identity 'does not imply rejection of outside influences. Rather, it should be a part of efforts to strengthen the capacity for autonomous decision-making, blending indigenous and universal elements in the service of a people-centred policy' (South Commission, 1990: 132). The Commission urged governments to adopt cultural development charters which articulate people's basic rights in the field of culture. Cultural policies should stress the right to culture, cultural diversity and the role of the state in preserving and enriching the cultural heritage of society (1990: 133).

Cultural exchange and cooperation

The Unesco General Conference adopted in 1966 (Resolution 8.1) a Declaration of the Principles of International Cultural Cooperation. The declaration refers in its preamble to the Unesco constitution and its emphasis on the wide diffusion of culture and to a variety of human rights instruments. It clearly states the human rights standards in connection with culture in Article I: 'Each culture has a dignity and value which must be respected and preserved. Every people has the right and the duty to develop its culture.' Among the aims of cultural cooperation the declaration mentions 'to enrich cultures, and to enable everyone to contribute to the enrichment of cultural life'. Cultural cooperation, which is seen as both a right and a duty for all peoples and all nations, is expected to contribute to the establishment of stable, long-term relations between peoples.

In a similar spirit the CSCE final act of Helsinki (1975) contains fairly elaborate provisions on cultural cooperation and exchange. In the part of the act dealing with humanitarian issues the participating states consider that cultural exchanges and cooperation contribute to a better comprehension among people and among peoples, and thus promote a lasting understanding among states. The states undertake to increase substantially their cultural exchanges in the conviction that this will contribute to the enrichment of their respective cultures. They declare to set themselves the following objectives: 'To develop the mutual exchange of information with a view to a better knowledge of respective cultural achievements. To improve the facilities for the exchange and for the dissemination of cultural property. To promote access by all to respective cultural achievements. To develop contacts and co-operation among persons active in the field of culture. To seek new fields and forms of cultural co-operation.'

Protection of cultural heritage, cultural property, return or restoration of cultural property

The United Nations General Assembly adopted in 1973 a resolution (UNGA Resolution 3148(XXVIII)) on the preservation and further development of cultural values. The resolution considers the value and dignity of each culture as well as the ability to preserve and develop its distinctive character as a basic right of all countries and peoples. In the light of the possible endangering of the distinctive character of cultures the preservation, enrichment and further development of national cultures must be supported. It is important that the resolution recognizes that 'the preservation, renewal and continuous creation of cultural values should be not a static but a dynamic concept'. It is recommended to the Director General of Unesco to promote research that analyses 'the role of the mass media in the preservation and further development of cultural values'. The resolution also urges governments to promote 'the involvement of the population in the elaboration and implementation of measures ensuring preservation and future development of cultural and moral values'.

A specialized instrument on the protection of the world cultural heritage was adopted by the seventeenth session of the Unesco General Conference in 1972. This was the Convention for the Protection of the World Cultural and Natural Heritage. The text noted that the world's cultural heritage is threatened, that this impoverishes the world and that effective provisions are needed to collectively protect the cultural heritage of outstanding universal value. In the convention the international protection of the world cultural heritage is understood to mean 'the establishment of a system of international cooperation and assistance designed to support States parties to the Convention in their efforts to conserve and identify that heritage'.

On the protection of cultural property, the world community has also adopted through Unesco the Hague Convention for the Protection of Cultural Property in the Event of Armed Conflict (1954), the Convention on the Means of Prohibiting and Preventing the Illicit Import, Export and Transfer of Ownership of Cultural Property (1970), and the Convention on the Protection of the World Cultural and Natural Heritage (1972). In 1973 the United Nations General Assembly adopted on its agenda the issue of restitution of works of art to countries that are the victims of expropriation. UNGA Resolution 3187(XXVIII) of 18 December 1973 sees prompt restitution of works of art as strengthening international cooperation and as a just reparation for damage done. To implement this, Unesco established the Intergovernmental Committee for Promoting the Return of Cultural Property to its Countries of Origin or its Restitution in Case of Illicit Appropriation. Throughout the 1980s the United Nations General Assembly stressed the issue, commended the work of Unesco done in this field and called upon member states to ratify the relevant convention. In 1986 the General Assembly proclaimed that the 1988–97 period would be the World Decade for Cultural Development. The objectives for the decade were formulated as the acknowledgement of the cultural dimension of development, the enrichment of cultural identities, the broadened participation in cultural life and the promotion of international cultural cooperation (UNGA Resolution 41/187, 8 December 1986).

Other approaches of the world community to the protection of cultural property include the safeguarding of traditional culture and folklore. In 1989 the General Conference of Unesco adopted a recommendation that stressed the need to recognize the role of folklore and the danger it faces. Folklore is defined as the totality of tradition-based creations of a cultural community. The recommendation urges measures for the conservation, preservation, dissemination and protection of folklore.

The position of cultural workers

In 1980 the Unesco General Conference adopted a recommendation on the status and position of artists. This instrument deals with the problems of artists in a context of very powerful cultural industries and important changes in the media of reproduction and distribution. Initially the drafting of regulations on artists was opposed by Western delegations. They argued that the freedom of the artist would be threatened by state regulation. Also some of the NGO lobbies such as the International Federation of Producers of Phonograms and Videograms opposed the recommendation. Others in the NGO community such as the International Federation of Musicians, the International Federation of Authors and Composers and the International Federation of Actors were in support of efforts to improve the status of artists as cultural workers. 'The NGOs concerned were repeatedly to stress their support for urgent adoption of an international instrument; and in so doing were also regularly to proclaim not only the duties of industry towards artists, but their own readiness to accept reference to artistic responsibility' (Wells, 1987: 168). The initial Western opposition mellowed, with the result that Western amendments weakened the text so that consensus adoption became possible. The Soviet bloc was in favour of regulation (although it wanted a somewhat stronger instrument) but went along with Western preferences, as did the Third World which was supportive although not satisfied with the level of attention to artists and culture in developing countries.

The positions
The major issues in connection with culture focus on the diffusion of culture, international cultural cooperation, the preservation and protection of culture and the defence of cultural identity. Many of the multilateral debates on culture have been embedded in a human rights approach to culture.

There has been a fair consensus in world politics about the importance of multilateral cooperation for the preservation, participation and promotion of culture. In concrete cases, such as the status of artists, countries have been divided on the need for and the strength of multilateral accords. The deepest controversy occurred in connection with the issue of cultural identity. On this issue the desire of the developing countries to establish solid protective measures was not accommodated. Recent developments suggest that the preference of the most powerful players for a commercial approach will guide the prevailing political practice.

Prevailing political practice
There is fairly extensive multilateral cooperation in the issue area of culture. This is guided by a combination of binding and voluntary accords which are weak. There are binding norms and rules in such treaties as the Beirut and Florence agreements or the Convention on the Protection of the World Cultural and Natural Heritage. These accords have no effective enforcement mechanisms. Other instruments, such as recommendations and declarations, are of an

informal nature. On the issue of cultural identity, multilateral cooperation has been hindered by a basic discord between players defending cultural sovereignty and those promoting unrestricted market access for cultural producers. The issue was very prominent in the 1970s debates on the Third World demand for a new international information order. It also figured in the negotiations on satellite television broadcasting. The Unesco Declaration of Guiding Principles on the Use of Satellite Broadcasting for the Free Flow of Information, the Spread of Education and Greater Cultural Exchanges provides in Article VII that cultural programmes should respect the distinctive character, the value and the dignity of all cultures. The IDTBS principles of 1982 also refer to the respect for the cultural integrity of states.

Notes

1 In the 1970s the problem of cultural invasion or imperialism was also perceived as 'cultural synchronization' (Hamelink, 1984). This approach made the point that cultural uniformity and threat to cultural identity were not merely the result of imperial processes, but also needed the support of the recipient communities. Synchronization also occurs in situations where coercive power is not the main variable. In many developing countries, for example, the local elites have been very helpful to the transnational business corporation in introducing their consumer society standards.

7

Development

In this issue area, two issues have achieved agenda status: the development of communication capacity in developing countries and the international transfer of technology.

Mass communication capacity

In the earliest meetings of the Economic and Social Council of the United Nations the inadequacy of information facilities in the less developed countries was highlighted. Diplomats representing these countries stressed that with the existing disparities there could be no reciprocity and equality in world communication. Several resolutions by the Council and by the General Assembly expressed the need to improve information enterprises in the less developed countries, and in 1957 the General Assembly requested the ECOSOC Commission on Human Rights to 'give special consideration to the problem of developing media of information in under-developed countries'. One year later the United Nations General Assembly requested ECOSOC to formulate 'a programme of concrete action and measures on the international plane which could be undertaken for the development of information enterprises in under-developed countries'. The specialized agencies were invited to contribute to this initiative.

Unesco was asked to study the mass media in the less developed countries and to survey the problems involved in the development of communication. This was no new terrain to the organization. In its early history there had been an effort to reconstruct and develop mass communication media in war-devastated countries. At its third General Conference in 1948 a resolution was adopted that added to this 'the provision of raw materials, equipment and professional training facilities . . . for under-developed areas' (Resolution 7.221, 1948). This was the beginning of assistance to Third World countries which received special impetus when in 1958 the General Conference explicitly requested the Director General 'to help develop media of information in the under-developed countries'. In response to the request of the General Assembly, Unesco organized a series of expert meetings (in Bangkok 1960, Santiago 1961 and Paris

1962) to assess communication needs and to design ways to meet these needs. The organization also prepared a report that was presented to the GA in 1961. This report, *Mass Media in Developing Countries*, formulated minimal levels of communication capacity and concluded that for some 70 per cent of the world population this minimum was not available (Unesco, 1961).[1]

The report recommended that communication development should be considered part of the overall United Nations development effort and thus be incorporated in the UN Technical Assistance Programme. In response to the report ECOSOC suggested in 1961 that the developed countries should assist the developing countries in the 'development of independent national information media, with due regard for the culture of each country'. In 1961 ECOSOC recommended to the General Assembly that the Unesco programme should have a place within the efforts of the First United Nations Development Decade.

In 1962 the UNGA confirmed this by stating that 'development of communication media was part of overall development'. Herewith a multilateral programme of technical assistance to the development of mass communication capacity was launched that was unanimously supported by the UN member states. Also in 1962 the Unesco General Conference reinforced this by asking the Director General 'to promote the formation, in the developing countries, of professional organizations in the fields of press, film, radio and television'. The General Conference also proposed the organization of regional seminars for media training and expert meetings on the development of mass communication in Africa, Asia and Latin America.

The technical assistance programme that lasted throughout the 1960s was primarily oriented towards the transfer of resources and skills. Only in 1970 was the programme complemented with a policy planning component when the sixteenth Unesco General Conference authorized the Director General to 'assist Member States in the formulation of their policies with respect to mass communication media'. The technical assistance programme lasted throughout the 1960s and made Unesco into a forum of consensus on information matters.

In the 1970s the non-aligned countries recognized that this technical assistance did not alter their dependency status, that 'information famine' persisted and that in fact their cultural sovereignty was increasingly threatened. They therefore opened the debate on the need for normative standard setting regarding the mass media. The key agenda issue for this debate was the demand for a new international information order. This demand expressed the Third World concern about disparity in communication capacity along three lines.

There was concern about the impact of the skewed communication relations between North and South on the independent cultural development of the Third World nations. In fact the first non-aligned summit in Bandung, Indonesia in 1955 had already referred to the impact of colonialism on culture: 'The existence of colonialism in many parts of Asia and Africa, in whatever form it may be, not only prevents cultural cooperation but also suppresses the national cultures of the peoples . . . Some colonial powers have denied their dependent peoples basic rights in the sphere of education and culture.' The 1973 non-aligned summit at Algiers expressed its concern about cultural colonialism as the effective successor to the earlier territorial modes of colonialism.

Then there was concern about the largely one-sided exports from the North to the countries of the Third World and the often distorted or totally absent reporting in the media of the North about developments in the South. The Algiers summit called for the 'reorganization of existing communication channels, which are a legacy of the colonial past and which have hampered free, direct and fast communication between developing countries'. This disequilibrium in the exchange of information between the North and the South controlled by a few Western transnational information companies began to be criticized by the non-aligned movement as an instrument of cultural colonialism. The Tunis symposium of 1976 stated: 'Since information in the world shows a disequilibrium favouring some and ignoring others, it is the duty of the non-aligned countries and other developing countries to change this situation and obtain the decolonization of information and initiate a new international order of information.' The New Delhi Declaration on Decolonization of Information stated that the establishment of a new international order for information is as necessary as the new international economic order.

A third line of concern addressed the transfer of media technology. On balance it was concluded in the early 1970s that preciously little technology had been transferred and that by and large only technical end products had been exported from the industrial nations. This was often done under disadvantageous conditions so that in the end the technical and financial dependence of the receiving countries had only increased.

As from its Algiers summit in 1973 the non-aligned movement continuously articulated its position of strong support for the emancipation and development of media in the developing nations. Unesco became the most important forum for this debate.

In 1970 the minutes of the Unesco General Conference read: 'Delegates from a number of developing countries stressed the need to ensure that the free flow of information and international exchanges should be a two-way operation. They asserted that the programme must continue to emphasize the rights of less privileged nations to preserve their own culture.' In a first phase (1970–6) the debate was characterized by the effort to 'decolonize'. In this period political and academic projects evolved that fundamentally criticized the existing international information order and that developed proposals for decisive changes. Several years of declarations, resolutions, recommendations and studies converged into the demand for a new international information order (NIIO). The concept surfaced at the Tunis information symposium in March 1976. With this concept (formally recognized by non-aligned heads of state in August 1976 in Sri Lanka) a clear linkage was established with the proposal for a fundamental restructuring of the international economy that was put forward in 1974 (the new international economic order, NIEO).

Although the precise meaning of the NIIO was not defined it was evident that its key notions were national sovereignty and cultural autonomy. The NIIO reflected the non-aligned aspiration to an international information exchange in which states that develop their cultural system in an autonomous way and with complete sovereign control of resources fully and effectively participate as independent members of the international community. From 1976 the Western news media began to take a critical attitude towards the demand for an NIIO. The majority of the international mass media expressed their opposition to the non-aligned initiative. In various commentaries the following points were recurrently made. There is no relation between the demand for a new economic order and that for a new information order. The core of the problem of disequilibrium lies in the Third World itself and is caused by paucity of technical and financial resources. The NIIO proposal is authoritarian by nature and under the pretext of aiding the Third World it attempts to undermine Western liberties. Proposals for reform coming from Third World countries are necessarily influenced by governments and are therefore unacceptable. The NIIO is basically inspired by Soviet interests.

During the nineteenth General Conference of Unesco in 1976 at Nairobi, a draft resolution proposed by Tunisia was discussed and adopted. The resolution invited the Director General 'to pay special attention to the activities of the bodies responsible for coordinating and implementing the information programme of the non-aligned countries . . . to strengthen the intellectual, technical and financial resources provided for under the Regular Programme through an appreciable and appropriate increase in the proposed growth rate for communication and information activities'. The resolution was adopted with 73 votes for, none against and three abstainers.

Also a resolution concerning the 'free and balanced flow' (Resolution 100, paragraphs 22 and 23) was adopted in which 'The General Conference . . . stresses the importance of free and balanced circulation of information and the need vigorously to intensify the efforts to put an end to the imbalance which, as regards capacity to send out and receive information, typifies the relationship between the developed and developing countries, by helping the latter to establish and strengthen their own communication and information infrastructures and systems, so as to promote their development . . . and their ability to play a full part in the international dissemination of information.'

The twentieth General Conference of Unesco in 1978 at Paris adopted a request to the MacBride Commission to propose measures that could lead 'to the establishment of a more just and effective world information order'. In fact, this conference was a turning point in the debate in so far as at this meeting the hostile opposition towards the idea of a new order was softened. There began to be almost unanimous acceptance that Third World countries had justifiable complaints and that concessions must be made by the industrialized states. The original formula coined by the non-aligned movement, NIIO, was replaced by the proposal for a 'new, more just and effective world information and communication order' (NWICO). According to the interpretation of United States Ambassador John Reinhardt at the 1978 General Conference, this new order required 'a more effective program of action, both public and private, to suitable identified centers of professional education and training in broadcasting and journalism in the developing world . . . [and] a major effort to apply the benefits of advanced communications technology . . . to economic and social needs in the rural areas of developing nations'. The NWICO that was now acceptable to all Unesco member states was mainly interpreted as a programme for the transfer of knowledge, finances and technical equipment. The problem of the international information structure was being reduced to mere technical proportions. In response to this an intergovernmental programme for support to the development of communication was launched as a Western initiative in 1980.

The 21st General Conference in 1980 at Belgrade adopted by consensus a resolution concerning the establishment of the International Programme for the Development of Communication

(IPDC). Also a Venezuelan resolution was adopted (without consensus and against mainly Western opposition) that proposed study into the new information order. The resolution aimed 'to initiate studies necessary for the elaboration of principles related to a New World Information and Communication Order'. The Venezuelan resolution was adopted with 53 votes in favour, six against (among them the USA, the UK and Switzerland) and 26 abstainers.

During the Unesco General Conferences of 1976, 1978 and 1980 the Western minority managed to achieve most of its policy objectives against the expressed preference of the majority of member states. In the end the debate did not yield the results demanded by the developing countries. Their criticism of the past failures of technical assistance programmes was answered by the creation of yet another such programme: the International Programme for the Development of Communication. By many Third World delegates this programme was seen as an instrument to implement the standards of the NWICO. The Unesco General Conference of 1980 had stated (Resolution 4.19) that among these standards were the elimination of the imbalances and inequalities which characterize the present situation; the capacity of the developing countries to achieve improvement of their own situation, notably by providing infrastructure and by making their information and communication means suitable to their needs and aspirations; and the sincere will of developed countries to help them. The IPDC was not going to meet these expectations. Apart from the inherent difficulty that IPDC did represent a definition of world communication problems that had in the past not worked to the benefit of Third World nations, the programme would also from the outset suffer a chronic lack of resources.

Moreover, in 1981 there were clear indications that the opponents of the Third World demand for a new information order had not yet been satisfied. They continued to see dangers to the liberties of the Western mass media. At Talloires in France (15–17 May 1981) a Voices of Freedom Conference of Independent News Media was held. The conference was attended mostly by representatives of publishers' interests (from 21 countries). There were no representatives of the international journalists' federations. The conference participants adopted the Magna Charta of the Free Press which stated:

> We believe the time has come within Unesco and other intergovernmental bodies to abandon attempts to regulate news content and formulate rules for the press. Efforts should be directed instead to finding practical

solutions to the problems before us, such as improving technological progress, increasing professional interchanges and equipment transfers, reducing communication tariffs, producing cheaper newsprint and eliminating other barriers to the development of news media capabilities . . . We are deeply concerned by a growing tendency in many countries and in international bodies to put government interests above those of the individual, particularly in regard to information. We believe that the ultimate definition of a free press lies not in the actions of governments or international bodies, but rather in the professionalism, vigor and courage of individual journalists.

The International Federation of the Periodical Press (FIPP) reinforced this position at its meeting in Washington on 20 May 1981. In the same year the first signs of the later (1984) US withdrawal from Unesco (in 1985 followed by the UK) became visible, and in fact the US made reference to the Talloires meeting. A letter by President Reagan to the House of Representatives (17 September 1981) said: 'We strongly support – and commend to the attention of all nations – the declaration issued by independent media leaders of twenty-one nations at the Voices of Freedom Conference, which met at Talloires, France, in May of this year. We do not feel we can continue to support a Unesco that turns its back on the high purposes this organization was originally intended to serve.' The US withdrawal was subsequently officially announced on 29 December 1983 in a letter by Secretary of State George Schultz. According to the letter, 'Unesco has extraneously politicized virtually every subject it deals with, has exhibited hostility towards the basic institutions of a free society, especially the free market and the free press, and has demonstrated unrestrained budgetary expansion.'

In the effort to maintain a fragile international consensus the Unesco General Conference began to erode the original aspirations of the NIIO proponents and shifted from the need to establish a regulatory structure to the new order as 'an evolving and continuous process' (Paris, General Conference, 1982, Resolution 3.3). In September 1983 Unesco convened a round table on a new world information and communication order at Igls, Austria. The meeting focused strongly on assistance to developing countries for the development of their communication infrastructures. A second, and last, round table on the NWICO took place in 1986 (April) in Copenhagen, Denmark.

Although the concept of a new order remained central for some years to come, nothing was done in regard to its implementation. Gradually Unesco withdrew support from all research, documentation or conference activities intended to contribute to the establishment of a new information order and moved towards a 'new strategy' (for the medium-term plan 1990–5) with an emphasis on the free flow of information and the freedom and independence of the media, on giving priority to operational activities, and on the importance of information technology. Whereas the non-aligned summit in Belgrade (September 1989) reiterated its support for the NIICO, the Unesco General Conference strove hard to reach consensus on formulations that represented conventional freedom of the press, pluralism of the media, freedom of expression, and free flow of information positions. According to the Unesco Director General (in 1989) plans for a new information order no longer existed in Unesco.

In 1978 the United Nations General Assembly had expressed its support for the establishment of a new world information and communication order in Resolution 33/115. The General Assembly 'affirmed the need to establish a new, more just and more effective world information and communication order, intended to strengthen peace and international understanding and based on the free circulation and wider and better-balanced dissemination of information'. In part C of the same resolution the General Assembly had established the Committee to Review United Nations Public Information Policies and Activities. In the report of this Committee submitted to the 1979 meeting of the General Assembly, it was stated that the review of United Nations information policy should be 'a part of the wider undertaking involving the general evolution of the question of a new world information order'. In the same year the General Assembly adopted Resolution 34/182 (of 18 December 1979) by which the Committee to Review was renamed the United Nations Committee on Information and in which the mandate for the Committee was formulated. Pursuant to the resolution the Committee would continue 'to examine United Nations public information policies and activities, in the light of the evolution of international relations, particularly during the past two decades, and of the imperatives of the establishment of the new international economic order and of a new world information and economic order'. The Committee was also 'to promote the establishment of a new, more just and effective world information and communication order intended to strengthen peace and international understanding and based on the free circulation and wider and better balanced dissemination of information and to make recommendations thereon to the General Assembly'.

Since Resolutions 33/115 and 34/182 (of 1978), the General Assembly has each year confirmed the importance of the effort to establish a new, more just and more effective world information and communication order. Support for the effort was also expressed by the European Economic Community, as its representative to the

1985 meeting of the Committee on Information stated that the ten members of the EEC 'reaffirmed their commitment to a more just and more effective world information and communication order, which should emerge through an evolutionary process'. In 1990 the resolution forwarded by the UN Committee on Information to the General Assembly shifted its language to a recognition of the call for a new world information and communication order as an evolving and continuous process.

When the intergovernmental community in essence removed the demand for a new order from its agenda, non-governmental actors moved into the arena. Two non-governmental forums in particular were dedicated to a revitalization of the information order debate in the light of contemporary developments. These were the World Association for Christian Communication (WACC) through its periodical *Media Development* and its Manila Declaration (adopted during the WACC world congress of 15–19 October 1989 in Manila, the Philippines) and a loose collection of individuals and non-governmental organizations assembled in the MacBride round tables on communications. Since 1989 round tables have taken place in Harare, Zimbabwe (1989), Prague, Czechoslovakia (1990), Istanbul, Turkey (1991), Guarujá, Brazil (1992), Dublin, Ireland (1993), and Honolulu, USA (1994). Several of these meetings took place in conjunction with scientific conferences of the International Association for Mass Communication Research. The Harare round table in 1989 'noted that economic and technological disparities still characterise the current international system. The rapid advances in communication technologies in the affluent parts of the world have widened that gap between the "haves" and "have-nots". Urgent investment is needed to improve the communication infrastructure in many developing countries. Appropriate technologies must be developed in the countries of the South, and bilateral and multi-lateral programmes should be initiated to remedy these disparities and imbalances.'

According to the round table of Prague, 1990, the debate on NWICO 'is now in the arena of professional organisations, of communication researchers and, most importantly, in the arena of grassroots movements, representing ordinary men, women and children who are directly affected by our current cultural and communication environment'. The meeting expressed concern about the state of communication in the South:

> The rapid development of communication technology, which has drasti-
> cally increased the capacity for information in industrialised countries,
> has bypassed many countries in the South. Essential technical infrastruc-
> tures for communications are still not available there or are inaccessible

to most of the people. Instead, foreign communication enterprises have, in alliance with many governments and elitist interests, created an artificial commercial culture which is accessible only to an affluent few. This trend prevents the achievement of cultural emancipation and sound development policies. To reverse this situation, South–South cooperation is imperative. This calls for new structures to promote collective self-reliance and solidarity. At the same time, a new basis and new methods for North–South cooperation must be found which ensure greater equality and more genuine partnership.

The round table of Istanbul, in 1991, observed with growing concern 'the rapidly increasing concentration, homogenisation, commercialisation, and militarisation of national and world cultures. The principles of the MacBride Report have been countered by the virtual monopoly of global conglomerates over the selection, production and marketing of information and entertainment products, including crucial scientific and technical data and information rights; by the transnational industrial-media complex under its American protectorate; and by the weakening of multilateral relations and international organisations.'

The sixth MacBride round table took place in Honolulu, Hawaii, 20–3 January 1994. This meeting gave special attention to the inadequate communication capacity of the so-called Fourth World within the Third World, the indigenous peoples. The round table participants recognized 'that the indigenous peoples of the world are marginalized from communicative links in the world and within countries'. The meeting also addressed the issue of the plans for 'information superhighways' to be constructed by the USA, the EU countries and Japan. As the participants stated in the final document: 'No "information superhighway" is planned for the developing world . . . It is likely that the new information highways will widen the gap between the information rich and information poor, both within individual countries and between rich and poor regions of the world, to such an extent as to render it unbridgeable in the foreseeable future' (IAMCR, 1994: 5–6).[2]

The positions
The concern about North–South disparity has found almost universal recognition in the world community. The most vocal agents of the concern have been the representatives of Third World countries, often supported by the Eastern European governments (representatives of the professional and academic groups), and staff members of some intergovernmental institutions (such as Unesco). The concern was strongly motivated by the conclusion that communication disparities seriously hamper processes of national development in Third World countries, impair the chances of these

countries defending local culture and mastering technological capacity, and could in the long run also negatively affect the interests of the Western countries.

This consensual concern met contending positions on its accommodation. A claim to a legal-political solution confronted a claim for a mainly technical solution. The origins of this controversy about the solution of global information inequality are to be found in the immediate post-war years at the time of the incipient United Nations. This controversy is rooted in an early 'division of labour' within the United Nations system that embodied a distinction between political and technical tasks in dealing with international information questions.

Early in the history of the United Nations system it was a rather common claim among the Western member states that the specialized agencies of the UN should be technical rather than political. Political issues were to be dealt with by the UN General Assembly, whereas the other agencies, and among them Unesco, were supposed to provide technical assistance to the implementation of the normative principles elaborated by the political body. In the field of information this meant that the UN General Assembly would be responsible for news and freedom of information, and Unesco would deal with the improvement of the technical conditions for news production and exchange and promote the free circulation of educational and cultural materials. As a result of this division of labour, Unesco began to implement a programme of technical assistance. Moving away from the imposed 'technical' mandate was perceived by the Western member states as undue 'politicization'.

The Western delegations formulated the following claims. The adoption of a legally binding instrument on the new international information order should be avoided. A regulatory instrument could only be adopted if it would reflect Western preferences, and a consensus on the primacy of technical assistance in information matters should be maintained.

The NIIO proponents claimed that a legally binding instrument on the information relations in the world should be formulated, conditions of technology transfer advantageous to the Third World countries should be created, and independent cultural development in the South needed protection. The NIIO claims were supported by such non-aligned principles as the application of the fundamental principles of international law, the recognition of the rights of every nation to develop its own independent information system and to protect its national sovereignty and cultural identity, and the right of every nation to participate at governmental and non-governmental level in the international exchange of information under favourable conditions in a climate of justice, equality and mutual advantage. In line with the NIIO claims an adequate accommodation of the concern about disparities in world communication would also imply a recognition of the responsibility of various actors in the process of information for its truthfulness and objectivity, as well as for the particular social objectives to which the information is devoted.

The claimants for a technical solution argued for this approach because they believed that a political solution would not be in their economic interests and would undermine such international norms as the freedom of information. Their opponents argued that a mere technical solution would only deepen their dependency and would not contribute to the structural transformation they deemed necessary.

Prevailing political practice
There is a limited form of multilateral cooperation on the issue of mass communication development. This is not supported by a binding and robust accord on the need to develop mass communication capacity in developing countries.

There is discord on fundamental principles and a general unwillingness in the rich regions of the world to provide a type of assistance that would resolve the problems that were reported as early as 1961 by the Unesco study. There is an informal accord for multilateral cooperation through the IPDC. This remains however largely ineffective since the most powerful players do not live up to their promises. In 1992 the IPDC received in total contributions the amount of US $5,599,566. In 1992 and 1993 together a total of 45 projects were financed with US $6,837,718. For the biennium 1994–5 Unesco proposed to spend a grand total of US $24,278,100 for the development of communication.[3]

Telecommunication capacity

As in the area of mass communication, so too with telecommunication the concern about international disparity has been firmly placed on the agenda of world politics. Major efforts to meet the concern about international development assistance were launched by the UNDP, the UPU and the ITU. Assistance has particularly concentrated on the development of human resources, the support to national telecommunication authorities and the establishment of regional networks. The Universal Postal Union has carried out development assistance projects within its mandate to contribute to the organization and development of postal services and the fostering of international postal cooperation. Through UNPD the UPU has contributed to various training programmes and institutions for postal administrations and to technical cooperation among developing countries. Since the mid 1960s the United Nations Development Programme has spent considerable amounts of money on projects in the field of telecommunication. An important actor also became the World Bank with its provision of development assistance to telecommunication infrastructures.

In 1952 the ITU became involved with the United Nations development assistance programmes, and in 1959 the ITU convention made reference to the need for cooperation and coordination related to development assistance. Article 13 in the International Telecommunication Convention (Plenipotentiary Conference of 1959) required the ITU consultative committees (the CCIR for radio communication and the CCITT for telegraph and telephony) to pay due attention to the formulation of recommendations directly connected with the establishment, development and improvement of telecommunication in new or developing countries in both the regional and international fields. In 1960 a special division within the Secretariat General was established to deal with issues of development assistance.

The 1965 Plenipotentiary Conference provided in Article 14 that 'There shall be a World Plan Committee, and such Regional Plan Committees as may be jointly approved by the Plenary Assemblies of the CCIs. These Plan Committees shall develop a General Plan for the international telecommunication network to help in planning international telecommunication services. They shall refer to the CCIs questions the study of which is of particular interest to new or developing countries and which are within the terms of reference of those Consultative Committees.' Already in 1964 at the CCITT Plenary Assembly several special autonomous groups (GAS) had been set up; some of these turned out to be of special interest to the developing countries, such as GAS 3 (economic and technical comparison of transmission systems) and GAS 5 (economic studies at the national level in the field of telecommunications). Much later, in 1985, more GAS were established, some of which were intended to specially cater to the developing countries' needs. These included GAS 7 on rural telecommunication and GAS 10 on basic planning data for traffic forecasting and forecasting methods for long-term planning.

Since 1965 governments of new or developing countries have been encouraged to participate in the work of the consultative committees. This has met with little success. The major reasons for the limited participation by developing countries have been lack of expertise and lack of funds. Developing countries have also been generally critical of the CCI agendas and decision making as too little geared towards the needs and interests of these countries. A case in point has been the increasing attention CCITT has given, since the early 1980s, to the development of such projects as the integrated services digital network (ISDN). 'What is hardly acceptable to developing countries is that, on the one hand, CCI work, so critical to developed countries, is an integral part of the ITU budget, and as this work expands, so will ITU budgetary allocations. On the other hand, allocations for ITU technical assistance, of critical importance to developing countries, come from the shrinking UNDP budget; the prospect of the ITU contributing to this budget appears slim, as the largest contributors, the industrialized countries, have so far been unwilling to increase ITU income' (Renaud, 1989: 60).

At the 1965 ITU Plenipotentiary Conference several Third World countries had proposed that development assistance should be increased through: '(1) the creation of a special ITU development assistance fund separate from that under the auspices of the United Nations; (2) the establishment of regional ITU offices to aid local administrations with their telecommunications problems; and (3) the creation of a new ITU technical assistance organ similar in structure to the ITU Consultative Committees, with its own elected director' (Codding, 1990b: 140). These proposals never reached the plenary as they were defeated in committee meetings.

In 1973 the ITU Plenipotentiary Conference had decided to establish a 'special fund for technical cooperation'. The fund was to be financed by member states. The developed nations turned out to be rather unready to contribute. However, the Technical Cooperation Department of the Secretariat General had within the framework of the UNDP developed a programme through which technical advice and training had been provided to many developing countries in the field of both terrestrial and space telecommunications. The proposal for a separate development organ was again defeated in the committee meetings and did not reach the plenary.

An important ITU Plenipotentiary Conference with regard to the development concern was the 1982 meeting. The conference decided to incorporate development assistance into the ITU objectives and established a Special Voluntary Programme for Cooperation. The resolution of the programme was initiated by technologically advanced countries – the UK, the USA, Japan and Germany – in a bargaining effort to respond to Third World demands while maintaining their agendas for the consultative committees. The initiatives were intended to, once again, defeat the attempt (since the 1970s) to finance development assistance from the regular budget. The Special Voluntary Fund was established in 1984. Funding had been expected from private industry but money came late and in small quantity. This reflected the ambiguous attitude of the developed member states. Although they solemnly promised full support for the development objective, they never lived up to this promise.

In 1989 the Plenipotentiary Conference at Nice adopted the formalization of ITU's role as both executive agency for UNDP-funded telecommunication development programmes and as a development institution in its own right. The Nice conference created the Bureau for Telecommunications Development (BTD) and gave it a mandate that included among other things the following tasks: 'to raise the level of awareness of decision-makers concerning the important role of telecommunications in the national socio-economic development programme, and provide information and advice on possible policy options; to promote the development, expansion and operation of telecommunication networks and services, particularly in developing countries; to encourage participation by industry in telecommunication development in developing countries; to provide support in preparing for and organizing development conferences' (Nice Document 508-E, 19 June 1989, R.3/12). The Nice conference also decided that the BTD would have the same status as the other permanent organs of the Union, and regarding the budget it was resolved that the Bureau would get 15 million Swiss francs in 1990 and that this would increase to 22.5 million Swiss francs by 1994. The Nice constitution contained a provision on the BTD that stated that it is to 'facilitate and enhance telecommunications development by offering, organizing and co-ordinating technical cooperation and assistance activities'.

In terms of the role of the ITU *vis-à-vis* the development concern, the Nice conference resolved that the Union should '(1) continue to work for the harmonization, development and enhancement of telecommunications throughout the world, (2) ensure that technical and operational standards for all forms of telecommunications are established, and (3) encourage promotion of technical cooperation among ITU member states'. The conference also recommended that the Unesco IPDC would receive support and that 'developed countries should take into account the requests for favourable treatment made by developing countries in service, commercial or other relations in telecommunications, thus helping to achieve the desired economic equilibrium conducive to a relaxation of present world tensions'.

The earlier conference of 1982 had established an independent commission to study the problem of world-wide telecommunications development. In 1984 the so-called Maitland Commission produced a report entitled *The Missing Link* (Independent Commission for World Wide Telecommunication Development, 1985). The report recommended more investment in telecommunications in developing countries and more resources for training and transfer of technology. The Maitland report contained four major conclusions (Maitland, 1992): higher priority had to be given to investment in telecommunications; the effectiveness of existing systems had to be improved; financing arrangements had to recognize that foreign exchange is scarce in many developing countries; and the ITU should play a more effective role. In response to the Maitland report the ITU established the Centre for Telecommunications Development (CTD) in 1985, which was in 1991 within the BTD. The CTD was expected to contribute in a significant way to telecommunication development. It failed to meet the expectation. The limited and sporadic funding that was provided may have played an important role in this. The Centre fell victim to the ambiguous attitude of the developed members of the Union.

Recently the organizational structure of the ITU has changed and the development activity is now lodged in a special sector. The High-Level Committee (21 members chaired by Gaby Warren of Canada) appointed by the Nice Plenipotentiary in 1989 to prepare structural changes in the ITU reported in April 1991 in *Tomorrow's ITU: The Challenges of Change* (HLC, 1991). Among its many recommendations, the HLC supported the need for increased funding for telecommunication development in Third World countries. Recommendation 4 provided, for instance, that 'the ITU should play a more clearly defined catalytic role, as envisaged in Nice Resolution no. 14, by working cooperatively with international, regional and bilateral development and financial agencies'. The resolution also especially mentioned the least developed countries where the 'gap is widest, requiring exceptional efforts from multilateral cooperation'. The Committee had 96 recommendations for changes in the organization.

This report was submitted to the ITU Administrative Council in May 1991, whereupon the Council decided to convene an Additional Plenipotentiary Conference to be held in Geneva in December 1992. This APC accepted most of the recommendations for change and adopted a new ITU constitution and convention which reflect these changes. These new instruments entered into force on 1 July 1994. In the new structure the substantive work of the Union is organized in three sectors: radiocommunication, standardization and development. The development sector incorporates the work of the earlier Bureau for Telecommunications Development and is responsible for enhancing telecommunication development. In between the plenipotentiary conference held every four years, there will be one world telecommunication development conference.

The positions
There is consensus in the international community on the concern for telecommunication development. This is motivated by the double function of telecommunication as an economic sector in its own right and as the key infrastructural support to other economic activities. In this dual role, telecommunication is an essential ingredient of national socio-economic development. Other motives include the expectation that development of telecommunication contributes the international economic equilibrium that is conducive to a relaxation of world tensions. The developed countries have also used the concern as a concession to the Third World in exchange for the maintenance of their own agendas.

With regard to the accommodation of the consensual concern there have been the rival claims to increase support to the Third World from the regular budget versus the claim to generate external funding for this. At the 1989 Plenipotentiary Meeting there was a challenge to the Third World position that the establishment of a separate development organ was necessary since the development objective of the ITU had not been given enough emphasis and status (equal to standardization and regulation) and that funding had been insufficient. The rival claim from the developed countries was that such an institution would be too expensive, inefficient and unnecessary since the organization was already doing a splendid job.

Prevailing political practice
There is a limited form of multilateral cooperation in the field of telecommunication development. A set of provisions in the ITU constitution, in resolutions of the Plenipotentiary Conference in Nice, 1988, and in the decisions of the 1992 APC constitute the essence of a largely voluntary and weak accord. It remains to be seen what the new development sector of the ITU will achieve. With the increasing importance of mobile satellite services there is also a growth of multilateral cooperation in this field. A key player in this is Inmarsat, the international maritime satellite organization. The Inmarsat programme of cooperation with developing countries has over the past years actively involved representatives from

developing countries in seminars, workshops and working groups. Developing countries have also been encouraged to take part in Inmarsat decision making on the development of new telecommunication services. For the time being this remains a limited form of multilateral cooperation without a comprehensive accord on the development of telecommunication capacity.[4]

International transfer of technology

Participation in world communication requires that actors have access to the technologies that make cross-border movements of data, information and knowledge possible. Given the stark disparity in communication capacity between the industrialized countries of the North and the Third World countries, there has been (since the early 1950s) considerable concern about Third World acquisition of communication technology. This issue occurs in the broader context of the international production and dissemination of technical knowledge and information. The problems of the international transfer of technology are analysed here in the context of world communication politics since technology (often equated with its end products only) is in essence the know-how (the technical knowledge) to produce artifacts, to innovate production processes and to render services. This technical knowledge is made available (communicated) in such forms as models, plans, instructions, blueprints, computer software, training and engineering designs.

The paramount concerns in this field are related to the conditions of access to knowledge and the terms of its transfer, to the adverse business practices by large transnational technology producers, to the monopolization of technical knowledge through the international patent system, and to the development of independent technological capacity in the Third World. The larger background to these concerns is the quest of Third World countries to complete the decolonization process and to achieve a level of self-reliant development.

The access to technical knowledge became a concern for the Third World countries only in the 1970s. Earlier on most of the newly independent countries were mainly interested in attracting foreign investors, particularly transnational corporations, with the expectation that they would transfer the much needed scientific and technical know-how. It was assumed in the 1950s that science and technology, which had lifted the advanced industrial countries to unprecedented levels of material wealth, would do the same for the Third World. In the remarkably rapid economic growth that North

America and Western Europe experienced after the industrial revolution, science and technology were crucial factors.

Since the North had progressed through laborious and expensive trial-and-error processes, it seemed a well advised policy for those who came late to exploit the most recent state of the art. 'Rarely did the countries at each stage of the decision-making process raise basic questions such as: does the country have the technology? Can it develop it? Can it adapt imported technology? How long will it take? What resources will be needed? What are the trade-offs between importing technology now and waiting to develop it at home? Why not import now, but plan in such a fashion that there will be no more repetitive imports in the future?' (UNCTAD, 1985: 162). By and large policy makers in the developing countries were concerned with the availability of maximum volumes of technological products rather than with the more complex problems of their political, economic and cultural integration. Little or no attention was given to the infrastructural requirements for a productive assimilation of imported science and technology in the recipient countries.

Throughout the First United Nations Development Decade it did seem that the transfer of the latest and the best from the developed countries to the Third World was the optimal instrument for rapid development. In the course of the 1960s there was a considerable increase in the volume of technology transferred between the developed market economies and the developing countries. In the process many recipient countries became aware that the transfer usually consisted of end products rather than of technology *per se*, that much of the transfer took place as intra-firm movements, that the conditions under which transfer took place were often disadvantageous for them, and that much of the technology was inappropriate, obsolete, over-priced or all of these together. A response to remedy this situation was often sought in national legislation that would address such issues as limitations on activities and ownership of foreign companies, adverse business practices on the part of the technology suppliers, patent policies, the promotion of national technological capacity and the settlement of disputes.

In the multilateral forums there was remarkably little focus on the transfer of technology concern. At the second session of the UNCTAD in 1968 (New Delhi) a draft resolution on issues connected with science and technology was presented, but was passed on for further consideration since other matters were considered more important. 'There was no time for science and technology . . . Quite clearly, UNCTAD too was, as yet, unprepared to grapple with technology questions' (UNCTAD, 1985: 163).

In 1970 the tenth session of the UNCTAD Trade and Development Board decided to establish an Intergovernmental Group on Transfer of Technology (IGGTT). At its first session the IGGTT drew up a programme of work for UNCTAD in the field of transfer of technology. Herewith a strong involvement of UNCTAD in technology issues began that would soon lead to such activities as the negotiations on an international code of conduct on the transfer of technology and the revision of the industrial property system. These activities were part of a broader movement towards the adoption of a multilateral instrument on the international transfer of technology that began in the early 1970s.

In 1973 the UN Advisory Committee on the Application of Science and Technology (ACAST) proposed the idea of an international code of conduct (1973). This proposal was taken up by the 1974 Programme of Action on the NIEO (UNGA Resolutions 3201 and 3202) and the Declaration on the NIEO. Part IV of the Programme of Action proposed:

> To formulate an international code of conduct for the transfer of technology corresponding to needs and conditions prevalent in developing countries, to give access on improved terms to modern technology and to adapt that technology, as appropriate, to specific economic, social and ecological conditions and varying stages of development in developing countries, to expand significantly the assistance from developed to developing countries in research and development programmes and in the creation of suitable indigenous technology, to adapt commercial practices governing transfer of technology to the requirements of the developing countries and to prevent abuse of the rights of sellers, to promote international cooperation in research and development in exploration and exploitation, conservation and the legitimate utilization of natural resources and all sources of energy.

Also in 1974 (12 December) the Charter of Economic Rights and Duties of States was adopted (UNGA Resolution 3281(XXXIX)) with 100 states voting in favour, six against and ten abstaining. Article 13 of the charter stated in paragraph 1: 'Every State has the right to benefit from the advantages and developments in science and technology for the acceleration of its economic and social development.' And paragraph 3 provided: 'Accordingly, developed countries should cooperate with the developing countries in the establishment, strengthening and development of their scientific and technological infrastructures and their scientific and technological activities so as to help expand and transform the economies of developing countries.' The major technology leaders voted against this appeal.

The transfer of technology issue was also raised in connection with the efforts to design a code of conduct on transnational corporations. UNGA Resolution 3201 on the NIEO called for 'regulation and supervision of the activities of transnational corporations by taking measures in the interest of the national economies of the countries where such transnational corporations operate on the basis of the full sovereignty of these countries'. The motivation for the development of such supervision was twofold. There was a recognition that the positive role of the TNCs should be strengthened. There was also a conviction that it was necessary to provide guidelines for their conduct. From the beginning the Third World and socialist countries focused on the need to develop standards for TNC conduct in order to restrain their adverse practices. The developed countries, although not rejecting the need for standards on TNC conduct (as was manifest in the ICC Guidelines of 1972, the ICC Rules of Conduct on Extortion and Bribery in International Transactions of 1978 and the OECD Guidelines for Multinational Enterprises of 1976), were interested in a minimalist arrangement that would also address the ways in which host countries would have to treat the corporations.

The formulation of a code of conduct became the mandate of the United Nations Commission on Transnational Corporations (established pursuant to UNGA Resolution 1913(LVII) of 5 December 1974) with the assistance of the United Nations Centre on Transnational Corporations. In January 1977 an intergovernmental working group began preparations for a draft code which was submitted to the Commission in 1982. The code, which is designed as a voluntary arrangement, is still on the Commission's agenda as no consensus has been reached on some outstanding issues. In the latest version of the draft code the provisions on technology read that: '(a) Transnational corporations shall conform to the transfer-of-technology laws and regulations of the countries in which they operate . . . (b) Transnational corporations in their transfer-of-technology transactions, including intra-corporate transactions, should avoid practices which adversely affect the international flow of technology, or otherwise hinder the economic and technological development of countries, particularly developing countries. (c) Transnational corporations should contribute to the strengthening of the scientific and technological capacities of developing countries' (United Nations Centre on Transnational Corporations, 1990).

As the science and technology issues moved on to an essential position in multilateral negotiations, it also became clear that there were important differences in the positions taken by the developed and the developing countries. These were largely based upon the conflicting interests of the protection of knowledge as private property versus the availability of knowledge as public resource. The Third World countries began to claim a right of access to scientific and technological (S&T) information in the early negotiations on the UNCTAD code of conduct on the transfer of technology where they stressed the definition of S&T information as a common good. They claimed that knowledge resources should be transferred to them. These claims were expressly formulated in UNGA Resolution 3201 (Declaration on the Establishment of a New International Economic Order, 1 May 1974) and UNGA Resolution 3202 (Programme of Action on the Establishment of a New International Economic Order, 1 May 1974).

Resolution 3201 observed that 'The benefits of technological progress are not shared equitably by all members of the international community.' Therefore it was seen as imperative to give 'to developing countries access to the achievements of modern science and technology and the creation of indigenous technology for the benefit of the developing countries in forms and in accordance with procedures which are suited to their economies'. The developed countries opposed these claims and did not support the NIEO programmes and declaration.

Despite Western opposition the UNGA resolutions on the NIEO led to the preparations of the United Nations Conference on Science and Technology for Development. This conference was eventually held in Vienna in 1979 and on 31 August the UNCSTED adopted the Programme of Action on Science and Technology for Development. The Vienna programme responded to Third World demands for access to and transfer of knowledge and addressed the creation of conditions under which the developing countries could improve their autonomous capacity for research and development. The programme contained a series of action proposals for the resolution of the North–South disparity in scientific and technical information. Its essential components were strengthening scientific and technological capacities of the developing countries, restructuring the current pattern of international scientific and technological relations, strengthening the role of the UN with regard to science and technology for development, and creating the financial provisions to this end.

The programme is only a set of recommendations, without legal force. In the course of the 1980s it turned out to have little or no impact on the international relations in science and technology. On 19 December the UNGA adopted by Resolution 34/218 the final report of the Vienna conference. An Intergovernmental Committee on Science and Technology for Development was established. A

Centre for Science and Technology for Development was created. A separate UN financing system for science and technology for development was established. In spite of all these efforts, by 1986 it had to be concluded that the implementation of the Vienna proposals had remained short of initial expectations (United Nations, 1986). The financial targets had not been met and in 1987 the office for fund raising was closed.

Meanwhile, the UNCTAD IGGTT had adopted at its third session (26 July 1974) a resolution on the possibility and feasibility of an international code of conduct in the field of transfer of technology; the UK, the USA, the Federal Republic of Germany and Switzerland voted against. In the same year the *ad hoc* IGGTT was transformed into a permanent body of UNCTAD, and became the Committee on the Transfer of Technology (CTT). In 1977 the United Nations convened by UNGA Resolution 32/188 the United Nations Conference on an International Code of Conduct on the Transfer of Technology to negotiate a code of conduct under the auspices of UNCTAD. Since 1978 the conference has held several sessions and discussed versions of a draft code. Only in 1983 did one basic text emerge that was to become the focus of consultations and negotiations that continued through the 1980s and the early 1990s. Since major controversies on outstanding issues (such as restrictive business practices and the settlement of disputes) could not be resolved, no agreement has been reached yet.

In the preparations of the first draft code the Pugwash conference played a significant role. A special working group of the Pugwash Conferences on Science and World Affairs adopted in April 1974 a draft code which was to become the basis for the UNCTAD negotiations (UNCTAD, 1974). A Pugwash workshop at Turin (11–13 October 1990) on Reviving the North–South Dialogue on Technology Transfer recommended the renewal of the stalled negotiations on the code to complete the text for ratification by the UN diplomatic conference.

Consultations to resolve the impasse in the code of conduct negotiations continued to fail in 1991 and 1992. The remaining key issues were how restrictive business practices in technology trans-actions should be treated in the code, and questions about the applicable law in technology contracts and dispute settlement procedures. In the 1991 negotiations on the terms of reference for a group of experts that was to make recommendations for the resolution of the impasse, the divergent positions were very clear. With regard to restrictive business practices (which include restric-tions on the purchase of spare parts, and on exports, production, sales and distribution; price fixing practices; limitations on the use of patents after expiration; and anti-competitive activities) Third World countries claimed that these should be judged by the development criterion. This meant that it was necessary to assess how far such practices affect the development of the recipient countries. The Western countries held the opinion that transfer of technology and related business practices should be assessed in the light of whether they contribute to international competition among TNCs. With regard to applicable law Third World countries claimed that national law and jurisdiction should prevail, whereas the Western countries stressed the respect for the freedom of contract among parties to transfer of technology. Although some of the Latin American and African countries felt that some concessions might have to be made to the West in order to resume the negotiations, the Asian countries felt very strongly that 'they were not prepared to accept a code, even voluntarily, which would specifically pre-empt their sovereignty' (*Third World Economics*, 1991: 4).

In April 1991 the UNCTAD Committee on Transfer of Technology adopted a resolution that called upon the world community 'to increase technology flows to developing countries and facilitate access of those countries to technology, in particular those new and advanced technologies of critical importance for their development, with a view to reducing the existing technological gap between developed and developing countries'. The resolution also pointed to the export restrictions that developed countries imposed on key technologies, thus avoiding competition from Third World countries. In the Committee the Group of 77 had emphasized that the pressure from developed countries to impose stricter conditions on industrial property protection made the need for 'an international framework of principles and standards for technology transfer on fair and equitable terms to both suppliers and recipients' more urgent. This was, according to the Group of 77, 'also the rationale for the validity and usefulness of an international code of conduct on the transfer of technology (*Third World Economics*, 1991: 4). The Group of 77 considered the impasse in the code of conduct negotiations particularly threatening at a time when Third World countries faced the decline in technology transfer during the 1980s (as a result of recession, debt crisis and protectionism) and increased international competition in the field of advanced technology on the world market.

The patent system and the transfer of technology
In the 1960s developing countries began to challenge the international patent system. They supported a demand for the revision

of the 1883 Paris Convention for the Protection of Industrial Property with the following arguments. The patent system contributes to the reinforcement of TNC technical dominance. These companies own five out of six patent applications in the LDCs. The complicated and costly system of administration militates against protection of local innovations. Often the patent system does not recognize the information sector technology. A large part of patents do not lead to the working of inventions in host countries; they are often used by their owners to protect an import monopoly and to hinder local production. They control local markets since the patented product is imported from a company's headquarters. The patent system encourages protection rather than transfer of technology. In fact the protection granted bestows monopoly rights that hamper a broad diffusion and utilization of knowledge. Patents are often used by foreign firms to make high profits and they limit the dissemination of know-how, even if information about patents is publicly available. Patents do not include the vital information needed to produce and thus the system does not really diffuse knowledge for technical manufacturing. Foreign-owned patent registration hampers the development of local technological capacity.

The Third World demands for revision of the patent system were raised very strongly in the early 1970s. Since 1974 the WIPO began to explore the possibility of revising the Paris convention in the light of Third World concerns. In the preparatory process of the envisaged revision the Group of 77 made several proposals for the accommodation of Third World interests. Although four diplomatic conferences (between 1980 and 1984) addressed the Paris revision, the concerns of the developing countries were not accommodated.

One of the concessions the Third World countries were able to achieve in the negotiations was the introduction of compulsory licensing of intellectual property. Compulsory licensing aims at preventing owners of rights to intellectual property from refusing to exploit those rights and at forcing right owners to allow competition subject to the payment of reasonable royalties or licence fees. Among the motives for this provision are the expectation that it compels technology suppliers to transfer technology and that it limits the possibility for suppliers to restrict the use of technology after the expiration of transfer agreements. Compulsory licensing caused much controversial debate in the international community, but on balance very little use has been made of the provision. This can be partly explained by the fact that the compulsory licence does not automatically include the necessary knowledge that enables the recipient to reproduce an invention independently.

Apart from the concession on compulsory licensing, the Third World concerns were put on the back burner as the industrial nations managed to deadlock the negotiations and shifted the forum of debate from the World Intellectual Property Organization to the GATT. Since the prevailing agreements on intellectual property protection were seen as the main culprits in causing billions of dollars damage to trade interests, the industrialized countries and their TNC lobbies began to put pressure on the developing countries to adopt more strict intellectual property legislation and to harmonize their domestic laws with Western models. In 1985 and 1986 the USA, the EC and the TNC lobbies began to persuade the GATT membership to include in the GATT an agreement on trade-related intellectual property rights (TRIPs). The preference for GATT over WIPO was partly argued on the basis of the perceived inadequacies of the Paris and Berne conventions administered by the WIPO. These agreements would not provide for an effective mechanism of implementation and sanctions. Moreover, they were seen as insufficient to stop the extensive world-wide trade losses caused by counterfeiting and piracy. GATT on the contrary has a mechanism for the settlement of disputes and for the imposition of penalties (retaliation and cross-retaliation sanctions) when GATT rules are broken. Other arguments were that Berne and Paris were too permissive on granting compulsory licences, and had no express provisions on full compensation for compulsory licences. Basic to the expressed preference for GATT as a negotiating forum was the choice to view intellectual property protection as a key trade issue.

At the ministerial meeting in Puenta del Este (Uruguay, September 1986) where the new GATT round of multilateral trade negotiations (Uruguay Round) was initiated, the ministerial declaration (issued on 20 September 1986) stated on TRIPs:

> In order to reduce the distortions and impediments to international trade, and taking into account the need to promote effective and adequate protection of intellectual property rights, and to ensure that measures and procedures to enforce intellectual property rights do not themselves become barriers to legitimate trade, the negotiations shall aim to clarify GATT provisions and elaborate as appropriate new rules and disciplines. Negotiations shall aim to develop a multilateral framework of principles, rules and disciplines dealing with international trade in counterfeit goods, taking into account work already undertaken in the GATT. These negotiations shall be without prejudice to other complementary initiatives that may be taken in the World Intellectual Property Organization and elsewhere to deal with these matters.

The Third World countries, particularly India and Brazil, argued that WIPO was the proper forum for negotiations on intellectual property rights and that a GATT framework would be detrimental to their interests. However, a working group on IPR was established and by April 1989 the Third World countries had agreed to let negotiations proceed. At the Montreal meeting (December 1988) for mid-term Uruguay Round talks the Third World countries were still insisting that WIPO would be the correct forum for talks on intellectual property. They also expressed a preference for non-enforceable conventions and they expressed the fear that a GATT agreement on IPR would restrict trade and allow certain firms to exercise monopolistic power through their patents.

In April 1989 the Trade Negotiations Committee (TNC) adopted decisions among others on the principle of establishing standards, enforcement and dispute settlement procedures on trade-related aspects of IPR including trade in counterfeit goods. The developing countries, spearheaded by India and Brazil, dropped their insistence that the WIPO should have exclusive jurisdiction in IPR matters and that the GATT should have no role in setting norms and eliminating theft of copyrights, patents and trade marks. At the April meeting the trade ministers agreed that IPR negotiations would address such issues as the applicability of the basic principles of the GATT, the provision of adequate standards and principles concerning the availability, scope and use of trade-related intellectual property rights, the provision of effective and appropriate means for enforcement of trade-related intellectual property rights, and the provision of effective and expeditious procedures for the multilateral prevention and settlement of disputes between governments, including the applicability of GATT procedures.

Against the rather successful movement to incorporate TRIPs in a GATT agreement, a large meeting of NGOs maintained that such an agreement would seriously hinder the diffusion of technical knowledge to Third World countries, hamper local technological innovation and benefit mainly transnational corporations. The New Delhi NGO statement on intellectual property rights and obligations (March 1990) claimed: 'The free flow of scientific knowledge and information within the scientific community would be severely restricted. It would therefore obstruct the very development of science and technology in the public interest . . . The TRIPs proposals aim at reserving the domestic markets of the Third World countries for the manufactured goods of the developed countries. The proposals would arrest the promotion of indigenous technological capabilities.'

The global harmonization of IPR protection that is proposed by the new GATT agreement is supported with the argument that this will increase technology transfer to Third World countries and will facilitate access to advanced technology. Given their export orientation many developing countries have accepted to change their IPR domestic regulation to a level defined by the industrialized countries. Many of them will adopt the GATT accord on TRIPs which determines minimal norms for protection. Several countries have already revised their IPR laws. There is a clear shift from the earlier position taken by the Third World countries. Most of them feel now that only the adoption of the proposed harmonization can reduce the North–South technology gap. In connection with the technology gap many countries have begun to focus on export strategies and the common expectation is that improved IPR protection will reinforce this economic policy through transfer of technology and cooperation in science and technology. Countries have also been coerced (usually through bilateral negotiations with the USA or the EU) to change their position through threats of sanctions from Western trading partners. The real policy decisions have often been taken not in the multilateral GATT forum but in these bilateral encounters. A classical case is that of Mexico, where President Carlos Salinas de Gortari, who wanted a North American Free Trade Agreement (NAFTA) was put under enormous pressure by US copyright industries which threatened not to support the agreement if Mexico would not toughen its intellectual property protection. US trade pressures also forced Mexico to enact a Law for the Promotion and Protection of Industrial Property (effective 28 June 1991) that provides for patent protection for plant varieties. Mexico was rewarded for its accommodation of US interests by removal from the US blacklist of trading partners.

It is still far from clear whether the shift in position will indeed benefit the Third World. In any case, given the great differentiation among Third World countries, the effects are likely to be different across countries. It may well be that a very few countries will benefit through the new IPR regime and have more technology imports, more domestic innovation and more R&D investment. The likelihood is, however, that the majority of countries will not see any such benefits and may even confront strong drawbacks. It is likely, for example, that prices for the products of biotechnological engineering will increase. The GATT TRIPs agreement sanctions that the biotechnology industry commercializes and privatizes the biodiversity of the Third World countries. This industry uses the genetic resources of the Third World as a free common resource and then transforms them in laboratories into patentable genetically engineered products. In the process the industry manipulates life forms that are common heritage. This means that whereas formerly plants and animals were excluded from the IPR regime, biotechnology has changed this. Life can now be the object of ownership. This has many perplexing implications, one of which is that thousands of years of local knowledge about life organisms are devalued and replaced by the alleged superior knowledge of Western scientists and engineers.

The Pugwash Executive Committee, in its meeting in Turin (11–13 October 1990), argued that intellectual property rights should not only benefit the industrial nations, but also stimulate free innovation in the Third World. There should be a proper balance between safeguards for intellectual property rights and global welfare. The Committee warned that the provisions of the TRIPs accord under the GATT would not strengthen the technological capabilities of the South, but would rather strengthen the control of TNCs over technology and reinforce the monopolistic rights of technology providers. The pressure to create a uniform system of IPR protection was seen by the Committee as a constraint on the flexibility that Third World countries need to adapt their IPR system to their specific needs and interests.

Extensive multilateral cooperation supported by a binding and robust accord in the area of transfer of technical knowledge has become even more urgent as Third World countries are rapidly losing their natural resource leverage in international negotiations. This is largely due to recent developments in technology. 'Discoveries in new materials and processes lower the demand for many raw materials traditionally supplied by developing nations. Automation and quality-control requirements make unskilled and semi-skilled labour a relatively less important component of manufacturing costs, decreasing the advantage of locating operations in labour surplus countries' (United Nations Centre on Transnational Corporations, 1990: 10). The new patterns of foreign direct investment (FDI) suggest 'the emergence of a type of technological "convergence club" of the world's leading industrialized nations, plus perhaps a small group of advanced developing or newly industrializing countries which are positioned to make similar progress' (1990: 11). As technological capacity is an important factor in determining the direction of FDI flows, a majority of Third World countries are left behind in the new world order shaped by the members of the 'convergence club'. This is particularly worrying as current trends indicate that access to technology is getting more and more difficult for the Third World. Restrictions on technology exports and stricter rules on the protection of industrial property make the acquisition of technical knowledge from the North more expensive and less likely.

The positions

Concerns about the international transfer of technology have focused on the conditions and terms under which Third World countries could acquire technical knowledge and could control the adverse practices of technology suppliers. The monopoly control over technical knowledge through the international patent system has also aroused serious concern in the world community. The main agents of these concerns have been the developing countries. Quite different concerns have been expressed by the technology supplier countries and their transnational corporations. These agents were concerned that prevailing instruments for the protection of intellectual property were grossly inadequate in protecting their proprietary interests and in facilitating international trade. They were also concerned that the international adoption of restrictive measures in connection with the transfer of technology and the conduct of TNCs would stifle international trade.

These divergent concerns were motivated largely by development considerations versus market considerations. Third World concerns were inspired by the aspiration of acquiring technological capacity for independent development, and were based upon the conception of technology as a common good. The industrialized countries' concerns were based upon the wish to retain technology leadership and to expand markets. In their conception, technology is primarily private property.

In the multilateral negotiations rival claims were put forward. In relation to the international code of conduct on the transfer of technology, restrictive and permissive positions were on a collision course. The Group of 77 countries claimed for instance that the code should be an internationally legally binding instrument, and the group of developed market economy countries claimed that it should be a non-binding arrangement of a voluntary and general nature. The restrictive approach was oriented towards national development and the permissive approach focused on international competition. With regard to the settlement of disputes, for example, the restrictive claim would defend the supremacy of the domestic law of the recipient country. The more permissive approach would insist on formulations that stressed the respect for the freedom of contract (i.e. the free choice of applicable law) among parties to transfer of technology. The Third World countries as the main claimants for the development approach refused to accept this since they claimed that this would erode the power of national governments to regulate technology transfer and to determine jurisdiction in cases of dispute.

The industrial countries, the main claimants for the competition approach, claimed that the principle of competition should be the sole criterion by which to judge restrictive business practices. In other words, practices should be regarded as restrictive business practices and prohibited if they restrict competition. The Third World countries claimed that these practices should be judged in the light of how they affect the development of recipient countries. In other words, practices should be prohibited as restrictive business practices if they restrict trade and/or adversely affect the transfer of technology since this conduct hampers the development of recipient countries.

In relation to the international patent system the claim to a revision of the system of 'right of access' and the claim to a revision based upon a 'trade' framework confronted each other. These claims were largely based upon conflicting arguments about the availability of knowledge resources as common good versus the protection of knowledge as private property. The argument from developing countries for a 'right of access' revision has been that the conventional patent system encouraged protection rather than diffusion or transfer of technology. Their opponents, the industrial countries and the large private technology suppliers, have argued that without the provision of strict industrial property protection there would be no transfer of technology at all. Against the claim to practices that would primarily protect the property rights of knowledge producers, the obligations of rights holders have been emphasized. Such obligations could include the duty of disclosure, the obligation to provide information and supporting documents concerning corresponding foreign applications and grants. The right holders should be obliged to work the patent in the country where the patent is granted and could be required to refrain from engaging in abusive, restrictive or anti-competitive practices.

Prevailing political practice
There is only limited multilateral cooperation in the field of transfer of technology. This is not supported by a binding and effective multilateral accord. Current provisions are found in a series of declarations, resolutions, programmes of action and draft codes of conduct. All these lack binding provisions and effective implementation measures. The most powerful constituency of technology suppliers offers no support for the establishment of effective multilateral cooperation. There remains a basic discord on fundamental principles as the stalled negotiations on the UNCTAD code of conduct demonstrate.

In connection with the protection of intellectual property the conventional patent system is considered inadequate by all players, albeit with divergent arguments. As a result of the Uruguay Round of multilateral trade negotiations a binding and robust accord has emerged on the protection of intellectual property. Developing countries have considered this accord to be disadvantageous to their interests. It can be expected however that the majority of these countries will adapt to the norms and rules of an accord that accommodates a trade claim rather than a development claim.

Notes

1 As minimal standards the report proposed: for every 100 inhabitants of a country a distribution of 58 newspapers, 94 radio sets, 13 cinema seats and 32 TV receivers. 'Under-developed' meant an availability of less than ten newspaper copies, five radio sets, two cinema seats and two TV sets. In 1960 some 100 states (representing some 66 per cent of the world population) had less than these minimal levels of media available.

2 A source for the MacBride round table statements is Traber and Nordenstreng (1992).

3 Compare this figure of approximately US $18 million with the profit figures for some of the world's leading communication industries in 1992, e.g. News International Corporation US $360 million, Reuters US $407 million, Walt Disney US $817 million.

4 David Wright, manager of regional programmes for Inmarsat, has explained that the efforts of Inmarsat to establish multilateral cooperation are not for purely altruistic reasons. 'Our forecasts show that a large percentage of the Inmarsat market, especially with the advent of personal satellite communications, will be in developing countries in the future. Thus we want them to be strong supporters of our system' (Wright, 1994: 11).

8

Transborder Data Flow

The major issues that emerged in the area of transborder data flow (TDF) are related to national sovereignty, privacy, data security and computer crime. The agenda status of TDF issues is primarily caused by the technological convergence of telecommunication and computers (telematics). This merger made it possible for private actors to combine these technologies into integrated networks. Existing political practices however hindered this and as a result strong pressures to deregulate the TDF environment emerged. One important aspect of the new technological possibilities was the threat to conventional territorial control over data. Data of different kinds could now easily be shipped in and out of countries without the authorities knowing, let alone controlling. This raised the issue of national sovereignty. TDF also gave rise to concerns about the protection of privacy.

In the 1970s the TDF issue was placed on the agenda of such international institutions as the OECD and the Council of Europe. In fact, the term 'transborder data flow' was probably invented by an OECD expert group that wondered in 1975 whether this new area 'constituted a problem sufficiently important in its implications for national sovereignty for governments to propose regulation' (Gassman and Pipe, 1976: 27). TDF issues are today still on the agenda because of the economic importance of electronic data interchange (EDI) and electronic funds transfer (EFT).

In the course of the 1960s computer communication networks were created that consisted of computers with communication channels attached to them which linked computers to computers or to telecommunication terminals. The networks were constructed as centralized systems in which data were transported for processing, storing or forwarding to central computers. They were also designed as distributed systems that facilitated data traffic between decentralized computers or terminals. Transmissions through these networks commenced with the first circuits for defence purposes and airline reservations. During the 1960s and 1970s they were increasingly applied also for international banking, credit control, data banks and intergovernmental cooperation. In world politics concerns about TDF were first addressed by the OECD through two high-level OECD conferences on TDF which took place in 1977 and 1983. 'The TDF issue initially arose in the OECD because of some experts' concerns that individual privacy would not be protected if name-linked information was passed to other countries with less stringent data protection laws' (McDowell, 1989: 20). The OECD concern led to the adoption of the 1980 guidelines on privacy. In the early 1980s emphasis was put on the movement of economic data in particular, and in 1985 a declaration on TDF was adopted that promoted a liberal, 'free flow of information' approach to TDF issues.

The Intergovernmental Bureau for Informatics took TDF issues on the agenda as part of its concern with the development of national informatics capacity. The TDF debates sponsored by the IBI (for instance the world conferences in 1980 and 1984) were motivated by the IBI concern about the TDF impact on national strategies and policies for informatics. In spite of its attempt the IBI did 'not achieve the objective of becoming a universal forum for discussing these issues or advancing a broad multilateral approach to the TDF issue' (1989: 21).

The United Nations became involved through the United Nations Centre on Transnational Corporations which produced several studies on TDF in the 1980–5 period. 'The UNCTC research program investigated TDF use by transnational corporations, and the effect of this use on corporations' relations with developing nations' (1989: 21). The UNCTC work on TDF was severely hampered by declining budget resources and the unwillingness of the most powerful players to support it. The other UN agency involved is the United Nations Commission on International Trade Law (UNCITRAL). This Commission focused on issues connected to electronic funds transfer (EFT) and electronic data interchange (EDI). In 1988, it produced a set of rules for interchange of trade data by teletransmission (UNCID rules) which provide the basis for international EDI agreements.

On the regional level, in particular, the Council of Europe addressed TDF issues in the context of its convention on the protection of privacy (Article 12 of the 1981 convention). In the mid 1980s the GATT became an important forum for world politics on transborder data flows. In 1986 also Unesco established a special Intergovernmental Informatics Programme within its Science Division. Among the tasks of the programme were the development of telematic networks providing electronic mail and access to data banks.

National sovereignty

National sovereignty can be defined as the capacity to influence allocative decisions regarding national resources. Transnational data flows export data that are essential to such decisions and move these beyond the jurisdiction of national governments. TDFs imply a threat to national sovereignty since they facilitate the control over critical national decisions by foreign actors.

Control over locations where vital data are processed and stored is an important factor in national and world politics. If a country lacks data about itself – whether it has no capacity to collect them or to process them – its decision making capacity is seriously impaired. 'This can result in a national self-perception of impotence, an inability to effect one's vital choices, and the effective erosion of one's political sovereignty' (Gotlieb, Dalfen and Katz, 1974: 247).

TDFs imply increasing chances to escape governmental control on the international flow of capital, for example. It was always difficult for governments to control capital flows, but the development of telematics challenged national sovereignty most fundamentally. The awareness of the TDF threat to their national sovereignty inspired many Third World countries to strive towards multilateral rules on this phenomenon. Using the IBI as their forum they tried to achieve a common accord on TDF. The most powerful players considered this undesirable and favoured an arrangement that would be based upon free trade standards.

Data protection

The concern about data protection emerged originally as a mainly domestic issue. It was first expressed in the 1970s through legislation in Germany, Sweden, Norway, France and the USA. These countries designed laws that dealt with the protection of person-linked data. Their origin was motivated by the increasing application of computer technology to data collection, storage and processing. This was seen to possibly lead to such centralized control that the privacy of citizens could seriously be endangered. The application of computer technology enormously expanded the capacity of information capture, processing and storage. The potential to handle large volumes of information according to the specific and detailed requirements of their users increased dramatically. A precise tracing of an individual's movements became possible through the 'electronic trace' people leave behind as they use credit cards, rent cars, buy airline tickets, and purchase items in department stores. In most of the affluent countries people began to give their privacy away when signing up for credit cards, mortgages or driver's licences. As Robert Ellis Smith, editor of the *Privacy Journal*, stated; 'For very little cost, anybody can learn anything about anybody' *(Business Week*, 1989: 32). In many countries it became increasingly difficult to know who held what information on whom and for what purposes. Rapidly increasing volumes of personal information could be collected, stored and sold through vast electronic systems. As a result national and international markets for personal information emerged. As economic activities converged, for example in the banking and insurance sectors, there was a strong incentive to share the personal information that banking and insurance companies had been collecting. These companies also began to realize that the information resources they possessed not only could be used for internal purposes, but also had a general market value.

As banking and insurance internationalized, their trading of personal information also became global business. When more data on more citizens were held in more countries and were transported between more countries, the concern about data protection became an international issue in need of international regulation. The extension of domestic data protection also became necessary since national legislation could be evaded by the installation of data processing centres across the border.

The data protection laws that were adopted during the 1970s have several common features, such as 'setting limits to the collection of personal data in accordance with the objectives of the data collector and similar criteria, restricting the usage of data to conform with openly specified purposes, creating facilities for individuals to learn of the existence and contents of data and have data corrected, and the identification of parties who are responsible for compliance with the relevant privacy protection rules and decisions' (OECD, 1980: 11).[1] Differences between national laws existed in particular with reference to licensing requirements and control mechanisms, the definition of sensitive data, and the provision of individual access.

When in the 1970s the data protection concern internationalized, the prime forums for negotiation were the Council of Europe, the European Communities and the OECD. Already in 1973 and 1974 the Committee of Ministers of the Council of Europe had adopted two resolutions concerning data protection. The recommendations suggested that member countries would take steps to implement basic principles of protection relating to the collection of data, the quality of data, and the rights of individuals to be informed about data and data processing activities. Following this the COE began to prepare for an international arrangement through a convention.

In the 1970s the EC also began to study the possible harmonization of legal rules in connection with TDF, and in 1978 the European Parliament held a public hearing on data processing and individual rights. The subcommittee responsible for the hearing prepared a report that was submitted to the European Parliament in 1979 with a resolution on the protection of individual rights in view of data processing.

The OECD programme goes back to the late 1960s and its studies on computer usage. In 1977 the OECD Data Bank Panel held a symposium in Vienna to discuss privacy problems in the context of TDF. The symposium presented a number of guiding principles that recognized '(a) the need for generally continuous and uninterrupted flows of information between countries, (b) the legitimate interest of countries in preventing transfers of data which are dangerous to their security or contrary to their laws on public order and decency or which violate the rights of their citizens, (c) the economic value of information and the importance of protecting "data trade" by accepted rules of fair competition, (d) the need for security safeguards to minimise violations of proprietary data and misuse of personal information, and (e) the significance of a commitment of countries to a set of core principles for the protection of personal information' (OECD, 1980: 14). In 1978 a new expert group on transborder data barriers and privacy protection was initiated and was instructed to work closely with COE and EC to 'develop guidelines on basic rules governing the transborder flow and the protection of personal data and privacy' (OECD, 1980: 14). The work of the expert group led to the OECD guidelines that were adopted in 1980. Although there are similarities with the COE convention, the main difference is that the guidelines are a non-binding instrument. Another distinction is that the guidelines apply to all personal data, including those handled manually; the COE convention addresses only automatically processed data.

In the 1980s a new forum for data protection developed in the conference of data commissioners (TDR, 1989: 5–8). This is an informal body that brings together those public authorities that are mandated to supervise personal data registers and generally supervise enforcement of the data protection legislation. Over the past years the conferences of the data commissioners have acquired increasing importance and the conference has evolved into an unofficial regulatory institution. The 1989 conference addressed among other issues the commissioners' concern about the lack of control over TDF and the need for equivalent safeguards in transmitting and receiving countries. Special attention was also given to the privacy implications of the evolving integrated services digital networks (ISDNs). 'This development means that considerably more personal data are processed by network operators as well as by service suppliers than was the case with previous networks. This development calls for national and international measures to ensure the protection of personal data' (Riley, 1989: 7–8).

The data protection concern has typically developed as a domestic issue addressed by domestic legal disciplines. Because of the different national legal approaches to data protection the design of an international approach has been hampered. An obstacle is also posed by the rapid development of innovations in information technology. This quickly renders legislation obsolete and makes constant revision necessary. The issue of data protection emerged when computer applications began to proliferate throughout society. When it became clear that national rules could not adequately protect privacy against the possibility of moving data to countries with permissive attitudes towards data protection, the concern internationalized and led to calls for international measures to protect personal data. Data protection needs effective multilateral cooperation since world-wide there has been an increase in ways of intruding upon people's privacy.

The positions
The claim that there should be a strong protection of individual privacy has been countered by the claim that restrictions on data traffic impede free trade, hamper the free import and export of information and could be used in protectionist ways.

The 1985 OECD Declaration on Transborder Data Flows reflected the fear that protection of TDFs could in effect imply non-tariff trade barriers. This became a concrete issue in the 1980s with the protective legislation in Brazil that imposed restrictions on data processing abroad. And in response to the draft directive of the EC on data protection, commercial firms have claimed that the provisions of the directive pose 'excessive and unjustified restraints on their freedom of action' (Rodotà, 1992: 266). The OECD Guidelines on Protection of Privacy have tried to find a balance between the rival claims to the protection of individual privacy and to the recognition of the free flow principle.

There have also been rival claims with regard to the scope of protection. Originally, data protection standards would pertain to natural persons and the question has been raised about their extension to legal persons. In several of the national laws that were enacted in the 1970s protection had been extended to include also legal persons (e.g. in Austria, Denmark, Norway and Luxembourg). The claim in favour of extension has been defended with the arguments that data collections on legal persons contain person-linked data; that in the absence of protection companies could label person data as company data; that unauthorized use of legal person data may have important economic effects; and that data registered by companies should be correct, especially in cases where big firms hold data on smaller companies.

It took some time before the large users woke up to the ramifications of privacy regulation and started an effective lobby against the inclusion of legal persons. The main argument against legal person protection has been that this would imply access to data and in this way crucial (marketing, financial, product development) information would be given to competitors. The International Chamber of Commerce (1984) has stated repeatedly that existing legislation – tort laws, laws on intellectual property, laws on theft of industrial secrets – provides sufficient protection for legal persons. The OECD guidelines contain no provisions for the application of privacy protection to legal persons. The COE convention opens in Article 3.2(b) the possibility to apply its provisions to companies.

Data security

At the heart of TDF is a high-risk technology. Errors in computer software, malfunctioning of computer systems, or incorrect trans-mission can cause physical harm and economic loss. If digital information technology is tampered with, airline passengers may die in a crash, hospital patients may be seriously injured, or companies may go bust. Computer software error and the related liability issues were raised in the late 1980s in a poignant way by Vanden-berghe. In an article entitled 'Software bugs: a matter of life and liability', he pointed to the possibility of death and serious injuries as a result of malfunctioning computer systems. Vandenberghe warned that 'With the ever increasing importance of software and firmware in traffic control, airplanes, cars, production machines, medical devices, etc., it can only be expected that these kinds of events will occur more often' (1988: 18).

Herewith the concern was expressed that with the increasing dependence on digital systems for vital social functions, such as international finance and transport, a critical vulnerability had been created in the case of system malfunction or deliberate obstruction. This vulnerability to technology failure in many social areas was seen as particularly serious because of the inherent unreliability of digital computers (Forester and Morrison, 1990: 68–87).[2]

Among some of the earlier signals that pointed at the problem of technology vulnerability was the 1978 report by the Swedish

Ministry of Defence Committee on the Vulnerability of Computer Systems (SARK), *The Vulnerability of Computerized Society*. In 1981 the Organization for Economic Cooperation and Development (OECD) held a workshop in Sigüenza (Spain) on the Vulnerability of the Computerized Society. In 1984 the American Federation of Information Processing Societies published a report on the matter, and in the same year the Information Task Force of the Commission of the European Communities published *The Vulnerability of the Information-Conscious Society: European Situation*. In 1986 the Norwegian Vulnerability Commission presented a report called *The Vulnerability of a Computer Dependent Society*. In 1989 a committee of the British Computer Society reported that current skills in safety assessment were inadequate and therefore the safety of people could not be guaranteed (Forester and Morrison, 1990: 3).

These various commissions and reports began to identify the risks that the use of international computer systems entailed. Such risks could be incorrect transmissions either by technical malfunction or by the intentional act of an intruder. Incorrect transmissions could include the transmission to the wrong address, or of the wrong content, or of both. Transmissions could also be afflicted by delays or by the unexplained loss of data.

Another risk could be unauthorized access to the data traffic or the data themselves or both. A third type of risk could be communicating with fraudulent persons (Redeker, 1989: 19). Risks could also be caused by malfunctions of networks that take care of electronic funds transfer, and such malfunctions may be caused by environmental factors, by equipment failures, by errors in design architecture, or by human errors in data processing. Such errors could cause inadvertent changes in the contents of payment instructions.

Vulnerability for societies can also be a result of the increased speed of transactions. As businesses use greatly reduced response time to lower their stocks of goods (space parts, components) a computer virus could close down a factory if something goes wrong in the electronic communications between manufacturer and supplier. The Michelangelo virus of early March 1992 did not create as much damage as it could have since there was timely warning across the world. Several reports did mention however that some 10,000 computers had been hit world-wide. The virus did wipe out the contents of the hard disks of the infected computers.

The users of TDF are increasingly confronted with urgent and complex security problems that need measures against both inadvertent error and deliberate fraud.

Since the risks of digital technology may lead to considerable damage, a call for international rules that would establish liability and damage compensation emerged. This concern for the adoption of international arrangements on data security confronted a host of complex problems. In conventional practice, for example, the operators of international networks could not be held liable for damages caused as a result of transmissions. In many countries the PTT has been the main network operator and in most national legislations the PTT cannot be held liable. As Redeker states for the German case, 'the PTT is practically never liable for damages, except in the case of gross negligence of a very high ranking officer of the PTT' (1989: 20). In the Netherlands, for example, the law on telecommunications operations (law of 1988, Article 12) provides a very restricted liability for the public network operator with limits on compensatory payments. Also in international law, there are no provisions for liability in case of damage.[3] The convention of the International Telecommunication Union (in Article 21) simply excludes any liability for international connections.[4] Just as it has been a long-standing tradition with telecommunication carriers to refuse any liability for losses caused by their deficiencies, so too have banks been very reluctant to accept liability. The pertinent articles in the International Chamber of Commerce (ICC) Uniform Customs and Practice Rules provide (Article 17) 'Banks assume no liability or responsibility for the form, sufficiency, accuracy, genuineness, falsification or legal effects of any documents', and (Article 18) 'Banks assume no liability or responsibility for the consequences arising out of delay and/or loss in transit of any messages, letter or documents, or for delay, mutilation or other errors arising in the transmission of any telecommunications.'

Recently, however, there has been a growing awareness in the international community that in time the interests at stake may necessitate the regulation of liability for network operators. The complexity of liability for risks is also compounded by the sharing of information in networks when separate systems become interconnected and lines of responsibility blur. It is difficult to establish who is accountable for errors in the use of distributed information processing facilities offered by third parties. Another problem with creating solid legal provisions on information system liability has been the concept of information itself. The definition of this intangible phenomenon, and the determination of the nature of its ownership or control (and by implication accountability for acts involving information), has turned out to be much more difficult than was the case with tangible products.

With the increasing reliance on computer systems and the magnitude of potential harm, the question has arisen of the recognition of strict liability for information systems. In strict liability the plaintiff does not have to provide evidence of negligence by the defendant. A plaintiff in a products liability case must show that the defendant manufactured or supplied a product that was defective when it left the defendant's control, that the plaintiff was injured by the product, and that the defective condition was the proximate cause of the injury. There is a growing volume of case law in the USA in which the courts accept product liability for products containing defective information, for example defects in the instrument approach chart that may cause an aeroplane crash. Typically, the First Amendment has been cited to argue that subjecting information products to liability law would restrict free speech. Courts have acted differently on this. Increasingly, countries adopt consumer protection acts that impose liability on providers of defective products. There is a general tendency to shift from the classical rule of *caveat emptor*, which places full responsibility with the buyer, to a *caveat* for the producer. However, in most cases this new liability still tends to follow the conventional division between products and services. For example, the EC Directive on Product Liability of July 1985 does not apply to services.

In conventional law the issue of liability is addressed from the angle of physical harm. There is little provision for indirect economic loss that may be caused by a negligent delivery of information. 'This means that in the context of information technology, one is more likely to succeed under the present rules for personal injury caused by a robot malfunction than the failure of a business due to defective software' (Saxby, 1990: 226). Only recently have there been indications that courts may be willing to go beyond the classical compensation for bodily injury and physical damage. In some countries, like Germany, strict liability for information has been accepted. One could also argue that product liability for information is at least indirectly provided in the EC directive since a defect in the information concerning a product can be considered a defect of the product (Vandenberghe, 1988: 20). The *ratio legis* of the directive is the protection of the consumer, and from the consumer's angle hardware and software are identical. As Vandenberghe has argued, the defence by a manufacturer that software cannot be produced without errors and that often the defect cannot be discovered is weak. 'If the state of scientific and technical knowledge at the time he put the software into circulation was not such as to enable him to discover the existence of a defect which could endanger life and property, was it then not reckless to put such a product into circulation?' (Vandenberghe, 1988: 22). A product may be held defective because of a failure to provide adequate warning as to (reasonably foreseeable) dangers that may result from its use. This does raise the question of whether, for example, software producers should provide warnings against the possible presence of viruses.

Computer crime

With the spread of computer applications a new type of crime emerged which, as data processing became international, raised new issues for regulators. Several highly publicized cases in the late 1980s (such as access to computer systems in Canada from New York or access to NATO information systems in Norway from the USA) have shown that 'the prevention of computer crime is of great significance as business, administration and society depend to a high degree on the efficiency and security of modern information technology' (Sieber, 1990: 119).

With the proliferation of computer users and the growth of knowledge about computer operations, the chances of computer abuse have drastically increased. There are however no reliable data on the spread of computer crime or on the extent of possible damage caused by it. There is a relatively small number of known computer offences and probably a much higher figure for undiscovered abuses. Sieber attributes this

> first to the low proportion of computer offenses which become known due to the specific difficulties of detection and proof in the DP sector. Second, many of the offenses that are discovered are subjected to the internal disciplinary procedures of the companies concerned rather than being reported, due mainly to a fear of damage to the company's reputation and loss of confidence by investors, shareholders, and customers or in order to facilitate the compensation for the damage done. Third, cases reported to the law-enforcement agencies are not always systematically prosecuted since effective treatment requires special knowledge as well as high expenditure in terms of time and money. Finally, it is a matter of chance whether reported cases of computer crime are discovered among other cases of fraud and breach of trust, because the criminological term 'computer crime' does not appear in official legal administration statistics. (1986: 33)

Studies indicate that 'losses in computer crime are much more severe than those in traditional crime' (1986: 34) and 'the problems caused by computer crime are bound to intensify in the future' (1986: 35).

The phenomenon of computer crime has raised some difficult juridical questions, like whether taking data from a computer system constitutes theft. In the conventional juridical sense theft refers to tangibles. It means taking away tangible property with the intention of deprivation. Can data be owned and taken away? Can an owner of data be deprived of data? Traditionally legal experts have been hesitant in awarding information the status of property. Whenever this happens in criminal or civil law, there is the tendency to restrict exclusive property to a time limit. Other questions are whether one can steal from something that remains unaltered. Is the owner of a data bank deprived of property if the data stay in the data bank? If data theft is legally recognized, then how can the damage to the victim be assessed? Extending exclusive proprietary rights to data and protecting them from disclosure (for instance through trade secret provisions) can cause monopolization of data and thus imply unfair competition. Other unresolved issues deal with search, seizure and evidence procedures. If in a case of alleged computer crime the crucial data have to be accessed on the suspect's computer system, does conventional search and seizure extend to the right to use the accused's equipment? Can law enforcement officers search foreign data collections? Since this does not require their physical presence on foreign territory, is an electronic *droit de poursuite* necessary? Can the accused or witnesses be required to generate data electronically from their systems? Does police tapping of computer data collections require the same provisions as conventional telephone tapping?

A 1986 OECD study referred to computer-related crime having an international dimension owing to the internationalization of information and computer services. The study pointed to the need for an international response since 'international cooperation in the repression of computer-related offences . . . would facilitate transborder data flows' (OECD, 1986: 7). In the summary the study stated that international cooperation is recommended in the areas of both civil and penal law. 'As far as civil and administrative economic law is concerned, international harmonized solutions are necessary also in order to secure equal conditions of competition, to facilitate transborder data flow, and to avoid the transfer of undesirable or detrimental actions in foreign countries . . . It is important to develop common approaches to penal and procedural law in order to protect the international data networks, to enable the functioning of international instruments of cooperation in criminal matters and to guarantee that evidence gathered in one country is admissible in court in another country' (1986: 64). The report stated very clearly that any other solution 'would lead to "data havens" and "computer crime havens" and therefore lead to restrictions in transborder data flow' (1986: 64). The purpose of international cooperation would be the repression and prevention of computer crime. To this end it is especially important to resolve current problems related to possibilities for extradition. Both international extradition treaties and national extradition legislation will have to be amended to include computer-related crime. Harmonization of regulation on computer crime is made difficult since countries follow different legal approaches and use divergent legal conceptualizations. It has been increasingly realized that international cooperation in the field of law enforcement and computer crime would demand directives regarding the conditions under which several states would be entitled to prosecute the same case, the law enforcement authority on foreign territory and the harmonization of criminal sanctions. Harmonization is required if the emergence of computer crime havens is to be prevented.

Since 1984 the OECD has addressed the issue of computer crime in a series of *ad hoc* meetings and through studies conducted by the secretariat and Ulrich Sieber. From this work the 1986 study on computer-related crime which resulted addressed the approaches in member countries, gave a classification of acts to which the label computer-related act could be ascribed, and provided an analysis of the international dimension of computer-related crime. In 1986 the OECD proposed as a definition of computer crime 'any illegal, unethical or unauthorized behaviour relating to the automatic processing and the transmission of data' (OECD, 1986: 7).

In 1990 a committee of experts of the Council of Europe recommended a computer crime list of eight points.[5] These were computer fraud, computer forgery, damage to computer data or programs, computer sabotage, unauthorized access, unauthorized interception, unauthorized reproduction of a protected computer program, and the unauthorized reproduction of topography. On an optional list the committee listed as four more crimes the alteration of computer data or computer programs, computer espionage, unauthorized use of a computer and unauthorized use of a protected computer program (Council of Europe, 1990).

The positions
Transborder data flows have made it possible to commit computer burglaries irrespective of borders. Computer crime has become an international problem as it can easily be committed through technology in one country with effects in another country. This has raised concern about its impact, repression and prevention across national borders. Special concern has been raised since countries operate different legal practices. This makes international cooperation very difficult. In cases where countries have different definitions of

computer crime, or in cases where computer crime is not recognized by the domestic legal system, the possibility of extradition is unlikely.

Therefore, the need for an effective common response has been stressed in a series of international gatherings and publications. 'The special need for a close international harmonization of (criminal and non-criminal) information law primarily originates from the mobility of data in automated information systems' (Sieber, 1990: 127). Not only are data mobile, but today's technology makes control over data flows practically impossible and national measures utterly futile. Great differences in national policies would rather contain the risk of creating 'computer crime havens' (1990) and would tend to hamper international data flows. 'Differing legal regimes would also provoke governments to restrict data flows to countries with less developed protective systems . . . These national restrictions would imperil privacy, trade secrets and the free economic development of an international information market' (1990: 127).

In very general terms there is a distinction between those countries that claim that existing legislation sufficiently covers acts related to automated processing and transmission of data and those countries that claim that legislative initiatives are needed. The latter prefer either to incorporate computer crime into existing law or to establish completely new rules. In the legal articulation of the issue there are divergent emphases on such concepts as property, forgery and access.

Electronic data interchange (EDI)

The proliferation of automated data processing has caused changes in the nature of essential documentation in international trade. Paper documents are being replaced by electronically produced, transmitted and reproduced documents, and document authentication is changing from the handwritten signature to electronic means.

Examples of affected documents are rail consignment notes, bills of lading, goods declarations, airway bills, documents required by port and customs authorities and documents issued by operators of transport terminals. Paper-based records are increasingly replaced by digital media in finance, transport and commerce. Computer-to-computer communications are increasingly used to make payments, issue invoices and transmit contracts. Bills of lading, bills of exchange, airway bills and letters of credit are digitally transported. 'Paperless trading' or electronic data interchange (EDI) is rapidly expanding into the dominant mode of business communications in the 1990s. In 1990 a world market exceeding US $1 billion made use of electronic trade, with such major users as banks, transport and shipping companies and governments (Ritter, 1991). Since participation in international trade becomes dependent upon access to EDI technology, this new form of transmission adds to the difficulties for developing countries seeking to improve their trade opportunities. 'The inability to access such interchanges will be the equivalent of an absolute barrier to international trade' (Robinson Sauvant and Govitrikar, 1989: 112).

The greater utilization of EDI necessitates the inter-operability of networks and requires standardization of communication, system integration, message definition and distributed networking. To facilitate data communication between information systems the International Organization for Standardization (ISO) has developed the open systems interconnection (OSI) model. The ISO has also developed a standard for the structure (or syntax) of messages, the EDIFACT standard. In fact the EDIFACT was adopted by the working party on facilitation of international trade procedures (working party of the Economic Commission for Europe of the United Nations) in 1986 and the OSI was adopted in 1987.

Serious problems for the development of EDI are also caused since not all traffic is necessarily error-free. The International Chamber of Commerce (ICC) has designed rules of conduct for data traffic, but these Uniform Rules of Conduct for the Interchange of Data by Teletransmission (UNCID) do not contain provisions on liability in case of damage caused by transmission errors. They are mere guidance for parties that enter into an interchange agreement.

The widespread utilization of EDI is hampered by the lack of harmonization on rules relating to the question of whether documents can be placed in intangible format under the legislations of both sender and receiver, and to differences in evidential and signature requirements. The specific regulatory issues that surfaced address the legal value of computer records and the legal value of electronic authentication. Key questions are whether electronic documents are admissible in court proceedings and whether they have an evidential value comparable to paper documents. Can electronic documents be authenticated through digitized signatures? Will their reliability be challenged in courts? Since in the civil laws of many countries computer documents will be considered hearsay evidence, their admission as evidence faces difficulties.

In international trade, documents have been transported by telegraph and telex for more than 100 years. The conventional point of view has tended to consider these telecommunications much like paper-based documents. Where legal provisions required that documents must be presented in writing, the paper copies held by the sender and the receiver of the telegraphic or telex traffic would be considered as sufficiently meeting those provisions. Evidently this traffic did not provide for written authentication. However, in most cases sufficient confirmation as to the source could be given (for instance through call-back procedures) although opportunities for fraud were always present. With the advent of computer communications networks, paper-based documents could be transformed into electronic messages and reproduced at distant locations as similar paper-based documents. Among the issues this raised was the possibility of unauthorized alteration of records.

In 1984 the United Nations Commission on International Trade Law decided to put the topic of legal implications of electronic data processing in international trade on its agenda. In 1985 a report was submitted to the Commission by the secretariat which was based upon material collected from two investigations. One dealt with the use of computer-readable data as evidence in court proceedings, and another (in cooperation with the Customs Cooperation Council) on the acceptability to customs authorities of goods declarations in computer-readable form and the use of such declarations in court proceedings. Practically all countries that responded indicated that they had legal rules that would permit computer records as evidence and that would allow courts to evaluate the legal significance of such records. The report observed that an important legal problem regarding electronic data in international trade was caused by the requirement that documents must be signed or must be in paper-based form. At its meeting in 1985 the UNCITRAL recommended to governments: (i) to review the legal rules affecting the use of computer records as evidence in litigation in order to eliminate unnecessary obstacles to their admission, to be assured that the rules are consistent with developments in technology, and to provide appropriate means for a court to evaluate the credibility of the data contained in those records; (ii) to review legal requirements that certain trade transactions or trade-related documents be in writing, whether the written form is a condition to the enforceability or to the validity of the transaction or document, with a view to permitting, where appropriate, the transaction or document to be recorded and transmitted in computer-readable form; (iii) to review legal requirements of a handwritten signature or other paper-based method of authentication on trade-related documents with a view to permitting, where appropriate, the use of electronic means of authentication; (iv) to review legal requirements that documents for submission to governments be in writing and manually signed with a view to permitting, where appropriate, such documents to be submitted in computer-readable form to those administrative services which have acquired the necessary equipment and established the necessary procedures. Moreover, the Commission recommended 'to international organizations elaborating legal texts related to trade to take account of the present Recommendation in adopting such texts and, where appropriate, to consider modifying existing legal texts in line with the present Recommendation'.

In the development of rules for the use of computer records in international trade, a number of other international organizations became involved. Among them was the International Maritime Organization which has adopted several amendments to the Convention on Facilitation of International Maritime Traffic (signed at London, 1965) in order to facilitate the use of electronic data. The International Rail Transport Committee (IRTC) began in 1985 a study of legal conditions for replacing rail consignment notes by electronic data transmission. A report submitted in September 1985 to the Governing Committee of IRTC stated that the Convention Concerning International Transport by Rail (signed in 1985) did permit the transport of goods under the cover of electronic transmission of data. The Customs Cooperation Council resolved in 1986 that in view of the need to facilitate the greatest possible use of electronic data techniques in international trade a legal framework for the acceptance of international trade data transmitted by electronic or other automatic means as evidence in court proceedings had to be created. The Council noted that existing legislation often refers exclusively to traditional paper documents, and suggested the review of legal requirements concerning documents and signature and the modernization of legislation in order to ensure the acceptability of teletransmitted data as evidence in court proceedings.

Important in the debate on the use of electronic data in trade has also been the working party on facilitation of international trade procedures of the UN Economic Commission for Europe. At its sixteenth session in September 1982 the working party decided 'that there is an urgent need for international action to establish rules regarding legal acceptance of trade data transmitted by telecommunications'. Also the International Chamber of Commerce has promoted the acceptance of documents produced by electronic techniques. In its 1983 revision of the Uniform Customs and Practices for Documentary Credits it is stated that 'Unless otherwise stipulated in the credit, banks will accept as originals documents produced or appearing to have been produced by reprographic systems, by, or as the result of, automated or computerized systems' (Article 22(c)). Although there are at present different national legal approaches to court evidence of computer records, and to the requirement for handwritten authentication, the general regulatory trend is towards the legal acceptability of electronic transmissions.

Since EDI messages often contain person-linked data, there is a privacy problem that needs to be addressed. A question, for example, is whether the existing arrangements for the protection of privacy would in principle also apply to EDI traffic. A current policy issue in the European region is how far EC draft directives on the protection of privacy in electronic information systems may unduly hamper the development of EDI systems.

A still unresolved issue is that of liability. Obviously, parties and third persons can suffer damage as a result of failures in transmissions, corruption of data or improper access to data. In such cases questions of liability and compensation should be clarified. This is particularly important in the field of electronic funds transfer.

Electronic funds transfer (EFT)

EFT has raised concerns about the protection of consumers in the case of incorrect charges, unauthorized access to their accounts, the non-delivery of electronically ordered goods, or the delivery of defective goods. EFT has also brought up regulatory issues in connection with methods of identification and the inter-operability of systems to ensure a wide use of electronic payment cards. In the case of loss, EFT raises the complex problem of whether the transferor banks are liable, or whether the public carriers or private communication services are liable, or whether loss can be contractually allocated between different actors? Should there be a general disclaimer of liability on the part of the banks, or should this be restricted to cases where one could not reasonably expect the bank to have been able to avoid or reduce errors? Another difficult question relates to the burden of proof. When a debit to an account is unauthorized, in the customer's opinion, should the customer prove this or can the burden of proof be shifted to the bank? This question has come up especially in the context of so-called customer activated terminals where fraudulent access is a widespread problem. As a consequence of delays in the international transfer of funds, customers can incur damage, and the problem of liability comes up again as a complex issue, particularly as intermediary banks may be involved. Under what conditions could a transferor or intermediary bank be held liable for delays.

Electronic funds transfer is funds transfer that involves electronic messages and computer processing. Most funds transfers today involve both paper-based and electronic techniques. The concern about the vulnerability of EFT arose with the development of new closed-user networks for funds transfers in the 1960s. As it turned out, credit transfers (for which telegraphy had been used for over a century) could be efficiently handled by electronic means, particularly in cases where regular large-scale payments had to be made, for instance salaries or social security benefits. Debit transfers to those transferees to whom many customers would owe debts on a regular basis could effectively be processed by computers.

EFT has a domestic and an international dimension. The link between transferor and transferor bank is a national act as is the link between transferee and transferee bank. The link between transferor and transferee is international. This has raised the question of whether separate arrangements for domestic and international components or a single agreement for the whole process would be preferable.

In 1982 the UNCITRAL decided to prepare a legal guide on EFT, which was published in 1986 (UNCITRAL, 1986). This *Legal Guide on Electronic Funds Transfers* was the beginning of work towards model rules on electronic funds transfers. A working group on International Payments undertook the work and submitted in 1988 draft provisions for model rules on electronic funds transfers. At its 1988 session in New York (July 1988) the working group decided to rename its draft and call it draft provisions for model rules on credit transfers. The draft left the matter of the protection of consumer rights to national discretion and provided (in Article 1.2) that 'A State may adopt supplementary legislation dealing with the rights and obligations of consumers.' On the question of liability a rather general exoneration was provided for (in Article 10) 'if the bank proves the failure was due. . . . to interruption of communication facilities or equipment failure'.

In 1988 the Convention on International Bills of Exchange and International Promissory Notes was adopted by the United Nations General Assembly as an annex to Resolution 43/165. The provisions of the convention govern the funds transfer instruction issued by the transferor and all the transactions to implement this instruction. The convention also provides that the rights and obligations of an intermediary bank would be governed by it. The implication is that the domestic transfer between a transferor bank and an intermediary bank in the same country would also be governed by international rules. The scope of the convention is restricted (Article 1) as its provisions are only applicable if parties have indicated that their bills of exchange are 'international bills of exchange'.

The positions
For both EDI and EFT there is a concern about the legal validity of computer records in an international context. Both forms of data communication also raise concerns about standardization of systems, harmonization of legal rules, and vulnerability of electronic systems to failure. Agents of such concerns have been governments of countries involved in electronic trading and finance, transnational trading corporations, banks, and business interest organizations such as the International Chamber of Commerce. Representatives of consumers in particular have raised concerns about liability in cases of failure and compensation in cases of damages resulting from such failure.

The players currently involved have argued the case for a common agreement on legal rules to govern EDI and EFT. There has been some disagreement as to whether current provisions on data protection should be applied to these transmissions. There have also been rival claims as to the level of liability to be allocated to the different parties involved in EDI and EFT. Banks and telecommunication operators tend to claim a general exoneration of liability and consumer organizations prefer a more restrictive approach that protects consumer rights more adequately.

Prevailing political practice
In 1987 Kirby wrote that with reference to the COE convention and the OECD guidelines 'it must, in all frankness, be said that little else has been achieved in the move towards an international regime within which the TDF phenomenon will continue to grow' (1987: 81). This continues to be the state of affairs. There is to date no common comprehensive agreement on TDF. The situation is that of a patchwork of separate regulatory instruments and forums that address fragmented concerns raised by TDF.

In the 1974–86 period there were different forums without any one of them achieving the status of a world forum. Some regulatory instruments were developed, none of which was comprehensive in scope and application. The policy efforts in the 1974–86 period were to a limited extent influenced by public good considerations. This shifted from 1986 onwards towards a market orientation motivated by commercial considerations. The effort of the Intergovernmental

Bureau for Informatics to develop a common agreement on TDF
was not perceived by the major players (the data-resource-rich
countries and the leading TNCs) as in their interests. There was a
strong desire on the part of the powerful players to move towards a
consensus within a trade framework that would facilitate a permissive arrangement supported by the strong constituency of the
world's leading data technology producers, data service providers
and data network users, and the governments of data-resource-rich
countries. These forces began to promote a collective practice in
which trade barriers are reduced, the operations of TNCs are
unhindered, and international data service transactions are treated
in non-discriminatory fashion. The concern about a liberalization of
data trade became the motivating force behind the emergence of a
robust and effective common agreement that serves in particular the
key players in world data communication.

On the issue of national sovereignty there was basic discord. The
developing countries got involved in the TDF debate through the
International Bureau for Informatics (originally established by
Unesco in 1951) which was to become their main forum. Some 37
developing countries opened TDF discussions in the IBI with the
participation of France, Spain and Italy. In conferences held
between 1978 and 1984 the issue of the TDF threat to national
sovereignty was the priority on the agenda. This was very clear at
the Second World Conference on TDF in 1984 where much
discussion focused on the need to control TDF. The call for a TDF
regulatory framework was reinforced by a variety of studies that
pointed to the additional threats TDF posed to economic and
cultural sovereignty (Hamelink, 1984: 64–73). However important
all these issue were, 'by the mid-1980s, the majority of them had
been eliminated from the international agenda, while most of those
that remain are consistent with the corporate demand for unrestricted TDF' (Drake, 1993b: 293).

In the 1970s the private actors were hardly involved in the debate.
This changed in the early 1980s when Third World positions on the
sovereignty issue began to worry the transnational TDF user
community. First the US-based companies began to lobby Congress
and State Department for a policy position protective of their
interests. This was reinforced through the mobilization of international coalitions of users. Among the most vocal groups emerged
the International Telecommunications Users Group (INTUG), the
International Chamber of Commerce (ICC), and the Business and
Industry Advisory Committee (BIAC) of the OECD. Against these
lobbies the governments that were pro regulation were plagued by
the question of whether regulation was indeed practicable. As any

regulation would imply some form of data flow monitoring, the utilization of direct satellite connections, advanced encryption techniques and random routing of fragments of messages suggested that it would be technically impossible to control TDF (Hamelink, 1984: 99). A basic problem was also, as Drake observes, 'that neither governmental nor independent analysts were able to produce much hard evidence that the anticipated negative effects of TDF were occurring at the time' (1993b: 296).

Around 1983–4 the new emphasis became clear. The new issues were trade barriers to TDF and the demand for TDF politics based upon trade principles. The concept of sovereignty was no longer there when in 1985 the OECD adopted its non-binding declaration on TDF. The declaration was introduced as 'the first international effort to address issues raised by the information revolution. It addresses the policy issues arising from transborder data flows such as flows of data and information related to trading activities, intracorporate flows, computerized information services and scientific and technological exchanges. These flows are playing an increasingly important role in the economies of member countries and international trade and services.' OECD ministers declared their common intent to 'promote access to data and information and related services, and avoid the creation of unjustified barriers to the international exchange of data and information'. And as Drake has suggested, even the term 'transborder data flow' seems to have lost against such concepts as 'information trade' (1993b: 302). The IBI was dismantled (there were also internal problems that sped up this process), the emphasis shifted and the prospect of a multilateral agreement on transborder data flow disappeared.

On the issues of data protection and data security, limited forms of multilateral cooperation have been established. They are limited to restricted membership forums and are not supported by binding and robust accords.

Data protection
'One basic concern at the international level is for consensus on the fundamental principles on which protection of the individual must be based. Such a consensus would obviate or diminish reasons for regulating the export of data and facilitate resolving problems of conflict of laws. Moreover, it could constitute a first step towards the development of more detailed, binding international agreements' (OECD, 1980: 12). Such a binding common agreement has not yet been developed and adopted by the international community.

Current collective practices are constituted by the OECD declaration and guidelines and the Council of Europe Data Protection Convention. The OECD instruments are non-binding; they define very general principles for a minimal international consensus; they contain no enforcement procedures; and their constituency is limited (although powerful). The Council of Europe Data Protection Convention is a binding legal instrument for states that ratify it. As the Council is a regional body, the constituency of the convention is limited, although the instrument is open for accession by all countries. The basic principles of the convention are the right to confidentiality, the right to be informed about the existence of data collections, and the right to data quality. The convention is formulated rather generally and leaves the methods to deal with these principles to national legislation. The convention does not say how people are to know about data being collected about them or how to obtain remedy when data registers refuse either access or rectification.

There are also serious questions about the adequacy of the concepts that are used in the convention. A core concept is the automated personal file. This was based upon the early situation in which large mainframe computers would hold files that could be accessed and processed by different users. Today files are ubiquitous; they are in personal computers, for instance. One can hardly apply the rules to all automated files. Also the notion of 'machine readable' has changed with the application of optical scanners.

The concern about the quality of data (COE convention Article 5 or OECD guidelines, part two, paragraph 8) led to the formulation of a right of access for the data subject. This is insufficient if the data subject wants to get all the data correct. The data in different collections may be in and by themselves correct, but their combination may create inaccurate statements. If you take from one data base correct data on gross income and combine them with correct data from another data base on net income and present them as income, the outcome is no longer accurate. There is also the development towards more automated data collection devices. The data subject himself or herself does not provide the information which is collected by electronic systems, such as traffic control systems.

The convention deals with the sensitivity of data (Article 6) and refers to health, sex and crime. Is this sufficient? How about data on political affiliation? Or data about race and religion? Sensitivity increases with the potential for discriminatory use of the data. What guarantees does the convention provide against collective surveillance, for example the surveillance of suspect populations? 'The majority of those subject to surveillance are not actually criminals, but only persons qualified by coincidence as members of the suspect population' (Bing, 1992: 256).

There is also a problem with the provision of the right of access as a fundamental right of citizens. The question is whether this really functions as an instrument of control. 'It is a disappointing international experience that very few citizens make use of the right to access, regardless of how comprehensive this right is outlined in the different national statutes' (Blume, 1992: 17). Yet there is sufficient evidence to suggest that 'citizens feel very strongly about data protection and are worried about the extent of knowledge that public authorities and large private firms can acquire about them in our modern, information society' (1992: 17). Blume suggests that the fact that access has to be a personal initiative constitutes a major barrier to use this means of control. An alternative might be a system in which citizens would be informed about the data held about them. 'Denmark has discussed such a system. However, besides the practical difficulties of such a system, a file of files would also create political problems. It would mean that the state had one big file or database containing all available information on all citizens, which when seen from the point of privacy would be very dangerous' (1992: 18).

In addition to the OECD and COE instruments, one could also refer to the United Nations Guidelines on Privacy. These are meant to propose the minimum guarantees that national legislation should adopt. Like the COE convention only general principles are defined and implementation is left to national domestic law. Although criminal sanctions are proposed as remedies, the scope and application is left to national legislators. Basic principles are lawfulness and fairness of collection, accuracy of data, specification of purpose, non-discrimination and the right of access. The guidelines provide for exceptions to these principles in cases of the protection of national security, public order and public health. These exceptions are very broadly defined.

The prevailing practice consists of limited multilateral cooperation based upon a voluntary and weak agreement. The effectiveness of any agreement is under threat from the actual conduct of the major players who display a growing interest in data collections and their commercial value.

Data security

In October 1989 the OECD secretariat submitted to the Committee for Information, Computer and Communications Policy (ICCP) a report on Information Network Security. The preparation of this report had been approved by the ICCP in October 1988.

Following the report the ICCP appointed a group of experts to draft guidelines for information system security. Between January 1991 and September 1992 this group met six times and prepared a recommendation for the OECD Council (ambassadors of the 24 member countries) on Guidelines for the Security of Information Systems, the guidelines themselves, and an explanatory memorandum. On 26 November 1992 the OECD Council adopted the recommendation and the member countries adopted the guidelines. In its recommendation to the member countries the Council pointed to the 'increasingly significant role of information systems and growing dependence on them . . . the sensitivity and vulnerability . . . due to risks arising from available means of unauthorized access, use, misappropriation, alteration and destruction'. In the memorandum annexed to the guidelines the group of experts has highlighted the growing dependence on information systems and its concern for the possibility of information system failure. 'Failures of information systems may result in direct financial loss, such as loss of orders or payment, or in losses that are more indirect or perhaps less quantifiable by, for example, disclosure of information that is personal, important to national security, of competitive value, or otherwise sensitive or confidential' (OECD, 1992: 17). The group expressed its deep concern at the growing gap between the need to protect information systems and the current measures of protection. The concern is an international issue 'because information systems and the ability to use them frequently cross national boundaries. It is a problem that may be ameliorated by international cooperation.' Pursuant to this consideration the Council – in its recommendation – called for 'international collaboration to develop compatible standards, measures, practices and procedures for the security of information systems'.

Other initiatives to formulate rules of data security have meanwhile been developed by the meeting of the Data Protection Commissioners (first meeting in Australia, November 1992), the Commission of the European Communities, which has proposed a Council directive on data protection, and the Council of Europe.

'The early completion by the OECD of its project seems likely to ensure that the OECD Guidelines are influential in shaping national and international laws and policies on this topic' (Kirby, 1993b: 28). The guidelines are presented as a general framework within which member countries can develop laws, codes of conduct, technical measures and user practices. Central to the instrument is a set of nine principles. The accountability principle provides that the responsibilities and accountability of those involved with information systems should be stated explicitly. The awareness principle which provides that those interested should have access to information about measures for the security of information systems in order to foster confidence in such systems. The ethics principle implies that the provision and use of information systems and the security of information systems should take into account the legitimate rights and interests of others. The multidisciplinary principle states that the development of security measures and practices should take the whole range of pertinent viewpoints and forms of expertise into account. The proportionality principle suggests that security needs vary and security measures should be in line with the value of information systems and the severity of potential harm. The integration principle says that security measures should be coordinated and coherent security systems should be designed. The timeliness principle proposes that the timely response to security breaches is vital. The reassessment principle suggests that the dynamic development of information systems renders a periodical assessment of security measures necessary. The concluding democracy principle says that the security measures should be in line with legitimate interests in use and flow of data and information. The guidelines conclude with a set of recommendations to member countries on the implementation of security measures through policy development, education and training, enforcement and redress, exchange of information, and cooperation.

At present, the OECD guidelines represent the core of an emerging political practice in connection with the concern about data security. The normative provisions of the guidelines are non-binding (they are indeed just guidelines), the constituency is very limited (although the OECD member states are powerful actors), and there are no enforcement mechanisms. There is however the potential for development into a robust and effective agreement.

Notes

1 In Sweden, Germany, France, Austria, Denmark, Norway and Luxembourg.

2 Forester and Morrison (1990) argue that, unlike analogue devices, digital systems can suddenly fail totally or behave erratically. As digital systems are discrete state devices, they can be in an infinite number of states and the execution of each state depends upon the earlier state to be correct. The magnitude of possible discontinuities is mind-boggling. Software bugs, systems malfunction, computer crime and hacking can costs millions of dollars – and human lives. Computer software errors may cause over-billing, false arrest, but also loss of life and grave injury.

3 The reasoning for this refers to the risks involved in the public policy to connect users to the network and the low revenues this yields. Arguments also point to the need to facilitate technological development and the fact that risks of damage are very different for different categories of network users (De Graaf, 1990: 66).

4 The ITU constitution of 1989 states in Article 25: 'Members accept no responsibility towards users of the international telecommunication services, particularly as regards claims for damages.'

5 The full descriptions of the listed crimes are as follows:

Computer fraud   The input, alteration, erasure or suppression of computer data or computer programs, or other interference with the course of data processing that influences the result of data processing, thereby causing economic or possessory loss of property of another person with the intent of procuring an unlawful economic gain for the perpetrator or for another person.

Computer forgery   The input, alteration, erasure or suppression of computer data or computer programs, or other interference with the course of data processing, in a manner or under such conditions as prescribed by national law that it would constitute the offence of forgery if committed with respect to a traditional object of such an offence.

Damage to computer data or programs   The erasure, damaging, deterioration or suppression of computer data or computer programs without right.

Computer sabotage   The input, alteration, erasure or suppression of computer data or computer programs, or interference with computer systems, with the intent to hinder the functioning of a computer or a telecommunication system.

Unauthorized access   Access without right to a computer system or network by infringing security measures.

Unauthorized interception   Interception, made without right and by technical means, of communications to, from and within a computer system or network.

Unauthorized reproduction of a protected computer program   Reproduction, distribution or communication to the public of a computer program which is protected by law.

Unauthorized reproduction of topography   Reproduction without right of the topography, protected by law, of a semiconductor product, or the commercial exploitation or the importation for that purpose, done without right, of topography or of a semiconductor product manufactured by using the topography.

9

Standardization of Consumer Electronics

'The development of public policy towards standardisation is not always inclined to take explicit account of non-technical factors. Historically, the preferred public face of standardisation was that of an activity transacted by technical experts within a purely technical discourse, and directed essentially at devising collective solutions to shared technical problems' (Mansell and Hawkins, 1992: 45). International standardization was initially a largely technical issue. In the past decades it has become increasingly clear however that standardization is not only a technical process, but is also influenced by political and commercial considerations.

In the past decade the development of new technologies and related information services has significantly increased the international demand for standards. At the same time, however, political and economic interests often hampered multilateral co-operation. This means that the players involved tend towards the adoption of multiple standards or of no standards at all. 'Increasingly, as the necessary standardization has moved to the multilateral arena and the numbers of interests involved have increased, so it has become more difficult to reach consensus. Sometimes no agreement is reached' (Hills and Papathanassopoulos, 1991: 147).

Standardization used to be largely a national process. The international dimension was restricted to the cross-border linkage of national systems. The globalization process in trade and finance has put more emphasis on world-wide standardization which then subsequently affects national systems. What happened was a shift from the construction of domestic grids to be interconnected to each other to the development of a global grid to which domestic networks must adapt.

Through this internationalization more players became involved in the standardization process. In addition to the PTTs and the RPOAs (like AT&T), the International Telecommunication Union and its consultative committees, CCITT and CCIR, the International Organization for Standardization, the International Electrotechnical Commission, the regional standards institutions and the large organized users, such as INTUG, became active contributors. The regional standards organizations became increasingly important. They held their first inter-regional conference in 1990, the Interregional Telecommunications Standards Conference with attendance mainly from Europe, North America and Japan. To a large extent the developing countries are just observers in the politics of standardization. There has been mounting pressure on them to align with the major powers in respective regions. This effectively excludes a large number of countries from the inter-national decision making process. Governments have become increasingly involved in the standardization process. This is largely due to their concerns about national sovereignty, the protection of national industries and the promotion of national trade.

The multilateral standardization process is often long and compli-cated. Recommendations for standards are made after lengthy deliberation and consultation in a process in which consensus is sought. As a result standards have been often developed outside the official standards institutions by the market leaders, such as large electronics manufacturers. This implies a conflict between propri-etary *de facto* standards and internationally agreed standards. 'Until the 1980s, the computer industry was dominated by the *de facto* world standard of IBM, achieved through market dominance' (Hills and Papathanassopoulos, 1991: 146).

As was suggested, political and economic factors play decisive roles in the politics of standardization. Among the political factors are such considerations as national security and prestige. In the struggle for a world-wide standard on colour television in the 1960s, the world-wide adoption of a US, French or German standard was clearly perceived by the respective countries as a political victory. In that same standards battle, the Soviet Union first sided with the French standard since it wanted to support neither the US nor the German standard. As negotiations went on, the Soviets felt that instead of adopting the French norm in full, it would be politically better to present a version they could claim to be their own.

Among the economic factors are such considerations as the use of standards as non-tariff trade barriers against market entry by foreign competitors. This was very much French policy in the 1960s in order to keep foreign TV manufacturers out of the domestic market. An essential economic factor is the access to markets. For companies that provide services their access to global markets depends upon interconnectivity. Also for companies providing equipment, standards equivalent to national and regional standards facilitate their access to local markets.

The extent to which national standards are compatible with international standards determines the compatibility and intercon-nectivity of equipment and thus the access to global markets. The choice of a standard for videotex provides a good illustration of how national economic interests could obstruct the achievement of international standardization. Since the USA did not develop its own videotex standard the US market was in principle open to the rival Canadian, French and British systems. Illustrative cases of world standardization politics are the standard setting for colour TV, videotex, HDTV and Internet.

The colour TV war of the 1960s

The first operating colour TV system was that of the National TV System Committee. The NTSC standard was operational from 1954. In the late 1950s Henri de France developed sequential encoded colour amplitude modulation (SECAM); with superior colours. In 1962 AEG-Telefunken developed – using the best elements of NTSC and SECAM – a system called phase alteration by line (PAL).

The 1965 CCIR Plenary Conference at Vienna was to decide the world-wide standard for television. All three systems had big economic stakes in the process and had their voting blocs. France and the Soviet Union voted for SECAM, Germany for PAL, and the USA for NTSC. 'The Soviet-French agreement established SECAM as a major contender for the title "world colour television system". The Americans and West Germans reacted by hastily combining PAL and NTSC support into a package called QUAM, which sought to eliminate technical differences between PAL and NTSC through creating one compatible system' (Savage, 1989: 191). The conference did not resolve the issue. SECAM received 21 votes against 18 for QUAM. Following political and economic interests the CCIR delegates voted in support of domestic industrial interests. These were considerable since many countries had not yet decided for a specific standard. They were therefore potential export markets for the winner of the world standard.

As a result of the deadlock the standards issue was taken up again by the eleventh Plenary Assembly of the CCIR in 1966 at Oslo. To add to the confusion, the Soviet Union presented to this meeting its modified version of SECAM (SECAM-IV) as a fourth option. 'The conference, like that in Vienna one year earlier, ended without an agreement on the European colour television system. The CCIR resigned itself to the irrevocable and entrenched existence of three incompatible standards' (Savage, 1989: 192). Eventually, the CCIR issued a multiple standards that made it possible for the three systems to coexist.

The TV standard issue was typically approached from limited, national perspectives. 'The determination of whether it is necessary as well as desirable to adopt standards compatible with other nations will be based upon an evaluation of several factors involving the national interest. These include national political strategy, national technical needs, public opinion, estimates of the value of services, economic status, balance of payments, the costs of not agreeing, history and experience' (Crane, 1979: 8).

The videotex conflict of the 1980s

Just as in the case of colour television, three competing, incompatible systems emerged: the Canadian Telidon system, the British Prestel, and the French Antiope. 'While AT&T had toyed with the idea of developing an alternative of its own, by 1980 it was apparent that the United States would not be developing its own videotex system, thus opening their market for the Canadian, British, and French systems' (Savage, 1989: 202).

For the respective governments – all three pursuing world-wide promotion of their standard and investing heavily in the effort – obtaining CCITT approval was essential. The CCITT convened in 1983 a series of conferences in order to achieve a world-wide unified videotex standard. At the 1984 CCITT eighth Plenary Assembly in Malaga-Torremolinos, it had to be concluded that no standard had been achieved and that stark divisions remained between the contenders. Eventually, after seven years of study, negotiation, and disagreement, the CCITT issued a multiple standard recommendation.

High-definition TV

In 1982 a CCIR interim working party recommended adoption of a single world standard for high-definition television, a new technological development that would bring a spectacular improvement in imagery and sound. The first HDTV system was developed by the Japanese NHK and Japan was keen to have its system adopted as the global standard. The NHK system offers video pictures of 35 mm film quality. It is however not compatible with existing TV systems and requires replacement of all TV sets. This system was initially supported by the Americans. The US position was motivated by the expectation that a single standard would facilitate the US export of TV productions. This changed later in view of the large volume of exports to Europe and in connection with the film community's concern about HDTV and incompatibility with 35 mm film. Meanwhile, the Europeans became worried about the prospect of a dominance of Japanese hardware and American software. Their opposition was led by Philips and Thomson.

At the 1986 CCIR conference in Dubrovnik the Japanese system was not adopted as the standard. The Europeans now developed their own standard, called multiplexed analogue component (MAC). Its major advantage was compatibility with existing analogue TV systems. The European Commission has been actively involved in furthering the European standard. Its 1986 Directive ordered the adoption of the MAC family of standards. There emerged some quarrels in the family between the C-MAC variant of the UK and the D2-MAC variant of France and the Netherlands. In 1990 the CCIR meeting was confronted with the Japanese wish that its standard be global, with the Europeans wishing theirs to be the global standard and the Americans wishing neither standard to be global. In early 1992 the European Commission decided to give up its own analogue HD-MAC norm and to concede space for a digital HDTV standard. In April 1993 the European Parliament decided that the European industry should explore the possibilities for digital television as it increasingly felt that analogue TV was out.

Among the problems that HDTV faced in Europe was that when colour TV was introduced in Europe, the broadcasting companies were very helpful by starting broadcasts in colour before households had access to colour sets. By the 1990s however the European broadcasting landscape had changed and public monopoly systems in many countries had given way to commercial, competitive stations. The main beneficiaries of European HDTV would be Thomson (France) and Philips (the Netherlands). The British obstructed the European standard as their commercial stations and cable operators would have to meet the additional expense of adapting their equipment to continental European norms. It may be that the British obstruction was a blessing in disguise, as it stopped the European Communities sinking more funds into an analogue production system and a transmission system that would quickly be obsolete. By June 1993 the European Communities decided to continue their investment in the development of HDTV, but at a lower rate. In 1992 the European Commission proposed a budget of more than US $1 billion annually (for five years) and in 1993 this changed to US $300 million annually for four years. The EC subsidies would go to TV companies, programme producers and programme distributors, provided their national governments support 50 per cent of the HDTV projects.

In 1994 it has to be concluded that no world-wide standard on HDTV has been achieved, and that the consumer electronics industry in several countries has been hit seriously by the HDTV failure. In the 1990s the consumer electronics industry was in need of new markets – given saturation of the VCR and CD markets – and the economic stakes in a world-wide HDTV standard were high. There is a potential world market of US $650 billion TV sets. These enormous economic interests made HDTV a matter of 'high politics'. 'As with black-and-white and colour television in the past, establishing an HDTV standard has inevitably become increasingly political and an instrument for protecting domestic hardware manufacturers as well as audio-visual productions' (Joosten, 1993: 28). The early HDTV operators, the Japanese and Europeans were losing the battle before it had really begun. They had selected an analogue production standard and a transmission mode which both turned out to have little future in the light of the increasing digitization of TV production and the use of optical fibre cables and microwave video distribution systems.

In early 1993 an advisory panel for the Federal Communications Commission (FCC) recommended that a choice would have to be made among four systems developed by three industrial consortia. It was expected that in early 1994 a decision would be made on the US standard. All four systems employ digital technology. The three consortia are Zenith jointly with AT&T; NBC with Thomson and Philips; and General Instruments with the Massachusetts Institute of Technology. The FCC began choosing a standard in 1987 in a process that combined a market-led strategy with some government coercion. The FCC has ordered that the winning consortium will license its technology at a price judged acceptable by the FCC to the contenders.

On 21 May 1993 the *New York Times* reported that the biggest computer companies (including Apple, Digital and IBM) in the USA had warned the FCC that they would develop their own standard if the administration supported the standard preferred by the broadcasters. The computer manufacturers pleaded for a high-definition TV system that would be compatible with the needs of computer users. By May 1993 three remaining rivals were close to an agreement to produce a unified system before the end of the year. This system would also cater to the requirements of the computer industry. The three teams that were to form the alliance were Zenith Electronics and AT&T; General Instruments and the Massachusetts Institute of Technology; and Philips, Thomson, NBC and David Sarnoff Research Center–Compression Labs Inc. On 25 May 1993 Associated Press quoted FCC chairman James Quello as saying 'It is great to see people working together to develop the best HDTV in the world.' Compared with Europe, in the US effort 'a much wider range of industries have participated in this essentially consensus forming process. This will reduce the risk of excluding certain interests and options outright as well as stimulate coordination and cooperation between the several participants. When the FCC decides on a standard at the end of this year [1993], American industry will be more likely to introduce HDTV successfully not only in their domestic market, but also abroad. Meanwhile, Japan still ponders over an obsolete analogue system and Europe remains even more divided than before' (Joosten, 1993: 30).

A crucial question for the success of HDTV is obviously what consumers want. So far in the process, consumers are not involved. Yet, they are decisive. Consumers may want better quality, but do they want to pay? Interestingly, the large-screen TV needs large and dimly lit rooms. There are likely to be extra charges for consumers (for new sets and transmission systems). Consumers may want programmes, and this is what is missing. Few productions are made for HDTV. In mid 1993 the estimates for HDTV sets were that they would cost consumers between US $1000 and US $2000 more than current large-screen, premium TV sets.

'There is also little hard evidence that viewers value the improvements in quality offered by HDTV. Compared to the introduction of colour television in the 1950/60s, HDTV offers relatively marginal quality improvements, including a wider "cinemascope" picture and clearer picture and sound quality. In reality, many viewers are happy to accept lower quality picture, on small or poorly tuned receivers for example, and it is hard to envisage such viewers being attracted by HDTV in large numbers. For those viewers who do want improved quality, intermediate widescreen technology (such as PALplus) may be sufficient, particularly as widescreen services are already becoming available, and at a much lower cost than HDTV' (Carse and Shurmer, 1993: 31). In their study on the future of HDTV, Carse and Shurmer estimate that by 2003 there could be a market (largely business and affluent households) of some US $7 billion. This takes into account 'the current uncertainty over standards, the likely indifference of both consumers and broadcasters to HDTV, and the availability of cheaper, intermediate widescreen improvements to picture and sound quality' (1993: 32). They project that if a world-wide digital standard were adopted this could increase up to US $15 billion by 2003. Even with the unlikely adoption of one standard, HDTV will only be a modest niche in the world market for TV sets.

The Internet battle

Computer networking has become an activity involving a rapidly growing number of users around the world. Today E-mail can be exchanged among some 127 countries with an estimated 20 million users. The development of international networks raises important questions about standardization. Presently there are two opposite preferences expressed by the community of users. Some prefer the transmission control protocol/internet protocol. 'Driven by user demand and elaborated in the market place, TCP/IP has been internationally adopted as the logical building block of the global Internet, and is employed in an estimated 75% of vendor independent enterprise networks' (Drake, 1993a: 643). Others favour the open system interconnection (OSI) designed by the International Organization for Standardization. OSI is primarily driven by European computer manufacturers and European telecommunication authorities. The TCP/IP approach reflects a market-driven, bottom-up process of standardization in which 'standards often arise within the electronic network from individuals and organizations who rapidly collaborate on design and testing on a global basis' (Drake, 1993a: 644). The OSI approach reflects a top-down planning method and involves formal multilateral institutions such as ISO and ITU. At stake in these different approaches is the basic issue of whether standard setting should be an open or a closed process.[1] At present the major standards organizations are not characterized by a great deal of transparency. Faced with a vastly expanding and dynamic community in cyberspace, this seems rather inadequate.

The positions
There has been a long-standing common concern in the world community about technical standardization. This has been largely motivated by the needs of interconnectivity and inter-operability of communication systems. In addition there have been important political motives in the sense of having a national standard declared the world-wide norm. Economic motives have also promoted the establishment of international standards as these would enable access to global markets and control over these markets. Economic concerns might have equally supported the adoption of national standards as a protective measure against foreign competition.

A peculiar complication in the area of standardization is the possible clash between standard setting and the protection of intellectual property rights. If a technology is commonly adopted as the international standard and if a company has patented this technology, then only the patent holder could produce the related equipment. Different positions on this issue have led to a conflict between the European Telecommunications Standards Institute (ETSI) and the Computer Business Equipment Manufacturers Association (CBEMA). ETSI has developed in recent years a policy whereby it expects companies to register an objection against having their intellectual property included in the development of standards. The objection should be lodged within 180 days. Several ETSI members, among them Apple, Digital Equipment Corp., Motorola and IBM have contested this policy. In July 1993 the General Assembly of ETSI decided to delay the implementation of its policy.

The standardization issue has often led to rival claims about the leadership of one standard against another. This would usually be argued on the basis of technological superiority or the *de facto* establishment of a standard outside the official forums. The claim that one standard should be adopted world wide has been defended from technical, corporate, political, and consumers' perspectives.

Prevailing political practice
There is multilateral cooperation on standardization of consumer electronics. Some of this is based upon formal and robust agreement through such forums as the ITU or the ISO. Some forms of cooperation have been based upon informal, *de facto* standard setting by market leaders or through voluntary but very effective accords among the major players. This has been the case with audiocassettes and compact disks. However, because of the political and economic stakes involved, the major players have often only agreed to disagree. The discord has been shown as sufficiently basic for actors to only agree on multiple standards. One may expect though that business actors will always be open to strike a deal when the price of disagreement is too high. The discord on standardization is in the end marginal and not inspired by principled motives.

Notes

1 A recent book on Internet (Malamud, 1992) contains a strong criticism against the standards organizations, the 'standards potatoes with their public standards cartels in Geneva' as the author calls them.

10

Analysis of Prevailing Practices

Different interests

Players in world communication often share a concern about the resolution of a specific issue. This does not necessarily mean that they are interested in multilateral cooperation or agree on the terms of a multilateral accord. In virtually all issue areas there are contending positions regarding the preferred type of political practice. If we summarize the political practices that prevail in the different issue areas, the situation is as follows.

In telecommunication, on the issue of availability all players share an interest in multilateral cooperation. They agree on the need for a formal and robust accord, but have divergent claims to its terms. The prevailing practice is extensive multilateral cooperation. There has been a stable practice from the mid nineteenth century which recently shifted from monopoly and fixed pricing to competition and cost-based pricing as a result of innovations in technology and strong lobbying by business interests. The new political practice that emerges supports extensive multilateral cooperation through a formal and robust trade accord.

On the allocation of natural resources there has been a formal and robust multilateral accord since 1906. Its terms shifted in the 1970s from a 'first come, first served' approach to an *a priori* planning approach. There is extensive multilateral cooperation on frequency and orbital slot allocation. The possibility of interference creates the need for coordination among all players.

On the issue of remote sensing there is basic discord on fundamental principles and on the question of whether cooperation arrangements should be binding or voluntary. The prevailing practice is that in spite of basic discord there are projects of multilateral cooperation. There is no strong need for the major players to coordinate.

On the issue of traded telecommunication services a cooperative practice is emerging based upon a formal and robust trade accord. The claims to the terms of the accord are divergent.

In the issue area of intellectual property protection there has been for a long time extensive multilateral cooperation based upon a formal but weak multilateral accord. With the increase of trading interests in IPRs a shift has emerged towards a new practice based upon a formal and robust trade accord. In the negotiations players have presented divergent claims.

In the area of mass communication the prevailing practice on issues of radio and TV broadcasting has been largely unilateral action, or bilateral and regional cooperation. No multilateral cooperation has been achieved and on fundamental principles there has been basic discord. Much of this was due to Cold War antagonism. It remains to be seen whether the decline of East–West tension will facilitate multilateral cooperation in the area of broadcasting.

On the issues of freedom of information and media responsibility the prevailing practice among professional groups is a weak and voluntary form of multilateral cooperation. There are some normative provisions in binding instruments, but no comprehensive accord as a basis for multilateral cooperation has been achieved. The claims of different players have been divergent.

On the issues of media ownership and trade in media services there is no multilateral cooperation. On ownership, basic discord exists mainly between the most powerful players and the less powerful players. On the trade issue marginal discord exists among the most powerful players.

In the field of culture there is extensive multilateral cooperation on such issues as cultural exchange and the protection of cultural property. This is largely based upon voluntary accords. Also in cases of binding treaty provisions there are no mechanisms to ensure compliance. On the issue of cultural identity no multilateral cooperation has been possible and the discord among players is basic.

For the development of mass communication and telecommunication capacity in developing countries there are forms of multilateral cooperation but no robust multilateral accords. The transfer of technology is an area of basic discord on fundamental principles.

With regard to transborder data flows there has been basic discord on the issue of national sovereignty. On the protection of privacy multilateral cooperation has developed but on the basis of a weak and voluntary accord. On other issues, such as security, crime, EDI and EFT, forms of multilateral cooperation are emerging.

All players share an interest in multilateral cooperation on the standardization of consumer electronics. The prevailing practice is often the adoption of multiple or no standards. This is largely so because the most powerful players will only agree to cooperate if their standard becomes the world standard.

Contending positions

On most issues in world communication politics players have taken contending positions. Where some players preferred multilateral cooperation, others favoured unilateral or bilateral action. Where some desired formal and robust accords, others wanted informal and weak agreements. When all players wanted cooperation, they could often only agree to disagree. The inevitable implication of these contentious situations is that prevailing political practices will serve some players better than others.

In the issue area of telecommunication all players need multilateral cooperation on availability and allocation, but have different preferences for the terms on which this takes place. The shift from political to trading terms has been strongly promoted by the most powerful players and is likely to benefit their interests more than those of the less powerful players. On resource allocation the terms of cooperation shifted in the 1970s to suit the interests of the less powerful players better. It would seem though that in reality the most powerful players follow their preference for terms they consider more beneficial.

The basic discord on remote sensing combined with some multilateral cooperation matches the positions the powerful 'sensing' players have taken. The incorporation of the trade in telecommunication services in a multilateral trade accord is particularly beneficial for the industrial countries and their large telecommunication users. The developing countries have contested the terms of the new accord, but with no success.

The GATT rules have been fixed to suit the most powerful trading parties. In the issue area of intellectual property protection the conventional type of multilateral cooperation was unsatisfactory to most players. Developing countries and IPR industries wanted a different arrangement. This evolved under the auspices of the GATT and was incorporated into the Uruguay Trade Round accord. The new trade-based practice that now emerges is likely to mainly benefit the corporate IPR traders.

In the issue area of mass communication some players (in particular the developing countries and the Soviet Union) wanted effective agreements on radio and television broadcasting. The prevailing lack of such accords meets the interests of the Western countries and their mass media industries. On the issues of freedom of information and media responsibility the world community established the weak types of accord that are preferred by the most powerful players. The prevailing discord on the media ownership issue serves the large transnational owners best. The trading of media services is yet an undecided issue. It seems reasonable to expect that if a multilateral arrangement emerges, this will be a trade-based GATT accord favouring the interests of media services exporting countries and transnational media producers.

In the field of culture multilateral cooperation has been established for cultural exchange and the protection of cultural property. Although there have been contending positions on the terms of cooperation, by and large the prevailing practice has served most players. The problem of the protection of cultural identity has been much more contentious and the efforts of the developing countries to establish multilateral accords have failed.

On the development of mass communication and telecommunication capacity in the developing countries, there are contending positions by donor and recipient countries. The preference of the developing countries to have formal and robust rules on multilateral development cooperation has not been accommodated. On the issue of the international transfer of technology the recipient countries have demanded formal and robust multilateral rules. The technology producing and exporting countries have shown little interest in meeting this demand. The present practice suits their needs best.

In the area of transborder data flows there is at present only a limited form of multilateral cooperation on the issue of data protection. On other issues, forms of multilateral cooperation are under negotiation. The claim of the developing countries to an effective agreement based on the norm of national sovereignty was lost against the preference of the most powerful players to establish a trade-based practice.

The politics of standardization is largely a playing-field for the most powerful players among themselves. Whether they agree or disagree is determined by the political and economic interests of these players.

The obvious conclusion is that in most cases the prevailing political practices serve the preferences of the most powerful actors. However, before we jump to obvious explanations, it should be pointed out that on some issues less powerful players managed to gain some benefits and that in several cases the most powerful players had to make concessions to less powerful parties.

Trends

The foregoing overviews allow us to draw conclusions about the major trends in world communication politics.

In the first place, world communication politics is increasingly shaped by trade and market standards and less by political considerations. There is a noticeable shift from a political to an economic discourse. The evidence is found in the growing emphasis on the economic importance of intellectual property and the related priority of protection for investors and corporate producers. In the telecommunication field the standards of universal public service and cross-subsidization have made way for cost-based tariff structures. In the area of transborder data flows, politics changed from a political argument about national sovereignty to trade rules. Around 1983–4 the new emphasis became clear. The real issues were trade barriers to TDF and the demand for TDF politics was based upon trade principles. The concept of sovereignty was no longer there when in 1985 the OECD adopted its declaration on TDF. The OECD ministers declared their common intent to 'promote access to data and information and related services, and avoid the creation of unjustified barriers to the international exchange of data and information'. As Drake has suggested, even the term 'transborder data flow' seems to have lost against such concepts as 'information trade' (Drake, 1993b: 302).

Secondly, there is the increasing significance of the private most powerful players. The locus of policy making shifts from governments to associations of private business actors. This was demonstrated by the decisive role the private sector played in the 1992 WARC negotiations. It has also manifested itself in the commercialization of remote sensing activities and the provision of telecommunication services. The standards issues are largely decided by the interests of powerful private actors.

The third trend is the increasing marginalization of the Third World. The developing countries become more and more the visitors of the arena and less the active participants they used to be. In the 1970s there was a Third World forum for TDF issues (the IBI) and debates in the world community focused on such Third World demands as the new international information order. In communication resource allocation the developing countries had a significant role in the 1970s. Today this is the business of the advanced economies and their corporate actors. When the 1992 WARC discussed the future shape of telecommunication services the developing countries were just bystanders.

A pragmatic explanation

The key analytical question these overviews and conclusions raise is: how can we explain the political practices that were adopted in the political arena? This search for an explanation invites the ambition of a grand theory of world communication politics. There are however some arguments to resist this temptation and to propose a more pragmatic approach which uses a variety of theoretical approaches in an eclectic manner.

This approach is inspired by the fact that the general study of world politics is not informed by one comprehensive theoretical framework. For the study of world politics a variety of theoretical positions has been developed, such as idealism versus realism, behaviouralism versus traditionalism, functionalism, systems theory, interdependence theory, transnationalism and regime theory. None of these approaches by itself is very satisfactory for our understanding of the realities of current world politics. There is at present no comprehensive theory of world politics. This is partly explained by the vastness of the field of study (Leroy Bennett, 1991: 20). 'The paradigmatic fragmentation that has occurred in the late twentieth century results in part from a rejection, necessary as it may be, of an international system with the state as its core unit' (Dougherty and Pfaltzgraff, 1990: 540). The challenges of the state-centric model implied that no longer would one theoretical approach prevail. This should not disconcert anybody since this fragmentation is very common to the whole field of the social sciences. With the heterogeneity of its objects of study, the essential contestability of all its concepts and the underdetermined nature of its theories, one can hardly expect a comprehensive paradigm to emerge. The field is so wide, complex and varied that one cannot expect to find one comprehensive theory that satisfactorily helps our understanding. Contending perspectives have developed with different units of analysis, key concepts and emphases. Different schools have focused on power, or interdependence, or dependency. Analysts have narrowed the political agenda to security issues or have diversified into economic, social and cultural issues.[1]

An additional consideration is that political practices emerge in the processes of multilateral negotiations. Such negotiations are a complex phenomenon for analysis since a large number of actors is involved, such as states and their diplomats, secretariats of inter-governmental organizations, technical experts, NGO lobbies and domestic constituencies. This complexity is reinforced since multi-lateral negotiations are not rational processes in the 'realist' sense. Bargaining in the political arena involves emotion, insecurity, misperception, prejudice and intuition. There are also factors of ambience such as the level of trust among parties or optimist versus pessimist attitudes. Actors also bring very different perceptions of the functions of the multilateral forum to the decision making process. In such perceptions the multilateral institutions vary from instruments for foreign policy to conduits for diplomatic symbolism. External publicity is also a component to be reckoned with. Important political changes at the home front of negotiators (such as a change of government) may decisively impact the outcome of the process. Many multilateral negotiations are no longer *ad hoc* events. They are often institutionalized in long-term processes, like the GATT multilateral trade negotiations. Negotiations may also take place simultaneously in different forums, for example in the GATT and the ITU.

A difficulty with the analysis of world politics is also that it is a 'two-level game'. 'At one level, representatives of different countries seek to reach or sustain international agreements; at a second level, those same representatives must build the political support required to sustain commitments and establish credibility' (Putnam in Haggard and Simmons, 1987: 516). Growing interdependence means that groups at the domestic level increasingly have interests in international arrangements.

A common agreement may indeed serve the solution of resolving problems of international coordination and cooperation, but actors may still avoid it unless the common agreement suits the interests of domestic political constituencies. Understanding compliance and defection requires an analysis of domestic political processes. In making choices about multilateral accords and compliance, governments calculate the domestic benefits and losses and will try to make the benefits greatest and losses smallest for the domestically most powerful groups. As a result there is often a gap between signing and implementing the provisions of an agreement. A large volume of provisions is adopted multilaterally with great unanimity, and then little of it is either ratified or implemented in domestic legislation. This reflects a basic tension between the aspiration to world community standards and very real domestic political preferences.

Multilateral negotiations can be looked at as playing-fields in which actors attempt to optimize the outcome. They can be conceived as games in which one party wins and the other loses or in which both parties win or both lose. From this perspective one may be inclined to involve game-theoretic approaches. A problem with these approaches is that they emphasize the rational conduct of actors, whereas in the reality of political bargaining conduct is often irrational. Another problem is that game theories may help explain situations with a limited set of actors (usually two-person games), but are inadequate in the complex processes of international negotiations that involve a multitude of actors. 'No single theory has yet been developed for *N*-person games' (Dougherty and Pfaltz-graff, 1990: 514).

Structural realism

It is an attractive option to explain the fact that on the majority of issues the most powerful players got what they wanted from a realist perspective. In the realist approach to world politics the interests of the most powerful states determine the choice for or against multilateral accords and influences the modality of such accords.

The realist perspective argues that the structural conditions of the arena of world politics determine the outcome of the political process. Political practices will be what 'hegemons' want them to be. As Keohane and Nye (1977: 50–1) state: 'stronger states in the issue system will dominate the weaker ones and determine the rules of the game'. The classical realist interpretation is most forcefully presented by Thucydides in his *History of the Peloponnesian War*: 'the strong do what they have the power to do and the weak accept what they have to accept' (1954: 400–8). Basically the realist approach rests on the variable of power and proposes that multi-lateral agreement or disagreement is imposed by the most powerful state actor(s).

The most powerful actors prefer a collective arrangement if this suits their perceived interests optimally, and they bargain effectively for its achievement even against the perceived interests of the less powerful actors who may be influenced to support the agreement. In this approach power and interest determine outcome, not beliefs, moral principles or procedures. In the realist approach the creation, maintenance and erosion of collaborative arrangements is linked with the existence and disappearance of a hegemonic power.[2] The hegemon determines the rules of the game and enforces com-pliance.[3]

The realist argument provides certainly part of an explanation. The more powerful actors pushed the agreements on trade in telecommunication services and trade in intellectual property rights. It can easily be observed that the development claims of Third World countries were not met since the Northern states and their transnational corporations had by and large no interest in accom-modating these claims. Moreover, politically powerful elites in the South – part of the international structural condition – have been willing to make compromises that suited their interests. In particu-lar, powerful states can influence the negotiating process through a variety of measures. In the 1980s the USA, for example, used threats of withdrawal from multilateral forums as well as preferential bilateral treatment to exert influence on the rule making process. Countries have also been coerced to change their position through threats of sanctions from large trading partners. Such pressure has usually been exerted in bilateral negotiations. The illustrative case of Mexico and the enormous pressure by the US government and its copyright industries was mentioned in Chapter 7.

It cannot be ignored that, in the implementation of agreed rules, coercive force remains a crucial factor. The market power of the largest players, the USA, Japan and the UK, has certainly decisively changed international telecommunication practices. The technological developments made a more liberal arrangement more attractive for the large players. The largest actors stood to benefit more from a competitive market-oriented arrangement than from the conventional monopolistic structure. The control of the advances in technology plus the considerable market power of the largest players provided extra bargaining strength in world politics.

The role of structural power has also been manifest in the cases where discord is the prevailing practice. The realist explanation will stress that a common agreement is unlikely if the more powerful actors can achieve their preferred outcome by unilateral action. They do not need a collective arrangement on remote resources sensing, for example, since they control the 'sensing' technology (Krasner, 1991: 350). The international transfer of technology is a clear case: weak states have much to gain and little to give and so have great incentives to participate in a multilateral accord, whereas strong states have no incentives although without them the whole enterprise is impossible. When there are winners and losers, the winners are less likely to have an interest in cooperating with the losers. The provisions of the draft code of conduct on the transfer of technology largely reflect the aims and interests of the powerful technology providers. This is certainly not unrelated to their position of power. These players have been successful in fighting against provisions that would proscribe certain practices by technology sellers and that would create an effective implementation machinery for such provisions.

A problem with the realist approach is that it tends to exclusively focus on the distribution of power among states which determines the outcome of the political process. Conventional realism does not recognize the significant role in the political process of non-state actors. A more adequate explanation should take into account the role of the international governmental organizations (IGOs) and the international non-governmental organizations (INGOs).

The IGOs play a significant role in political bargaining and perform in world politics as relatively autonomous actors. They foster coalitions, shape agendas and often provide support for less powerful states. Secretariats of IGOs have often very actively promoted links among governments, with governments and with NGOs. As Renaud states in connection with the ITU: 'In particular, international secretariats staffed with knowledgeable individuals may have the opportunity to place themselves at the centre of crucial communication networks and, therefore, to be influential as negotiators and brokers without having significant tangible sources of power' (1990: 195). Woodrow (1991b) has made the argument that the ITU, by shifting towards the acceptance of a trade arrangement, plays a significant role in reforming the conventional standards. There is a clear development within the institution from a cautious and somewhat hostile response to the adaptation of the ITU structure and rules to accommodate the new challenges.

The INGOs (and in particular the business associations) are formidable lobbying forces in the multilateral forums. The International Publishers Association has strongly lobbied for the recognition of a publisher's right. The International Federation of Phonogram and Videogram Producers (IFPI) lobbied actively for anti-copying devices and levying schemes. The Proprietary Rights Committee of the US Information Industry Association has been very active to bring the IPR concerns of the information industry to domestic and international forums. The Motion Pictures Association of America has been another powerful lobby. Together with companies such as American Express and IBM it has actively promoted the free trade discipline and unregulated market access, the right of national treatment and presence, and the definition of information as a commodity. With regard to its presence in the international regulatory forum the International Telecommunications Users Group (INTUG) has clearly striven towards a greater and more institutionalized contribution. INTUG trusts that by the late 1990s 'users will no longer be present as marginal observers in forums where telecommunications policy issues are determined, but as integral participants in all those committees, international, regional and national, where matters directly affecting the facilities that they pay for and depend upon are debated and settled' (*INTUG News*, October 1989).

In the preparations of the 1988 World Administrative Telegraph and Telephone Conference (WATTC) a group of major transnational corporations battled against draft regulations as submitted by the Preparatory Committee in 1987. In proceedings before the Federal Communications Commission IBM stated that the draft regulations were 'directly counter to the pro-competitive national policies of the US'. The company suggested that the USA contribute regulations that will 'not require that members regulate international enhanced services and international enhanced services providers' (Drake, 1988: 226). AT&T contended that the draft regulations would 'require changes in order to make (them) minimally acceptable to the US'. Also PanAmSat opposed the draft text that ITU Secretary General Richard Butler submitted in an effort to reconcile the widely divergent positions. It worded in its opposition to the text that this was 'an explicit attempt to bring within the ambit of the ITU's regulatory jurisdiction all of the private, non-carrier services and facilities that are outside of this jurisdiction' (1988: 231). In the preparations towards WATTC 1988 an international press campaign played an important role attacking the non-market claimants as illicit protectionists. The restrictive arrangement was made to look extremely threatening.

There was also a strong lobby from the business users community towards the GATT trade in services agreement. Important groups were the International Chamber of Commerce, the OECD affiliated Business and Industry Advisory Council and the Coalition of Service Industries (a grouping of national business coalitions from ten countries). Industry influence was also very prominent during the 1992 WARC. A formidable private lobby dominated much of the negotiations. This was clearly motivated by the fact that so many new services are privately operated and companies had to try to get frequencies allocated for their services. With the global outreach of these services, world-wide frequencies were required that could only be allocated by the WARC. Investments between US $1 billion and US $3.5 billion in global voice satellite systems were at stake. Corporations actively shaped the policy positions of their home governments and they participated in their governments' delegations to the conference. Companies tried in particular to get the support of developing country delegations who had no projects of their own. 'A common lobbying technique was to set up elaborate demonstrations of the proposed projects in hotels and invite delegates from smaller and developing nations to attend. These demonstrations were usually followed by expensive luncheons and the distribution of gifts and souvenirs' (Sung, 1992: 629).

The concessions of the less powerful

With the addition of the role of the non-state players, the realist perspective helps us a great deal but not enough. It does not recognize that 'the great powers today routinely find themselves in situations in which they must negotiate the terms of international regimes covering specific issue areas, whether they like it or not'

(Young, 1989: 355). Power in the sense of capabilities, physical resources, capacity to impose sanctions, and access to expertise and information does not equate to the ability to engineer collective choices. Even the hegemon cannot get the less powerful to agree solely on the basis of coercive power. The paradox is that often the costs of exercising such power are too great. In political bargaining the capacity to realize compliance also rests upon respect, status, success, moral position, legitimacy and public opinion. A robust agreement could be manufactured by the most powerful actors, but its effectiveness will often be dependent upon compliance by other actors, and sometimes by all actors. It is difficult to maintain this type of agreement if less powerful actors do not comply. Particularly with transborder problems there is the possibility also for less powerful players to undermine multilateral arrangements. The emphasis on coercive power cannot explain how unwilling players are massaged towards acceptance of an arrangement that they initially perceive as adverse to their interests. In the cases of the negotiations on the trading of telecommunication services and intellectual property rights the developing countries perceived a trade-based agreement as inimical to their interests. However, in the course of the negotiations initial Third World claims were given up and major concessions were made in order to accommodate industrial country claims. This can only be partly explained by the realist argument.

In the search for additional insights, cognitive factors offer a promising explanation. Jönsson alludes to the importance of cognitive factors when he observes that 'an agreement often requires a formula, a shared perception or definition of the problem' (1993: 209). A multilateral agreement is more effective if it is supported by a common belief. The existing telecommunication practice was seriously challenged when the belief that telecommunication should be a monopoly began to change to the belief that it should be competitive.

It was very crucial in the GATT negotiations that Third World countries accepted the belief that 'free trade' would be in their interest. An illustration of the effect of such a belief provided an editorial comment in the Kenyan daily newspaper *The Standard* of 8 December 1993. This presented an analysis of the negative effects the GATT results will have on the economies of Third World countries. However, the article concluded that in spite of all the dangers of the Uruguay package 'there is no doubt that the whole world will benefit'. The belief in the global benefit of the 'free trade' standard is accepted and overrides the very real damage the agreement may cause. In a similar tone the Kenyan daily *The Daily*

Nation (on 10 December 1993) explained that African countries will find themselves worse off with the agreement since their food prices will go up and the export prices for their commodities such as coffee will go down. Yet, the agreement was not rejected because of the belief that the failure of the Uruguay Round would lead to catastrophic trade wars. It is fascinating to see how successful the parties most interested in the agreement have been in introducing this notion of trade wars without any supporting evidence, as if it were an uncontrollable metaphysical process. Moreover, the belief that if such trade wars erupt they would damage the African countries more than the Uruguay accord is an equally magical notion that was widely disseminated through the slick use of public relations and largely uncritical international mass media.

A good example of the promotion of a new 'belief' was the introduction of the concept of 'market access' into the GATT negotiations. This was put on the regulatory agenda by the free trade claimants.

> Countries like the United States contend that to safeguard the existing trading system and update its rules and principles requires some form of guaranteed market access to service providers in some sectors. Although there is some attempt to downplay the fact, this would mean that all countries, developed and developing, which accepted this new principle would have to accept that their domestic sovereignty and national regulatory autonomy would be restricted to some extent. Market access would be more intrusive than national treatment into domestic decision-making. In short, participating countries would have to acknowledge that there is no way to revolt against economic interdependence. Countries such as Brazil and India . . . believe this is undesirable. They worry that new trade rules for services which might include guarantees of market access to foreign service providers are unneeded and perhaps detrimental to their influence and development prospects. (Aronson, 1989: 241–2)

The lobby of transnational services providers and users (the Coalition of Service Industries, the US Council for International Business, supported by the US government and the OECD) claimed that unless they could provide services abroad, they could not compete. They effectively pushed the principle on to the negotiating agenda. The Coalition of Service Industries (1988) urged that the services agreement should include the 'access to and use of distribution and delivery systems, including telecommunications networks'. An OECD report (OECD, 1988) stated that market access would imply the right of non-establishment, the right of commercial presence and the right to interconnect. 'Access also includes fair and equitable terms for interconnection to public networks, the provision of leased lines by telecommunications administrations, and the right to connect equipment which meets appropriate requirements to the network.' The Council for International Business published in November 1989 a document in which market access was also proposed as one of the key principles for a General Agreement on Trade in Services. Geze Feketekuty (counsellor to the US Trade Representative) proposed in a presentation at Montpellier, France, in November 1989, the need to include market access in an annex to the US designed draft services agreement. In his unofficial exposition of the annex, it was mentioned that market access would entail the right of establishment and the right of non-establishment. 'Under the right of establishment foreign providers of competitive telecommunications services covered by the progressive liberalization schedule would have the right to establish locally any facilities required to produce or distribute the covered services. Under the right of non-establishment foreign providers of covered services would be allowed to provide such services across the border from a foreign location via the telecommunications network, without being required to establish local facilities in the importing country' (TDR, 1989: 6). The right of non-establishment was a standard that the developing countries in particular felt very uneasy about. 'They may feel more protected from possible abuses if they impose investment requirements on foreign service providers so that they can keep a close eye on the providers, making sure that they are effectively regulated' (Aronson, 1989: 246). The proponents of the standard were powerful actors in the USA, the UK and Japan. In the course of the multilateral negotiations the most powerful players managed to promote the legitimacy of the 'market access' formula. Although it never was part of the GATT legal framework, it became a widely supported legal principle. Its general acceptance facilitated the necessary compliance of initially 'unwilling' players.

The 1970s negotiations on the Third World demand for a new international information order provided another example of the role of common beliefs. The original formula of a new international information order (NIIO) hampered the bargaining process. The concept was not commonly shared in the world community and its protagonists did not manage to promote the NIIO belief system successfully. A better formula was the new world information and communication order (NWICO) on the basis of which a consensus was reached. However, this concept had very different implications from the earlier proposal and was acceptable precisely because it posed less threat to the powerful players. The 1978 Unesco General Conference was a turning point in the debate in so far as at this meeting the hostile opposition towards the idea of a new order was softened. There began to be almost unanimous acceptance that

Third World countries had justifiable complaints and that concessions must be made by the industrialized states. The original
formula coined by the non-aligned movement (NIIO) was replaced
by the proposal for a new, more just and effective world information and communication order (NWICO). According to the
interpretation of United States Ambassador John Reinhardt at the
1978 General Conference this new order would require 'a more
effective program of action, both public and private, to suitable
identified centers of professional education and training in broadcasting and journalism in the developing world . . . [and] a major
effort to apply the benefits of advanced communications technology
. . . to economic and social needs in the rural areas of developing
nations'. The new formula (NWICO) was acceptable to all Unesco
member states. It facilitated consensus on a largely technical
interpretation of the world's information problems and by implication major concessions on the part of the developing countries.

In addition to cognitive factors, *quid pro quo* deals should also be
mentioned. The acceptance of adverse arrangements can be
brought about by the prospect of some future advantage. The
concession of the developing countries to a lesser arrangement than
the new information order they demanded was undoubtedly facilitated by the US promise that it would launch 'a Marshall plan' for
the development of communication media. Also in the GATT trade
negotiations the developing countries made major concessions to
the preferences of the industrial players. Most of them felt that their
adoption of strict intellectual property protection would improve
their export capacities. This was certainly helped by Western
suggestions that improved IPR rules would lead to more readiness
of technology exporters to share their resources.

The concessions of the powerful

Another question that realism fails to answer adequately is why the
more powerful players sometimes make concessions. Realism also
fails to explain why the most powerful players would consent to
accords they perceive as unnecessary or undesirable. How did the
developing countries manage to change the 'first come, first served'
rule on frequency allocation? How did they manage to get unanimous acceptance of the Unesco Mass Media Declaration although
most Western players did not want the instrument?

Such concessions can be explained by pointing to normative and
procedural factors, the building of coalitions and utilitarian considerations.

Norms and procedures
Although the world political arena is not known for its high moral calibre, it should be recognized that 'there are many international norms that derive their compliance pull from a shared sense of justice: human rights most notably, but also, for example, norms against armed conquest and the annexation of territory' (Hurrell, 1993: 65). In this context Hurrell remarks that there is a good deal of evidence to suggest 'that successful bargaining outcomes do not depend on the achievement of some notion of optimum allocative efficiency, but rather on the perception that the outcome meets some criterion of justice and equity' (1993: 68). The basic norms that are adopted by IGOs often reflect the interests of the less powerful actors since they stress such standards as justice and equality. These norms can be used to legitimize positions preferred by the less powerful and can make the opposition by the more powerful look unduly hostile and disrespectful.[4] In the negotiations on resource allocation and media responsibility normative factors played an important role. The developing countries used very effectively such norms as equal access, common heritage, and freedom of opinion. The general adoption of an accord on the basis of moral principles does not however guarantee an effective form of multilateral cooperation. The powerful players go along, but the agreement will be largely ineffective since they will not comply in actual conduct. Agreement contrary to the interest of the more powerful actors can also result from the tendency in international institutions to seek a consensus. There is a clear trend within many of the multilateral organizations to develop instruments that all parties can accept without the need for a formal general vote.

This desire to avoid disagreement implies the risk that pseudo agreements emerge, such as in the case of the Unesco Mass Media Declaration. All parties agreed, but many stated in the explanation of their support that they had serious reservations. The UNGA resolutions on the new international economic order were adopted by acclaim. However, many member states declared serious opposition to parts of the texts. In such cases the consensus is more ritual than a reflection of serious unanimity. Certain advantages for the less powerful, such as one state, one vote procedures, can also be undermined if the more powerful simply walk out and refuse participation in decision making.

The coalition approach
The first formal introduction of groups in multilateral negotiations was probably through the resolution that established UNCTAD

(UNGA Resolution 1995 (XIX) of 1964). This decision of the United Nations General Assembly provided for four regional groups: group A with African and Asian countries plus Yugoslavia; group B with the OECD countries; group C with the Latin American countries; and group D with the USSR and the socialist countries of Eastern Europe. The advantage of the group system is that negotiations tend to be more effective. 'The main advantage is that it permits the negotiating process to take place within a forum that is substantially smaller than the entire membership of the body concerned' (Dell, 1989: 54). The disadvantage is that when positions are divided within groups, 'it takes no more than a handful of strong and determined delegations to bring about deadlock in a large meeting despite the fact that in the absence of these delega- tions it would be possible to reach a satisfactory agreement' (1989: 56). There is always the risk of group inflexibility, 'which makes the negotiation of compromise agreements more difficult' (Kaufmann, 1988: 157). Group negotiations were the main approach in the UNCTAD discussions on the code of conduct on the transfer of technology. As Wilner observes, 'a major disadvantage of this approach to negotiation has been that groups of states are reluctant to drop or modify concrete positions, stated in specific terms, in provisions of their draft . . . on a number of occasions, groups have been stuck with a pre-determined position and it has taken great effort to bring about even modest changes' (1980: 179).

Kaufmann confirms that 'groups have become an essential feature of conference diplomacy' (1988: 146). There are regional alliances, political groups, and coalitions based upon formal international economic agreements (such as the European Union or the OECD) or on common interest (such as the Group of 77). According to Kaufmann the main functions of such alliances are to exchange information, to develop common positions with or without voting commitment, to agree on candidates for election or on common spokesmen, or to undertake joint lobbying campaigns (1988: 152-4). The developing countries have used the coalition approach to gain voting advantage over the more powerful countries. Their alliance of non-aligned countries played an important role in negotiations on technology transfer and the new international information order. Coalitions however can both be assets and liabilities. If they are internally divided, as the non-aligned movement was on many issues, or simply too big, they may not achieve their shared objective. Coalitions have a certain productive size, and when they grow too big their size may become counter-productive. Riker (1962) called this the 'size principle'. In his opinion coalitions should not exceed the size necessary to achieve the desired objective. The non-aligned movement had a problem of size and this contributed to its ineffectiveness.

Another problem is that actors tend to form alliances on very pragmatic grounds. These are often based on a calculation of costs and benefits. 'A decision to join an alliance is based upon perception of rewards in excess of costs. Each country considers the marginal utility from alliance memberships, as contrasted with unilateral action' (Dougherty and Pfaltzgraff, 1990: 450). The prevalence of pragmatic interests over ideological orientations in the building of coalitions may seriously weaken them. The illustration was the coalition of developing countries and the USSR in the information order debate. Very strange ideological bed-fellows allied in response to the perceived common threat of Western cultural imperialism. The coalition of the Third World and Eastern Europe did not help in improving the credibility of the Third World position on information matters. This created the threat of voting power, but never achieved the aspired multilateral agreement.

The utilitarian approach
Concessions by more powerful players can finally be explained by using a functionalist approach. As argued before, actors cannot always be coerced into effective cooperation. In fact, most multilateral arrangements would be less effective if today's world political arena resembled Thucydides' coercive empire. In some cases collective agreements emerge since all actors want them. In the case of the availability of telecommunication, for example, the common preference for an effective multilateral accord is best explained by a functionalist-utilitarian argument. If all actors share common aversions or common interests they are all better off if they act jointly than if they operate unilaterally (Stein, 1983: 127). If, for example, radio frequencies were not collectively protected against harmful interference, all actors in world communication would suffer a disadvantage. It would also be perceived by all actors in world politics as undesirable if national telecommunication standards were incompatible and thus effectively hampered international telecommunication traffic. The common interest in joint action may also be determined by certain external factors, such as the scarcity of resources. When, for example, resource scarcity emerged in the electro-magnetic spectrum (more demand than frequency capacity) there was a need to establish a robust cooperation arrangement. 'Broadcasting has long been a traffic problem requiring only coordination in order to facilitate access to airwaves. With greater congestion, however, it is rapidly becoming a dilemma of the commons, which requires a collaborative allocation of a

scarce resource' (Stein, 1983: 132). If all actors want multilateral cooperation and see the enforcement of this in their self-interest, there is a good probability that the most powerful players are ready to make concessions. It may be their perception that the alternative of non-agreement is less preferable, even if the common agreement has distinct disadvantages in their view. Accommodating the claims of less powerful actors may from the point of view of the more powerful actors be necessary and preferable to the damage caused by the alternative of no agreements. In the recent multilateral negotiations on telecommunication arrangements (for example WATTC 1988) the more powerful players have made concessions to the less powerful players. Multilateral cooperation with effective compliance, even on sub-optimal terms, was perceived by them as more beneficial to their interests than no agreement at all.

Summary

There is ample evidence to support a structural-realist explanation of prevailing political practices in world communication. This theoretical approach is useful but only to an extent. Hegemons do not always succeed. Sometimes even the less powerful manage to achieve their preferred goals and the more powerful make important concessions.

Additional insights are needed to offer a more satisfactory explanation. It was suggested that next to the structural conditions of the world political arena, cognitive and procedural factors, as well as the building of coalitions and utilitarian motives, should be called upon. We need the eclectic combination of these approaches to gain an understanding of the 'who gets what, why and how' questions of world communication politics.

Notes

1 For a very broad division of the field into three approaches – realists, pluralists and globalists – see Viotti and Kauppi (1993).

2 Classic realist studies provide the following comments. 'International politics, like all politics, is a struggle for power' (Morgenthau, 1966: 25). 'If there is any distinctive political theory of international politics, balance of power theory is it' (Waltz, 1979: 117). 'The distribution of power among states constitutes the principal form of control in every international system. The dominant states and empires in every international system organize and maintain the network of political, economic, and other relationships within the system and especially in their respective spheres of influence. . . . those states that have been called the great powers . . . establish and enforce the basic rules and rights that influence their own behavior and that of the lesser states in the system' (Gilpin, 1981: 29–30).

3 The development of common agreements in the field of human rights provides a good deal of support for the realist position. As Krasner concludes in his analysis of human rights regimes on religious toleration, slave trade, minorities and individual human rights: 'The differences in outcomes in these four cases are best explained by the capabilities and commitments of those states that supported each of these regimes. Only when powerful states enforced principles and norms were international human rights regimes consequential' (1993: 141). One example is the abolition of the slave trade, 'an exceptional triumph for human rights and freedom. . .that was made possible in large measure because of the commitment and power of Great Britain' (1993: 154). The protection of minorities in the nineteenth century and under the League of Nations was a complete failure. 'National governments ignored their obligations to protect the rights of minorities within their borders. Neither the major powers nor the League of Nations acted to enforce the regime' (1993: 155). It is clear that the enforcement of human rights agreements depends heavily upon the interests and powers of state actors. However, realism cannot provide the complete story. Other elements, such as moral purpose, have to be applied as well for an understanding of failure or implementation of human rights provisions.

4 In the formation of multilateral accords, not only political and economic advantage count, but also moral interests. Moral proselytism plays an important role. This is 'the compulsion to convert others to one's beliefs and to remake the world in one's own image' (Nadelman, 1990: 481). In this effort the 'transnational moral entrepreneurs' (TMEs such as Amnesty International and Greenpeace International) are essential. The role of moral concerns in shaping an international regime can be illustrated with the development of the regime against slavery and slave trading (1990: 491-8). In some areas the TMEs may be more successful than the conventional IGOs in achieving certain objectives: 'Most global prohibition regimes are promoted not only by states but also by transnational moral entrepreneurs who mobilize popular opinion and political support and lobby governments both within their host country and abroad. The norms they seek to internationalize are, in all cases, cosmopolitan in nature, relating not to the ways in which states treat one another but, rather, to the ways in which individual human beings are treated both by states and by one another' (1990: 524).

11

Towards a People's Right to Communicate

The final question of this book is how we go about the assessment of political practices against the standards of human rights. This normative assessment aims to establish the 'human rights content' of prevailing political practices. I do not pretend to offer a conclusive assessment. More important is my aspiration to present a new way of looking at the politics of world communication. I want to stimulate thinking on a people-centred approach to world communication.

Human rights content

For the purposes of the assessment I propose to rank the human rights content of prevailing practices as strong, weak, negligible, absent or adverse. This ranking is based upon the strength of human-rights-based norms, procedures to enforce these norms and the mechanisms for implementation (see Figure 11.1).

Norms can be binding, soft or absent. Norms that are articulated as treaty provisions are stronger than those found in non-binding instruments. The freedom of expression is a strong norm (articulated in the ICCPR); the norm of adequate communication capacity in developing countries is a guideline formulated by several non-binding statements.[1]

Procedures for enforcement can be very robust and imply sanctions; they can also be weak and only permit review and information exchange; or they can be absent. The institutional mechanisms for enforcement of human rights standards can vary from effective to ineffective, or can be absent.

From the overview in Table 11.1 we can conclude that in a majority of issue areas there are human rights norms, although mainly non-binding. Binding norms are found with regard to the protection of intellectual property, the freedom of information, media responsibility and culture. There are no procedures for enforcement except on the issues of copyright and patent law, the freedom of information, media responsibility and the development of communication capacity. These are however weak. Equally there are no implementation mechanisms except for these four areas

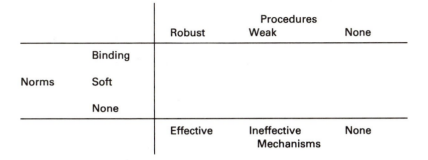

		Procedures		
		Robust	Weak	None
	Binding			
Norms	Soft			
	None			
		Effective	Ineffective Mechanisms	None

Figure 11.1   *Prevailing practices of world communication politics*

where these mechanisms are ineffective. In five areas there is no human rights content at all.

In none of the issue areas of world communication can we identify a strong human rights content. A weak human rights content is found in connection with copyright and patent law, freedom of information, media responsibility, culture, development and the development of communication capacity. In relation to issues such as telecommunication availability, allocation of resources, remote sensing, radio and TV broadcasting, culture, transfer of technology and transborder data flows the human rights content is negligible. No human rights content was found in the areas of trading of telecommunication services, traded intellectual property rights and media services, the concentration of media ownership and standardization of consumer electronics. It can be argued that in some cases the absence of human rights content is even adverse to the protection of human rights standards.

To illustrate some of these results I have selected the following cases: freedom of information, IDTBS, transfer of technology, standardization and TRIPs.

Weak human rights content: freedom of information
In the prevailing political practice on freedom of information there are binding normative provisions on freedom of information in international human rights law. Article 19 of the Universal Declaration of Human Rights is in the strict formal sense a non-binding standard, although it has important moral significance and is incorporated in a binding treaty as a legal standard. This is Article 19 of the International Covenant on Civil and Political Rights (1966) which provides that 'Everyone shall have the right to freedom of expression; this right shall include freedom to seek, receive and

Table 11.1   *Prevailing political practices and human rights content*

Issue areas	Norms	Procedures	Mechanisms	Human rights content
Telecommunication				
Availability	S	N	N	N
Allocation	S	N	N	N
Remote sensing	S	N	N	N
Trade in telecom services	N	N	N	A
Intellectual property				
Copyright/patent law	B	W	I	W
Trade in IPR	N	N	N	A
Mass communication				
Radio broadcasting	S	N	N	N
TV broadcasting	S	N	N	N
Freedom of information	B	W	I	W
Media responsibility	B	W	I	W
Ownership	N	N	N	A
Trade in media services	N	N	N	A
Culture				
Exchange	B	N	N	N
Identity	B	N	N	N
Development				
Capacity	S	W	I	W
Transfer of technology	S	N	N	N
Transborder data flows				
National sovereignty	S	N	N	N
Privacy	S	N	N	N
Standardization	N	N	N	A

Norms: B binding; S soft; N none.
Procedures: W weak; N none.
Mechanisms: I ineffective; N none.
Human rights content: W weak; N negligible; A absent or adverse.

impart information and ideas of all kinds, regardless of frontiers, either orally, in writing or in print, in the form of art, or through any other media of his choice.' The binding force of this provision is mitigated since it is a treaty rule and not all states have ratified the treaty. Moreover, in stating the articles that do not permit derogation (Article 4.2: 'No derogation from Articles 6, 7, 8 (paragraphs 1 and 2), 11, 15, 16 and 18 may be made under this provision') the freedom of information is not included. Also the Convention on the Rights of the Child (adopted unanimously by the United Nations General Assembly on 20 November 1989) gives the right of children to freedom of expression the force of international law. Article 13 of the convention states: 'The child shall have the right to freedom of expression; this right includes freedom to seek, receive and impart information and ideas of all kinds, regardless of frontiers, either orally, in writing or in print, in the form of art, or through any other media of the child's choice.' A strong provision is also formulated in the CSCE Helsinki final act (1975): 'The participating states make it their aim to facilitate the freer and wider dissemination of information of all kinds.' However, the act is not a binding treaty and it has been signed by only a limited number of states. Many resolutions by the UNGA and by the Unesco General Conference refer to the freedom of information. In 1945 Unesco adopted in its constitution the commitment 'to promote the free flow of ideas by word and image'. Repeatedly, the Unesco General Conference has adopted resolutions which invite the Director General 'to promote the free flow of information at international and national levels, press freedom, independent and pluralistic media, and a better balanced dissemination of information, without any obstacle to the freedom of expression' (for example Resolution 27/C.4.1.2).

The professional organizations have adopted standards on freedom of information in various documents. The Declaration of Tailloires on Freedom of the Press adopted by independent news organizations (17 May 1981) has in its preamble references to Article 19 of the UDHR, the constitution of Unesco, and the Helsinki final act. In Article 2 the declaration states: 'We believe that the free flow of information and ideas is essential to mutual understanding and world peace. We consider restraints on the movement of news and information to be contrary to the interests of international understanding, in violation of the Universal Declaration of Human Rights, the constitution of Unesco, and the final act of the Conference on Security and Cooperation in Europe, and inconsistent with the Charter of the United Nations.' And Article 3 provides: 'We support the universal human right to be fully informed, which right requires the free circulation of news and opinion. We vigorously oppose any interference with this fundamental right.' The International Federation of Journalists in its Sydney Declaration of February 1989 declares: 'A free, independent media reflecting diversity of opinion is a precondition of democratic societies' and 'the free flow of information is the lifeblood of communities whether they be based on geography, ethnic origins, shared values or common language.' The Declaration of Windhoek on Promoting an Independent and Pluralistic African Press referred in the preamble to the UDHR and to United Nations General Assembly Resolution 59(1) of 14 December 1946 which

stated that freedom of information is a fundamental right. Participants in this UN/Unesco-convened seminar declared that: 'Consistent with article 19 of the Universal Declaration of Human Rights,
the establishment, maintenance and fostering of an independent,
pluralistic and free press is essential to the development and
maintenance of democracy in a nation, and for economic development.'

Although not all the norms on the freedom of information are
formulated as treaty provisions, they are to an important extent
binding standards. The real significance of these standards will
depend upon the degree of their enforcement. 'The real test of the
effectiveness of a system of international protection for human
rights is whether it provides an international remedy for the
individual whose rights are violated' (Robertson, 1981: 357). The
remedial procedures related to freedom of information standards
are mainly based upon the optional protocol (OP) to the ICCPR
and Resolution 1503 adopted by the ECOSOC in 1970. The
protocol authorizes the Human Rights Committee to receive and
consider communications from individuals subject to its jurisdiction
who claim to be victims of a violation by that state party of any of
the rights set forth in the covenant. Individual complaints can only
come from nationals of states that are party to the OP (at present 66
states). The OP provides for communications, analysis and reporting, but not for sanctions.

Resolution 1503 recognizes the possibility of individual complaints about human rights violations. It authorizes the Human
Rights Commission to examine 'communications, together with
replies of governments, if any, which appear to reveal consistent
patterns of gross violations of human rights'. The 1503 procedure is
slow and confidential, and provides individuals with no redress. As
Donnelly concludes: 'The 1503 procedure is simply weak. The
strongest "enforcement" action possible is to make the evidence
that has been acquired, along with the commission's views on it,
publicly available. This is better than nothing. But rather than real
international enforcement, this involves at most a certain degree of
semi-independent international monitoring. And in practice, the
commission has never fully exercised even these weak procedures'
(1993: 60).

In the INGO community there are no procedures for the
enforcement of the freedom of information standard. Overall, the
assessment has to be that available procedures for enforcement of
the normative provisions on freedom of information are weak.

The institutional mechanisms for implementation are the UN
Human Rights Commission, and the human rights committees in

connection with the ICCPR, the Race Convention and the Convention on the Elimination of All Forms of Discrimination against Women. However important the work of these bodies is, they do not represent effective mechanisms for implementation.[2]

The UN Human Rights Commission is a permanent body of the ECOSOC. Its members are state representatives. Findings of the Commission have a certain significance but are not binding.

The Human Rights Committee consists of eighteen experts supervising the implementation of the ICCPR. The work of the Committee covers only parties that ratified the covenant (presently 114 states) and provides international monitoring on the basis of reports provided by states. In reporting to the Human Rights Committee many states confine themselves to mentioning that their constitution guarantees the freedom of expression. This is obviously a very inadequate basis for an opinion about actual conduct in connection with this right. The Committee's monitoring does not imply any sanctions, but it can generate some negative publicity on a country's human rights performance.

For the implementation of the Race Convention a Committee on the Elimination of Racial Discrimination has been established. The Committee can receive complaints among states, but only fourteen states authorize the Committee to receive communications from individuals.

The implementation body for the 1979 Convention on the Elimination of all Forms of Discrimination against Women is the Committee on the Elimination of Discrimination against Women. The Committee is not authorized to receive individual communications. At present, 'the supervisory mechanisms of the women's rights regime will remain significantly weaker than those of other international human rights regimes (which . . . are not terribly strong)' (Donnelly, 1993: 77).

The INGO community has no effective institutional mechanisms to provide adequate protection for the freedom of information standard.

Negligible human rights content: IDTBS and the international transfer of technology
In connection with the issue of direct TV satellite broadcasting there are strong references to human rights standards in the Unesco Declaration of Guiding Principles on the Use of Satellite Broadcasting for the Free Flow of Information, the Spread of Education and Greater Cultural Exchanges of 1972. The preamble refers to the Unesco purpose to promote the free flow of ideas by word and

image, to the Universal Declaration of Human Rights, in particular the articles on freedom of information, right to education and the right to freely participate in the cultural life of the community. Article IV.2 provides that 'account should be taken of the needs and rights of audiences, as well as the objectives of peace, friendship and cooperation between peoples, and of economic, social and cultural progress'. ArticleV.1 says that 'The objective of satellite broadcasting for the free flow of information is to ensure the widest possible dissemination, among the peoples of the world, of news of all countries, developed and developing alike', and Article V.2 stresses that 'every effort be made to ensure the factual accuracy of the information reaching the public'. Article VII focuses on cultural rights and states that cultural programmes 'should respect . . . the right of all countries and peoples to preserve their cultures as part of the common heritage of mankind'. Article XI concludes explicitly with the provision that the principles of the declaration shall be applied with due regard for human rights and fundamental freedoms. The Unesco declaration is a non-binding instrument and there are no provisions for enforcement and implementation.

The 1983 Principles Governing the Use by States of Artificial Earth Satellites for International Direct Television Broadcasting state on purposes and objectives: 'Activities in the field of international direct television broadcasting by satellite should be carried out in a manner compatible with the sovereign rights of States, including the principle of non-intervention, as well as with the right of everyone to seek, receive and impart information and ideas as enshrined in the relevant United Nations instruments. Such activities should promote the free dissemination and mutual exchange of information and knowledge in cultural and scientific fields, assist in educational and economic development, particularly in the developing countries, enhance the qualities of life of all peoples and provide recreation with due respect to the political and cultural integrity of States.' In the provision on the applicability of international law there is an explicit reference to international instruments relating to human rights. The principles state that all peoples should benefit from IDTBS and that 'access to technology in this field should be available to all States without discrimination'.

The United Nations General Assembly Resolution that contains the IDTBS principles is a non-binding instrument which was not adopted by the major actors. Its normative provisions on human rights are soft, and the instrument proposes neither procedures nor institutional mechanisms for the enforcement of human rights standards. It seems a fair conclusion that the prevailing political practice on IDTBS has a negligible human rights content.

A similar assessment applies to the international transfer of technology. There are implicit references to human rights standards in instruments such as the Charter on Rights and Duties of States, the UNGA resolutions on the NIEO, the Vienna programme and the UNCTAD code (preamble, paragraph 3). These norms have very little legal significance and are not supported by enforcement procedures or mechanisms for implementation.

Although the negligible human rights content is regrettable in both cases, the more serious problem concerns the transfer of technology. The current practice in this area effectively withholds knowledge from the majority of people and effectively negates such rights as embodied in the UDHR Article 27, the ICESCR Article 15, UNGA Resolution 3384(XXX) of 10 November 1975, and the Declaration on the Use of Scientific and Technological Progress in the Interests of Peace and for the Benefit of Mankind (preamble and Articles 1, 2, 5, 6 and 8). The absence of a strong human rights content directly affects the protection of human rights in an adverse way! The human rights standards that all people have the right to share in scientific advancement (UDHR Article 27) and to enjoy the benefits of scientific progress and its applications (ICESCR Article 15) demand robust rules on enforcement and effective institutions to implement these rules. This is particularly important in the light of the increasing privatization and commercialization of the production of scientific and technical knowledge. The creation and control of knowledge as private property seriously obstruct access to sources of knowledge that should be considered common heritage.

No human rights content: standardization and TRIPs
There is no human rights content in the political practices that govern such areas as the standardization of consumer electronics and the trading of intellectual property rights. Although a human-rights-based politics of standardization would benefit the interests of ordinary people, the more serious problem occurs with the recently adopted accord on TRIPs in the GATT negotiations. The emerging political practice on IPRs is adverse to the protection of human rights.

The TRIPs provisions exclude the knowledge and innovation generated by ordinary people from protection. Its definition of innovation, for example, favours transnational corporations. The formulation of the TRIPs agreement 'excludes all kinds of knowledge, ideas and innovations that take place in the "intellectual commons" – in villages among farmers, in forests among tribals and even in universities among scientists' (Shiva, 1993: 32). The specific restriction of IPRs to those capable of industrial application 'immediately excludes all sectors that produce and innovate outside the industrial mode of organisation of production' (1993: 32). A further reduction is to 'trade-related IPRs' which clearly benefits the TNC producers of knowledge. There is no adequate provision on the right to be informed. Farmers, for example, should have the right to be informed about IPR processes that affect the agricultural sector. The TRIPs provisions fail to guarantee adequate protection against the deprivation of knowledge. In fact, the provisions on the patentability of plant varieties make it possible for communities in the Third World to be robbed of basic knowledge resources.

There is no recognition of respect for the cultural resources of Third World communities, as 'TRIPs is based on the assumption of bioimperialism – that only knowledge and production of Western corporations need protection. If unchallenged TRIPs will become an instrument for displacement and dispensing with the knowledge, the resources and the rights of Third World farmers' (1993: 34). There is no recognition of collective claims. 'TRIPs recognises only the Western industrialised mode of innovation and has failed to recognise the more informal, communal system of innovation through which Third World farmers produce, select, improve and breed a plethora of diverse crop varieties. Farmers' seeds reflect the ingenuity, inventiveness and genius of our people. However, the protection of the collective intellectual property of Third World farmers does not even find a place in TRIPs' (1993: 34). There is in TRIPs no recognition of the collective intellectual property rights of Third World farmers that would protect their local knowledge.

The politics of world communication: people do not matter

If we take human rights content as an indicator of the representation of people's interests, we have to conclude that people do not matter in the politics of world communication.

This reflects fairly accurately the conditions under which this politics is shaped. The key players do not include ordinary people or organizations representing them. The most powerful players are dominant states and forceful lobbies of business interests. The needs of ordinary men and women do not usually figure prominently on the agendas of these players. There is certainly the pretence that states and business actors act on behalf of all people, and there is a common reference in many multilateral accords to the benefits of 'everyone'. In reality though the most powerful players have stood consistently in the way of robust human-rights-based political practices in the different issue areas of world communication. They pose serious threats to the freedom of information standard by their governmental and commercial forms of censorship and concentrated control over communication channels; they hinder the universal accessibility of common natural and human resources; they refuse liability for defective communication; and they deprive people of knowledge, cultural identity and privacy. In their operations, formidable interests are at stake. The implementation of human rights standards would deeply challenge these interests.

If we take human rights seriously, we should – against this reality – articulate and implement a politics of world communication 'as if people matter'. One approach to this aspiration is the design of a robust political practice on the people's right to communicate. This implies the formulation of binding norms, strong enforcement procedures and effective implementation mechanisms to secure the right of all people freely to participate in world communication, to share its benefits and to enjoy protection against its abuse.

The right to communicate: emergence and evolution

As early as 1969 Jean d'Arcy introduced the right to communicate by writing: 'the time will come when the Universal Declaration of Human Rights will have to encompass a more extensive right than man's right to information . . . This is the right of men to communicate.' The motivating force for the new approach was the conclusion that the adopted principles such as embodied in the Universal Declaration of Human Rights or the Covenant on Civil and Political Rights were inadequate to deal with the reality of two-way communication. Communication needs to be understood as an interactive process. The criticism was also that adopted rules focus too much on the content of the process. 'It is the information itself which is protected' (Fisher and Harms, 1983: 8). 'The earlier statements of communications freedoms . . . implied that freedom of information was a one-way right from a higher to a lower plane' (1983: 9). There is an increasing need for participation: 'more and more people can read, write and use broadcasting equipment and can no longer, therefore, be denied access to and participation in media processes for lack of communication and handling skills' (1983: 9).

The right to communicate is perceived by the protagonists as more fundamental than the information rights as accorded by current international law. It would have to be one of the non-derogable basic rights. The current liberties such as the freedom of expression would be seen as derived from this basic right. The essence of the right would be based on the observation that communication is a fundamental social process, a basic human need and the foundation of all social organization. The recognition of this right would also imply a strong ethical basis for resource-rich countries to share resources with poorer countries.

Since 1974 the notion has been included in Unesco's programme. At the eighteenth session of the Unesco General Conference a resolution was adopted (Resolution 4.121) that affirmed 'that all individuals should have equal opportunities to participate actively in the means of communication and to benefit from such means while preserving the right to protection against their abuses'.[3] The resolution authorized the Director General 'to study ways and means by which active participation in the communication process may become possible and analyze the right to communicate'. The right to communicate was an issue at the 1975 conference of the International Institute of Communications (IIC) at Cologne, Germany. The participants proposed that: 'Everyone has the right to communicate. [Communication] is a basic need and is the foundation of all social organization. It [the right to communicate] belongs to individuals and communities, between and among each other. This right has been long recognized internationally and the exercise of it needs constantly to evolve and expand. Taking account of changes in society and developments in technology, adequate resources – human, economic and technological – should be made available to all mankind for fulfilment of the need for interactive participatory communication and implementation of that right.'

In 1977 a publication edited by Harms, Richstad and Kie offered the substantial elements of a right to communicate. These included that everyone should have a right to get the information they need; there should be an appropriate, balanced information exchange between persons, regions and countries; the communication structure in a country should promote two-way communication at all levels; people should have basic communication skills and they should be taught them; and there should be room for active participation in society as well as individual privacy.

In May 1978 a first Unesco expert seminar on the right to communicate took place at Stockholm (in cooperation with the Swedish National Unesco Commission) (Unesco, 1978). Participants identified different components of the concept of the right to communicate. These included the right to participate, the right to access to communication resources and information rights. The meeting agreed 'that social groups ought to have the rights of access and participation in the communication process. It was also stressed that special attention with regard to the right to communicate should be paid to various minorities – national, ethnic, religious and linguistic' (Fisher, 1982: 43). The meeting was also in agreement that 'the development of the necessary new structures within the communication resource-poor communities would require inter-national cooperation and a more balanced exchange of hardware and software, reducing the gap between the resource-rich and resource-poor communities' (1982: 44). In summary the Stockholm meeting concluded that 'the right to communicate concept poses "big and messy" problems that require an outlook larger than that provided by any single cultural background, any single professional discipline, or any particular body of professional experience. And although some of the aspects of the concept were felt to be uncomfortable by some participants and observers, these same participants and observers also generally find the concept hopeful and encouraging' (1982: 45).

Whereas the Stockholm meeting provided largely an analysis of the right to communicate on the levels of the individual and the community, a second expert seminar focused on the international dimension of the right to communicate. This was the Meeting of Experts on the Right to Communicate at Manila. The meeting was organized in cooperation with the Philippine Unesco National Commission and took place 15–19 October 1979. The participants proposed that the right to communicate is both an individual and a social right. As a fundamental human right it should be incorpor-ated in the Universal Declaration of Human Rights. It has validity nationally and internationally. It encompasses duties and responsi-bilities for individuals, groups and nations. It requires the allocation of appropriate resources.

Meanwhile the Unesco Mass Media Declaration had been adopted in 1978 without a concrete reference to the right to communicate. The declaration implied the right by such formula-tions as: 'it is important that the mass media be responsive to concerns of peoples and individuals, thus promoting the participa-tion of the public in the elaboration of information'.

In its final report the MacBride Commission concluded that the recognition of this new right 'promises to advance the democratiza-tion of communication' (International Commission for the Study of Communication Problems, 1980: 173). The Commission stated: 'Communication needs in a democratic society should be met by the

extension of specific rights such as the right to be informed, the right
to inform, the right to privacy, the right to participate in public
communication – all elements of a new concept, the right to
communicate. In developing what might be called a new era of
social rights, we suggest all the implications of the right to
communicate be further explored' (1980: 265). The Commission
also observed that: 'Freedom of speech, of the press, of information
and of assembly are vital for the realization of human rights.
Extension of these communication freedoms to a broader individual
and collective right to communicate is an evolving principle in the
democratization process' (1980: 265). According to the Commission: 'The concept of the "right to communicate" has yet to receive
its final form and its full content . . . it is still at the stage of being
thought through in all its implications and gradually enriched'
(1980: 173).

From 3 to 5 March 1980 Unesco convened a study group on the
right to communicate in London. The group focused on three basic
questions: the 'why' of the right to communicate, the 'what' of the
right to communicate, and 'how' the right to communicate should
be developed. In its analysis of the substance of the right to
communicate, the group stressed a number of vital aspects. The
right to communicate should be seen as a dynamic and flexible
concept. It should be based on a positive notion of communication
and express such positive social values as democratization, public
participation and access, equality and self-management. The right
to communicate should recognize the relationship between communication and development and take into account individual and
communal levels of communication. The right to communicate as a
comprehensive concept should carry notions of duties and responsibilities (Fisher, 1982: 52–3). Also in 1980 the International Institute
of Communications organized with Unesco in connection with its
annual conference a working group on the right to communicate.
The working group agreed on the following formulation of the
concept: 'Everyone has the right to communicate. Communication
is a fundamental social process which enables individuals and
communities to exchange information and opinions. It is a basic
human need and the foundation of all social organization. The right
to communicate belongs to individuals and the communities which
they compose' (1982: 54). In 1980 a definition of the right to
communicate was proposed by Harms: 'Everyone has the right to
communicate. The components of this comprehensive human right
include but are not limited to the following communication rights: a
right to assemble, a right to participate, and related association

rights; a right to inform, a right to be informed, and related information rights; a right to privacy, a right to language and related cultural evolution rights. Within the world communication order, the achievement of a right to communicate requires that communication resources be available for the satisfaction of human communication needs.'

The 1980 Unesco General Conference in Belgrade confirmed the concept of a right to communicate in terms of 'respect for the right of the public, of ethnic and social groups and of individuals to have access to information sources and to participate actively in the communication process' (Resolution 4/19, 14(xi)). In 1981 a consultation at Strasbourg, convened by the International Institute of Communications together with Unesco, addressed the relationship between the right to communicate and a new world information and communication order. Participants claimed that: 'The universal recognition of this right for individuals, communities and social groups requires a new world information and communication order which will provide the freedom and the means for its exercise.'

The Unesco General Conference of 1983 in Paris adopted a resolution on the right to communicate, stating: 'Recalling that the aim is not to substitute the notion of the right to communicate for any rights already recognized by the international community, but to increase their scope with regard to individuals and the groups they form, particularly in view of the new possibilities of active communication and dialogue between cultures that are opened up by advances in the media' (Resolution 3.2). The 23rd Unesco General Conference in 1985 at Sofia requested the Director General to develop activities for the realization of the right to communicate.

In January 1985 a group of Unesco consultants prepared a status report on the right to communicate. The report observed that despite over a decade of debates, reports and meetings, a clear consensus had not been reached. However, it was possible to pinpoint the principal issues relating to the right to communicate: '(1) how it is to be described or defined – as an emerging concept, or one already proclaimed but not yet established, or one only requiring the synthesis of already established elements; (2) how, once established, it is to be implemented; (3) what is its relationship with some other concepts such as the right to development, and especially with the notion of a new world information and communication order'. According to the consultants:

> the diversity of opinions, ranging from pronounced opposition to enthusiastic support, has given the subject the stigma of a controversial

issue whose further development (evolution) risks to be paralysed at a time when it may be most needed. Particularly so when one considers the rapid development of new communication technologies and the opportunities they provide for better communication at all levels of society. On the other hand, it is becoming equally evident that the fundamental importance of the right to communicate stems from the fact that all of the major established human rights can be fully exercised and enjoyed only on the basis of genuine, comprehensive communication understood as an unalienable right of each human being. This dependence between established human rights and the as yet undefined right to communicate asks for further endeavours in this area.

In the early 1990s the right to communicate has practically disappeared from Unesco's agenda. In the medium-term plan for 1990–5 it is no longer a crucial concept. The right to communicate is mentioned but not translated into operational action.

The declarations of Unesco-convened meetings at Windhoek (1991) and Alma Ata (1992) made no reference to the right to communicate. The right to communicate continued to play a role in the meetings of the MacBride round table. The Harare statement of 29 October 1989 proposed: 'The core of the MacBride Report lies in the conviction that communication is a basic human right. Communication is both an individual human need and a social necessity – constituting the nervous system of society' (Traber and Nordenstreng, 1992: 26). The MacBride round table in Prague, meeting 21–2 September 1990, stated: 'In an era in search of greater democracy and respect for human rights, the right to communicate should be promoted as one of the fundamental principles of a democratic order. The right to communicate is, in the words of Sean MacBride, "the very foundation of other human rights" ' (1992: 29). A meeting convened in Lima, Peru by the World Association for Christian Communication and the Institute for Latin America (IPAL), 26–8 November 1990, referred to the people's right to communicate in connection with the problem of ownership of the infrastructures and media of social communications (1992: 39).

In 1992 Pekka Tarjanne, Secretary General of the International Telecommunication Union, took up the issue of the right to communicate and stated: 'I have suggested to my colleagues that the Universal Declaration of Human Rights should be amended to recognize the right to communicate as a fundamental human right' (1992: 45). In 1993 the International Association for Mass Communication Research provided support to the right to communicate through contributions to various expert seminars. One of these was held at Bratislava, Slovak Republic (10–11 June 1993) and generated the Bratislava declaration. In this document the participants proposed that relevant provisions on freedom of information 'be reviewed toward the goal of affirming and strengthening the right to communicate as an inalienable right of individuals and peoples and as a fundamental instrument in the democratization of society'. The Bratislava declaration was part of the preparatory materials for the NGO Forum on All Human Rights for All held during the United Nations World Conference on Human Rights in June 1993. The Forum pointed in its final report (A/Conf. 157/7. 14 June, 11) to 'The guarantee of the right to information as comprising the right to receive, to produce and to have access to impartial and uncensored information, free of monopoly.' In an additional document (A/Conf. 157/7Add. 1, 17 June, 8.9) the Forum recommended: 'Assertion of the rights to communication, investigation and reception of information and opinion. Establishment of the obligation of Member States to repeal all official censorship machinery and all penal measures which imply special protection for public officials in order to guarantee informational pluralism, facilitating access to the mass media by public media organizations, granting fixed slots in the State-run media, and ensuring pluralist administration of the State media separate from Governmental authority.'

In its evolution the right to communicate has not been without its critics. Throughout the debate the objection was repeatedly raised that 'communication is so integral a part of the human condition that it is philosophically unnecessary and perhaps wrong to describe it as a human right' (Fisher, 1982: 41). Another objection pointed to the possible use of the concept by powerful groups in society. 'The concept has to be interpreted, and this will be done by groups in power, not by the weak or oppressed. Limits will be fixed within which the right to communicate may be exercised. These borders will be defined on a political basis and will favour present power relationships in the world. The right to communicate is not a concept leading toward change; it is an attempt to give groups working for liberation a feeling of being taken seriously, while in practice the right to communicate will be used to preserve the present order in the world and to stabilize it even further' (Hedebro, 1982: 68).

Fisher has drawn attention to the fact that opposition to the right to communicate has come from different ideological standpoints. 'The concept of the right to communicate is distrusted by the "western" nations which see it as part of the proposals relating to new world information and communication orders, about which they are highly suspicious . . . In some socialist and Third World countries, opposition to the right derives from the fact that it could be used to justify the continuation of the existing massive imbalance in information flows and the unrestricted importation of western

technology and information and, consequently western values'
(Fisher, 1982: 34).

The socialist type of objection was expressed in a comment by
one of the MacBride Commission members, the USSR representative S. Losev: 'The right to communicate is not an internationally
accepted right on either national or international level. Therefore it
should not be discussed at such length and in such a way in our
report' (International Commission for the Study of Communication
Problems, 1980: 172). Also the US government opposed the right to
communicate and tried, in spite of the Soviet criticism, to denounce
the concept as a communist ploy. In the American rejection the key
feature was the link between the right to communicate and the
notion of people's rights. Although the reference to people and to
people's rights is very common in American political history, in
the context of Unesco this was seen as a defence of state rights
and a threat to individual rights. The irony of this position is clear
when one reflects on the opening phrase of the US constitution:
'We the people . . .'. As Colleen Roach observed: 'By rejecting the
term "people", American diplomats and the American press have
also turned their backs on the very history of the United States'
(1988: 20).

The right to communicate: the project of a multilateral accord

The recognition of a right to communicate 'for all people' is the
cornerstone of the human-rights-based world communication
politics. This could be achieved through the adoption of a robust
multilateral convention that provides the basis for people-centred
political practices in the issue areas of world communication.

This proposed multilateral convention on the right to communicate is not the common type of inter-state accord. It should be an
agreement between state and non-state actors (BINGOs and
PINGOs). The conference that would adopt the convention would
invite all United Nations member states to send delegations, each of
which would include one representative of the government, one
delegate representing business interests and one delegate representing people's interests. The convention text would be signed by all
members of delegations and would later be ratified through trilateral negotiations in the home countries of the delegations.

The idea of involving more than state players in issues of world
politics is not new. The International Labour Organization employs
the instrument of trilateral negotiations in formulating its policies.
The decision making labour conferences are attended by delega-

tions composed of representatives of governments, employers and workers. In several IGOs there is also a noticeable trend towards bilateral bargaining between states and business players. In recent years the non-state business actors have achieved a prominent position in such forums as the ITU, the GATT and the OECD.

The multilateral convention would in principle be designed around a set of basic standards, rules for the enforcement of these standards and institutional mechanisms to implement the standards and rules of the convention.

The norms

For the normative component of the right to communicate I propose four categories of binding standards. These are information rights, protection rights, collective rights and participation rights.

All the standards in these four categories are treaty provisions and thus contractual obligations for those parties ratifying the convention. It would seem realistic to propose that most norms would allow derogation in situations of public emergency. However, it can be argued that some standards on the right to communicate are peremptory and do not permit derogation. If we follow the provisions of the ICCPR on this (Article 4.1), certain norms on discrimination are peremptory.[4] The ICCPR prohibits discrimination on the grounds of race, colour, sex, language, religion or social origin. The formulation that discrimination 'solely' on these grounds is peremptorily prohibited could imply that discrimination would not be prohibited if other grounds, such as political affiliation, were also at play. By and large though it can be concluded from the human rights treaties and the literature that substantial forms of discrimination on the grounds mentioned in ICCPR Article 4.1 are binding international law (Hannikainen, 1988: 482). Article 4.2 refers to other human rights norms that equally permit no derogation. There is no derogation from ICCPR Articles 6, 7, 8:1.2, 11, 15, 16 and 18.

Under this absolute prohibition the right to freedom of thought, conscience and religion is also recognized as non-derogable. This provision should be extended to the right to hold opinions. This can be defended by arguing that the distinction between the freedom of thought and the freedom to hold opinions is unreal. Moreover, Article 19.3 of the ICCPR subjects to certain restrictions the right to freedom of expression, but not the right to hold opinions.

Other norms on the right to communicate may not be formulated in an equally absolutist manner. 'Even the seemingly absolute guarantees of the First Amendment to the US Constitution are considerably limited in practice by, for example, the clear and present danger test' (Örücü, 1986: 38). One can even claim that the very act of 'converting a freedom into a legal right, is in effect a regulation which fundamentally is also a limitation of a pure liberty' (1986: 40). However, while admitting to certain limitations, these should be clearly delimited. Limitations to the exercise of human rights can effectively destroy these rights. Therefore it is important to identify the limit to limitation. This is what Örücü has called the question of the 'irreducible minimum' (1986: 45). 'Every basic right requires a defined core and precise criteria for identifying encroachments' (1986: 55). The guiding principle here is that limitations are always formulated such as to increase the level of protection. 'One should always keep in mind that the ultimate objective of the limitation clauses is not to increase the power of a state or government but to ensure the effective enforcement of the rights and freedoms of its inhabitants' (Kiss, 1981: 310). In the light of this principle, limitations to human rights standards should be confined to those 'prescribed by international law and necessary in democratic societies'.[5]

The prescription by international law is essential since domestic laws are often more restrictive. This is why the Vienna declaration is inadequate when it states in Article 39: 'Underlining the importance of objective, responsible and impartial information about human rights and humanitarian issues, the World Conference on Human Rights encourages the increased involvement of the media, for whom freedom and protection should be guaranteed within the framework of national law' (25 June 1993). In many countries the national legislation allows for exceptions to the freedom of information which effectively erode the standard itself. Article 19(3) of the ICCPR uses the phrase that restrictions 'shall be only such as are provided by law'. This is equally unsatisfactory as it is too general. Evidently the law cannot violate any right or freedom recognized by the covenant (Article 5.1)[6] but it would be desirable to add explicitly that the law must be in accordance with the provisions of the United Nations charter and the Universal Declaration of Human Rights.

The provision that restrictions should be necessary in democratic societies is used in Article 10 of the European Convention for the Protection of Human Rights and Fundamental Freedoms (1950). In the convention this is linked with the following notions: 'in the interests of national security, territorial integrity or public safety, for the prevention of disorder or crime, for the protection of health or morals, for the protection of the reputation or rights of others, for preventing the disclosure of information received in confidence, or for maintaining the authority and impartiality of the judiciary'. These notions lend themselves to arbitrary interference, as 'All of them are difficult to define and imply a measure of relativity in that they may be understood differently in different countries, in different circumstances, at different times' (Kiss, 1981: 295). In the International Covenant on Civil and Political Rights (Article 19), 'national security, public order (*ordre public*) . . . public health or morals' are permissible grounds for limitation of the freedom of expression. All these principles with the possible exception of public health are controversial and difficult to interpret. Public morals for example suggests a uniform conception of morality which does not exist. Public morals tend to be the moral conception of the social elite.

National security is a permissible ground for limitation of the freedom of expression. The meaning of the principle of national security is not given and the obvious problem is that its interpretation will be determined by those accused of violating the standard.

Information rights
The category of information rights recognizes as binding norms the right to hold opinions, the right to freedom of expression, the right to receive, seek and impart information and ideas, and the right to reply.

The right to hold opinions   As argued above, this should be a non-derogable standard.

The right to freedom of expression   This standard implies the right to express opinions without interference by public or private parties. In the conventional interpretation of this right the emphasis is on governmental interference with the expressions of citizens. However, human rights have both governmental and private aspects. For example, 'torture and kidnapping may be practised not only by police but also by private groups, such as "death squads" ' (Nickel, 1987: 43). Conventional human rights thinking mainly focuses on the vertical state–citizen relation. This ignores the possibility that concentration of power in the hands of individuals can be as threatening as state power. Whenever citizens pursue different economic interests, individual human rights will be under serious threat. Citizens also need to be protected against each other. When freedom is mainly protected from state interference, the restrictions that fellow citizens can impose upon access to information are left outside the scope of the right. Human rights should have a horizontal effect. They should apply not only to state–citizen but also to citizen–citizen relationships. In the case of information provision there should be protection against information oligopolies organized by fellow citizens.

This so-called *Drittwirkung* or third-party effect of human rights means, for example, that information rights of people should be free from interference by public as well as by private parties. Already in the discussions leading to the human rights covenants it has been proposed that interference by private parties should be barred. The proposal did not acquire the status of legal provision. 'An individual has the right to freedom of opinion without interference by private parties as well, and the state is obliged to ensure that freedom . . It is doubtful, however, whether the complex problem of protecting a person's opinion against interferences by other individuals can be solved in this global and absolute manner' (Partsch, 1981: 218). In spite of these reservations, the defence of freedom of expression should go beyond state interference and incorporate the reality of situations in which private parties exercise power equivalent to if not exceeding that of the state.

The right to freedom of expression goes beyond this negative freedom from interference, however, and includes the recognition of positive free speech rights. If the freedom of expression is interpreted in more than the classical negative sense, the positive interpretation makes it necessary to define this right not merely as a liberty but as a claim right. A positive freedom to communicate implies the claim right to express opinions and the related entitlement to facilities for the exercise of this right. If the freedom of expression is viewed as a liberty in the Hohfeldian sense, there is no correlative duty to provide the facilities for expression.[7] The recognition of freedom of expression as a positive claim right is particularly important in situations where the voices of some people are systematically excluded. In such situations the mere freedom from interference does not enable people to participate in public communication (Barendt, 1985: 86).

The right to receive information   People have the right to receive opinions, information and ideas. This standard implies the right of people to be properly informed about matters of public interest. This includes the right to receive information which is independent of commercial and political interests, and the right to receive a range of information and cultural products designed for a wide variety of tastes and interests.

The standard that people should be properly informed correlates with a duty of information providers to impart information and ideas on matters of public interest. In its opinions on the right to receive information, the European Court of Human Rights has ruled that the media should not merely broadcast signals but should function as purveyor of information and as public watchdog. The right to receive information is usually understood as liberty and not as a claim right to the dissemination of information, ideas and opinions. In this sense it remains a soft standard that prolongs inequality between those who provide information and those who receive it. A strong norm implies that the necessary facilities and opportunities are provided to secure the reception of the widest possible choice of information and ideas. This implies legal measures in situations where the channels of communication are monopolized in order to secure the largest possible number of autonomous channels.

The right to seek information This standard implies the right of access to information on matters of public interests (held by public or private sources).[8] The right of access to information is in many Western countries protected through the enactment of freedom of information laws. The basic rationale for these statutes is that democracy requires an informed citizenry capable of judging decisions made by governments. The difficult question however is whether one can defend a 'right to know' under freedom of information standards if the speaker is unwilling to speak: 'recognition of a right of access would then be tantamount to the imposition of constitutional duties to disclose information' (Barendt, 1985: 108). In the case of the unwilling speaker the right of access is difficult to uphold as a claim right. This is so 'partly because the claims are generally made by a recipient against an unwilling speaker, upon whom it is sought to impose a duty to disclose information. It may be added that if such a claim were made against a private person or body, rather than government, that person or body's own First Amendment or privacy rights might be implicated' (1985: 112). Forcing an unwilling speaker to provide information may violate the speaker's constitutional right to remain silent. It is easier to see the grant of the right of access to information when the speaker is willing but hindered in the execution of constitutional rights.

The right to impart information This standard includes the right to access public means of distributing information, ideas and opinions. It provides for a claim right to individuals to speak. In other words it secures people's access to the public media. The recognition that the public should receive a multitude and variety of views held by ordinary people correlates with the requirement that these ordinary people should speak via the media.

The right to distribute information necessarily includes fair and equitable access to information distribution channels. This has consequences for the tariffs of telecommunication and computer networks.

The right of reply   This standard usually covers a range of situations in which people are injured by inaccurate or offensive expressions disseminated to the general public by means of public communication.[9] In different legislations the right to reply provides the entitlement to respond to critical opinions or only to factual allegations. It would seem a wise course to follow Barendt in his interpretation of the standard and 'to confine rights of reply to clear misstatements of facts, because it is easier to judge that one has been committed than it is to conclude that an account is generally distorted or contains an unfair attack' (1985: 101).

Protection rights
The category of protection rights recognizes binding standards on privacy, discrimination, presumption of innocence, independence and deceit. Under these standards the right to communicate should provide robust protection against the abuse of public communication.

The protection of privacy   The protection of privacy is a binding norm in international human rights law (ICCPR Article 17). It reinforces the sovereignty of the individual over a person-bound sphere of no intrusion. As a basic civil right it has not been explicitly formulated in relation to public communication. The complexity of the standard is obviously that it needs balancing against other norms such as the right to seek information. This is further complicated by the recognition that the protection of privacy can also imply the right not to know. This is relevant in the context of genetic information and people's right not to know that they are certain to develop some disease.

A robust formulation of the standard, in spite of these complications, is needed in the light of a growing abuse of people's privacies in public communication. It has become very common in many countries to obtain imagery of people without their consent and use this for entertainment purposes. An example is the use by TV stations of video material taken from rescue or emergency services. Privacy is also massively under threat in countries where electronic surveillance of people is widespread. In several countries governments are preparing legislation to prohibit the encryption of telecommunication and data traffic. This action against secret encoding of electronic communications facilitates for police forces the interception of communications by criminals. However, one of the results will be that people can no longer protect their private use of electronic communication. This leaves privacy unprotected and adds to the risks of the surveillance societies.

Basic to a right to communicate is the provision of the right to be protected against interference with people's privacy by the media of mass communication (publicly or privately owned), or by public and private agencies involved with data collections. Also people's private communications should be protected by law against interference by public or private parties.

Presumption of innocence   People's right to respect for the standard of due process is very essential in connection with the coverage of criminal cases by the media. This standard implies that the media should not declare defendants guilty before courts have established a verdict of guilt.[10]

Discrimination   An important normative standard of the right to communicate is the protection against forms of communication that are discriminatory in terms of race, colour, sex, language, religion or social origin. At present there are explicit provisions against racially discriminatory communication and against the advocacy of religious hatred (ICCPR Article 20; ICERD Article 4), but not on other forms of impermissible discrimination. The right to communicate requires provisions on the protection against discrimination on these other grounds as well.

People have the right to the protection by law against prejudicial treatment of their person in the media of public communication. This right to be treated in non-discriminatory ways implies that reporting by the media should refrain from the use of images that distort the realities and complexities of people's lives or that fuel prejudice by discriminatory descriptions of people and situations, and that neglect the dignity and ability of opponents in national, racial or ethnic conflict.

Deceit   People have the right to be protected against misleading and distorted information. This right concerns both the dissemination of news and the provision of consumer information. News dissemination should be based on accuracy and impartiality.

The provision of consumer information should be guided by the consumer's right to protection of health and safety, the right to protection of economic interests, the right of redress and the right of representation. Protection against injurious information is especially relevant with regard to children. The United Nations Convention on the Rights of the Child (1989) provides on this issue in Article 17 that states parties shall encourage the development of appropriate guidelines for the protection of the child from information and material injurious to his or her well-being. These guidelines should take into account the provisions on freedom of expression. The implication of a standard on defective information is that people have the right to hold information providers accountable for the accuracy of their information and establish liability when inaccurate information causes damage. This should however not construe undue limits for the freedom of expression, but, if it is proven in a court of law that an information provider has wilfully disseminated inaccurate or misleading information or has facilitated the dissemination of such information by gross negligence, people should have recourse to compensation when damage can be established.

Independence   The information rights mentioned above require the protection of the professional independence of employees of public or private communication agencies. Professional journalists obviously need a form of protection when they are out gathering information on dangerous missions. But they also need protection against interference by the owners and managers of the mass media. This implies the adoption of robust editorial statutes to protect journalists against owners and managers of news media.

Collective rights
Human rights have both individual and collective dimensions. 'There are also rights which present individual and collective aspects. Freedom of religion and freedom of expression are cases in point' (Boven, 1982: 54). Rights to language and religion are enjoyed in communities. They cannot be implemented by protecting individual rights only. Also the right to development demonstrates this relationship. UNGA Resolution 34/46 of 1979 states that 'the right to development is a human right and that equality of opportunity for development is as much a prerogative of nations as of individuals within nations'. As a result, in the discussion on the locus of human rights the individual and the community cannot be separated. Individuals do not exist in isolation and are members of communities. Communities do not exist outside the individuals that make up the collective. Sanders concludes that 'individual rights and collective rights are distinct ideas, they are separate categories.

Some individual rights can be vindicated without reference to collective rights . . . But other basic rights – such as freedom of religion – cannot be effectively vindicated without the recognition of collective rights' (1991: 383).

This does not exclude that in different cultural and ideological traditions there are conflicting emphases on the individual versus the collective. There may be conflicts between individual and collective rights. This needs careful balancing. An example is the collective right to cultural autonomy of a group that practises sexual discrimination through female circumcision. A guiding principle here is the provision of Article 5 of ICCPR and ICESR which prohibits any collective to engage in acts that are 'aimed at the destruction of any of the rights and freedoms' recognized in the covenants. The exercise of collective rights cannot imply the destruction of individual rights.

In international law there has been a remarkable evolution from an exclusive emphasis on sovereign nation-states, to individuals, to non-state social groups (peoples) and to humankind. There is still a strong tendency to give priority to individual rights, and states tend to be against the recognition of the collective rights of minorities as they usually favour assimilation over cultural autonomy. Even so, there is increasing recognition of collective rights. Following Sanders (1991), collective rights are claims on behalf of communities (for example ethnic minorities) that seek to protect their specific features, such as cultural or linguistic characteristics. Sanders distinguishes collective rights from group rights: 'the major limitation of group rights is that they only exist while the discrimination continues' (1991: 369). Groups are joined because of external discrimination, whereas collectivities are joined by internal cohesiveness. 'Collectivities seek to protect and develop their own particular cultural characteristics' (1991: 369). For example, 'cultural minorities seek more than the right of their individual members to equality and participation within the larger society. They also seek distinct group survival' (1991: 370).

The right to communicate should be recognized both as an individual and as a collective right. To put the right exclusively in either category limits unduly the rights of individuals as members of a community or the rights of the collectivity. Collective claims require provisions on the access to public communication on behalf of social groups. This is particularly important as so many social groups, e.g. women, minorities, youth, tend to be excluded from public communication.

In addition to this right of access for communities, collective claims also include the right of development, and the recognition of communal knowledge resources. The recognition of the development principle in world communication politics implies the entitlement to the development of communication infrastructures, to the procurement of adequate resources, the sharing of knowledge and skills, the equality of economic opportunities, and the correction of inequalities. The communal claim to intellectual property recognizes that knowledge resources are often a common good owned by a collective. Knowledge as common heritage should be protected against its private appropriation by knowledge industries. Collective claims also imply provisions on cultural identity, on the recognition of cultural diversity and linguistic variety, and on the cultural autonomy of communities.

Participation rights
The idea of human rights has to extend to the social institutions that facilitate the realization of fundamental standards. Human rights cannot be realized without involving citizens in the decision making processes about the spheres in which freedom and equality are to be achieved. This moves the democratic process beyond the political sphere and extends the requirement of participatory institutional arrangements to other social domains. In this extension also culture and technology should be subject to democratic control. This is particularly important in the light of the fact that current democratization processes around the world (the 'new world order' processes of deregulation) tend to delegate important areas of social life to private rather than to public control and accountability. Increasingly large volumes of social activity are withdrawn from public accountability, from democratic control, and from the participation of citizens in decision making.

The rapidly proliferating privatization of information provision and cultural production implies that more and more public space is taken over by corporate, commercial interests. This 'public to private' shift entails that the decisive criteria of people's access to information and culture are marketability and profitability.

The standard of extended participation implies the accessibility and affordability of communication facilities and services, but also the availability of communication skills. People have the right to acquire the skills necessary to participate fully in public communication. This requires programmes for communication literacy and critical media education. This right should enable people to become critical users and producers of information and culture.

Participation rights also entail people's right 'freely to participate in the cultural life of the community, to enjoy the arts and to share in scientific advancement and its benefits' (Article 27 of the

UDHR). The participation claim requires the creation of social and economic conditions that will enable people 'not only to enjoy the benefits of culture, but also to take an active part in overall cultural life and in the process of cultural development'. The Unesco recommendation on participation by the people at large in cultural life and their contribution to it (1976, nineteenth session of the General Conference), which articulates this requirement, also provides that 'participation in cultural life presupposes involvement of the different social partners in decision-making related to cultural policy'.

Participation extends beyond public participation in media production or media management into the areas of public decision making. The 1982 Unesco expert consultation in Bucharest, Romania (9–12 February; Unesco, 1982) emphasized that it is essential for a right to communicate 'that individuals and groups should be able to participate at all relevant levels and at all stages in communication, including the formulation, application, monitoring and review of communication policies'. This means that the standard requires that political practices provide for people's participation in public policy making on the provision of information, the production of culture and the production and application of knowledge. This means that there should be ample scope for public participation in the formulation and implementation of public information policies, of public policies on the generation and application of knowledge, of public cultural policies and of public technology policies and the adoption of technology standards.

Procedures

The right to communicate needs robust procedures of enforcement. The essential principles for this are the provision of effective remedy against acts violating the right to communicate, the establishment of accountability and the recognition of the horizontal effect of remedial measures.

Crucial for the protection of human rights is the notion that there can be no rights without the option of redress in cases of their violation. Rights and remedies are intrinsically related and, where human rights concepts do not provide accessible and affordable means of redress, they erode the effective protection of the rights they proclaim. The old adage of Roman law states: 'ubi ius, ibi remedium' (where there is law there is remedy). One can turn this around and propose that when no remedy is available there is no law. People should be able to seek effective remedy when state or private parties obstruct their right to communicate.

Human rights not only require mechanisms of redress, but also imply that those who rule on behalf of all are accountable, i.e. they are obliged to justify their decisions on behalf of all. It is a basic requirement of human rights standards that provisions on public policy imply a mechanism for accountability. 'The requirement that every citizen has a right to take part in the conduct of public affairs is satisfied if appointed officials are in some way responsible to elected representatives' (Partsch, 1981: 239). This includes rules on accountability for public policy makers and private parties involved in providing communication services, information networks and cultural products.

The realization of human rights requires limitations on the power of the state as well as a defence against 'horizontal' abuses of fundamental rights and freedoms. The implication is that the right to communicate should also be enforced *vis-à-vis* non-state players. People should have access to effective redress when private actors interfere with their privacy, distribute misleading information, threaten their cultural autonomy, fail to protect their intellectual property, or hamper their access to telecommunication and data networks.

On the basis of these principles (effective remedy, accountability and horizontal effect) the procedures for individuals and communities to seek redress have to contain at a minimum the following three components: the recognition of the formal right to file complaints when public or private actors do not comply with the adopted norms; the recognition of the competence of an independent tribunal which receives complaints and also with which non-state actors, both individually and collectively, have *locus standi*; the recognition that the opinions of the tribunal are binding on those who accept its jurisdiction.

Implementation mechanisms

Binding norms and robust rules on their enforcement are still no guarantee that all people will effectively enjoy a right to communicate. To improve the chances of compliance with the norms and rules, effective institutional mechanisms are essential. At a minimum this means the creation of an independent committee for monitoring and review, a special rapporteur, and an independent tribunal to receive complaints, to arbitrate and to adjudicate.

The independent committee could function much like the existing human rights committees of the United Nations. The members of this committee on the right to communicate would be elected and would serve in their personal capacity. The committee members would have experience in the field of human rights and special competence in the different issue areas of world communication. Nominations would be made by all parties ratifying the convention on the right to communicate and elections would be held at a review conference on the convention.

The committee would receive and consider communications from the parties to the convention about parties not fulfilling the obligations of the accord. The committee would also review regular reports by parties to the convention about their implementation of the obligations of the accord. The committee meetings would not be closed and all documentation related to communications from parties, review reports and so on would be accessible to all. The committee could appoint a special rapporteur on the right to communicate who could conduct independent study and assessment of the implementation of obligations by the parties involved.

The committee would also first receive all complaints filed by individuals and communities that may require adjudication by the tribunal. Much like the European Commission of Human Rights, the committee would receive, review and assess complaints about alleged violations of the right to communicate. In this way the committee would act as a filter for cases that would be settled out of court and those that would go to the tribunal. The independent tribunal would function like the European Court of Human Rights as a body that is above all parties and that can take binding decisions. The tribunal could be a special chamber of the International Court of Justice: there is a provision for this in the Court's statute.

Conclusion

The politics of world communication affects people's daily lives. Yet in the prevailing political practices of world communication people do not matter. A world communication politics that would be guided by a human rights perspective would require – as a cornerstone – a robust multilateral accord on the right to communicate.

This project cannot be left to the world's princes and merchants. As history has generously demonstrated, the defence of basic human rights cannot be entrusted to these players. People's interests will only be taken seriously when people themselves mobilize pressure upon the forces of state and market. This means that ordinary people will have to intervene in world affairs, which are typically perceived as an arena outside citizens' intervention and not in need of democratic control. This means that people have to confront the common fear that they would really mess up if they were allowed to run the world. They also have to deal with their own 'lack of needed information about their direct involvement in the world and . . . lack of visions about how they might play a more dynamic role in their relations with the world' (Alger, 1987: 385). A serious obstacle for civil society to get involved in world politics is that 'people everywhere are socialized in the view that world affairs is, and indeed ought to be, handled by a small elite in state capitals and world centers' (1987: 384).

In spite of these real reservations, we have seen in the past decade a remarkable increase in the number and scope of collective political actions by ordinary people. 'The eighties can be character-ized by the massive emergence of new movements which intervene directly in a field traditionally considered as exterior and closed to social movements: the international arena' (Hegedus, 1990: 263). In contrast to the social movements of the seventies, 'the movements of the eighties are basically global, planetary and transnational not only with regard to the issues they address but, above all, in their interventions. "Thinking globally, acting locally", the slogan of the peace movement, reflects exactly the genuinely new and multiple dimension of these practices which act simultaneously at an infra- and transnational level, and challenge the very framework of nation-states as well as the basic paradigm of an international world order, structured on the exclusive relations between states, blocs and military super-powers' (1990: 267).

The successful operations of peace and green movements have shown some essential features of a broad people's movement. The so-called new social movements can be characterized as non-hierarchical and decentralized with diverse, cross-ideological, and multicultural constituencies. Their activities have a strong ethical dimension and are problem centred (1990: 271). The movements demonstrate a basic concern for people's self-determination and individual responsibility. They enhance people's control, 'they engender a movement of citizen empowerment' (1990: 272). The movements address 'the basic question of people's empowerment to enter the political process directly and to "control their own history": that is, to manage in an autonomous manner their indi-vidual and collective destiny with respect to domestic and trans-national issues' (1990: 272). A significant element has also been the recruitment among scientific elites. Many scientists have for exam-ple joined the peace movement in the 1980s (Meier, 1990: 257).

In order to create world communication politics 'as if people matter' new civil initiatives are needed. If people's interests are to be accommodated, people will have to claim the right to communicate. So far, social movements have expressed their concern about the world in such fields as human rights, security, environment and development, but not in connection with world communication. Yet people's daily lives are affected by world communication in essential ways. We need therefore, much like the green movement and the peace movement, a communication movement. For the establishment of a world-wide communication movement it is essential that people acquire information about how they are involved and affected and about how they can make a difference.

Existing social movements are often already working on issues that touch upon the right to communicate, although they are not yet perceived as 'right to communicate' issues. Urban movements search for more communicative lifestyles and promote communication among people. Ethnic movements protest the destruction of cultural identities and resist cultural uprooting. Environmental groups fight against state control over information resources and corporate dispossession of people's knowledge. Feminists challenge the production and dissemination of pornographic images.

Although not articulated as such, all this activity attempts to shape world communication politics in accordance with people's interests. As Touraine has observed, the new social movements challenge the domination which 'controls not only the "means of production" but the production of symbolic goods, that is, of information and images of culture itself' (1985: 774).

The process leading to a world-wide communication movement needs to start with ordinary men and women in their local communities and with the effort to build bridges between these communities. This means that the sources of changes on the world level are in the local space. The resolution of world problems lies with what Rahnema calls 'the regeneration of local spaces' (Alger, 1990: 166). This implies a process of learning, of identifying issues as communication issues, of recognizing the micro/macro connection. The defence of local self-determination needs global action. Local spaces have to link transnationally to discover how people's right to communicate is curbed by current political practice. Linking can take place through telecommunication, and computer networks are more easily accessible than before. Computer conferences on the main concerns in world communication are a feasible project. Joint actions can be planned for intervention in the global arena in an autonomous manner. People across the globe can conclude private agreements and alternative treaties in the various issue areas of world communication.

A broad social movement in the field of world communication is the essential prerequisite to achieve genuine multilateral negotiations between princes, merchants and ordinary people. Only an alert and vibrant world civil society can begin to influence the other players towards the adoption of and the compliance with political arrangements for world communication that reflect people's interests.

I have no doubt that the formation of world communication politics from a human rights perspective is a tall order indeed. However, if we want all people to matter in the communication processes of the third millennium, we have to meet the challenge!

Notes

1 Human rights norms are the standards of behaviour that are articulated in a fairly extensive body of international human rights law. This encompasses a series of conventions adopted by the United Nations General Assembly including the ICCPR (and the optional protocol, 1966), the ICESCR (1966), the International Convention on the Elimination of All Forms of Racial Discrimination (1965), the International Convention on the Suppression and Punishment of the Crime of Apartheid (1973), the Convention on the Elimination of All Forms of Discrimination against Women (1979), the Convention against Torture and other Cruel, Inhuman or Degrading Treatment or Punishment (1984), the Convention on the Prevention and Punishment of the Crime of Genocide (1948) and the Convention on the Rights of the Child (1989); conventions adopted by the International Labour Organization including the Freedom of Association and Protection of the Right to Organize Convention (1948), the Discrimination (Employment and Occupation) Convention (1958), the Abolition of Forced Labour Convention (1957), the Equal Remuneration Convention (1951) and the Migrant Workers Convention (1975); conventions adopted by the General Conference of Unesco including the Convention against Discrimination in Education (1960) and the Convention for the Protection of the World Cultural and Natural Heritage (1972); and a series of declarations and recommendations adopted by the United Nations General Assembly, including the UDHR (1948), the Declaration on the Granting of Independence to Colonial Countries and Peoples (1960), the Declaration on Permanent Sovereignty over Natural Resources (1962), the Declaration on the Rights of Disabled Persons (1975), the Declaration on the Use of Scientific and Technological Progress in the Interests of Peace and for the Benefit of Mankind (1975), the Declaration on Social Progress and Development (1969), the Declaration on the Human Rights of Individuals Who are not Nationals of the Country in which They Live (1985) and the Declaration on the Right to Development (1986); declarations adopted by the General Conference of Unesco including the Declaration of the Principles of International Cultural Cooperation (1966) and the Declaration on Fundamental Principles Concerning the Contribution of the Mass Media to Strengthening Peace and International Understanding, to the Promotion of Human Rights and to Countering Racialism, Apartheid and Incitement to War (1978); declarations adopted by world conferences convened by the United Nations including the Proclamation of Tehran (1968), the Declaration of the World Conference to Combat Racism and Racial Discrimination (1978) and the Vienna Declaration and Programme of Action adopted by the World Conference on Human Rights (1993); and instruments adopted outside the United Nations system including

the Final Act of the Conference on Security and Cooperation in Europe (1975) and the Geneva Conventions on the Treatment of Prisoners of War and the Protection of Civilian Persons in Time of War (1949).

2 By 1994 it was still too early to judge whether the recently appointed United Nations High Commissioner for Human Rights may add to the strength of implementation of human rights standards and whether the recently appointed Special Rapporteur for Freedom of Expression can play a role in the implementation of freedom of information standards.

3 Full text of Resolution 4.121: 'Recalling that the recognition of fundamental human rights is at the origin of the Charter of the United Nations and is proclaimed by the Universal Declaration of Human Rights, Believing that communication is the foundation of all social organization, Bearing in mind the relationship between communication and culture, Taking account of the diverse developments in the technology of communication and the potential availability of an abundance of communication resources, although at the same time noting that there are unresolved problems in the control of and access to these resources, Bearing in mind the plurality and equality of cultures and the potential now existing for all groups and individuals in society to give full expression to their cultural values, Noting the growing human need for a wider variety of communication services in an interdependent world, Recognizing the emergence of a science of communication and the increased need for planning communication resources for the future, Convinced that all individuals should have equal opportunities to participate actively in the means of communication and to benefit from such means while preserving the right to protection against their abuses, Authorizes the Director General to study and define the Right to Communicate in consultation with competent organs of the United Nations and with professional organizations and other interested institutions, and to report to the nineteenth General Conference on further steps which should be taken.'

4 Article 4.1 of ICCPR: 'In time of public emergency which threatens the life of the nation and the existence of which is officially proclaimed, the States Parties to the present Covenant may take measures derogating from their obligations under the present Covenant to the extent strictly required by the exigencies of the situation, provided that such measures are not inconsistent with their other obligations under international law and do not involve discrimination solely on the ground of race, colour, sex, language, religion or social origin.'

5 The 1982 Unesco expert consultation in Bucharest, Romania, 9–12 February 1982 (*Right to Communicate: Legal Aspects*, Paris: Unesco) proposed 'that restrictions on the exercise of the right to communicate should be strictly confined to those authorized by international law.'

6 Article 5.1 of ICCPR: 'Nothing in the present Covenant may be interpreted as implying for any State, group or person any right to engage in any activity or perform any act aimed at the destruction of any of the rights and freedoms recognized herein or at their limitation to a greater extent than is provided for in the present Covenant.'

7 The Hohfeldian classical legal analysis (Hohfeld, 1919) distinguishes between rights as legal claims and rights as liberties. In the former case the right correlates with a duty. For example, person A is entitled to compel person B by legal process to act. If the right is a liberty then it correlates with a no-right of others. This means that B does not have the right to interfere with A's privilege.

8 The Steering Committee on the Mass Media of the Council of Europe as well as its Steering Committee for Human Rights have taken measures to extend freedom of

information to include the right of the individual to have access to official information.

In 1981 the Committee of Ministers adopted Recommendation R(81)19 on the access to information held by public authorities that stressed the desirability for member states of recognizing such a right: 'the right to obtain, on request, information held by the public authorities other than legislative and judicial authorities . . . subject only to such limitations and restrictions as are necessary in a democratic society for the protection of legitimate public . . . or private interests'. The Committee of Ministers has also examined the question of whether Article 10 should be amended to include the right to seek information. The consensus was that this right is already implicit in Article 10.

'The European Court has ruled that the right to receive information does not entail a general presumption of access to information held by the government, although a limited presumption, such as to information of general public interest, is by no means precluded' (Coliver, 1993: 231). The Court would not seem to support a claim right 'to know' but rather a Hohfeldian liberty that does not impose the obligation to provide information, but may bar state interference with for example media interviews with prisoners.

9 American Convention on Human Rights, Article 14, provides that: 'Anyone injured by inaccurate or offensive statements or ideas disseminated to the public in general by a legally regulated medium has the right to reply or make a correction using the same communication outlet, under such conditions as the law may establish.'

10 Article 14.2 of ICCPR: 'Everyone charged with a criminal offence shall have the right to be presumed innocent until proved guilty according to law.'

References

Aggarwal, V.K. (1985) *Liberal Protectionism: the International Politics of Organized Textile Trade*. Berkeley: University of California Press.

Akehurst, M. (1991) *A Modern Introduction to International Law* (6th edn). London: HarperCollins.

Alger, C. (1987) 'A grass-roots approach to life in peace', *Bulletin of Peace Proposals*, 18 (3): 375–92.

Alger, C. (1990) 'Grass-roots perspectives on global policies for development', *Journal of Peace Research*, 27 (2): 155–68.

Archer, C. (1983) *International Organizations*. London: Unwin Hyman.

Aronson, J.D. (1989) 'Market access and telecommunication services', in P. Robinson, K.P. Sauvant and V.P. Govitrikar (eds), *Electronic Highways for World Trade: Issues in Telecommunication and Data Services*. Boulder, CO: Westview Press. pp. 239–55.

Aronson, J.D. (1990) 'New directions in international telecom', *Transnational Data and Communication Report*, 13 (10): 20–2.

Barendt, E. (1985) *Freedom of Speech*. Oxford: Clarendon Press.

Baumgarten, J.A. (1991) 'What publishers need in international copyright treaties', *Rights*, 5 (3): 1–5.

BIAC (1988) *Statement on Trade in Telecommunications Network-Based Services*. Paris: OECD/BIAC.

Bing, J. (1988) 'Electronic publishing. Part One: Database publishing', *Media Law & Practice*, 9 (2): 57–67.

Bing, J. (1992) 'Data protection in a time of changes', in W.F. Korthals Altes, E.J. Dommering, P.H. Hugenholtz and J.C. Kabel (eds), *Information Law towards the 21st Century*. Deventer: Kluwer. pp. 247–59.

Blume, P. (1992) 'How to control data protection rules?', *International Computer Law Adviser*, 6 (6): 17–21.

Boven, Th. C. van (1982) 'Distinguishing criteria of human rights', in K. Vasak (ed.), *The International Dimensions of Human Rights*. Paris: Unesco. pp. 43–59.

Brownlie, I. (1990) *Principles of Public International Law*. Oxford: Clarendon Press.

Business Week (1989) 'Is Nothing Private?' 4 September, 32–7.

Buzan, B. (1993) 'From international system to international society: structural realism and regime theory meet the English School', *International Organization*, 47 (3): 327–52.

Carse, P. and Shurmer, M. (1993) 'Why the US standard will have the clearest "market focus" ', *Intermedia*, 21 (2): 30–2.

Cavalli, J. (1986) *Le Genèse de la Convention de Berne pour la Protection des Oeuvres Littéraires et Artistiques du 9 Septembre 1886*. Lausanne: Imprimeries Reunies.

Christol, C.Q. (1982) *The Modern International Law of Outer Space*. New York: Pergamon Press.

Christol, C.Q. (1990) 'Outer space exploitability', *Space Policy*, 6(2): 146–60.

Christopherson, S. and Ball, S. (1989) 'Media services: considerations relevant to multilateral trade negotiations', in UNCTAD, *Trade in Services: Sectoral Issues*. Geneva: UNCTAD. pp. 249–308.

Coalition of Service Industries (1988) *A Multilateral Agreement on Trade in Services*. 21 April. Washington DC.

Codding, G.A. Jr (1990a) *The Future of Satellite Communications*. Boulder, CO: Westview Press.

Codding, G.A. Jr (1990b) 'The Nice ITU Plenipotentiary Conference', *Telecommunications Policy*, 14 (2): 139–49.

Cohen Jehoram, H. (1987) 'Uitputting in het Auteursrecht', *Informatierrecht*, 2.

Cohen Jehoram, H. (1988) 'Critical reflections on the economic importance of copyright', *Rights*, 2 (4): 4–6.

Coliver, S. (1993) 'Press freedom under the European Convention on Human Rights', in Article 19, *Press Law and Practice*. London: Article 19. pp. 217–39.

COPUOS (1963) *Fifth Session Report*. A/5549/Add.1.

Council for International Business (1988) *Value-Added and Information Services Trade Negotiations*. New York: US Council for International Business.

Council for International Business (1989) *US Industry Proposed Approach for a General Agreement on Trade in Services. Applicable to the Telecommunications Services Sector*. New York: US Council for International Business.

Council of Europe (1990) *Computer-Related Crime*. European Committee on Crime Problems: Strasbourg.

Crane, R.J. (1979) *The Politics of International Standards: France and the Colour TV War*. Norwood: Ablex.

D'Arcy, J. (1969) 'Direct broadcasting satellites and the right to communicate', *EBU Review*, 118: 14–18.

De Graaf, F. et al. (1990) Juridische aspekten van netwerken. Utrecht: Netherlands Association for Computers and Law.

Dell, S. (1989) 'The United Nations Code of Conduct on Transnational Corporations', in J. Kaufmann (ed.), *Effective Negotiation: Case Studies in Conference Diplomacy*. Dordrecht: Martinus Nijhoff. pp. 53–74.

Donnelly, J. (1986) 'International human rights regimes', *International Organization*, 40 (3): 599–642.

Donnelly, J. (1993) *International Human Rights*. Boulder: Westview Press.

Dougherty, J.E. and Pfaltzgraff, R.L. (1990) *Contending Theories of International Relations*. New York: HarperCollins.

Drake, W.J. (1988). 'WATTC-88: restructuring the international telecommunication regulations', *Telecommunications Policy*, 12 (3): 217–33.

Drake, W.J. (1993a) 'The Internet religious war', *Telecommunications Policy*, 17 (9): 643–9.

Drake, W.J. (1993b) 'Territoriality and intangibility: transborder data flows and national sovereignty', in K. Nordenstreng and H.I. Schiller (eds), *Beyond National Sovereignty: International Communication in the 1990s*. Norwood: Ablex. pp. 259–313.

European Commission (1992) *Pluralism and Media Concentration in the Internal Market*. Brussels: European Commission.

Eyerman, R. (1992) 'Modernity and social movement', in H. Haferkamp and N.J. Smelser (eds), *Social Change and Modernity*. Berkeley: University of California. pp. 37–54.

Feij, J.N. (1989) 'The launching of the Uruguay Round of multilateral trade negotiations', in J. Kaufman (ed.), *Effective Negotiation*. Dordrecht: Martinus Nijhoff Publishers. pp. 93–108.

Feketekuty, G. (1989) 'International network competition in telecommunications', in P. Robinson, K.P. Sauvant and V.P. Govitrikar (eds), *Electronic Highways for World Trade: Issues in Telecommunication and Data Services*. Boulder, CO: Westview Press. pp. 257–85.

Fisher, D. (1982) *The Right to Communicate: a Status Report*. Series Reports and Papers on Mass Communication 94. Paris: Unesco.

Fisher, D. and Harms, L.S. (eds) (1983) *The Right to Communicate: a New Human Right?* Dublin: Boole Press.

Forester, T. (1987) *High-Tech Society*. Oxford: Basil Blackwell.

Forester, T. and Morrison, P. (1990) *Computer Ethics*. Oxford: Basil Blackwell.

Fuhr, J.P. (1990) 'Telephone subsidization of rural areas in the USA', *Telecommunications Policy*, 14 (3): 183–8.

Gassman, H. and Pipe, R.G. (1976) *Policy issues in data protection and privacy concepts and perspectives*. Proceedings of the OECD seminar, 20–4 June 1974. Paris: OECD.

Gershon, R.A. (1990) 'Global cooperation in an era of deregulation', *Telecommunications Policy*, 14 (3): 249–59.

Gilpin, R. (1981) *War and Change in World Politics*. Cambridge: Cambridge University Press.

Gotlieb, A., Dalfen, C. and Katz, K. (1974) 'The trans border transfer of information by communications and computer systems', *The American Journal of International Law*, 68(2): 227–57.

Guback, Th. H. (1969) *The International Film Industry*. Bloomington: Indiana University Press.

Gurtov, M. (1988) *Global Politics in the Human Interest*. Boulder: Lynne Riener.

Haggard, S. and Simmons, B.A. (1987) 'Theories of international regimes', *International Organization*, 41 (3): 491–517.

Hamelink, C.J. (1984) *Transnational Data Flows in the Information Age*. Lund: Studentlitteratur.

Hamelink, C.J. (1994) *Rules for World Communication: a Compendium*. Amsterdam: IFSCE.

Hannikainen, L. (1988) *Peremptory Norms in International Law*. Helsinki: Finnish Lawyers' Publishing Company.

Harms, L.S. (1980) *The Right to Communicate: Concept*. CIC Report 37.

Harms, L.S., Richstad, J. and Kie, K.A. (eds) (1977) *Right to Communicate: Collected Papers*. Honolulu: University Press of Hawaii.

Haufler, V. (1993) 'Crossing the boundary between public and private: international regimes and non-state actors', in V. Rittberger (ed.), *Regime Theory and International Relations*. Oxford: Clarendon Press. pp. 94–111.

Hedebro, G. (1982) *Communication and Social Change in Developing Nations*. Ames: Iowa State University Press.

Hegedus, Z. (1990) 'Social movements and social change in self-creative society: new civil initiatives in the international arena', in M. Albrow and E. King (eds), *Globalization, Knowledge and Society*. London: Sage. pp. 263–80.

Hills, J. (1989) 'Universal service: liberalization and privatization of telecommunications', *Telecommunications Policy*, 13 (2): 129–44.

Hills, J. and Papathanassopoulos, S. (1991) *The Democracy Gap: the Politics of*

322   *The Politics of World Communication*

Information and Communication Technologies in the United States and Europe.
New York: Greenwood Press.

HLC (1991) *Tomorrow's ITU: the Challenge of Change.* High-Level Committee.
Document 145–E. 26 April. Geneva.

Hobbes, T. (1651) *Leviathan.* Harmondsworth: Penguin (1968). Chapter 18, part II,
p. 233.

Hocking, B. and Smith, M. (1990) *World Politics.* New York: Harvester/
Wheatsheaf.

Hohfeld, W.H. (1919) *Fundamental Legal Conceptions.* New Haven: Yale University Press.

Hurrell, A. (1993) 'International society and the study of regimes: a reflective
approach', in V. Rittberger (ed.), *Regime Theory and International Relations.*
Oxford: Clarendon Press. pp. 49–72.

IAMCR (1994) 'Statement of the 6th MacBride Round Table on Communication',
IAMCR Newsletter, 4 (1): 5–6.

Independent Commission for World Wide Telecommunication Development (1985)
The Missing Link. Geneva: International Telecommunication Union.

International Chamber of Commerce (1972) *Guidelines for International Investment.*
Brochure 272. Paris: ICC.

International Chamber of Commerce (1978) *Rules of Conduct on Extortion and
Bribery in International Transactions.* Paris: ICC.

International Chamber of Commerce (1984) *Policy Statement on Privacy Legislation,
Data Protection and Legal Persons.* Adopted by the Council of the International
Chamber of Commerce at its 146th session, June 1984. Document 373/25 Rev.

International Chamber of Commerce (1988) *Services in the Uruguay Round.*
International Chamber of Commerce. Executive Board.

International Commission for the Study of Communication Problems (1980) *Many
Voices, One World.* Paris: Unesco.

International Organization of Journalists (1986) *International Information and
Communication Order Sourcebook.* Prague: IOJ.

Jasani, B. (1991) 'Remote sensing: an overview', in B. Jasani (ed.), *Outer Space.*
Tokyo: United Nations University Press. pp. 12–27.

Jasentuliyana, N. (1994) 'Ensuring equal access to the benefits of space technology
for all countries', *Space Policy,* 10 (1): 7–18.

Jönsson, C. (1993) 'Cognitive factors in explaining regime dynamics', in V.
Rittberger (ed.), *Regime Theory and International Relations.* Oxford: Clarendon
Press. pp. 202–22.

Joosten, M. (1993) ' "Let the market decide" – but can it?', *Intermedia,* 21 (2):
28–30.

Jowett, G.S. and O'Donnell, V. (1986) *Propaganda and Persuasion.* London: Sage.

Kaufmann, J. (1988) *Conference Diplomacy: an Introductory Analysis.* Dordrecht:
Martinus Nijhoff.

Keohane, R. and Nye, J. (1977) *Power and Interdependence.* Boston: Little Brown.

Kirby, M.D. (1987) 'The need for international informatics laws', in J. Becker (ed.),
Transborder Data Flow and Development. Bonn: Friedrich-Ebert Stiftung. pp. 77–
91.

Kirby, M.D. (1993a) 'Information, good government and social responsibility', in
TIDE 2000, *Improving Quality of Life in Asia with Information Technology and
Telecommunications.* Amsterdam: TIDE 2000. pp. 261–73.

Kirby, M.D. (1993b) 'Guidelines necessary', *Transnational Data and Communication Report*, 16 (2): 26–8.

Kiss, A.C. (1981) 'Permissible limitations on rights', in L. Henkin (ed.), *The International Bill of Rights*. New York: Columbia University Press. pp. 290–310.

Krasner, S.D. (1983) *International Regimes*. Ithaca: Cornell University Press.

Krasner, S.D. (1991) 'Global communications and national power: life on the Pareto frontier', *World Politics*, 43 (3): 336–66.

Krasner, S.D. (1993) 'Sovereignty, regimes, and human rights', in V. Rittberger (ed.), *Regime Theory and International Relations*. Oxford: Clarendon Press. pp. 139–67.

Kubka, J. and Nordenstreng, K. (1986a) *Useful Recollections. Part I*. Prague: International Organization of Journalists.

Kubka, J. and Nordenstreng, K. (1986b) *Useful Recollections. Part II*. Prague: International Organization of Journalists.

Kunczik, M. (1990) *Images of Nations and International Public Relations*. Bonn: Friedrich-Ebert Stiftung.

Ladas, S.P. (1930) *The International Protection of Industrial Property*. Cambridge, MA: Harvard University Press.

Lee, M.A. (1991) 'Arms and the media: business as usual', *Index on Censorship*, 10: 29–31.

Leroy Bennett, A. (1991) *International Organizations: Principles and Issues*. London: Prentice-Hall.

Lipson, C. (1991) 'Why are some international agreements informal?', *International Organization*, 45(4): 495–538.

Luther, S. Fletcher (1988) *The United States and the Direct Broadcast Satellite*. Oxford: Oxford University Press.

McDowell, S.D. (1989) 'The shaping of TDF policy', *Transnational Data and Communication Report*, 12 (5): 19–23.

McQuail, D. (1992) *Media Performance: Mass Communication and the Public Interest*. London: Sage.

Maitland, D. (1992) ' "The missing link" revisited', *Transnational Data and Communication Report*, 15 (6): 15–18.

Malamud, C. (1992) *Exploring the Internet: a Technical Travelogue*. Englewood Cliffs, NJ: Prentice-Hall.

Mansell, R. and Hawkins, R. (1992) 'Old roads and new signposts: trade policy objectives in telecommunications standards', in F. Klaver and P. Slaa (eds), *Telecommunication. New Signposts to Old Roads*. Amsterdam: IOS Press. pp. 45–54.

Matte, N.M. (1982) *Aerospace Law: Telecommunications Satellites*. London: Butterworth.

Meier, A. (1990) 'The peace movement: some questions concerning its social nature and structure', in M. Albrow and E. King (eds), *Globalization, Knowledge and Society*. London: Sage. pp. 251–61.

Mitchell, J.M. (1986) *International Cultural Relations*. London: Allen & Unwin.

Morgenthau, H. (1966) *Politics among Nations*. Chicago: University of Chicago Press.

Mowlana, H. and Smith, G. (1990) 'Tourism, telecommunications and transnational banking', in F. Go and R. Brent (eds), *Tourism and Transnationalization*. Special issue of *Tourism Management: Research, Policies, Practice*, 11 (4): 315–24.

Nadelman, E.A. (1990) 'Global prohibition regimes: the evolution of norms in international society', *International Organization*, 44 (4): 479–526.

Neelankavil, J.P. and Stridsberg, A.B. (1980) *Advertising Self-Regulation: a Global Perspective*. New York: Hastings House.

Nickel, J.W. (1987) *Making Sense of Human Rights*. Berkeley: University of California Press.

Nicolson, H. (1969) *Diplomacy*. London: Oxford University Press.

OECD (1976) *International Investment and Multinational Enterprises: Declaration by the Governments of OECD Member Countries*. 21 June. Paris: OECD.

OECD (1980) *Recommendation of the Council Concerning Guidelines Governing the Protection of Privacy and Transborder Flows of Personal Data*. C (80) 58 (Final). 1 October. Paris: OECD.

OECD (1986) *Computer-Related Crime: Analysis of Legal Policy*. Paris: OECD.

OECD (1988) *Telecommunication Network-Based Services: Implications for Telecommunication Policy*. ICCP/87.5. Paris: OECD.

OECD (1992) *Guidelines for the Security of Information Systems*. OECD/GD (92) 190. Paris: OECD.

Örücü, E. (1986) 'The core of rights and freedoms: the limit of limits', in T. Campbell, D. Goldberg, S. McLean and T. Mullen (eds), *Human Rights: from Rhetoric to Reality*. Oxford: Basil Blackwell. pp. 37–59.

Partsch, K.J. (1981) 'Freedom of conscience and expression, and political freedoms', in L. Henkin (ed.), *The International Bill of Rights*. New York: Columbia University Press. pp. 209–45.

Pentland, C. (1976) 'International organizations', in J.N. Rosenau, K.W. Thompson and G. Boyd (eds), *World Politics: an Introduction*. New York: Free Press.

Poskett, P. and McDougal, P. (1990). 'WARC 92: the case for mobile satellites', *Telecommunications Policy*, 14 (5): 355–63.

Raghavan, C. (1990) *Recolonization: GATT, the Uruguay Round and the Third World*. Penang: Third World Network.

Ramcharan, B. (1989) 'Universality of human rights in a pluralistic world', in *Proceedings* of the Colloquy organized by the Council of Europe in cooperation with the International Institute of Human Rights, Strasbourg.

Redeker, H. (1989) 'Liability in telecommunication systems: the German case', *International Computer Law Adviser*, 4 (1): 18–21.

Renaud, J.L. (1989) 'North, South and the CCITT', in J.M. McDonnell (ed.), *Reforming the Global Network: the 1989 ITU Plenipotentiary Conference*. London: International Institute of Communications. pp. 58–65.

Renaud, J.L. (1990) 'International organization and integration theory: the case of the International Telecommunication Union', in F. Korzenny and S. Ting-Toomey (eds), *Communicating for Peace: Diplomacy and Negotiation*. London: Sage. pp. 176–98.

Rights (1987) 'The right to publish', *Rights*, 1 (1): 1–3.

Rights (1992) 6 (1).

Riker, W.H. (1962) *The Theory of Political Coalitions*. New Haven: Yale University Press.

Riley, T. (1989) 'Commissioners stress TDF risks', *Transnational Data and Communications Report*, 12 (9): 5–8.

Ritter, J.B. (1991) 'Private data networks', *Transnational Data and Communication Report*, 14 (4): 15–20.

Roach, C. (1988) 'US arguments on the right to communicate and people's rights', *Media Development*, 35 (4): 18–20.

Robertson, A.H. (1981) 'The implementation system: international measures', in L.

Henkin (ed.), *The International Bill of Rights*. New York: Columbia University Press. pp. 332–69.

Robinson, P., Sauvant, K.P. and Govitrikar, V.P. (eds) (1989) *Electronic Highways for World Trade: Issues in Telecommunication and Data Services*. Boulder, CO: Westview Press.

Rodotà, S. (1992) 'Protecting informational privacy: trends and problems', in W.F. Korthals Altes, E.J. Dommering, P.H. Hugenholtz and J.C. Kabel, (eds), *Information Law towards the 21st Century*. Deventer: Kluwer. pp. 261–72.

Rutkowski, A.M. (1986) 'The new international telecommunications regulations', *Telecommunications*, November: 66–72.

Sanders, D. (1991) 'Collective rights', *Human Rights Quarterly*, 13: 368–86.

Saur, K.G. (1989) *Yearbook of International Organizations*. Munich.

Savage, J. (1989) *The Politics of International Telecommunications Regulation*. Boulder, CO: Westview Press.

Saxby, S. (1990) 'The role of law in the development of the information society' in H.W.K. Kasperen and A. Oskamp (eds), *Amongst Friends in Computers and Law*. Deventer: Kluwer. pp. 213–28.

Schiller, H.I. (1976) *Communication and Cultural Domination*. New York: M.E. Sharpe.

Shiva, V. (1993) 'Why we should say "No" to GATT-TRIPs', *Resurgence*, 39: 32–4.

Sieber, U. (1986) *The International Handbook on Computer Crime*. New York: Wiley.

Sieber, U. (1990) 'The emergence of criminal information law', in H.W.K. Kasperen and A. Oskamp (eds), *Amongst Friends in Computers and Law*. Deventer: Kluwer. pp. 117–30.

Skilbeck, J. (1988) *The Economic Importance of Copyright*. London: International Publishers Association.

South Commission (1990) *The Challenge to the South*. Oxford: Oxford University Press.

Stein, A.A. (1983) 'Coordination and collaboration: regimes in an anarchic world', in S.D. Krasner (ed.), *International Regimes*. Ithaca: Cornell University Press. pp. 115–40.

Stewart, M. LeSueur (1991) *To See the World: the Global Dimension in International Direct Television Broadcasting by Satellite*. Dordrecht: Martin Nijhoff.

Strange, S. (1983) 'Cave! hic dragones: a critique of regime analysis', in S.D. Krasner (ed.), *International Regimes*. Ithaca: Cornell University Press. pp. 337–54.

Strange, S. (1992) 'States, firms and diplomacy', *International Affairs*, 68 (1): 1–15.

Sung, L. (1992) 'WARC-92: setting the agenda for the future', *Telecommunications Policy*, 16 (8): 624–34.

Taishoff, M.N. (1987) *State Responsibility and the Direct Broadcast Satellite*. London: Frances Pinter.

Tarjanne, P. (1992) 'Telecom: bridge to the 21st century', *Transnational Data and Communications Report*, 15 (4): 42–5.

TDR (1989) *Transnational Data and Communications Report*, 12 (9).

Third World Economics (1991) Issue 17. May. Penang, Malaysia: Third World Network.

Thucydides (1954) *History of the Peloponnesian War*. Harmondsworth: Penguin.

Touraine, A. (1985) 'An introduction to the study of social movements', *Social Research*, 52 (4).

Traber, M. and Nordenstreng, K. (eds) (1992) *Few Voices, Many Worlds: towards a*

Media Reform Movement. London: World Association for Christian Communication.

Turkewitz, N. (1989) *Rights*, 3 (4): 6–7.

UNCITRAL (1986) *Legal Guide on Electronic Funds Transfers*. New York: United Nations.

UNCTAD (1974) *The Possibility and Feasibility of an International Code of Conduct in the Field of Transfer of Technology*. TD/B/AC.11/22. 6 June. Geneva: UNCTAD.

UNCTAD (1985) *The History of UNCTAD 1964–1984*. New York: United Nations.

Unesco (1961) *Mass Media in Developing Countries: A Unesco Report to the United Nations*. Series of Reports and Papers in Mass Communication. Unesco: Paris.

Unesco (1970) *Cultural Rights as Human Rights*. Paris: Unesco.

Unesco (1978) *Final Report of the Meeting of Experts on the Right to Communicate*. Stockholm, 8–12 May. Unesco: Paris.

Unesco (1982) *Right to Communicate: Legal Aspects*. Paris: Unesco.

Unesco (1989) *World Communication Report*. Paris: Unesco.

United Nations (1978) Document A/AC/105/218, Annexe 3, 13 April 1978.

United Nations (1986) *Report to the Intergovernmental Committee on Science and Technology for Development: Working Methodology for the End-of-Decade Review of the Implementation of the Vienna Programme of Action*. Document A/CN.11/69. New York: United Nations.

United Nations Centre on Transnational Corporations (1990) *The New Code Environment*. UNCTC Current Studies, Series A, no. 16. New York: United Nations.

Vandenberghe, G.P.V. (1988) 'Software bugs: a matter of life and liability', *International Computer Law Adviser*, 2 (9): 18–22.

Van Dinh, T. and Porter, R. (1986) 'Is the concept of national sovereignty outdated?', in J. Becker, G. Hedebro and L. Paldan (eds), *Communication and Domination*. Norwood: Ablex. pp. 120–8.

Viotti, P.R. and Kauppi, M.V. (1993) *International Relations Theory*. New York: Macmillan.

Waltz, K.N. (1979) *Theory of International Politics*. Reading, MA: Addison-Wesley.

Weber, G.A. (1924) *The Patent Office: its History, Activities and Organization*. Baltimore: Johns Hopkins Press.

Wells, C. (1987) *The UN, UNESCO and the Politics of Knowledge*. London: Macmillan.

Whitton, J.B. (1979) 'Hostile international propaganda and international law', in K. Nordenstreng and H.I. Schiller (eds), *National Sovereignty and International Communication*. Norwood: Ablex. pp. 217–29.

Widman, S.S. and Siwek, S.E. (1988) *International Trade in Films and Television Programs*. Cambridge: Ballinger.

Wijk, J. van and Junne, G. (1992) *Intellectual Property Protection of Advanced Technology*. Report prepared for the United Nations University Institute for New Technologies. Amsterdam: University of Amsterdam.

Wilner, G.M. (1980) 'Transfer of technology: the UNCTAD Code of Conduct', in N. Horn (ed.), *Legal Problems of Codes of Conduct for Multinational Enterprises*. Deventer: Kluwer. pp. 177–88.

WIPO (1988) Copyright, April, 174.

WIPO (1993a) *Memorandum Prepared by the International Bureau for the Third*

Session of the Committee of Experts on a Possible Protocol to the Berne Convention. 12 March. Geneva: WIPO.

WIPO (1993b) *Memorandum Prepared by the International Bureau for the FirstSession of the Committee of Experts on a Possible Instrument for the Protection of the Rights of Performers and Producers of Phonograms*. 12 March. Geneva: WIPO.

Woodrow, R.B. (1990) 'Telecom and trade in services – never the twain shall meet?', *Transnational Data and Communications Report*, 13 (4): 17–24.

Woodrow, R.B. (1991a) 'Tilting towards a trade regime', *Telecommunications Policy*, 15 (4): 323–42.

Woodrow, R.B. (1991b) 'Evolving institutional roles', in R.B. Woodrow and C. Brown (eds), *The Uruguay Round and Beyond: What Future for Services Trade Liberalization?* Geneva: Applied Services Economics Centre. pp. 149–58.

Wright, D. (1994) 'Mobile satellite communications in developing countries', *Telecommunications Policy*, 18 (1): 5–11.

Young, O.R. (1986) 'International regimes: toward a new theory of institutions', *World Politics*, no. 39: 104–22.

Young, O.R. (1989) 'The politics of international regime formation: managing natural resources and the environment', *International Organization*, 43 (3): 349–75.

Index

Index compiled by Meg Davies